A BRIEF HISTORY OF
SINGAPORE
AND MALAYSIA

**MULTICULTURALISM AND PROSPERITY:
THE SHARED HISTORY OF TWO SOUTHEAST ASIAN TIGERS**

CHRISTOPHER HALE

TUTTLE Publishing

Tokyo | Rutland, Vermont | Singapore

"Books to Span the East and West"

Tuttle Publishing was founded in 1832 in the small New England town of Rutland, Vermont [USA]. Our core values remain as strong today as they were then—to publish best-in-class books which bring people together one page at a time. In 1948, we established a publishing outpost in Japan—and Tuttle is now a leader in publishing English-language books about the arts, languages and cultures of Asia. The world has become a much smaller place today and Asia's economic and cultural influence has grown. Yet the need for meaningful dialogue and information about this diverse region has never been greater. Over the past seven decades, Tuttle has published thousands of books on subjects ranging from martial arts and paper crafts to language learning and literature—and our talented authors, illustrators, designers and photographers have won many prestigious awards. We welcome you to explore the wealth of information available on Asia at www.tuttlepublishing.com.

Published by Tuttle Publishing, an imprint of Periplus Editions (HK) Ltd.

www.tuttlepublishing.com

Copyright © 2023 by Christopher Hale

Front cover's images © f11photo/ Depositphotos.com (top); © Noppasin/ Istockphoto.com (bottom)

Library of Congress Cataloging in Publication Data

ISBN 978-0-8048-5420-7

Distributed by:

North America, Latin America & Europe
Tuttle Publishing
364 Innovation Drive
North Clarendon VT 05759 9436, USA
Tel: 1(802) 773 8930
Fax: 1(802) 773 6993
info@tuttlepublishing.com
www.tuttlepublishing.com

Asia Pacific
Berkeley Books Pte Ltd
3 Kallang Sector #04-01
Singapore 349278
Tel: (65) 6741 2178
Fax: (65) 6741 2179
inquiries@periplus.com.sg
www.tuttlepublishing.com

26 25 24 23
10 9 8 7 6 5 4 3 2 1   2211TP
Printed in Singapore

*Public opinion never reaches these equatorial jungles; we are grossly
ignorant of their inhabitants and of their rights ... unless some fresh
disturbance and another 'little war' should concentrate our attention
for a moment on these distant states, we are likely to remain so,
to their great detriment.... I felt humiliated by my ignorance.*

—Isabella Bird, 1879

*As human beings, we all have different experiences, different
feelings about the same thing, so we will definitely have different
views, different perspectives on things.... Because of this, there
will always be different stories about Singapore's history ...
because people will always have different views on certain
decisions made or certain historical events that happened.*

—Zain, Singapore student, 2018

*To the ordinary Englishman this is perhaps the least
known part of the globe. Our possessions in it are few
and scanty; scarcely any of our travellers go to explore
it; and in many collections of maps it is almost ignored,
being divided between Asia and the Pacific Islands.....*

—Alfred Russel Wallace, 1869

CONTENTS

VIETNAM

THAILAND

Sout

Perlis

Kangar

Alor Setar

Kedah

Kota Bharu

Georgetown

Kuala Terengganu

Penang

Kelantan

Terengganu

Perak

Ipoh

Pangkor Island

Pahang

Strait of Malacca

Kuantan

Selangor

Shah Alam

Kuala Lumpur

Negeri Sembilan

Putra Jaya

Seremban

Malacca

Malacca City

Johor

Johor Bahru

SINGAPORE

Equator

Sumatra

INDONESIA

Malay Peninsula

10°

5°

0°

100°

105°

Singapore and Malaysia

200 km
100 miles

hina Sea

Kota Kinabalu

Sabah

BRUNEI

Sarawak

Kuching

INDONESIA

Java Sea

110°   115°

INTRODUCTION

The Battle Box of the Past

I walked this morning round the walls and limits
of the ancient town of Singapore....
—John Crawfurd, *Journal of an Embassy from the Governor-*
General of India to the Courts of Siam and Cochin China, 1828

T he presumptuous historian who sets out to unfold a brief history of Singapore and Malaysia is instantly beset by challenges and contradictions. Today, both nations are not just proudly independent but avowedly different one from the other. I have often heard Malaysians scorn the manicured, litter-free perfection of the wealthy city-state on the other side of the Causeway while Singaporeans may seem condescending to a supposedly less developed neighbour. Secular, proudly diverse Singaporeans look askance at the Malaysian fixation with ethnic identity defined by religion. There are, indeed, tensions and even fractures between modern Singapore and Malaysia that might seem to undermine the premise of this brief, intertwined history. Even the most cursory glance at an atlas exposes the territorial gulf between the island state, fondly referred to by its citizens as the 'little red dot' and the sprawling terrain of the Malaysian peninsula and its eastern domain on the island of Borneo. Recent history is a story of estrangement, not unity. When Singapore became independent in 1963, it was as one part of a federal Malaysian nation. Two fractious years later, this tempestuous marriage ended in acrimonious divorce and Singapore and Malaysia went their separate ways. And, yet, the fundamental premise of this brief history is that even such a traumatic separation, which reduced Lee Kuan Yew, Singapore's first prime minister, to shed very public tears, cannot untangle the intricate tapestry woven from a deeper, longer and shared history.

For two centuries before they won independence, the peoples who occupied the island of Singapore, the Malay Peninsula and north Borneo had lived under British rule as subjects of empire. Generations of British historians told a story of how Singapore was founded by Sir Stamford Raffles in 1819, and a tiny fishing village blossomed into one of the great mercantile synapses of empire, the 'Clapham Junction of the East'. Since the turn of the present century, a new generation of historians and archaeologists has chipped away at this fusty narrative. The old statue of Raffles still stands on Boat Quay but his role in history has been politely demoted. In 2019, the Bicentennial Year, the Singapore government chose to dilute the prominence of the British colonialist by erecting four new statutes of Asian pioneers close to his statue. He would not be dumped in a storeroom or museum – his fate under Japanese occupation – but share space with his Malay translator 'Munshi' Abdullah, Indian businessman Narayana Pillai, Chinese merchant Tan Tock Seng and, reaching back a further 500 years, a visiting Srivijayan prince, Sang Nila Utama, who, according to the *Sejarah Melayu* ('Malay Annals'), bestowed on the island its Sanskrit name Singapura, the 'Lion City'. All the new statues represented safe, conservative picks. Three of the figures commemorated alongside Raffles were known as 'compradors' or, less politely, collaborators who happily threw in their lot with the British. It is Sang Nila Utama who challenges the old myths of Singapore history. He may inhabit a no-man's land between myth and history to be sure, but his presence on Boat Quay confounds the persistent image of Singapore as a kind of *tabula rasa*, or blank slate. How could a little fishing village possess a history worth talking about?

We now know, or should know, that long before Portuguese, Dutch and British buccaneers sailed across the Indian Ocean to conquer and plunder, an archipelago of thriving port cities had grown up along the coasts and rivers of Sumatra and the Malay Peninsula. Srivijaya, Temasek (later Singapura) and Malacca were richer and more cosmopolitan than sixteenth-century London or Amsterdam. The peoples of these port cities traded in a dazzling Babel of languages and dialects but many shared Malay as a lingua franca, the language of commerce. Srivijaya, Malacca and Singapura had grown and prospered over centuries. This was a mature Asian civilisation, and yet the European newcomers reported that the Malay world was uncivilised. They had eyes only for its precious metals and spices.

Go back even further in time to the beginning of the first millennium and the Malay Peninsula and the great elbow of islands that reaches out to Bali and beyond were woven together in a vast network of trade that connected the Mediterranean with India and China. For many centuries, the voyagers and traders who communally spun this intricate and interconnected web historians call the 'Silk Road of the Sea' knew nothing of nation states and national identities. They had no use for hard-edged borders. This communal and fluid world would be quickly eroded. European newcomers quarrelled and fought over competitive spheres of influence which would eventually distil as modern nations. From the perspective of deep time, the peoples of Malaysia and Singapore, whatever their origin, share that common inheritance, that shared history.

The Past is a Foreign Country

The irony is that the Europeans who came to rule over the Malay world were fascinated by the histories of the peoples they conquered. Raffles himself had restored the majestic ruins of the great temple of Borobudur when he was governor of Java, and published a richly illustrated *History of Java* two years before he sailed into the Singapore harbour. His friend Dr John Leyden translated the *Sejarah Melayu*, known as the 'Malay Annals', a semi-mythic history of the Malacca sultanate commissioned in the early seventeenth century by the regent of Johor. As Raffles makes all too clear in his introduction to Leyden's translation, the old tales told by the regent's scribes exposed the sinister power of 'Mahometanism', and that under the baleful influence of Islam the so-called 'native states' had fallen into 'apathy and indolence'. The relics of the past told, Raffles' alleged, a story of decline and decay that only superior Englishmen could reverse and reform. As representatives of the East India Company, the main instrument of empire-building until the mid-nineteenth century, Raffles and his successors were driven above all by mercantile interests. Nevertheless, the quest for profit was underpinned by what came to be known as the 'white man's burden' – the mission to civilise the uncivilised. These profit-obsessed missionaries set out to control the future of the peoples of Southeast Asia, and that meant shaping how they saw the past.

Early on the morning of 3 February 1822, John Crawfurd, who, like Raffles, was employed by the British East India Company, stopped off in Singapore. A somewhat irascible Scot, who was, it was said, frequently impatient and quick of temper, Crawfurd was on his way to Siam (now Thailand) and Cochinchina (now Vietnam) to seek out new trading opportunities for the Company he served. He was close to Raffles and both men shared a vision of Singapore's future glory as a Company base, a hinge between east and west, a bastion of prosperity and civilisation. Crawfurd would become the second 'Resident' of Singapore with the power to impose his vision. Like Raffles, Crawfurd imagined himself as a scholar. He was fascinated by the languages, history and peoples of the region of the world they now hoped to rule. These hard-headed Company men understood that knowledge was power: to know is to first own and then to dominate. By the time they arrived on the island of Singapore, Raffles and Crawfurd were veterans of brutal conquest. In 1811, they took part in the conquest of Java, wresting the island from its Dutch rulers, humiliating its sultans and plundering their palaces. Raffles and Crawfurd shared tremendous ambition. They believed that to own the future meant possessing the past. So it was that on that broiling morning 200 years ago, Crawfurd set out in search of the ancient history of Singapore.

From the broad mouth of the Singapore River, Crawfurd skirted a sandy beach and arrived at a creek known simply as the 'Freshwater Stream'. The creek has long since been paved over, but early maps of Singapore show that Crawfurd was on the seaward side of the present-day Padang: 'The inclosed [sic] space is a plain, ending in a hill of considerable extent, and a hundred and fifty feet in height. The whole is a kind of triangle, of which the base is the sea-side, about a mile in length....' All that the remains today of the 'Freshwater Stream' is a humdrum concrete drain at the junction of Bras Basah, Handy Road and Orchard Road. It was that 'hill of considerable extent' called Bukit Larangan, the 'Forbidden Hill', by locals that intrigued Crawfurd. Crossing the sandy beach, Crawfurd turned west

and then began climbing, following the vegetation-encrusted path of
a mysterious earthen rampart. On maps this was labelled the 'Malay
Wall'. Crawfurd was encumbered by his thick company jacket, and
it was hot, uncomfortable work. Above, in the forest canopy, little
armies of macaques leapt noisily from branch to branch uttering un-
earthly screams. Crawfurd was not the first Company man to ascend
the Forbidden Hill. Two years earlier, a British engineer, one Lieutenant Ralfe, had dug into the old wall and exhumed a cache of brass
coins. It turned out that the coins had been minted under the Song
emperors of China. The implications were astonishing. As Crawfurd
drily noted, 'The discovery of these coins affords some confirmation
of the relations which fix the establishment of the Malays at Singapore, in the twelfth century.' As he toiled upwards through thickly
woven forest following the rampart towards the summit of the Forbidden Hill, Crawfurd was hurtling back in time.

When he finally reached the summit of the Forbidden Hill, Crawfurd noticed other relics of Singapore's ancient history. He could
make out tumbledown brick walls that he imagined as 'a sepulchre
and a supposed temple'. As the macaques screamed overhead, Crawfurd conjectured: 'I look upon the building to have been a place
of worship, and from its appearance in all likelihood, a temple of
Buddha. The other relics of antiquity on the hill are the remains of
monasteries of the priests of this religion. Another terrace, nearly of
the same size, is said to have been the burial place of Iskandar Shah,
King of Singapore.' Crawfurd had read about Iskandar Shah in the
'Malay Annals': 'This is the prince whom tradition describes as having been driven from his throne by the Javanese, in the year 1252 of
the Christian era, and who died at Malacca. Over the supposed tomb
of Iskandar, a rude structure has been raised, since the formation
of the new settlement, to which Mohammedans, Hindus, and Chinese, equally resort to do homage.' Crawfurd noticed another tell-
tale relic. 'It is remarkable,' he reported 'that many of the fruit-trees
cultivated by the ancient inhabitants of Singapore are still existing,
on the eastern [i.e. southern] side of the hill, after a supposed lapse
of near six hundred years. Here we find the durian, the rambutan,
the duku, the shaddock, and other fruit trees of great size; and all so
degenerated ... that the fruit is scarcely to be recognised.'

Even in Crawfurd's matter-of-fact reporting, this long-abandoned orchard is especially evocative. Who might, centuries earlier, have tasted its fruits? Scattered everywhere between the gnarled old trees Crawfurd noted shards of Chinese pottery. Whoever had occupied the old palace on the Forbidden Hill centuries earlier had known and traded with merchants and emissaries of Imperial China, the most powerful and sophisticated civilisation on earth.

In early 1822, Singapore was already changing fast. In his *Journal*, Crawfurd described dining with the British Resident, Colonel William Farquhar, a fellow Scot. After dinner, Farquhar took his visitors on a tour of the new settlement. There was, Crawfurd wrote, 'universally an air of animation and activity ... the habitations were so numerous and the population so great that we could hardly imagine that the whole was the creation of three short years.' As Singapore grew and prospered, what remained of its long history would be erased and forgotten. The Forbidden Hill became Fort Canning. For Singapore's new masters, history began in 1819.

History would prove hard to repress. In the summer of 1854, English naturalist and explorer Alfred Russel Wallace arrived in the old port of Malacca. Malacca was a British possession and, along with Singapore and Penang, one of the 'Straits Settlements'. Wallace had spent years exploring and collecting in the Amazon rainforest and was about to embark on a journey across the Malay Archipelago that would lead him to identify the faunal divide now known as the 'Wallace Line' and to develop the theory of natural selection independently of his contemporary Charles Darwin. After spending a few months in Singapore, Wallace complained that birds and 'most other animals' were scarce, so he travelled north to explore the deep forests of the Malay Peninsula and climb Mount Ophir. Wallace was immediately fascinated by the antiquity of the port city and the astonishing diversity of its peoples. In his marvellous book *The Malay Archipelago*, Wallace conjures up Malacca like this: 'At present a vessel over a hundred tons hardly ever enters its port, and the trade is entirely confined to a few petty products of the forests. The population of Malacca consists of several races. The ubiquitous Chinese are perhaps the most numerous, keeping up their manners, customs, and language; the indigenous Malays are next in point of numbers, and their language is the Lingua-franca of the place. Next come the descendants of the Portuguese – who still keep up the use of their mother-tongue, though ruefully mutilated in grammar; and then there are the English rulers, and the descendants of the Dutch, who all speak English. In costume these several peoples are as varied as in their speech. The English preserve the tight-fitting coat, waistcoat, and trowsers [sic] and the abominable hat and cravat; the Portuguese patronize a light jacket, or, more frequently, shirt and trowsers only; the Malays wear their national jacket and sarong (a kind of kilt), with loose drawers; while the Chinese never depart in the least from their national dress, which, indeed, it is impossible to improve for a tropical climate.'

Through Wallace's eyes, we still glimpse in the diversity of its tongues and peoples, an ancient Malay port rich with history whose English rulers, encased in abominable hats and cravats, are merely presumptuous strangers.

700 Years

After 1819, the Forbidden Hill became Government Hill, then Fort Canning, then Fort Canning Park. Relics of the centuries-old port city were soon obliterated by the churn of modernity as Singapore was transformed by Crawfurd and his successors into 'the crowning port jewel of the Eastern Seas'. The past became a foreign country; Crawfurd and his successors turned their faces to the future. For the next 200 years, the British rulers promoted a foundational myth of Singapore that began in February 1819 when Stamford Raffles claimed the 'little fishing village' on behalf of the British East India Company. It was not only Singapore's former colonial masters who colluded in this mythological story. Sinnathamby Rajaratnam, one of the founders of the People's Action Party, which has held power in the city-state since independence, insisted that 'Nothing very much appears to have happened in Singapore before Raffles landed in this unpromising island.' The leaders of that first generation of Singaporean leaders, the 'men in white', confronting an uncertain future after winning independence, were loath to exorcise the spirit of Raffles.

Thanks to the work of a new generation of historians and archaeologists, we now know that the myth of Singapore deliberately masked a deeper history. This is the story I will tell in this book,

THE BATTLE BOX OF THE PAST

and I hope it will make amends for two centuries of myth-making. Singaporeans are becoming historians. Follow Crawfurd's footsteps today to the summit of Fort Canning Park and few can doubt that the ground is shifting. Singapore's deep history is being recovered. Deep beneath the Forbidden hill is the 'Battle Box', an exhibition about the British defence of Singapore in 1942. In 2019, not far from this colonial relic, I visited a spectacular exhibition which fleshed out the deep history of 'Singapura' as a stirring tale of Asian princes, traders, soldiers and sultans. Singapore chose to celebrate the Bicentennial of Raffles' landing with a dizzying hi-tech journey into the past. The foundation myth was jettisoned; a mere two centuries became seven.

And, yet, this radical myth-busting vision of 'Singapura' must compete with a contrarian vision of Singapore extravagantly flaunted in Kevin Kwan's novel *Crazy Rich Asians* and the hit film it spawned. In both book and movie, the gateway to the city-state is not the Singapore River and Boat Quay but Changi International Airport, which has become a kind of pilgrimage site devoted to the bling gods of the shopping mall. Changi and the iconic towers of Downtown and the Bay symbolise a nation that punches above its weight and turns its collective face more resolutely to the future than the past. The producers of the American TV series *Westworld* cleverly transformed downtown contemporary Singapore into a futuristic dystopia. The series designer explained: 'It's a wonderful place and it parallels the future of Westworld really well. There's this shiny exterior to everything, and there is a dark undercurrent as well.' It would seem that crazy rich Asians have little time for the past and even repeat the old mythologies. As one character in the movie proclaims: 'The Chinese came to Singapore when there was nothing but jungle and pig farmers. There was a snake here, eating an apple. You know what I mean? And they built all of this. Now, they're the landlords of the most expensive city in the world.'

On the other side of the narrow Causeway that connects Singapore to its neighbour Malaysia, history is remembered differently. As modern Asian nations, Singapore and Malaysia have been shaped by shared histories as colonial possessions. Singapore, and what was once 'British Malaya', were both governed by the Colonial Office in London. Colonial administrators set national borders and

later negotiated independence inside those borders. After independence, the Malaysian government turned Malacca into a shrine of
Malay identity and a living memorial to the old Malay sultanate. The
centrepiece of the plan would be the fifteenth-century Istana, the
palace of Sultan Mansur Shah. But there was a problem. Five centuries earlier, the Portuguese had incinerated the palace and driven
its royal occupants into exile. The Istana had been obliterated by
the fire of conquest.

There was a solution, however, and it was discovered in the
pages of the *Sejarah Melayu*, the 'Malay Annals'. The scribes who
compiled this reverential chronicle of Malay rulers had described
the sultan's palace in such exquisite detail that a team of modern
architects turned words into a blueprint, and at huge cost began
rebuilding the long-vanished palace. What we see when we visit
Malacca today is a perfect replica. The Istana both memorialises
and affirms the symbolic power of Malay tradition. You will find the
same message enshrined in the National Museum in Kuala Lumpur
and the everyday rituals of the royal courts that every five years elect
a new supreme ruler, the Yang di-Pertuan Agong. I first travelled to
Malaysia to document the elaborate and expensive rituals of kingship. I soon discovered that these traditions were almost entirely a
modern invention. They teach Malaysians a lesson that only Malays
truly belong as *Bumiputera*, 'sons of the soil', and social relations are
all about the reverence of the people for their rulers.

Why do modern Singaporeans and Malaysians think of their
shared history so differently? I hope at the end of this brief history,
we will have some answers. The winds are picking up and the time
has come to hoist sails and set off on a journey across the Silk Road
of the Sea into the deep past. We begin our journey 12,000 years ago
when vast sheets of ice extended across the northern hemisphere
and, at the equator, the islands and archipelagos of Southeast Asia
are all joined in a single landmass.

CHAPTER 1

Messages from Our Forgotten Ancestors

Defining Southeast Asia

W hat's in a name? The story of Singapore and Malaysia unfolds in a region of the world we now call Southeast Asia. It has been said that the idea of 'Southeast Asia' as a distinct region was a recent invention of the British wartime organisation, the Southeast Asia Command, or SEAC, but this is not true. European scholars were referring to Southeast Asia as a distinct region long before World War II. Two thousand years ago, the Greek geographer Claudius Ptolemy called the forested, club-shaped peninsula separating the Indian and Chinese oceans the Golden Chersonese or Golden Khersonese, the 'golden peninsula'. The Sanskrit epic the *Ramayana*, known in Hindu tradition as the 'first poem', and other Indian literary sources also refer to an enticing 'land of gold' 'situated at the very rising of the sun.' These early geographers and storytellers seem to have understood the most fundamental characteristic of this golden land. Ships from India and China sailed for the Golden Chersonese on one monsoon and returned on the other. This meant that they had to wait for the change at some sheltered harbour on the Malayan coast. The peninsular form of the Golden Chersonese that created a barrier between the two great civilizations of the ancient world compelled the development of entrepôts, where goods could be stored from one season to the next. At the southern extremity of the peninsula, Ptolemy's *Geography* depicts the emporium of Sabara, perhaps the first and oldest reference to Singapore.

'Southeast' begs the question – southeast from where and according to whose compass setting? And the answer would be the Europeans who, a few hundred years ago, set sail across the Indian Ocean to conquer and plunder. There were other terms too. The British called Burma 'Lower India' – the lands of the great peninsula and long chain of islands reaching out to Australia and the Pacific were merely protuberances attached to India, the 'Jewel in the Imperial Crown'. The Victorian naturalist Alfred Russel Wallace called the lands between Asia and Australia the Malay Archipelago, 'situated upon the equator, bathed by the tepid water of the great tropical oceans'. For him, this 'least known part of the globe' was a pristine paradise teeming with 'natural productions which are elsewhere unknown' and 'the richest of fruits and the most precious of spices'. For a naturalist, even a Victorian one, there were no artificial, territorial borders: 'The Malayan type of vegetation', Wallace observed, 'spreads over all the moister and more equable parts of India, and that many plants found in Ceylon, the Himalayas, the Nilghiri, and Khasia mountains are identical with those of Java and the Malay Peninsula.' It was European empire-builders who etched hard, possessive lines on their maps.

In other words, the naming game reflects power. It is the powerful who draw lines on maps and define regions of strategic significance. In the aftermath of World War II, the region was redefined in a tropical storm of acronyms. Under the auspices of the world's new superpower, the United States, SEAC gave way to SEATO, the Southeast Asia Treaty Organisation, defined as a region vulnerable to communist aggression, which included Pakistan. It was only in 1967 that the independent states of the region seized the naming initiative by creating ASEAN, the Association of Southeast Asian Nations. For the foreseeable future, ASEAN defines Southeast Asia as consisting of ten modern states: Indonesia, Malaysia, Singapore, Myanmar, the Philippines, Thailand, Vietnam, Laos, Cambodia and Brunei.

What I hope this brief history will show is that the human story of modern Singapore and Malaysia propels us back in time to a world that knew nothing of border controls, passports, customs officers and all the restrictive paraphernalia of modern political borders. Long before Portuguese, Dutch and British ships sailed across the Bay of Bengal and into the Strait of Malacca, the Chinese emperors called modern Southeast Asia the Nanyang, which means 'Southern Ocean'. For the Hindu rulers of ancient Java, the Malay Archipelago was the Nusantara, or 'outer islands'. Most poetic is the Malay term *di-bawah angin*, meaning 'below the wind'. The origins of the term are lost but the *Sejarah Melayu*, or Malay Annals, records that under Sultan Muhammad Shah (r. 1424–44), as Malacca prospered its fame spread from 'below the wind to above the wind'. These famous winds have blown up quite a storm of scholarly speculation. Does the term refer to the typhoon belt or the monsoon season? Did 'under the wind' mean west and 'above the wind' east, since the wind was described as rising with the sun? The modern consensus now seems to be that 'below the wind' has nothing to do with typhoons but refers to lands leeward of the prevailing monsoon winds. Scholars noted that the Malay chiefs of the peninsula were known as *orang di-bawah angin*, the 'leeward peoples' while those arriving from 'above the wind' were westerners, or 'windward people'.

For centuries until the coming of steam, the monsoon not only dictated shipping schedules but defined identities and the many different ways people interacted with each other. Traders and seaman waiting for the wind to change in a foreign port would, for a few months, join the port community. These sojourners of the monsoon brought prosperity to the people of the port because they needed supplies and accommodation. Some married local women and put down roots. The monsoon created a richly interactive human and commercial economy. The word comes from the Arabic *mawsim*, meaning 'season', and the great rhythm of the winds was well known from very early times to Roman, Greek and Arabian sailors. The monsoons are generated by the relative temperatures of the Asian landmass and the Indian Ocean. In the summer months, warm air rising over the land creates a high pressure system that sucks strong winds and torrential rains from the southwest. In winter, the land cools and a low pressure system builds over the Indian Ocean. This draws the northeast monsoon winds from China and Japan towards the Strait of Malacca. The monsoon resembles a huge meteorological bellows, the engine of trade. As the monsoon winds filled their sails, mariners did not hesitate, when the winds were in their favour, to venture across thousands of miles of open ocean. These daring shipmasters, riding the winds, acquired a complex knowledge of the ocean. As early as the third century BCE, the writer of a Buddhist text known as the *Jakartas* praised the skills of an elderly captain:

'… he recognised all the tell-tale signs around him … such clues as the fish, the colour of the water, the birds and the rocks.'

These fluid and shape-shifting wayfinders imply that 'Southeast Asia' is a modern chimera, a creation of minds, maps and political power rather than the natural order of things. But names and labels possess enormous power, especially when they are slapped onto maps. They can shape lives, minds and identities. They compel allegiances. The history that flows is all about the way we are all prisoners of maps – and maps change all the time. We should recognise, before we voyage any further, that diversity and change are definitive of the lands above and below the winds – of mountains and rivers, ethnicities, languages, flora and fauna. This kaleidoscopic topography of peoples, oceans, rivers, mountains and ferocious volcanoes is the creation of the ancient energies of the earth, and it is in geology and climate, earth, sea and sky, that we must seek the deepest roots of our story.

The Lost World of Sundaland

Over millions of years, the infinitely slow convergence of the vast tectonic plates that float, like an immense jigsaw puzzle, on top of the earth's rocky interior threw up a chain of volcanic mountains encircling a vast slab of rock known as the Sunda Shelf. The enclosing arc of volcanic peaks, known as the Ring of Fire, was violent and unpredictable. Eruptions, like the cataclysm that destroyed Mount Toba tens of thousands of years ago, had the power to disrupt climate and change the course of human history. When Mount Tambora on the Indonesian island of Sumbawa erupted in 1815, the vast cloud of dust that encircled the earth led to a 'year without a summer' in Europe and massive crop failures. Gloomy, overcast days and spectacular sunsets inspired painters like Caspar David Friedrich and William Turner. In Southeast Asia, erupting volcanos darkened the skies, poisoned water sources and ruined crops, but laid down a thick carpet of dark, fertile soils that lured farmers to till and sow some of the most hazardous places on earth.

In August 1883, a volcano on the island of Krakatoa that lies between Sumatra and Java, erupted, ripping the island apart and belching, at twice the speed of sound, a plume of smoke that reached 17 miles into the atmosphere. The tremendous power of the eruption generated a deadly tsunami with waves reaching over 100 feet that swept away 165 coastal villages and settlements. The Dutch colonial authorities estimated that the tsunami killed over 40,000 people. When Krakatoa exploded, a British ship called the *Norham Castle* was just 40 miles away. 'So violent are the explosions,' the captain recorded in his logbook, 'that the ear-drums of over half my crew have been shattered. I am convinced that the Day of Judgement has come.' Earthquakes, eruptions and tsunamis are powerful and capricious. A sudden slip at the meeting point of tectonic plates discharges tremendous amounts of destructive energy, but science has yet to come up with a reliable way to predict when these devastating events might occur. Only the rhythm of the monsoon seasons are predictable in the lands below the winds.

Modern science has transformed the way we understand deep time and the story of the past. A hundred thousand years ago, our ancestors, who had first evolved in Africa, ventured overland across the Sinai Peninsula, separating the Mediterranean from the Red Sea, or crossed the Bab al-Mandeb, the 13-mile-wide strait at the southern end of the Red Sea, and followed the coast of the Indian Ocean, over tens of thousands of years, to eventually reach China 25,000 years ago. During the last Ice Age, which ended about 9,500 years ago, huge volumes of water were locked up in immense ice sheets and glaciers that extended from the polar regions. Sea levels were some 400 feet lower than today and huge expanses of today's relatively shallow seabed were dry land. The many thousands of islands that now form the western Indonesian archipelago were, when our ancestors first arrived in Southeast Asia, a continental extension of Asia now known as the Sunda Shelf. At the southern extremities of this vanished world lay stretches of open ocean that separated this fertile and teeming land bridge from a single landmass geologists call Sahul, or Greater Australia. By about 50,000 years ago, the first human seafarers had leapfrogged, perhaps using rafts and paddles, the chain of islands that stretched from Sunda to Sahul.

The lost landmass of Sundaland would have provided the land bridge taken by these 'First Australians'. But we should not imagine cohorts of intrepid ancient humans setting a course like Victorian explorers searching for the source of the River Nile or the South

Pole. Our ancestors had no maps. Human migration was incremental and infinitely slow. Its only goal was survival. These long-ago humans would exhaust the resources of a home range and set off to find a fresh new one. Then the cycle would be repeated again and again. They might lose out in a competitive struggle with other groups of humans or be overwhelmed by catastrophe. Some 75,000 years ago, the eruption of Mount Toba on Sumatra must have swept away innumerable human settlements and turned settled humans, if they survived, into refugees. Human migration was a story of endless renewal and endurance. Over time, a lot of time, these bands of humans would creep across the surface of the earth taming singular and challenging landscapes as involuntary explorers and pioneers.

The Sunda Shelf was the equatorial stage of dramatic developments in the story of life on earth. Here our ancestors found a fertile landscape of streams, valleys and deltas. Here on the very edge of the world, they might have settled on a shoreline and wondered what lay beyond the far horizon. They hunted other mammals and reaped the riches of the sea. And then everything changed.

Some 12,000 years ago, the world began to warm and the great ice sheets that had covered the northern hemisphere began to release their icy grip. Unimaginable volumes of melt water gushed into the oceans of the world, drowning the lush plains of Sundaland to create a new world of islands, archipelagos and shallow seas. In the Greek myth, a mighty flood destroys Atlantis and scatters its people to the end of the earth. In the lands below the winds, the end of the Ice Age turned ancient landlubbers into sailors and navigators. And these ancient voyagers became the ancestors of generations of traders and merchants who would build a unique maritime civilisation.

The Ancestry of Modern Southeast Asians

Who were the early peoples who ventured into this turbulent world? To answer that question, we turn to another modern science – genetics. The study of our own genes as well as the remnants of genes extracted from human fossils has revolutionised human history. The British geneticist Steve Jones compares the genes in our cells to a biological language that sends messages from the very dis-

tant past. The reason is that every one of our genes has an ancestor, and the human genome, the map of our genes, can be used to
piece together the story of living things. Every one of us is, in fact,
a *living fossil*: our genes are a book of the past that reaches back far
beyond the beginnings of our own species. The DNA molecule, the
famous double helix that was identified a few years after the end of
World War II, is based on a simple alphabet of four letters, the DNA
bases A, G, C and T, which are arranged in 'words' of three letters,
such as TGG or ACT. These genetic words are codes for amino ac-
ids, the building blocks of bodies. We all share 50 per cent of mum
and dad. Our parents, in turn, shared the genes of their parents and
grandparents and great-grandparents, and so on back into the past.
Our cells are like echo chambers of innumerable long-dead generations. The human genome, then, is a map of ancestral relations that
reaches across time and space.

What, then, is the message spelled out by the genes of modern
Southeast Asians? We now know that the people who first ventured
into the long arm of the Malay Peninsula some 50,000 years ago
were modern humans just like ourselves who had evolved hundreds
of thousands of years earlier somewhere in Africa. These newcomers
are the remote ancestors of modern aboriginal peoples who survive
in fragile communities in the Andaman and Nicobar islands and in
the forests of Malaysia and the Indonesian archipelago.

The first genetic studies of Southeast Asians strongly suggested
that the next wave of immigrants were originally rice farmers who
had mastered the art of sailing and navigation and migrated about
4,000 years ago from the island we now call Taiwan to the far-flung
corners of the Pacific and Indian oceans. Like other new arrivals in
Southeast Asia, these first navigators had no doubt fled famine or
some kind of conflict. These intrepid sailors brought with them not
only their genes, but their languages. The new arrivals spoke one
or more of a huge family of languages known as Austronesian. The
word derives from the Latin *auster*, meaning 'south' and the Greek,
nesos, 'island'. Language families, like our genes, are connected
like relatives or kin. The vast majority of speakers of Austronesian
languages are island dwellers. People, languages and genes travel
together over time creating a huge web of connections. Today, the
Austronesian family includes Malay, Javanese and the indigenous

language of the modern Philippines, Tagalog.

In the last decade or so, geneticists have harvested a lot more data which has, to some extent, filled in the picture of these long-ago migrations. Most significantly, they have used exciting new technologies to extract DNA from fossil remains. This is an impressive achievement because fossil DNA, as it is called, is only very rarely preserved in wet equatorial climates. According to these new studies, using a lot more data, the pendulum backs the 'Out of Taiwan' model, but with a fascinating twist.

Professor Eske Willerslev at the University of Cambridge says that the evidence points to an even more complex story. Many modern Southeast Asians derive ancestry, he says, from at least four ancient populations. The evidence is impressive. As well as samples from modern Southeast Asians, Willerslev and his team extracted DNA from 8,000-year-old fossilised skeletal remains – twenty-six in all. This was an astonishing achievement, simply because fossil remains tend to decay in acidic tropical soils. According to the new data, both the hunter-gatherers of Sundaland *and* East Asian farmers from Taiwan contributed to the diverse genetic identity of the first Southeast Asians. We can see the interlacing flows of different human groups in this genetic map.

The black lines represent the first arrival of modern humans in the region. The red lines show the dispersal of hunter-gatherers who had thrived in the lost world of the Sunda Shelf, and the purple lines reveal the dispersal of those East Asian Austronesian peoples from the north.

The peoples of modern Singapore and Malaysia have become a great deal more mixed up since the time of the great Austronesian migrations. Genetically, we can say that the Malays and Indonesians are a mixture of Austronesian, while the original inhabitants are the darker-skinned 'Sundaland' people who were present for tens of thousands of years and who were the ancestors of the Nicobar and Anaman islanders, the Papuans and the Australian aboriginals. We have to keep in mind that only about 15 per cent of Singapore's current inhabitants are Malay and even Malaysia has only around 60 per cent Malays. Just a few decades ago, the Malays only formed 50 per cent of the total population. Even among the Malays there is a huge variation between Kelantanese, Javanese, Bugis, Minangkabau and Acehnese immigrants, along with yet more groups who migrated from the regions of modern Thailand, Cambodia and Vietnam in both ancient and more recent times. This is to say nothing, as we will see below, of the large groups of Middle Eastern peoples, Jews and Indian Muslims who have their own stories. Southeast Asian identity has been continuously stirred and mixed by time and chance like the churning sea of milk in Hindu mythology, and there is no reason to imagine that this human blending and roiling will ever cease.

Modern peoples are, for better or worse, more mobile than they have ever been in history. Mobility covers a multitude of lifestyles, both voluntary and involuntary. But the human condition has always been defined by such peripatetic impulses. Before the end of the last millennium, those early Southeast Asians had spread east and west from the Malay Peninsula to reach as far as Madagascar and some of the most distant islands in the Pacific. Sometime between 1000 and 1300 CE, the descendants of these same peoples reached New Zealand, the last place on earth to be settled by modern humans. The history unfolded here is in the deepest sense of the word a maritime one inhabited by mariners and merchants that challenges fixed terrestrial borders. It is a world evoked by the second-century Tamil epic the *Cilappatikaram*, the 'Tale of an Anklet', where the city of Puhar 'prospers from the wealth of the ocean … in this expanse of white sand is the wealth brought in by ships of men who have voyaged from their native lands to live here … beacons are lit up to guide ships … overburdened with a profusion of fresh produce from the seas and the hills.'

In the next chapter, we take our story forward to show how the descendants of these early seaborne peoples became the masters of the Silk Road of the Sea.

CHAPTER 2

The Silk Road of the Sea: Maritime Trade in Ancient Southeast Asia

S hipwrecks are time machines. In the warm shallow seas of Southeast Asia, archaeologists have discovered scores of decaying wrecks resting in layers of sand that tell the story of the Silk Road of the Sea, a term borrowed from Professor John Miksic, the American archaeologist who has done so much to uncover Singapore's long history. The 'Silk Roads' refer to the fabled overland routes that connected the Mediterranean world to Central Asia and China, evoking images of leathery-skinned merchants leading strings of heavily laden camels across the deserts of Central Asia to seek out the riches of China. Silk made in China was once worth its weight in gold.

The fame of the overland Silk Roads has overshadowed the intricate web of maritime networks that were spun by mariners and traders between Africa, Arabia, China and Japan from the beginning of the first millennium. By the year 1000 CE, the flow of raw materials like metals and spices, manufactured goods, cultures and peoples, was globalised. In 1225, a Chinese trade official, Zhao Rukuo, documented forty-one different products sold in Mediterranean ports, East Africa, India and Southeast Asia. To imagine the Silk Road of the Sea, then, replace camels with ships and bone dry deserts with the immensity of oceans and seas. So, too, was the ceaseless traffic in ideas, customs and faiths that transmuted hearts and minds in the lands below the winds. First came the great religions of India – Buddhism and Hinduism – as well as Indic law and statecraft. These beliefs and philosophies inspired the development of 'temple states' in Burma, Cambodia and Java and the building of the colossal stone monuments of Pagan, Angkor and Borobudur.

By the eighth century, Islam was the dominant faith that reached across an arc of the ancient world from Portugal to the Indus Valley. In Central Asia, the 'Dar al-Islam' encountered the western borders of Tang China. Then, political upheavals that broke out simultaneously in the Muslim caliphates and the Chinese Middle Kingdom sent merchants scurrying from Central Asia to the Silk Road of the Sea. On the monsoon seas, mariners and the merchants who filled their ships, became more ambitious and confident. Local rulers in the ports they stopped at, such as the Chola Kingdom in southern India and Srivijaya on the island of Sumatra, began amassing wealth, prestige and power. So it was that the Silk Road of the Sea diffused both goods, peoples and cultures across thousands of miles in an oceanic virtuous circle.

The Miracle of the Belitung Shipwreck

Sometime in the ninth century, a merchant ship entered the Gelasa Strait, close to the island of Belitung in the Java Sea. It had sailed four weeks earlier from one of the Chinese ports and was heavily laden. It carried a ballast of lead ingots as well as a tightly packed cargo that altogether weighed some 300 metric tons. Its captain and crew were probably Malay or Indian and it may have carried a handful of passengers, including a Chinese monk whose inkstone, engraved with the image of an insect, was found in the wreck. Some of the crew or their passengers filled long hours at sea playing dice and a board game. These glimpses of life on board were also found on the wreck. As the ship entered the narrow Gelasa Strait, perhaps at night, disaster struck. The jagged rocks of an underwater reef known as Batu Hitam, or 'Black Rock', ripped open the hull. The ship would have begun to founder very fast. We can imagine the terrified and panic-stricken shipmaster, his crew and passengers, some woken abruptly, leaping from the violently pitching vessel into the roiling surf breaking on the reef. They left behind, sluggishly settling on the sea floor, a treasure trove, a time capsule of the Silk Road of the Sea. And there, for eleven centuries, the ship and its cargo lay undisturbed.

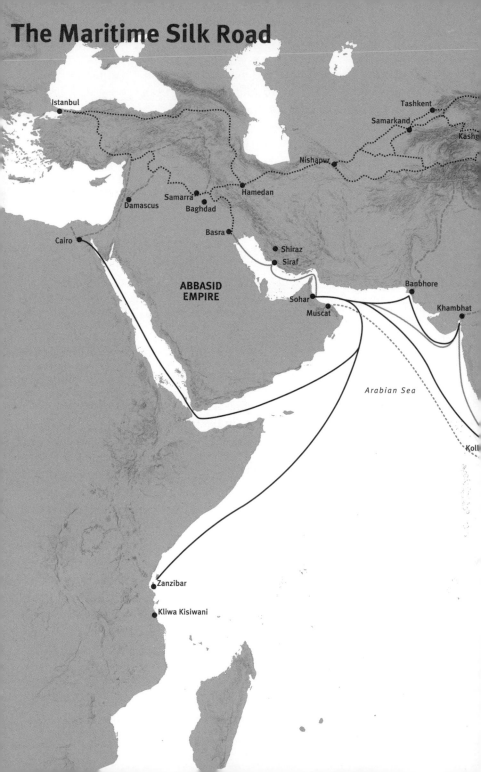

The Maritime Silk Road

Istanbul

Tashkent
Samarkand
Kashg

Nishapur

Damascus
Samarra
Baghdad
Hamedan

Cairo

Basra

Shiraz
Siraf

ABBASID EMPIRE

Banbhore

Sohar
Muscat

Khambhat

Arabian Sea

Koll

Zanzibar

Kliwa Kisiwani

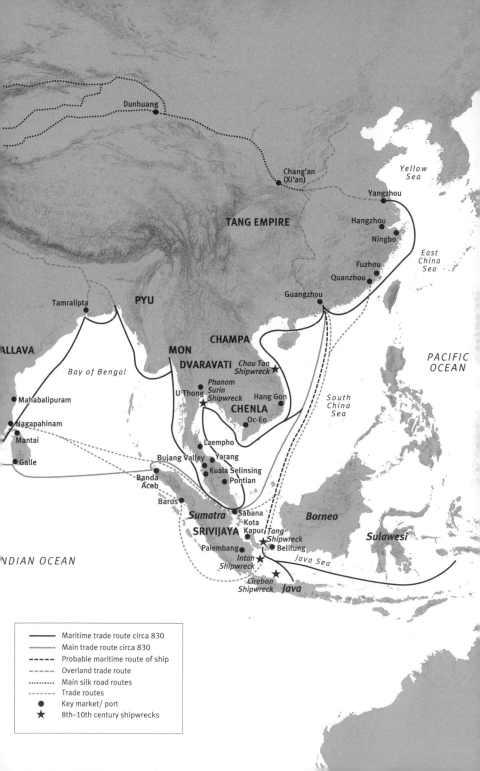

Dunhuang

Chang'an
(Xi'an)

TANG EMPIRE

Yangzhou

Hangzhou

Ningbo

Fuzhou

Quanzhou

Guangzhou

*Yellow
Sea*

*East
China
Sea*

Tamralipta

PYU

CHAMPA

MON

DVARAVATI

*Chau Tan
Shipwreck*

PACIFIC
OCEAN

Bay of Bengal

*Phanom
Surin
Shipwreck*

U Thong

Hang Gon

CHENLA

*South
China
Sea*

Mahabalipuram

Oc-Eo

PALLAVA

Nagapahinam

Mantai

Laempho

Galle

Bujang Valley

Yarang

Kuala Selinsing

Pontian

Banda
Aceb

Barus

Sumatra

Sabana

Kota
Kapur

SRIVIJAYA

*Tang
Shipwreck*

Borneo

Sulawesi

Palembang

Belitung

*Intan
Shipwreck*

Java Sea

INDIAN OCEAN

*Clrebon
Shipwreck*

Java

——	Maritime trade route circa 830
——	Main trade route circa 830
- - - -	Probable maritime route of ship
– – –	Overland trade route
· · · · ·	Main silk road routes
- - - -	Trade routes
●	Key market / port
★	8th–10th century shipwrecks

Then in 1998, as the Asian financial crisis wreaked havoc in Indonesia, fishermen from villages on the island of Belitung, began diving for sea cucumbers, a species of marine worm much prized in Chinese wet markets. Local villagers had long known of a reef some two nautical miles from the shore 'in which jars are growing' and the divers became curious about a large mound on the seabed close to the reef. When they began scraping away at layers of thick, crusted sediment on the surface of the mysterious protuberance, it was immediately obvious that they had found something remarkable. Here was a sunken hoard of Chinese ceramics, silver and gold – and much more valuable than sea worms. News of the discovery spread fast and local people, battered by the rip tides of recession, raced to the site to dive for treasure. And here the story of the Belitung wreck becomes very murky.

The fisherman's discovery had also caught the attention of German businessman and treasure hunter Tilman Walterfang. Taking advantage of the political crisis unfolding in Jakarta, Walterfang set up a partnership with an Indonesian salvage company, seized control of the wreck site and began excavations. In the course of two seasons, Walterfang's teams unearthed some 47,000 artefacts which were sent to a private conservation facility in New Zealand. How the Tang hoard ended up in New Zealand and then Singapore is a rather murky story. In 2005, it was reported that the Singapore government and the Sentosa Leisure Group, a private company, had bought the entire hoard for an eye-watering US$32 million, beating off bids from museums in China and the Middle East. It was a price worth paying, the government argued, because the 'Tang Treasures' would make Singaporeans proud of the history of the island's port. And yet the Tang treasures never quite overcame the musty odour of commercial pillage.

In 2012, the Smithsonian Institution in Washington, DC withdrew from hosting the Tang treasures citing UNESCO guidelines that 'underwater heritage shall not be traded, sold, bought or bartered as commercial goods'. Walterfang insisted that his prompt action prevented the spectacular hoard from falling into the hands of looters and disappearing into the illicit market of plundered antiquities. After all, there are few museum collections that can claim purity of origin, and is archaeology so very different from treasure hunting?

When we enter the Tang Treasure gallery in Singapore's Asian Civilisations Museum today, it would be churlish to dwell for long on its murky origins. The exhibition is both profoundly moving and crammed with surprises which tell a complex story about the maritime trading networks of the ninth century. The Belitung ship was indeed laden with 'treasures'. In the wreck, archaeologists found showpieces of Chinese artistry such as gold and silver vessels, including the largest gold cup of Tang origin ever discovered, bronze mirrors and a large bowl decorated with a marvellous image of a huge sea monster devouring a ship. These high-value luxury items might have been 'return gifts' sent from the Chinese court to a Javanese king who had sent tribute to the emperor.

The bulk of the cargo tells a different story. The ship carried some 55,000 ceramic pots and bowls, carefully packed in storage jars made in Vietnam or wrapped in wood shavings to protect them from storms of the Southern Ocean. This spectacular collection is testimony to a globalised economy of mass production, tailored to international market tastes and fashions. One of the museum guides remarked: 'These are the IKEA products of the ninth century ... mass-produced to order and in a hurry.' They were all fired in the kilns that had mushroomed across the Changsha area of present-day Hunan Province in southern China in the late Tang period: one bowl was inscribed with the equivalent Chinese date of 826 CE. The rise of the Changsha ceramic industry was driven by foreign demand. There were also hundreds of matching inkpots, spice jars and short spouted ewers, all mass-produced 'types' or lines. This mix of mass-produced ceramics and one-off high-value products suggests a commercial enterprise of impressive sophistication.

Here, then, was an intact cargo of mass-produced and elite commodities manufactured in ninth-century China, despatched to customers in Southeast Asia and the Persian Gulf. On many of the bowls, the Changsha potters inscribed geometric designs and inscriptions in a pseudo-Arabic style for Muslim customers. (They are not literally quotations from the Koran.) The Belitung ship and its cargo was a spectacular snapshot of an interconnected maritime economy of extraordinary sophistication. Other batches were decorated with lotus flowers to appeal to Buddhists, while green-splashed bowls were designed with Persian consumers in mind. A lot of marketing wisdom went into the design of the Tang treasures.

And there is a puzzle, too. There was no shortage of skilled potters in the Near East, but for reasons we cannot completely understand, it made perfect economic sense to the merchants in the ports and cities of the Arabian Gulf to import Chinese-made goods across thousands of miles of perilous ocean. The important point is that more than a thousand years ago, between the seventh and eleventh centuries, Indian Ocean mariners laid the foundations for a remarkable and barely interrupted growth in maritime trade and trading networks that has endured to the present day.

There is one other point to make about the Belitung wreck. Since its discovery, the ship was widely assumed to resemble an Arab dhow and likely to have been built in Muscat or another port in the Persian Gulf. The ship had been constructed from a number of different kinds of wood, such as mahogany, teak and two different species of the genus Afzelia. Neither of the Afzelia species grow in Arabia and it was assumed that the wood was imported from west or central Africa to build the ship: Afzelia, it was argued, is native only to Africa. In 2019, historian Stephen Haw noticed some fundamental problems with this theory about the origins of the Belitung boat. There is no evidence of trade in wood products between Africa and Arabia in the ninth century and, in any case, Arabian shipbuilders used local woods wherever possible. Archaeologists also claimed that Afzelia is native to Africa and only Africa but, as Haw discovered, this is not true. There are no fewer than four species of Afzelia that grow in Sumatra, Myanmar and other parts of Southeast Asia and these were widely used by early shipbuilders. Haw concluded that the material evidence that linked the Belitung ship to Arabia was flimsy. On the other hand, with a single exception, all the wood types, fibres and resins used in the construction of the ship can be found in Southeast Asia, strongly suggesting that it was built by Southeast Asian craftsmen, almost certainly in Sumatra. Haw suggests that the Belitung ship may have been sailing into the Sunda Strait on its way to the port of Barus in northwest Sumatra. It is conceivable that here its cargo would have been unloaded and sold to merchants from the Persian Gulf. From Barus, the Tang treasures might have sailed in another ship to markets in Arabia. None of this evidence is conclusive and we may never know the full story of the Belitung ship, but the evidence of its remains firmly locates the ship and its crew in Southeast Asia.

The Malay Entrepôt World

By the time the Belitung ship foundered on the black rock of the Gelasa Strait in the ninth century, a distinctive pattern of development shaped the world of the Southern Ocean. It was a pattern formed at the deepest level by the catastrophic end of the last Ice Age. When the huge Sunda Shelf was engulfed by floodwaters as the ice sheets collapsed 12,000 years ago, the peoples who had thrived in its plains and river valleys had to master a novel new world of oceans and waterways. Southeast Asia is unique among the world's major zones since most of its land surface lies within 125 miles of tide water. We can imagine that for its early peoples, it was a case of sink or swim, prosper or drown. And there was another natural impetus to exploit the new seas, rivers and oceans – the rainforest.

In the equatorial rainforests that shroud Peninsular Malaysia and Borneo, the exuberant profusion of primordial nature can appear overwhelming. The British colonial administrator Sir Hugh Clifford recalled his astonishment: 'The trees which form them grow so close together that they tread on one another's toes. The branches cross and recross, and are bound together by countless parasitic creepers, forming a green canopy overhead. The air hangs heavy as remembered sin and the gloom of a great cathedral is on every side. Everything is damp, and moist, and oppressive.' It has been said that 'the jungle is neutral': in other words, abundant but indifferent.

When our ancestors first encountered the wet, dark and tangled rainforests, they met a teeming, tangled world inimical to settlement. Here the sun rarely penetrates to the forest floor, and the soils are clays of meagre fertility. Topsoil is essential for agriculture, but in the deep forest nutrients contained in leaves falling to the forest floor are instantly sucked up and recycled by the vast web of entangled trees and shrubs, or washed away by torrential downpours. Even for resourceful hunter-gatherers, rainforests at low altitudes offer few edible wild plants or game. It is only in mountainous rainforests that cooler temperatures and a cycle of dry seasons provide an open forest pattern that can support larger mammals and bigger human communities.

It was in fertile, flatter riverine floodplains where rice could be grown that the monumental Asian kingdoms emerged. At Angkor, Pagan and Borobudur, where rich volcanic soils were laced with springs and streams, the colossal temples and palaces of god-kings were built on the stooped backs of rice farmers. As early as 250 CE, Chinese officials Kang Dai and Zhu Ying travelled through the flatlands bordering the Mekong and Bassac rivers. They reported back, describing a civilisation ruled by kings in walled cities, who used a script of Indian origin and depended on the labours of armies of rice farmers. Many centuries later, in 1687, a French ambassador sent by Louis XIV to the court of King Narai at Ayutthaya, then capital of Thailand, observed the astonishing industry of local rice farmers. Aristocratic lineages vied for supremacy by building impressive monuments to the gods of the Indian pantheon, above all Siva, who had the power to confer divine qualities on mere mortals. The climax of Southeast Asian rice cultures was the establishment of Angkor in the early ninth century. The foundation endowment of the temple of Rajavihara by the Khmer ruler Jayavarman VII in 1186 CE, depended on some 80,000 people living in 3,000 villages, 6,000 officiants, including priests and temple dancers to perform ritual functions year round, who all had to be provided with camphor and sandalwood and fed on rice. When you watch the sun rise over Angkor Wat, remember the forgotten generations of rice farmers whose back-breaking labours nourished the stonemasons who constructed this spectacular mausoleum for a living god whose name, Suryavarman II, means the 'Sun King'. When the king goes out, a Chinese visitor reported, he stands, sacred sword in hand, on an elephant 'whose tusks are encased in gold'.

The Enigma of Srivijaya

The archaeologist and historian John Miksic remarks that ships 'leave no tracks in the sea'. Unlike the rulers of Angkor, the lords of the monsoon seas erected palaces and temples of wood, not stone, and showed off their wealth in perishable commodities – spices, textiles and, of course, people. Across the Silk Road of the Sea, slaves were common currency. When once-bustling ports fell into decline, quays and warehouses emptied and then rotted into estuarine muds. As the English poet Percy Shelley wrote of the fallen status of Ozymandias, 'nothing beside remained'. The history of the monsoon ports must be pieced together from Chinese records and chronicles and the painstaking work of a new generation of archaeologists who have begun unearthing the relics of these fragile maritime cultures from their muddy hiding places.

The rise and fall of the ancient port states that flourished and fell in Sumatra, the Malay Peninsula and Java were driven by the rhythms of the monsoon winds and the rising flood of trade between the hustling, bustling markets of the Arabian Peninsula, India and China. Early in the first millennium, the port of Ubulla at the head of the Persian Gulf was famous as 'the port to al-Bahrain, Oman, al-Hind [India] and as-Sin [China]'. In 673 CE, a monk named Yijing arrived in the Chinese port of Guangzhou to arrange passage on a Persian ship 'for the south'. Some of our best sources are Asian monks on pilgrimages. In 725 CE, Huichau, a Korean Buddhist, described the people of the 'country of Lions', that is Sri Lanka, as 'bent on commerce', sailing the southern sea in 'big craft' to Kunlun [the Malay Peninsula] to 'fetch gold' and on to 'the country of Han' [Guangzhou] for 'silk piece goods and like ware'.

In the fifteenth century, the Muslim rulers of Malacca traced their descent from a mysterious Sumatran kingdom that had flourished on the banks of the Musi River in south-eastern Sumatra. The divine ancestors of the kings of Singapura and Malacca, it was said, had descended from heaven to alight on a sacred hill close to Palembang, now the capital of the Indonesian province of South Sumatra. This kingdom was called Srivijaya. The Chinese called it San Fo Chi, and reported that its rulers wore jewel-encrusted gold crowns and 'great ships' left the city every year bound for Guangzhou and Quanzhou. Arabic geographies describe a land of wonders called Zabaj midway between Arabia and China. In the nineteenth century, French archaeologists and scholars began searching for remains of this enigmatic civilisation and found almost nothing on the muddy banks of the Musi. The glories of Srivijaya, if it even existed, were, it seemed, entirely literary – preserved in documents, not artefacts. And, yet, for a long time European historians proclaimed the existence of a mighty Sriviyanan empire that rose and fell over

seven centuries. Frustrated by the lack of material remains, recent
researchers began to wonder whether the Srivijayan empire was a
chimera. The problem was the word 'empire'. The historical Srivijaya bore little resemblance to the colonial empires of the nineteenth
century, or even Angkor in Cambodia. Its rulers built in wood, not
stone. The source of its wealth and power was for the most part perishable. Its more tangible remains lie deep beneath the concrete towers and asphalt streets of modern Palembang. At the beginning of
the tenth century, the rulers of Srivijaya began sending emissaries to
China, bringing gifts to the emperor as tribute. In 980 CE, Chinese
records show that a merchant sailed from Srivijaya to the southern
coast of China to trade a cargo of rhinoceros horns, perfumes and
spices. The Chinese valued aromatic benzoin oil from Sumatra as
much as Arabian myrrh and frankincense: 'This perfume is found in
great quantities at San-Fo-Chi,' wrote one Chinese traveller.

In the period of the Song Dynasty, the Chinese trader and historian Zhao Rukuo (1170–1231) described Srivijaya in his two-
volume *Zhu Fan Zhi*, 'Description of the Barbarians'. This is not an
eye-witness account, for Zhao never left China and instead used
older geographies and gathered information from sailors and merchants in ports. Nevertheless, the length and colourful detail of
Zhao's descriptions show conclusively that Srivijaya was, from the
Chinese point of view, a powerful and exotic trading partner. Zhao
portrays Srivijaya as a kingdom of many provinces or dependen-
cies ruled from Palembang, its capital city, that was surrounded by
an impressive wall. The king wore a heavy jewel-encrusted crown
and was protected by guards carrying gold lances. Royal tradition
dictated that the king ate only sago. The death of kings, Zhao reported, was mourned by every one of the king's subjects who were
required to shave their heads. Many of the ruler's courtiers leapt into
the flames of the royal funeral pyre. One of the very rare inscriptions recovered by archaeologists close to Palembang is in the Malay
language but written in Sanskrit and the influence of Indic cultures
on Srivijaya was evidently very powerful. The sago nourished kings
who dedicated shrines to the Buddha and expected their subjects to
bring worthy offerings, such as golden vases.

The rulers and merchants of Srivijaya traded and fought with
other maritime kingdoms in Java and other sides of the Indian Ocean.

All these entrepôt kingdoms of the Southern Ocean profited from the monsoons, for the north-east winter monsoon prevented ships returning to China until the south-west monsoon of the summer months filled their sails for the journey home. No merchant or sailor could simply pass through the labyrinthine straits of the Southern Ocean. Journeys from China to Malaya and India were slow; it took three years to sail from China to India and back. Slow, interrupted journeys enriched the entrepôt kingdoms of the monsoon world.

These commercial relations were fiercely competitive and seem to have provoked serious conflict. Srivijaya was a state ready to go to war if its commercial trade was threatened. Its rulers could deploy an army and something like a navy. In 1025, Rajendra 1, the ruler of the Chola Kingdom in southern India, launched a naval attack on a number of ports in Sumatra on the grounds that the ruler of Srivijaya was blocking trade through the Sunda and Malacca straits. Srivijaya frequently clashed with the rulers of Javanese kingdoms. And all the maritime states that ringed the Southern Ocean competed for the favour of the Chinese emperor.

This is why the rulers of the competitive entrepôt kingdoms despatched so many emissaries to the faraway ruler of China. By paying tribute, they acknowledged the overlordship of the emperor of the 'Heavenly Kingdom'. By becoming vassal kingdoms, the rulers' status and power was enlarged and amplified to their subjects and competitors. In 992 CE, the Javans invaded Sumatra and soon afterwards sent an embassy to China. Not to be outdone, the ruler of Srivijaya despatched an embassy to China a few years later to inform the emperor that he had built a Buddhist shrine in Palembang where priests would pray for the emperor's long life. Such assiduous cultivation of the emperor paid impressive dividends. The Srivijayans returned home with belts covered in gold leaf, and in 1016 the emperor granted Srivijaya the coveted rank of 'first-class trading state'.

When he wrote his 'Description of the Barbarians' two centuries later, Zhao Rukuo had no doubt why Srivijaya was so rich and so important to China. He wrote: 'The country is an important thoroughfare for the traffic of foreign nations, the produce of all other countries is intercepted and kept in store there for the trade of foreign ships.' Like the powerful Chinese 'Superintendents of Barbarian Shipping' (ya fan bo shih), who scrupulously registered all the goods flooding into Chinese ports, the rulers of Srivijaya kept a check on foreign merchants, ships and goods that entered their waters. To deter pirates, the Srivijayan port authorities stretched an iron chain across part of the Musi River.

Arabian traders and geographers were just as fascinated as the Chinese by Srivijaya and its commercial allure. From the Persian Gulf, the land they called *Zabaj* could be reached by sea in a month. Merchants like Abu Zayd Hassan described a land of wonders – and cannibals. Here grew enormous camphor trees 'under which a hundred men might take shelter'. In the court of the Christian king Roger II who ruled Sicily in the twelfth century, the celebrated geographer and map-maker Al-Idrisi described how the Chinese invested in 'Zabaj' and 'other islands dependent on it': 'They became,' he went on, 'friendly with its inhabitants, for they admired their equity, their good behaviour, the agreeable nature of their custom and their good business acumen.' It would seem that the people of Srivijaya/Zabaj understood the significance of soft power.

Srivijaya was also a place of pilgrimage, and the journals of Chinese travellers who came here for spiritual succour cast a different light on life in the walled city and suburbs of Palembang. In the seventh century, a Buddhist monk named Yijing sailed from Guangzhou on a merchant ship and eventually reached the land he called *Sanfoqi*. (Chinese texts also refer to Srivijaya as *Shili foshi* and *Sanfoqi*.) Yijing describes his journey across the South China Sea to Sumatra in graphic detail: 'At this time, the first monsoon began to blow, when the ship proceeded towards the Red South [Southeast Asia, red is south in Chinese topography], with the ropes a hundred cubits [probably a translation of *chi*, the Chinese foot] long, suspended from above two by two…. The pair of sails flew away, leaving the sombre north behind. Cutting through the immense abyss, the great swells of water like a mountain on the sea … the massive waves like clouds clash against the sky.' These were hardy vessels!

As if writing for a seventh-century TripAdvisor, Yijing recommended Palembang to other religious wanderers: 'Buddhist priests number more than 1,000, whose minds are bent on learning and good practice. They investigate and study all the subjects that exist just as in India; the rules and ceremonies are not at all different. If a Chinese priest wishes to go to the West in order to hear and read the original scriptures, he had better stay here one or two years and practise the proper rules.' Then, when the monsoon winds blew from the East, it was time to find a ship bound for India. Every ship he sailed in, Yijing tells us, was a Srivijayan vessel. One, he wrote, was 'the king's ship'. This one stopped off in Jambi to the north of Palembang, and then Kedah on the north coast of the Malay Peninsula. Yijing spent the next eighteen years studying in Nalanda, the great Buddhist 'university' in the state of Magahda, Bihar in modern India.

Srivijaya can be rediscovered in the words of merchants, travellers and pilgrims. It has frustrated generations of archaeologists. Recently, however, archaeologists have discovered the fragile, eroded remains of wharves and warehouses that seem to have stretched for several miles along the northern bank of the Musi River. The ordinary people of ancient Palembang appear to have lived in sprawling suburbs of stilted dwellings outside the walled palace of the king. Many others lived on houseboats moored on the riverbank. In November 1862, Alfred Russel Wallace journeyed along the Musi River to Pelembang, discovering a riverside town that had changed little in a thousand years: 'The city is a large one, extending for three or four miles along a fine curve of the river, which is as wide as the Thames at Greenwich. The stream is, however, much narrowed by the houses which project into it upon piles, and within these again there is a row of houses built upon great bamboo rafts, which are moored by rattan cables to the shore or to piles, and rise and fall with the tide. The natives are true Malays, never building a house on dry land if they can find water to set it in, and never going anywhere on foot if they can reach the place in a boat. A considerable portion of the population are Chinese and Arabs, who carry on all the trade.' The English naturalist's sharp-eyed observations are the closest we will ever come to the watery world of medieval Srivijaya.

The Spice Race

Gold, ceramics and silk as well as numerous other commodities flowed back and forth along the maritime trading routes of Southeast Asia. One kind of raw material more than any other nourished the economic muscle and political clout of Srivijaya. For more than a thousand years, the taste, scent and profit of spices possessed a magnetic commercial allure for both Asians and Europeans. While pepper was grown all over South and Southeast Asia, the most valuable spices – nutmeg, cloves and mace – grew only on a cluster of tiny remote islands in the Java Sea, now known as the Moluccas. These were the Spice Islands – mere pinpricks in the ocean that had all the allure of the mythical gold kingdom of Eldorado. The source of the islands' wealth and legendary prestige were two tight-leaved evergreen trees that botanists call *Myristica fragmans* and *Caryophyllus aromaticus*. In plain English, from the seeds and flower buds of these fragrant trees come nutmeg and cloves. Nutmeg trees provide another spice – mace – which is the lacy, protective coating of the seed.

These rare and coveted luxuries had, over thousands of years, an impact on global trade that has only been exceeded by the colossal impact of natural gas and oil in our own times. As with the viscous 'black gold' that powers modern economies, the quest for these withered little seeds provoked unscrupulous competition and vicious trade wars. Spices were worth dying for and whoever controlled the harvesting and export of such prized raw materials might pull the strings of globalised economic power. In Venice and the other Mediterranean spice markets, pepper and ginger, mainly imported from India accounted for the bulk of cargoes, but cloves, nutmeg and mace commanded by weight much higher prices. In Elizabethan England, there was a nutmeg boom when doctors claimed it was the only certain cure for plague. In his 2000 book *Nathaniel's Nutmeg*, Giles Milton tells us that in Elizabethan London a single sack of nutmeg could 'set a man up for life' with a splendid house in the City and an army of servants. In 1665, the diarist Samuel Pepys, who was secretary of the Admiralty, reported that a small quantity of smuggled nutmeg and cloves had been sold for a 'sackful of gold'.

The London merchants who raked in huge profits importing nutmeg from Venice and other Mediterranean ports had no idea where these precious seeds were grown. Mediterranean merchants, in turn, bought spices in Constantinople, modern Istanbul, from traders who plied the Persian Gulf and Indian Ocean. In the ports of southern India and Sri Lanka, they did business with the monsoon magnates from Sumatra, the Malay Peninsula and Java. Even for Venetians, the masters of the Mediterranean, the fabulous Spice

Islands or 'spiceries' were blanks on the far side of the world. By the fifteenth century, greedy European merchants were competing in a long drawn-out search to discover and seize control of this Eldorado of tiny islands in the East.

Today, the Spice Islands lie within the Indonesian provinces of North and South Maluku to the east of Sulawesi. The islands that so fascinated European adventurers are sprinkled over an area that measures over half the size of Europe, but two time zones east of Jakarta, the Malukus [Moluccas] are regarded as remote even in Indonesia. Many of the islands, which range in size from small to tiny, are active volcanoes and the archipelago is scattered across one of the most seismically volatile regions of the world. And yet the Malukus were once centre-stage in global history thanks to volcanic soils and those miraculous trees. There is a traditional saying that 'nutmegs must be able to smell the sea, and cloves to see it.' It was the temperamental fussiness of spice trees about climate and the volcanic soils that generated the astounding value and repute of the spices they produced. Spice trees were *rarities*. The rulers of the northernmost islands of Tidore and Ternate fought for centuries to retain control of the spices that flourished in their island kingdoms. Four hundred miles to the south were the rocky and forbidding Amboyna and Ceram islands, famed for sweet-smelling cloves and, a few hundred nautical miles further sailing, the most far-flung and richest spiceries, the Banda Islands of Run and Neira. Today, the *Times Atlas of the World* has no entry for Run, but, thanks to its nutmeg and mace, this forgotten volcanic atoll was once fought over by the most powerful nations on earth. In the Anglo-Dutch wars that periodically flared up in the seventeenth century, the Dutch exchanged Run for New Amsterdam which the British renamed New York! We have jumped ahead of our story here, but it is vital to grasp just how momentous was the impact of the spiceries on world history.

Spices generated the wealth that underlay the power of kingdoms like Srivijaya in Sumatra and its neighbours in the Malay Peninsula and on the island of Java. It is the story of these early kingdoms, enriched by the cargoes that flowed through the Negara Selat, the world of the Malacca Strait, that will bring us to the ancient origins of Singapura, Johor and Malacca. According to the *Sejarah Melayu*,

it was a ruler of Srivijaya who may have been the real founder of
the island kingdom.

The Story of the 'Annals'

There is another important literary source of information about
Srivijaya, written many centuries after its wealth and power faded,
that we need to draw on to explore the connection between Srivijaya and the rise of ancient Singapore. I have used the word 'literary'
here for a reason. The *Sejarah Melayu*, the 'Malay Annals', is a story
of origin, the origin not of a people but of their semi-divine rulers
who descend, it is claimed, from the Macedonian conqueror Alexander the Great. The Annals were originally titled *Sulatus Salatin*,
the 'Genealogy of Kings'. The work was commissioned in the early
seventeenth century by the regent of the Malay state of Johor and
written in Classical Malay.

The Annals are not a record of facts as modern historians might
understand an event like the Battle of Waterloo, but rather a recita-
tion of royal sagas and tales that venerate the rulers of the port city
of Malacca. This is not to say that the Annals are fairy tales. Like
the legends of King Arthur in English mythology, the Annals serve
as royalist propaganda that affirm the power and sanctity of Malay
rulers, encapsulated in the word *daulat*.

In modern Malaysia, you will see a great many roadside posters portraying state sultans and sultanas arrayed in full regalia and
royal yellow, proclaiming *Daulat Tuanku!* I once discussed the exact
meaning of *daulat* with a young Malaysian and he dismissed it as
'aristocratic fiction'. We will have a lot more to say about the Annals
as well as Malay sultans in due course, but for now we should note
that the writers of the Annals regarded Srivijaya as the birthplace
of Malay culture. The first Malay ruler was the semi-divine Sang
Superba, or Sri Nila Pahlawan, who, accompanied by his younger
brothers Sri Krishna Pandita and Sri Nila Utama, made a miraculous
appearance in a blaze of white light atop the sacred hill of Bukit Seguntang, not far from Palembang. The authors of the Annals also
narrate that it would be the descendants of Sang Superba who would
go on to found the Malay kingdoms of Singapura and Malacca.

CHAPTER 3

The Pivot: The Influence of China and India

The Impact of Indic Cultures

C enturies before Chinese merchants drew the peoples of the Nanyang, the 'Southern Ocean', into a vast web of globalised trade, it was India and Indic cultures that had the most powerful and long-lasting influence on the peoples of Southeast Asia. India, of course, was not a unified state but an amalgam of competitive Hindu states such as the Chalukya, Chola, Pallava, Chera, Pandyan and Western Chalukya empires. In southern India, the maritime Chola Kingdom of Tamil Nadu became especially important to long-distance trade to the Middle East, Southeast Asia and China. Chola merchants were highly organised through assemblies known as *nagarams* and guilds that dominated the lucrative trade in pepper and spices. Wealth inspired ambition. At the beginning of the eleventh century, Rajendra Chola I sent naval expeditions to conquer the Maldives and then Sri Lanka to capture the all-important Indian ocean port of Mantai. Rajendra campaigned in Bengal, famed for its cotton manufactures, and then in 1025 launched a naval expedition from the south Indian port of Nagapattinam against Srivijaya and its vassal kingdoms in Sumatra. A Tamil inscription describes how the Chola king 'despatched many ships in the midst of the rolling sea and captured the "war gate" of the extensive city, Srivijaya with the "jewelled wicket-gate" adorned with great splendour and the "gate of large jewels."'

By the 1060s, the rising Buddhist kingdom of Pagan in Burma had loosened the Chola grip on Sri Lanka and Srivijaya. For much of the first millennium, the immense influence of Indic cultures flowed through trade and was rarely imposed at the point of the sword. What has been called the Indianisation of Southeast Asia that began in the first century CE was almost entirely peaceful and in stark contrast to European colonialism, which was characterised by local adaptation, borrowing and initiative.

We should understand the early empires of South Asia as huge reservoirs of Buddhist and Hindu religious philosophies and traditions that seamlessly wove together faith, law and political governance. Indian legal texts such as the *Manusmriti*, 'Laws of Manu', became the most influential legal text in early Southeast Asia. The edicts or Dhamma of the Mauryan emperor Ashok (304–232 BCE) spread the moral doctrine of the Buddha governing the most intimate behaviours, while the Sanskrit treatise, the *Arthashastra*, or the 'Science of Wealth', covered statecraft, political science, economic policy and military strategy. This Indic culture would revolutionise the world of the monsoon seas. China may have wielded immense commercial heft, but it was Indic ideas, set out in Sanskrit or Tamil writings, that had the most powerful impact on law, governance and personal morality and shaped the emergence of states and ways of ruling – and being ruled.

The Lost World of Funan

The earliest Southeast Asian state emerged in the Mekong Delta of southern Vietnam in the first century BCE and was called Funan by Chinese cartographers. For a few centuries, Funan dominated the Gulf of Siam and the shores of eastern Malaya, and was the main intermediary between China and India. Chinese sources tell the story of a local princess called Lin Yeh who led a raid on a passing merchant ship and ended up marrying one of the passengers who had the Brahmin name of Kaundinya and who had sailed from 'a land beyond the seas' – India, in other words. By marrying Lin Yeh, the Brahmin prince became king of Funan and the overlord of seven chieftains of settlements in the Mekong Delta.

Until quite recently, the material existence of Funan was as elusive as the remnants of Srivijaya in southern Sumatra. In the 1940s, French archaeologists, using novel aerial surveys, discovered Funan's mercantile centre at Óc Eo in the coastal Vietnamese province of An Giang at the top of the Gulf of Siam. The evidence revealed a huge trading centre built inland at the heart of a network of canals that criss-crossed the Mekong Delta linking the coastal settlements to the sea and the Funan capital Vyadapura, which may have been located close to Angkor Borei, now in modern Cambodia. The oldest archaeological layers show that Óc Eo was once a little Malay fishing village. According to Chinese accounts, in the middle of the third century CE, a king of Funan named in Chinese sources as Fan Shiman (or Fan-man) began expanding his kingdom in the delta, seizing huge tracts of land for rice cultivation and engaging in lively trade with Indian and Chinese merchants.

At some point in his reign, Fan Shiman led armies into the Kra Isthmus to conquer a Malay kingdom referred to in Chinese sources as Tun-San. This lay somewhere at the top end of the South China Sea on the Malay Peninsula. For Chinese merchants and travellers, the conquest of Tun-San made the journey to India quicker and easier: they could sail to the main port of Tun-San and then trek across the narrow waist of the isthmus to the west coast of the peninsula. No wonder the Chinese wrote of the newly conquered port as a place where great crowds from East and West met together to exchange precious goods and merchandise. Chinese visitors complained that at least 500 Indian families and thousands of Brahmins resided in Tun-San but 'they do nothing but study the sacred canon and practise piety ceaselessly.' It was these Indian traders and settlers, regarded by the Chinese as 'parasites', that brought Hindu and Buddhist cults and the language of Sanskrit from across the Bay of Bengal to the kingdoms of early Vietnam.

Centuries later, the rulers of Angkor claimed descent from the Brahmin prince Kaundinya and the kings of Funan. While Brahmin priests were welcomed, Funan and its port city were always richly cosmopolitan. Here, Khmers, Indians, Malays and Chinese rubbed shoulders, living lives ruled by trade and manufacture. They imported gold to make high-value ornaments and jewellery decorated with diamonds, rubies, opals and jet. Inside their walled city, the rulers of Funan invested in shipbuilding and spent lavishly on temples, libraries and archives. They used Sanskrit as the state language and erected statues to the Hindu gods they worshipped. The Chinese reports tell us that the Funanese king 'had large ships built, and sailing all over the immense sea he attacked more than ten kingdoms.' The king's subjects lived in 'walled villages, palaces, and dwellings. They devote themselves to agriculture ... they like to engrave ornaments and chisel. Many of their eating utensils are silver. Taxes are paid in gold, silver, pearls, and perfumed wood. There are books and depositories of archives and other things.'

In the fifth century, Funan appears to have entered a long period of decline. Its canals silted up, its gem manufactories stopped work and the rice paddies of the delta shrank. Funan was doomed by the rise of the spice trade. Merchants now turned their attention to the Moluccas and the emerging port states of the Indonesian archipelago.

For an earlier generation of historians such as George Coedès and other scholars, 'Indianisation' was a kind of Hindu colonialism and Hindu 'colonists' brought a package of Indic culture and civilisation that they foisted on the peoples of Southeast Asia. These historians thought in terms of a model of colonialism which led to the aggressive imposition of European legal, political and cultural norms. Recent scholarship tells a different story. Indianisation was never colonisation. It was voluntary and reflected the needs of local rulers.

Imagine Southeast Asia in the early centuries of the first millennium. Funan is flourishing in the Mekong Delta, but just about everywhere else the largest social and political units are villages ruled by chiefs. Population density is low and people live by hunting animals and gathering wild plants from the vast tropical forests. In many parts of Southeast Asia, these villagers engage in 'swidden agriculture': they cut and burn trees and plants to make space to grow crops. Over time, soils become impoverished and people move on. In the same way, hunters exhaust tracts of rainforest. Regardless of how they lived, these early societies were highly mobile and accustomed to living in transitory settlements. For the more ambitious village chieftains, this semi-nomadic way of life was hardly conducive to building power and holding onto it. They had many rivals.

We do not have a clear picture of how this happened, but over time these aspiring chiefs met Indian merchants and priests lured by the natural riches of the forest or simply out of curiosity. To lubricate these profitable exchanges, some village chiefs learned to use Sanskrit, Tamil or other Indic languages. They could record commercial transactions and correspond with other quick-learning chiefs. In the early centuries of the first millennium, all over Southeast Asia we see a dramatic increase in recorded inscriptions, many scratched into rock surfaces. These humble scratches mark the beginning of Indianisation before Indic languages and cultures swept through the courts of those ambitious rulers. For it was the Hindu and Buddhist faiths of Indic culture that proved to be most prized to Southeast Asian rulers. For in Indic philosophy, rulers may become gods.

Soon the rulers of Southeast Asian kingdoms took the vital next step by summoning learned Brahmins from the kingdoms of southern India so that they and their courtiers could learn and *refashion* Indic statecraft, law and mythology. We have already noticed the impact of Indian culture in the Mekong Delta with the rise of Funan. As early as the third century, Indian scholars knew of Hindu kingdoms in Java and Sumatra, and in the *Ramayana* Rama sends emissaries to Java to seek out the goddess Sita. From the fifth century, the Hindu Brahmins were joined by Buddhist emissaries to Southeast Asia who vied with both Brahmanism and older animist traditions. Monks accompanied traders and brought with them objects of power and protection, such as relics and images, as well as magical texts and chants. Hot on the heels of the Brahmins came Buddhist priests with a different message. The intricacies of Buddhist history and theology need not detain us here. The important point is to understand *why* these Indic traditions had such pervasive and powerful influence.

The most convincing explanation is that Indic traditions of religion, law and, above all, statecraft offered the early rulers and dynasties of the brash new kingdoms that had sprung up along the maritime trading networks of the peninsula and islands a way to amplify power and sanctify legitimacy to rule. By borrowing and adopting the elaborate symbols and rituals of power, tribal chiefs could represent themselves as *Devaraja*, god-kings. Some identified with the Hindu god Siva who, in Indic mythology, is supreme lord of the universe and guarantor of fertility.

It may surprise Western Buddhists to learn that Buddhism is a faith of power. According to the doctrines of Theravada Buddhism, the world is imperfect and requires correction by a person of great comeliness, vision and wisdom, who brings harmony to chaos. This ruler or king is referred to in classic texts as *Mahasammata*, because he is chosen by the people; he is a king or raja because he rules by the Dhamma, the sacred order of things, and Khattiya, lord of the fields. Social order depends on the righteous ruler who is charged with upholding the peace, harmony and well-being of the people. The great monuments of Pagan, Angkor Wat and Borobudur represent the cosmic Mount Meru that binds royal power with the Dhamma, the basis of all reality. It is no wonder, then, that the rajas of Southeast Asia embraced a faith that legitimated kingship and represented rulers as Buddharajas, or incarnate Buddhas.

In this early period, villages and ports dotted across the Malay world began to grow in power and social complexity to become 'temple states' dominated by charismatic rulers who represented themselves as living embodiments of gods. In these states, rulers donated gifts and land to eye-catching temples, where they publicly performed rituals as living gods. Under strong rulers, these early states swelled like balloons. If the ruler was weakened for some reason, then his kingdom deflated. We can see this pattern repeated again and again in the history of the rulers of Srivijaya, the Shailendra kings who built the great temple of Borobudur and the rulers of the Javanese empire of Majapahit. Indic cultures conferred on kings who ruled the lands below the winds the power of gods. In the turbulent ebb and flow of history, even divine power could be fragile and temporary.

China and the Southern Ocean

By the end of the first millennium, China became the most globalised kingdom on earth. China sucked in raw materials from Southeast Asia and transformed them into artefacts the world wanted, exporting exquisite ceramics and other manufactured goods to India, Africa, Arabia and the lands of the Mediterranean. The influence of Indian cultures on the emerging kingdoms of Southeast Asia was profound, extensive and long-lasting. Indic ideas shaped how Southeast Asians thought about the cosmos, how they built, how they wrote, what they wore and how they were ruled. The monuments and relics of this cultural exchange can still be seen and admired at Pagan and Angkor in mainland Southeast Asia and at Borobudur on Java, the largest and most elaborate Buddhist monument in the world. These fabulous temples are mute testimony to the emergence in Southeast Asia of temple states, godly rulers and a caste of priests who, whether Hindu or Buddhist, were the curators of Indic faiths, power and law.

The relationship between China and Southeast Asia was, above all, *commercial*. China, however, often proved a fickle partner, and the prosperity of the maritime silk road waxed and waned as Chinese dynasties rose and fell, convulsed by the fall of dynastic rulers, invasion or civil strife. The long, turbulent drama of Chinese history shaped and then reshaped the worlds of Southeast Asia and its peoples. And, of course, incalculable millions of Chinese *became* Southeast Asians when they fled China to escape famine and war or to seek better lives. Migrations have always been the lifeblood of Southeast Asian culture and prosperity.

Private Trade and Tribute

There was another dimension of Chinese culture that acted as a break on the mercantile ambitions of its peoples. Unlike their Indian and later Muslim counterparts, Chinese merchants were not by and large proselytisers. They had no interest in converting foreigners to one of the great Chinese faiths of Confucianism or Daoism. Although many Chinese embraced Buddhism which had first developed in India, it was the philosophy of Confucius (551–479 BCE) that held Chinese minds in an iron grip. It was Confucius who formalised the 'divine right of kings' as *Tianming*, or the 'Mandate of Heaven', which represented the secular authority of an emperor as granted by the gods. In return, rulers were accountable to the people and had to uphold Confucian values of austerity, military prowess, social conformity and isolationism. While Buddhists encouraged money-making, Confucians believed trade was disreputable. Confucian thinking infused the all-powerful imperial bureaucracy and merchants were regarded with disdain as parasites. This was a dilemma for Chinese emperors and the imperial court who coveted rare and precious commodities to affirm their status and prestige. In short, imperial power depended on trade and yet the Confucian bureaucrats despised its practice.

The solution was ingenious. This was the tribute system that cleverly yoked together diplomacy and commerce. In fact, the term was invented by Western historians: there is no word in Chinese that refers to tribute. Nevertheless, the practice was very real and defined China's relations with the rest of the world until it was overturned by Western colonial powers in the nineteenth century. The tribute system, in brief, refers to the ritualised and highly regulated exchanges between the Heavenly Kingdom and representatives of 'barbarian' states. The tribute givers, such as the rulers of Srivijaya and its rivals, recognised the ultimate authority of the emperor and the superiority of Chinese civilisation. This fitted with Confucian ideals of natural hierarchy and respect. Once representatives or embassies of the tributary state had 'kowtowed' to the emperor and presented sufficiently impressive gifts, which were often natural products, rare plants or animals special to their realm, they formally acknowledged the overlordship of China and accepted its protection. Chinese officials would then present gifts to the visiting emissaries which typically included books, embroidered silk and ceremonial artefacts that expressed both the sophistication of Chinese civilisation and the tributary's right to rule. They conferred power, or the symbols of power, not wealth. For a tributary ruler, an exquisitely crafted sceptre could become a potent symbol of power; his courtiers would be robed in Chinese silk. So it is important to recognise that the symbolism of tribute was more significant than the commercial value of the exchange. The emperor's reciprocal gifts often exceeded in value the offerings of a 'barbarian' state.

The ingenuity of the system is that diplomatic tribute offered a cover for business. Official diplomatic exchanges between the tributary embassies and the imperial court acted as a screen that concealed the lucrative private or unofficial interactions between the retinues of visiting embassies and Chinese merchants. Once a foreign state was admitted as a tributary, it was permitted to send ships for commercial purposes. The tribute system has been described as a convenient fiction that reconciled Confucian dogmatism with the development of a globalised trading empire. China exported vast quantities of precious metals, notably copper as well as manufactured ceramics and silk textiles. The imperial court craved luxury goods both for its own use and as rewards for the ruling clans, nobles and the silk-clad army of officials. China sucked in exotic goods from across the Indian Ocean and the South China Sea. A Chinese report describes how 'interpreters', who were usually palace eunuchs, sought out 'the merchant ships of the Barbarians' to exchange gold and silk for 'bright pearls, glassware, rare stones and strange things' and commodities they classified as *xiang*, or aromatics. Chinese aristocrats were obsessed by odour and spent fortunes on changing the way both they and their homes, furniture and possessions smelled and tasted. They burned aromatic woods to perfume rooms and steamed clothes with scented water. Scents were even personalised so that competitive Chinese elites made themselves recognisable with a bespoke perfume. China was the empire of odour and the demand for aromatic woods from all over Southeast Asia was insatiable.

The tribute system was more honoured in the breach than in strict Confucian observance. In the Song period that spanned the tenth to thirteenth centuries, China turned seawards and aggressively embraced overseas trade. The reason is that in 1126 CE, the Song were overwhelmed in their northern territory and capital at Kaifeng by tribes known as the Juchen, who established a rival dynasty, the Jin. The Song retreated south of the Yangtze to found a new capital at Hangzhou. Political turbulence failed to dim the flowering of culture, commerce and technology under the Song emperors. This was a time when the Chinese population grew and poverty was reduced. Internal trade flourished along the Yangtze and the Grand Canal, the longest artificial river in the world. Canal traffic was improved with the invention of a new lock system, and under the Song technological innovation was spectacular. Like liberalisation of the Chinese economy under Deng Xiaoping in the 1970s, the Song commercial revolution opened China to a wider world, and we can even pinpoint the birth of the revolution. In 982 CE, Chinese consumers complained so vociferously about a shortage of foreign aromatics that the imperial court agreed to release thirty-seven perfumes from government control, thus permitting trade outside official markets. Then, in 989 CE, the government lifted restrictions on Chinese merchants so that they could sail and trade abroad as long as they returned to the same port within nine months and submitted their goods to be weighed and taxed by the *Shibo*, or customs offices. Initially, international trade was restricted to the ports of Hangzhou, Mingzhou and later Guangzhou, but in 1090 the government agreed that merchants could use any port that issued a permit. Finally, in 1074, the government abolished a ban on the export of copper cash, which freed merchants from barter and exchange. Now they could pay and be paid in cash.

As Confucian restrictions were slowly relaxed and then abandoned, the government doubled duty on trade goods from 10 to 20 per cent. Evidently, the engineers of the Song revolution grasped the fundamental fiscal doctrine that taxation was more lucrative than government control.

One of the most striking examples of Song cosmopolitanism was the rise of Kaifeng as the centre of Jewish culture and commerce in East Asia. Mizrahi Jews from Persia flocked to the old capital where they built a synagogue, libraries and burial grounds. Few Westerners knew much about the Jews of Kaifeng until the Jesuit missionary Matteo Ricci revealed their existence in his journal *De Christiana expeditione apud Sinas*. In 1605, when Ricci was in Beijing, he was visited by an unusual young man named Ai Tian who had just passed the daunting civil service examination and hoped to secure a position in the imperial court. After a confusing conversation about the Virgin Mary and the Twelve Apostles, Ricci realised that Ai Tan knew only the Old Testament and that he was a Jew. When Ai Tian went back to Kaifeng, he was accompanied by a party of Jesuits. They reported that the Jews in Kaifeng observed the Sabbath, celebrated all the Jewish holidays, circumcised their boys and shunned pork. In the synagogue, Ai Tan showed his Jesuit friends the community's precious Hebrew manuscripts, including Torah scrolls.

Many other merchants were of non-Han descent. Many were Muslims who had come from Persia like the Jews of Haifeng. In Quanzhou, a Chinese magnate, Cai Jingfrang, began encouraging Arab and Persian merchants to set up in the port city. Some, like Pu Shougeng, had spectacular success: he rose to become superintendent of maritime trade; Pu Luoxin, whose birth name was Abu'l-Hassan, made a fortune importing frankincense from Srivijaya. The success of these pioneers transformed Quanzhou into a global trading hub. In Arabic, Quanzhou was known as *Zaytun*, the 'Olive City'. Merchants arrived in its port from the Philippines, Sumatra, Java, Cambodia, Korea and from as far away as Bahrain in the Persian Gulf. Its success inspired the Song emperors to build new harbours such as at Shanghai, which were strung like pearls along the coast of southern China. In Quanzhou, new canals and breakwaters were built and rivers dredged. Huge warehouses were offered to foreign merchants. The imperial government was not a mere bystander. It invested in naval patrols to protect convoys of merchant ships from pirates, and made sure that merchants spread their favours between different destinations to guarantee a balance of imports. 'I assure you,' wrote Marco Polo 'that for one ship load of pepper that goes to Alexandra or elsewhere, destined for Christendom, there come a hundred such, yes, and more too, to this haven of Zaytun; for it is one of the greatest havens in the world.'

The Song commercial revolution and the astonishing technological innovations of the period were driven by the dynasty's desperate need for revenue. The Song emperors invested heavily in grandiose new projects in Hangzhou, the southern capital, and had to fight off armies of the rival Jin Dynasty when they intruded across the Song frontier. The Song emperors realised that commerce profited the state as well as merchants and so invested in building new shipyards and harbours to promote the trade that helped fund the security of the empire. As China opened up to the wider world, Chinese merchants sailed south from Quanzhou, Fuzhou, Guangzhou, and Xiamen and set themselves up in the ports of the Southern Ocean in Java and the Malay Peninsula. They visited Johor, the Riau Islands and almost certainly Singapore. They formed partnerships with Malay merchants and some married local women. The new generation of ambitious Chinese merchants shed centuries of old restrictions and cumbersome regulations but could not escape the rigours of the monsoon. They dared not flout government rules obligating them to return within nine months. This was just a single monsoon cycle and so the Song merchants rarely ventured beyond the Strait of Malacca or the west coast Sumatran port of Barus. Confined to the realm of the Southern Ocean, the Chinese developed a closely woven web of commercial bonds with Malay, Javanese and Thai traders.

As Song Dynasty China flourished, new port cities would spring up in the world of the Southern Ocean to rival Srivijaya. One of these brash, new ports lay at the southern entrance of the Strait of Malacca. It was called Temasek.

CHAPTER 4

The Rise and Fall of Medieval Singapore

The World of the Straits

I n Malay, *Negara Selat* means the 'Realm of the Straits'. For millennia, the great elbow of the Malay Peninsula and the vast archipelago of thousands of islands that stretch eastwards formed a formidable barrier between India and the civilisations of China, Japan and Korea. The *Negara Selat* was the maritime bridge that connected West and East Asia – the thoroughfare of a globalised trading network. The rhythm of the monsoons compelled merchants, sailors and priests to become sojourners in a network of ports that grew as prosperous and powerful regional states by controlling the gush of trade goods that flowed across the Indian Ocean and the South China Sea through the Malacca and Sunda straits. These were hazardous maritime highways. For centuries, the waters around Singapore and other islands in the Riau-Lingga Archipelago were notorious as a graveyard of ships. Sailors relied on local Orang Laut, 'sea peoples', to navigate through the labyrinth of narrow straits and hidden reefs. Dutch navigators tersely named the southern end of the straits as *gebroken eilanden*, meaning 'broken, or fragmented, islands'. For many centuries, mariners shunned the Strait of Malacca. The Portuguese admiral Afonso d'Albuquerque likened it to the Homeric monsters Scylla and Charybdis, and had to depend on 'Moorish' (meaning Muslim) pilots to reach the port city of Malacca. According to another Portuguese navigator, the straits were full of uncharted and treacherous mudbanks, shallows, salt marshes and small islands and were notorious for 'transverse and unreliable winds'. An immobilised ship would become defenceless prey to marauders in smaller craft.

It is more likely that for many centuries Indian Ocean ships took the longer sea route along the west coast of Sumatra and then through the shorter, wider Sunda Strait into the South China Sea. Palembang, the main centre of the Srivijaya Kingdom that lay on the Musi River in southern Sumatra, is closer to the Sunda Strait than the Strait of Malacca. The Belitung wreck was discovered midway between Sumatra, Java and Borneo; the tenth-century Intan wreck, which was carrying a cargo of raw tin, bronze staffs used by Buddhist priests and bronze masks, was also discovered off south-eastern Sumatra. The perils of the Strait of Malacca may well explain why the port states of Temasek/Singapura at the southern end of the narrow waterway, and Malacca, which lies further north-west, developed much later than Srivijaya and its Javanese rivals which could be much more easily reached from the Indian Ocean through the Sunda Strait. The rise of the *later* entrepôt states in the Malay Peninsula, on the island of Singapore and along the Riau-Lingga Archipelago may reflect the growing confidence of Asian mariners and navigators sailing through the gullet of the Strait of Malacca on monsoon winds.

For a long time, the story of medieval Singapore was veiled by myth. Real history seemed to be as elusive as those ruined ramparts and palace walls that John Crawfurd discovered 200 years ago when he toiled up the tangled slopes of Fort Canning. For Crawfurd and Stamford Raffles, the evidence of an older Singapore was merely the inert relics of an irrelevant antiquity. Future profit was what mattered to the mercantile barons of the East India Company. After 1819, the British rulers of Singapore controlled the way its peoples thought about the past. Many were new arrivals like the British, and few had any reason to ponder the short-term memories of their rulers. Even after independence, the new leaders of Singapore were comfortable sharing the amnesia of their former masters. There seemed little point probing beneath the captivating story of the 'little fishing village' that grew to become the ultimate globalised city. In the first two decades of the twenty-first century, Singaporeans have woken up to the past. Historians and archaeologists have begun to tell a longer story. Teams of archaeologists led by John Miksic have toiled in broiling heat and equatorial downpours to unearth the remains of a medieval port city hidden beneath the concrete, steel and glass of Singapore's central business district. In the Bicentennial year of 2019, a coalition of historians published an assertively titled volume, *Singapore, a 700-Year History: From Early Emporium to World City*. Long before the Bicentennial made '700 Years' semi-official, even fashionable, many Singaporeans had begun rediscovering their history and campaigning to protect it from relentless development. When I worked for Channel News Asia at its old headquarters, I became fascinated by the shrines and graves of Bukit Brown Cemetery. I took an unofficial tour with Raymond Goh, who showed me tombs dating back to 1826. Goh is not just a tour guide. He is well known as the 'Tomb Whisperer' and fought to save the huge cemetery from the ravages of a new four-lane highway. He calls Bukit Brown an 'open-air classroom': 'You learn things the books don't teach you.' Developers are less sentimental. Singapore is 'too small' to indulge the past.

Even if past and present jostle uncomfortably together in Singapore, the past is no longer a foreign country. The new archaeology that is exposing tell-tale relics of the medieval emporium that grew up seven centuries ago in the shadow of the Forbidden Hill has revived interest in much older stories about the past, stories that appeared to be mere fabulations. In fact, all myths are nourished in the rich loam of history.

Once Singapura was Temasek, which may be derived from the Malay root word *tasek*, which means 'lake', suggesting, perhaps, a piece of land surrounded by water. In the fourteenth century, Temasek is mentioned in early Vietnamese documents and in the great navigator Wang Dayuan's travelogue, *Description of the Barbarians of the Isles*. According to the Javanese historical chronical, the *Pararaton*, or 'Book of Kings', Gajah Mada, prime minister of the medieval kingdom of Majapahit, vowed to conquer numerous rival states, including Temasek. Then Temasek seems to vanish from historical records. The Portuguese, who seized Malacca in 1511, refer only to Singapura. But intriguingly, there are many different *Singapuras* in early Southeast Asia.

Singapura has origins in Sanskrit: *simha* is 'lion' and *pura* 'city', thus Lion City. The lion god Narasimha is a powerful and sometimes terrifying figure in Hindu mythology. Lions are just as important in Buddhist and, of course, Chinese culture: 'When Sakyamuni Buddha was born, he pointed one hand to heaven and one hand to earth and said with a lion's roar: I alone am the honoured one in the heavens and on the earth.' We find the name in old Indian stories like the *Ramayana* which tells of Rama, the hero, searching for his lost wife Sita in a faraway city called Singapura. As early as the fourth century, there was a Singapura in the area of Tra Kieu in central Vietnam. Later, Chinese documents refer to a Singapura in central Thailand under the Angkorian Empire. An inscription discovered in Surodakan in Java lists Singapura as a vassal of the Majapahit Empire. The number of these 'Lion Cities' scattered across Southeast Asia reflects the spread of Indic cultures and Sanskrit as a language of power. So changing the name of Temasek, a Malay word, to Singapura was a logical decision for whoever ruled the island in the twelfth century. We can find out more about these aspirational rulers of medieval Singapura in the pages of the *Sejarah Melayu*, the 'Malay Annals' that so fascinated Raffles.

The Sejarah Melayu ('Malay Annals')

Commissioned in 1612 by the then regent of Johor, Raja Abdullah, the Annals extol the long line of hereditary Malay rulers and celebrate the resourcefulness and cunning of the Malay character. The text was also referred to in Arabic as the *Sulalatus Salatin*, the 'Genealogy of Kings', and the authors trace the dynastic line of Malay rulers all the way back to Alexander the Great, or Raja Iskandar, 'the Two-Horned, son of Raja Darab, a Roman of the country of Macedonia'. It may seem surprising that Malay rulers would claim descent from a pagan emperor, but in late antiquity Christians, Jews, Buddhists and Muslims all revered the Macedonian 'world conqueror'. Some Islamic scholars believe that in Sura 18 of the Koran, Alexandar is named as the prophet Dhul-Qarnayn [Dzulkarnain], 'he who has two horns'. Iskandar Shah was simply the most illustrious ancient ancestor that the Malay writers of the 'Annals' could claim as the founder of the *Sulalatus Salatin* – the genealogy of Malay rulers.

Given the pervasive influence of Indic culture in the Malay world, it is not surprising that the earliest stories in the Annals are mainly set in an Indian kingdom, and it takes the authors quite a few chapters to reach Temasek. Once there, the storytellers have a splendid tale to tell which mixes up fact and fantasy with impressive panache.

The hero is an Indian prince called Raja Chulan, who has made 'every prince of east and west his vassal', every ruler, that is, except the Chinese emperor. So Raja Chulan sets out with his army and navy to conquer the celestial empire. The story of Raja Chulan in the Annals no doubt sounds rather familiar. The scribes who compiled the Annals were clearly alluding to Rajendra Chola 1, the ambitious ruler of the Chola Kingdom in southern India who, in 1026, 'despatched many ships in the rolling sea' to subdue Srivijaya.

Meanwhile, the Chinese emperor gets wind of the raja's presumptuous plan and devises a ruse to put him off – and this is where Temasek comes into the story. The Chinese send a rickety boat manned by decrepit old men and loaded with fruit trees to meet the raja's forces before they reach China. The fateful encounter happens midway between India and China in the Malay port of Temasek. Here, the old men spin a tale for the rather credulous raja. They set off from China, they tell him, aged just twelve in a ship loaded with seeds. Now look at us – we have become hoary old men and the seeds have grown into mature trees. The message, of course, is that so distant is China that the raja and his forces will also be feeble old men by the time they reach their destination – hardly in a fit state to conquer an empire. The deception is a spectacular success: 'When should we ever get there?' the raja wonders, and gives up his plans of conquest. The story now takes a fantastical turn with a twist worthy of Jules Verne. Raja Chulan decides to prolong his time in Temasek and, in a glass submarine, descends to an underwater city where he befriends a sea prince. The two rulers get on so well that Raja Chulan agrees to wed the sea prince's daughter. The happy couple live together under the sea for three years and bring up three sons. But their subterranean idyll cannot last. Raja Chulan has responsibilities back home. So mounting a winged horse, he is flown back to his kingdom in India. This rather beautiful story of royal hubris, love, duty and abandonment has intriguing resonances with the real history of Rajendra Chola I and his naval assault on the kingdom of Srivijaya and firmly places Temasek at a strategic junction between India and China.

Founder of Singapura?

When Raja Chulan departs for India, the story moves from Temasek to 'a very great city' on the banks of the Musi River in southern Sumatra. This is, of course, Palembang, the capital of the kingdom of Srivijaya. Here, on the summit of Bukit Seguntang, the three sons who were born to the raja and his sea princess bride magically reappear in a blaze of light. The miraculous event is witnessed by two widows planting rice who 'beheld three youths of great beauty. All three of them were adorned like kings and wore crowns studded with precious stones, and they rode upon white elephants.' The princes reassure the widows that they are not 'genies or fairies' but descended from Raja Iskandar. In due course, the three youths are adopted by the Raja of Palembang and two become rulers of different kingdoms. The youngest remains in Palembang, becomes the new ruler of Srivijaya and is given the name Sang Utama. Sounds familiar? In 2019, the government of Singapore erected a statue of the same Sang Nila Utama alongside the old Raffles statue on Boat Quay to commemorate the first founder of Singapore. Confusingly, the Annals next tell us that a 'silvery white' cow owned by the two widows who witnessed Sang Utama's miraculous descent spews up foam, by the will of God, that turns into a human being who is called Bath. Bath extravagantly greets Sang Utama and gives him the title of Sri Tri Buana. 'And,' the Annals tell us, 'Sri Tri Buana became famous as a ruler; and all mankind, male and female, came from every part of the country to pay their homage to him.' So this renaming is highly significant, for Sri Tri Buana is a Sanskrit term in Buddhist cosmology meaning 'Lord of the Three Worlds'.

So here we have Sang Nila Utama becoming Sri Tri Buana, lord of three worlds, and we next find him making a 'solemn oath' that as a Malay ruler he will never shame his subjects who, in return, 'shall never be disloyal or treacherous.' Sri Tri Buana is warned that if he dishonours his oath, his house will be 'overturned and its roof laid to the ground'. Once Sri Tri Buana has agreed to this pact, he is allowed to marry. The royal nuptials are then described in sumptuous detail. When the festivities are at last at an end, Sri Tri Buana presents his chiefs with 'robes of honour'. Marriage firmly entrenches Sri Tri Buana as the ruler of Palembang. The Annals is not merely a picaresque tale, but a manual of statecraft that sets out a solemn, contractual bond between the ruler and his subjects. According to this pledge, the ruler cannot inflict injustice on his people; they, in turn, must be loyal and obedient.

The scene now shifts away from Srivijaya. Sri Tri Buana tells his bride that he plans to find a site for a new city. And so the ruler of Srivijaya sets forth in a 'golden yacht' with a fleet so vast that there seemed no counting it; the masts of the ships were like a forest of trees. Sri Tri Buana reaches the island of Bintan in the Riau Archipelago. Here he is adopted as son and heir by Queen Sakidar Shah who installs him as her successor 'to the beat of the drum of sovereignty'. The queen had hoped to marry Sri Tri Buana until she discovered 'he was very young'. As it turns out, this interlude in Bintan is a kind of throat-clearing prelude to a much more momentous event.

With the queen's permission, Sri Tri Buana goes hunting. He sets off with his consort and his entire fleet – the royal yacht, kitchen boats, floating bath houses and all. Once ashore, the princess and the wives of the chiefs collect shellfish and the menfolk go hunting. When he pursues a wounded deer to a high rock, Sri Tri Buana 'saw that the land on the other side had sand so white that it looked like a sheet of cloth.' 'What land is that?' he asks. 'That, your highness, is the land called Temasek.' And the story now gathers pace.

The shining beach was such a powerful lure that Sri Tri Buana set sail across the strait towards the distant island. Soon afterwards, a violent storm blows up and the raja's ship begins to founder. Much is thrown overboard, the Annals tell us, but the ship cannot be righted. So Sri Tri Buana hurls his crown into the water crying, 'Overboard with it then!' and, miraculously, the storm subsides. No detail in the Annals is incidental. Sri Tri Buana is ruler of Palembang and he throws the symbol of his power into the sea as he approaches Temasek. Power is flowing away from Srivijaya to the island with the shining beach.

What happens next is a familiar and oft-told tale, perhaps rather worn in the telling. But like the story of the lost crown, every detail has significance. We know Sri Tri Buana well enough now to know that his first act after landing on Temasek will be to go hunting. His party approaches Kuala Temasek, the mouth of the Singapore River: 'And they all beheld a strange animal. It seemed to move with great speed; it had a red body and a black head; its breast was white; it was strong and active in build, and in size was rather bigger than a he-goat.' This very odd creature seems to have beaten a hasty retreat, leaving Sri Tri Buana and his party scratching their heads. Surely, they concluded, it must be a lion. The animal described in the Annals does not by any stretch of the imagination resemble a lion, besides which lions have never roamed Southeast Asia. But the tale is not about natural history. The point is that for Sri Tri Buana, the beast definitely *was* a lion, and so he resolved then and there to build a new 'City of the Lion' on the spot where the beast had been spotted: Singapura. Singapura thus inherits the power of Srivijaya: 'And Singapura became a great city, to which foreigners resorted in great numbers so that the fame of the city and its greatness spread throughout the world.'

Sri Tri Buana rules Singapura for forty-eight years and is buried with his consort on the hill of Singapura. The 'Malay Annals' are full of cunning narrative rhymes. The hill of Singapura would become the Forbidden Hill, today's Fort Canning Park. Sri Tri Buana is lord of three worlds – and the number three is symbolic in early Malay literature. Sri Tri Buana, the first ruler of Singapura, descends with his siblings on the hill of Bukit Seguntang in a blaze of light. He is buried on Bukit Larangan, the Forbidden Hill in Singapura, and his descendants will found Malacca in the shadow of another hill, Bukit Bendera, now St Paul's Hill. All three royal capitals have the same basic topography: a hill overlooking an estuary. Remember, too, that Sri Tri Buana first spies Singapura from a high rock. The symbolic power of these high places that link Srivijaya with Singapura and Malacca reflects the maritime foundation of Malay culture. These sacred hills overlooking estuaries were fixed points that Malay navigators could use to orient themselves. In the Malaysian state of Kedah, at the northern end of the Strait of Malacca, the peak of Gunung Jerai overlooks the Merbok estuary and the Muda River. Archaeologists have discovered a cluster of sites scattered across the broad, flat estuary of the Bujang Valley where the remains of temples, palaces, villages and a port show that this was once a major trading centre. This chain of ports and sacred elevations from Kedah to Singapura defined the topography of the Malay world.

Munshi Abdullah, Raffles' Malay teacher, describes in his autobiographical *Hikayat Abdullah*, that his British employer was convinced that he had discovered the legendary Singapura he had read about in the 'Malay Annals' for, according to the local ruler or Temenggong, Bukit Larangan or 'Forbidden Hill' was the site of 'palaces' and a royal bath (Pancur Larangan or Forbidden Spring) built by the 'kings of ancient times'. On 6 February 1819, Raffles wrote to a colleague in the East India Company that Malay sultans 'will hail with satisfaction the foundation and the site of a British establishment, in the centrical and commanding situation once occupied by the capital of the most powerful Malayan empire then existing in the East'. Soon after he negotiated a lease on the south coast of the island with the Temenggong, Raffles reported to the Supreme Government in Calcutta that 'a British Station, commanding the Southern entrance of the Straits of Melaka, and combining extraordinary local advantages with a peculiarly admirable Geographical position, has been established at Singapore the ancient Capital of the Kings of Johor.' That he had leased the island's *history* as well as its territory is a recurring theme in letters after February 1819. In June, Raffles wrote that he had 'planted the British Flag' on the ruins of the ancient Capital of "Singapura" or "City of the Lion" at the 'Naval of the Malay countries.'

Digging Up the Past

For more than two decades at the turn of the last century, teams of archaeologists led by Professor John Miksic have toiled in scorching heat, drenching humidity, crashing thunder, crackling lightning and torrential downpours to dig and scrape away layers of detritus to expose the relics of a fourteenth-century trading emporium. Like human DNA, these relics of the past have to be decoded. In the shadow of Singapore's downtown skyscrapers, Miksic and his teams unearthed buried layers of ceramics, beads, coins and other rare treasures. Medieval Singaporeans, it seems, loved the high-quality blue-and-white Chinese porcelain that was brought here from one of the great sea ports of Imperial China – Quanzhou in Fujian Province. It was in here, in 1973, that Chinese archaeologists discovered the famous Quanzhou ship, buried deep in the mud of the bay. Coins found inside the rotten timbers dated the ship to the

collapse of the Song Dynasty when the armies of Kublai Khan conquered southern China at the end of the thirteenth century.

The richest finds have come from sites on the steep flanks of Fort
Canning, evidence that this was the location of the ruler's court.
Other impressive artefacts have come to light lower down the hill,
closer to the Singapore River. This was where ships from the islands
of the Southern Ocean, India and China docked and unloaded their
cargoes. Here stood the wharves, warehouses and homes of Singapura's merchants. This would have been a worldly, cosmopolitan
community. Some would be settled subjects of the ruler. Many others would be 'birds of passage' waiting for the monsoon winds to
continue their journey or return home. They would have needed
accommodation and food – and company. Some would have local
wives and families.

The large number of Chinese coins and other artefacts found
by Miksic and his teams does not mean that Chinese merchants
dominated trade with medieval Singapura. It is simply that Chinese
export trade goods were by their nature more durable (ceramics,
coins, metal implements, etc.) than perishable Indian or Southeast
Asian trade goods like textiles, forest products, spices, food products and aromatics.

Here, seven centuries ago, we would have heard the sounds of
all of Asia and the Middle East. Here we would have glimpsed the
rich diversity of the peoples from above and below the winds. Medieval Singapura was a vibrant and prosperous mercantile hub. It was
ruled by kings who built their palace on it and were buried in grand
tombs. At its peak, some 10,000 souls may have lived in Singapura.
The huge number of coins and imported luxuries found by Miksic's
teams of archaeologists show that many of these medieval Singaporeans enjoyed what we would now call 'high capita worth'. Modern
Singaporeans would have felt at home in medieval Singapura.

Singapura under Threat

Conflict and conquest preyed on the minds of the Malay scribes who
compiled the 'Malay Annals'. The world of the straits was a perilous
region as competitive kingdoms vied for power. Even before the
arrival of well-armed Europeans, Srivijaya had come under attack

from the rulers of the Chola Kingdom in southern India and was frequently at war with richer and more powerful Javanese kingdoms. According to the Annals, it was the kingdom of Majapahit that would prove most dangerous to the prosperity of Singapura. In the mid-fourteenth century, the Catholic missionary and explorer Odorico da Pordenone reported on the magnificence of the Majapahit capital: 'This [Java] is thought to be one of the largest islands in the world, and is thoroughly inhabited; having great plenty of cloves, cubebs [a kind of pepper], and nutmegs, and all other kinds of spices, and great abundance of provisions of all kinds, except wine. The king of Java [the ruler of Majapahit] has a large and sumptuous palace, the loftiest of any that I have seen, with broad and lofty stairs to ascend to the upper apartments, all the steps being alternately of gold and silver. The whole interior walls are lined with plates of beaten gold, on which the images of warriors are placed sculptured in gold, having each a golden coronet richly ornamented with precious stones. The roof of this palace is of pure gold, and all the lower rooms are paved with alternate square plates of gold and silver.'

This truly was an imperial power. When Odorico visited Trowulan, the capital of Majapahit, the ambitious prime minister Gajah Mada was busy conquering most of Java and other neighbouring kingdoms. According to the curious *Sumpah Palapa*, or 'Palapa Oath', sworn by Gajah Mada to Queen Tribhuwanatunggadewi, 'If Nusantara [the outer islands] are lost, I will not taste fruits or spices. I will not, if the domain of Gurun, domain of Seram, domain of Tanjungpura, domain of Haru, Pahang, Dompo, domain of Bali, Sunda, Palembang, Tumasik [Singapura], in which case I will never taste any spice.' In other words, he would not consume spices until he had succeeded in conquering a vast swathe of territory. Gajah Mada meant business. Majapahit's network of vassal states extended as far as Singapura.

Far to the north, an even more formidable power threatened the trading empires of Sumatra and the Malay Archipelago. In the twelfth century, Thai peoples began migrating south from China into the Chao Phraya River valley to found the kingdom of Sukhothai in what is now north-central Thailand. The Thai rulers were, to begin with, vassals of the Khmer Empire of Angkor but soon broke away to dominate the Chao Phraya region as far south as the Malay Peninsula. As Angkor declined, a second Thai kingdom, Ayutthaya, emerged in the lower basin of the river, just north of the Gulf of Thailand. The Ayutthayan kings ferociously exploited the maritime trade in the region and Ayutthaya soon became China's most important trading partner in the region. By the fifteenth century, Ayutthaya had absorbed Sukhothai in a single Thai kingdom and its navies dominated the Malay Peninsula, frequently raiding ships in the Strait of Malacca. The Thai kings were fearsome rulers who saw themselves as avatars or earthly incarnations of the Hindu god Vishnu. Many Thai rulers took the name of Rama, the 394th incarnation of Vishnu.

For the authors of the 'Malay Annals', the fall of Singapura is the prelude to the rise of Malacca. The chronicler tells the story as follows. The ruler of Majapahit is angered when he hears that Sri Tri Buana refuses to acknowledge him as overlord. He sends him a curious gift – a long wood shaving rolled up to resemble a girl's earring. The meaning of the gift is as difficult to understand as the rejoinder. Sri Tri Buana orders a carpenter to shave a boy's head with a wood cutting tool to demonstrate that he was as skilled as any Javanese craftsman. The ruler of Majapahit interprets this as a threat to shave the heads of his subjects and orders his navy to punish Singapura. The attack is beaten off. Soon afterwards, Singapura is blighted by a plague of dangerous garfish that leap out of the sea and stab people walking by the seashore. According to the Annals, 'thousands die' and Sri Tri Buana despairs. Then a young boy proposes building a fence along the shore made from the stems of banana trees. The garfish are thwarted – but Sri Tri Buana is so envious of the boy's success that he has him killed. 'The guilt of his blood was laid on Singapura.' Time passes and a new ruler succeeds Sri Tri Buana. Confusingly, the Annals call the new king Iskandar Shah but in other sources he is named Paramesvara, meaning 'supreme lord' in Sanskrit. It remains unclear after much scholarly debate whether Iskandar Shah changed his name to Paramesvara or vice versa – or even whether the names can be attached to the same individual. In any event, it is Iskandar Shah and/or Paramesvara whose impulsive actions will now lead to the fall of Singapura.

The story begins when Iskandar Shah discovers that one of his concubines has been unfaithful and has her stripped naked and displayed in the marketplace. He will regret imposing such a humiliating punishment, for her father is the royal treasurer. He is so enraged by the ruler's treatment of his daughter that he sends a vengeful message to the ruler of Majapahit, promising to help depose Iskandar Shah. And so it was that for the second time a Javanese fleet is sent to attack Singapura. The royal treasurer unlocks the city gates and soon 'the streets are awash with blood'. Iskandar Shah flees ... leaving Singapura in the hands of its more powerful Javanese rival.

The Rise of Malacca

The 'Malay Annals' tell us that Iskandar Shah, the last ruler of Singapura, fled the island and travelled north following the coast of the Malay Peninsula. Like his ancestor Sri Tri Buana, the ruler of Palembang, he was in search of an auspicious site to build a new city. He eventually arrived at a fishing village on the estuary of a large river, Sungai Bertam, and following the family tradition immediately set off on a hunt in the forest. When one of his hounds was attacked by mouse deer, Iskandar declared: 'This is a good place, when even its mouse deer are full of fight. We shall do well to make a city here.' His chiefs all heartily agreed. Iskandar Shah then enquired, 'What is the name of the tree under which I am sitting? The chiefs answered in unison, 'It is called Malacca, your highness.' He replied, 'Then Malacca shall be the name of the city.' 'Malacca' may have something to do with the Arabic for a meeting place, *malaquah*. But it was not uncommon for place names in Southeast Asia to refer to names of trees, and there is indeed a 'pokok Malacca' tree which has the scientific name *Phyllanthus embica*. In Sanskrit, the tree is called *amalaki* and is associated with Buddhist lore.

This is the story told in the 'Malay Annals' and it completes the hereditary chain that links Srivijaya with Singapura and finally Malacca. For many Malay scholars, Malacca is – in the words of historian Tim Harper – 'the focal point in a continuum of Malay history'. It was here that on 20 February 1956, Tunku Abdul Rahman, who was to become Malaysia's first prime minister, announced the date of the country's independence from British colonial rule. As the Annals tell us, Malacca was the apogee of Malay history. In Malay his-

toriography, the Annals is an account of the foundation of Malacca
as a renowned empire and emporium of trade. But it is not the only
account we have of the history of the city. The *Suma Oriental* was
written in Malacca between 1512 and 1515 by a Portuguese apoth-
ecary called Tomé Pires. Portuguese forces had captured Malacca in
1511. Although the *Suma* might be seen as a record of conquest, it
has genuine scholarly value. It was completed in Malacca some time
earlier than the Annals and so Pires was closer in time and place to
actual events and to people who remembered them. Pires wrote the
Suma for the Portuguese king, Manuel 'the fortunate', and he comes
across in the *Suma* as a meticulous researcher. He used a Javanese
chronicle, which he was convinced was the most reliable text at his
disposal and checked and double-checked information he collected
from merchants, sailors and officials.

Following his Javanese source, Pires tells the story of Paramesvara, the ruler of Palembang, who seems to be identical to Iskandar
Shah in the 'Malay Annals'. Pires, however, adds some intriguing details. He tells us that at the end of the fourteenth century, Paramesvara led a rebellion to oust the Javanese who had become overlords
of Palembang. Soundly defeated, Paramesvara fled across the Strait
of Malacca to Singapura 'where he arrived with all his junks'. Here,
without further ado, he slew the ruler and took power with the
backing of the Orang Laut, the 'sea people'. Pires tells us: 'Paramesvara was lord of all and governed the channel and islands ... and he
had no trade at all except that his people planted rice and plundered
their enemies....' So it seems that the piratical Paramesvara was an
even less savoury character than the Iskandar Shah of the Annals.

The story told in the *Suma* echoes many ingredients of the Annals but with intriguing twists. According to Pires, it is a Thai king
who launches an attack on Singapura. He tells us that the Siamese
army was so formidable that Paramesvara 'did not dare wait for him,
and fled with about a thousand men'. At this point, the story merges
with the narrative unfolded in the Annals: Paramesvara and his entourage sailed north along the Muar River, which brought them to
a 'plain surrounded by beautiful mountain ranges and abundant
waters'. And then one day, Paramesvara's son Xaquem Daxa goes
hunting. His dogs and greyhounds chase 'an animal like a hare' to
a hill, 'where there is the fruit of the Malays'. Here, the harelike

creature fiercely turns on the prince's hunting dogs. Later, Xaquem Daxa returns to his father and tells him the story of the hunt and the 'Malay' fruit trees. Paramesvara asks, 'Xaquem Daxa, where do you want to settle? and the son said on this hill of Malacca. The Father said it should be so. And at the said time he built his houses on top of the hill where the kings of Malacca have had their dwelling and residence until the present time.'

These variations on a theme are fascinating in their own right. The important point to take from both the Annals and the *Suma* is that in Malay legend there is an hereditary line that binds together Srivijaya, Singapura and Malacca. All three cities can be understood as mirror images of each other. They are all situated on rivers and the history of each revolves around events that take place on a hill – Bukit Seguntang in Palembang, where the godlike ancestors of the Malay rulers descended in a blaze of light; Bukit Larangang, the Forbidden Hill, in Singapura, the site of the royal palace and burial place; and St Paul's Hill in Malacca. Rivers and estuaries are the primary arteries of trade and prosperity. Hills and mountains are the birthplace of myths, echoes of Mount Meru, the sacred mountain of Hindu, Jain and Buddhist mythology, revered as the home of the gods and the axis of the world.

Before the catastrophic Portuguese conquest, Malacca prospered as a richly cosmopolitan maritime state. The *Sejarah Melayu*, ('Malay Annals') and other Malay texts such as the *Hikayat Hang Tuah* and the *Undang-Undang Melaka*, or 'Malacca Laws', established Malacca as an exemplar of Malay statecraft and a cultural reference for successor states in Johor-Riau, Perak and Penang that competed to inherit its mantle. In the meantime, Singapura vanishes from history and legend. What happened? There is no reason to doubt the Malay chroniclers. Singapura may well have been attacked by the much more powerful rulers of Majapahit and the Thai kingdom of Ayutthaya.

The Fall of Singapura

There are intriguing clues about the fate of Singapura in the archaeological finds made in the modern city. The ceramics unearthed under Fort Canning were mainly Chinese, and all but a handful of the finds have been dated to the Yuan or Mongol-led Yuan Dynasty which ruled China in the thirteenth century. The fifth Yuan emperor, Kublai Khan, who had completed the conquest of China begun by his grandfather Genghis Khan, promoted trade and welcomed foreign emissaries. Among these visitors was Marco Polo, the Venetian merchant who later acted as the emperor's agent. He established a new capital at what is now Beijing, known then as Dadu, which means 'Great Capital'. As emperor, Kublai Khan waged endless wars of conquest and demanded tribute from Burma, Java and Japan. On the surface, Kublai's China was a commercial hot house celebrated by Marco Polo for the use of paper money as the sole medium of exchange. This was a time of unprecedented prosperity that mainly benefited privileged foreign merchants who traded with the such kingdoms of the Nanyang as Singapura.

Then came catastrophe. In 1368, the Mongol Yuan Dynasty collapsed. Under the Ming emperors (1368–1644), the Confucian contempt for merchants and trade was back with a vengeance. For three centuries, China turned its back on the oceans. According to an edict of 1371, 'not even a little plank is allowed to drift to sea'. Under the Ming, foreign trade all but dried up, and so too did the wealth of Singapura and many smaller ports in the Southern Ocean. Majapahit remained the dominant trading kingdom in the region for some time, with near exclusive access to the Spice Islands. The fourteenth-century chronicle, *History of the Kings of Pasai*, describes people 'thronging in vast numbers' in the Majapahit capital of Trowulan on the Brantas River southeast of modern Surabaya: 'There was a ceaseless coming and going of people from the territories overseas which had submitted to the king, bring their offerings of beeswax, sandalwood, massoia bark, cinnamon, cloves and nutmeg piled in heaps.'

In the early fifteenth century, the imperial ban on trade went into reverse, for a few decades at least. Between 1405 and 1433, the third Ming emperor, Zhu Di, who took the regnal name of Yong-le ('perpetual happiness'), dispatched six enormous fleets of hundreds of ships and tens of thousands of soldiers across the Southern Ocean to India, the Red Sea, the Persian Gulf and East Africa. These remarkable naval expeditions, unprecedented in imperial history, were led by Admiral Zheng He and inspired an early Chinese novel, written by one

Luo Mao-deng in 1597 with the wonderful title *The Grand Director of the Three Treasures Goes down to the Western Ocean*. Zheng He is a fascinating individual, but like the expeditions he led he is encrusted by myth and speculation. We know for certain that he was born to a Muslim family in Bukhara, an important destination on the ancient Silk Road trading route. His father and grandfather were 'Hajji', devout pilgrims who had travelled to Mecca in the Arabian Peninsula. When the Ming armies invaded Yunnan, Zheng He's father was killed and his very young son was captured, taken to the imperial court and castrated. This was more an honour than a punishment. As a court eunuch, Zheng He rose to become a very powerful government official and must have had the ear of the emperor. After his death, Zheng He was deified by expatriate Chinese. Today, prayers are still offered to the admiral inside the Cheng Hoon Teng Temple in Malacca.

There is a huge and controversial literature about the Ming expeditions and Zheng He himself. What can be said with a high degree of certainty is that he was neither explorer nor imperial conqueror, and it is unlikely, as some historians have speculated, that he was a Muslim missionary. We know that he happily joined his crews to pray to the Chinese sea goddess Tianfei, known in some dialects as Mazu. So, if the Ming fleets were not voyages of exploration or conquest, what were they? As historian Donald Ellegood points out in his biography *Perpetual Happiness*, Emperor Yong-le made his intentions very clear: 'The four seas are too broad to be governed by one person. To rule requires delegation of powers.' Chinese emperors claimed the 'mandate of heaven' to rule as 'master of the world'. This was the rationale of the tribute system which required lesser states to acknowledge the overlordship of the emperor. Since Chinese emperors could not hope to *literally* rule every 'barbarian' kingdom, they had to find ways of compelling lesser rulers to acknowledge the imperial mandate. It was soft power with a very hard edge. When the Ming fleets sailed into the harbours of Malacca, Calicut, Aden and Mogadishu, the spectacle would have triumphantly affirmed the power and prestige of the Ming emperor.

Most prominent would have been the 'Treasure Ships'. These had been built in shipyards in Nanjing and carried a huge cargo of gifts to present to vassal rulers in the Southern Ocean and beyond. When Zheng He returned to China, he was accompanied by emissaries who presented tributes to the imperial court. Zheng He reported that 'we have traversed over a hundred thousand *li* [a traditional unit of measurement, about one-third of a mile] of vast ocean and have beheld great ocean waves, rising as high as the sky and swelling and swelling endlessly.... We spread our cloudlike sails aloft and sailed by the stars day and night.' Zheng He seemed to describe the weather phenomenon of St Elmo's fire in another passage: 'When we met with danger, once we invoked the divine name [Mazu], her answer to our prayers was like an echo – suddenly there was a divine lamp which illuminated the mast and sails, and once this miraculous light appeared, then apprehension turned to calm.'

As well as Zheng He's reports, and that rather curious novel mentioned earlier, we also have accounts of the Ming voyages written by Ma Huan, an interpreter of Persian and Arabic, and a soldier named Fei Xin. (Both Ma Huan's *The Overall Survey of the Ocean's Shores* and Fei Xin's *The Overall Survey of the Star Raft* are available in English translation.) These eye-witnesses left detailed descriptions of the topography, peoples and customs of the lands of the monsoon. It is telling that the chroniclers of the Ming voyages do not refer to Singapura and may only have sailed through the Singapore Strait, and may even have circumnavigated the Riau Archipelago since the strait was held to be notoriously treacherous. Be that as it may, it was the port city of Malacca and its ruler Paramesvara that fascinated the Chinese.

When Zheng He sailed into Malacca in 1412, the port town was rapidly emerging as the main trading centre on the straits. For Zheng He and his captains, Malacca was a vital base, where its ships could be repaired, and an important tributary power. The rise of Malacca in the fifteenth century owed everything to the power of the Ming emperor.

The Chinese were meticulous record-keepers, and in the *Ming Shih-lu* ('Veritable Records of the Ming') and the *Yung-lo Shih-lu* ('Veritable Records of the Emperor Yong-le') there are frequent references to Malacca. When the Chinese first came to Malacca and met its ruler Paramesvara, he was a vassal of the Thai empire – and it was Ming power that released Malacca from Siamese bondage. The *Yung-lo Shih-lu* tells us in journalistic detail what happened when the emperor's first emissary, Yin Ch'ing, arrived in Malacca two years before Zheng He: 'At the time, the envoys said that their king [Paramesvara] admired righteousness and wished to be like one of China's prefectures and annually offer tribute. The king asked that one of his mountains be designated the Grand Mountain of the State. The emperor commended this and ordered the officials of the Ministry of Rites thus, "The ancient rulers honoured the mountains and rivers, determined the boundaries, conferred nobility and set up feudal states in order to show special favour to distant peoples and demonstrate that no one is left out. We name the country's western mountain as the State Mountain and set up an inscription".

Malacca was brought under the protection of the world's wealthiest and most powerful state. The bond between China and Malacca was sealed when Zheng He's Treasure Ships sailed into the port two years later and the admiral decided to make the port city his regional 'base'. Ma Huan's account reveals what this meant in practice: 'Whenever the treasure ships of the Middle Kingdom [China] arrived [in Malacca], they at once erected a line of stockades, like a city wall and set up towers for the watch drums at four gates. At night they had patrols of guards carrying bells; inside, again they erected an inner stockade, like a small city wall, within which they constructed warehouses and granaries; and all the money and provisions were stored there. The ship which had gone to various countries returned to this place and assembled there. They marshalled the foreign goods and loaded them in the ships; then waited till the south wind was perfectly favourable ... and returned home.'

The Princess Bride

The authors of the *Sejarah Malayu*, the 'Malay Annals', have much to say about Paramesvara, that is to say, Iskandar Shah and his successor. They spin the relationship with China in a very different direction. In the story told in the Annals, it is not China but Malacca that holds the upper hand. The Emperor Yong-le, the 'Raja of Heaven', sends a shipload of needles to his counterpart in Malacca, one for every house in the realm. The message is that the Chinese are innumerable and that 'there are no greater Rajas than ourselves.' The Sultan of Malacca will have none of this and despatches a ship to China loaded with grains of sago to make the same point about his own subjects. So impressed is the emperor that he proclaims 'Great indeed must be this Raja of Malacca!'

The story has a quirky charm – but its authors had a very serious purpose. They were obliged to show off the prestige of the Malay rulers, not the Ming emperor. Another detail in the Annals version of the Pax Sinica is just as intriguing. Contemplating the sultan's gift of sago and what it suggested about the great power of Malacca, the emperor declared, 'It would be well that I should marry him with my daughter!' And so the captivating figure of the Chinese princess Hang Li Po steps gracefully into our story. Or does she?

Today, Hang Li Po's Well is a popular tourist attraction in Malacca, and for many Malaysian Chinese the Ming princess who lived among Malays and bore the ruler's children remains a meaningful historical figure. So when Malaysian historian Khoo Kai Khim claimed that poor Hang Li Po was a fabrication, he stirred up a paper tempest. Khoo pointed out that there is not a single reference to Hang Li Po in the many Chinese accounts of relations with Malacca. The single source of the story is the *Sejarah Melayu* ('Malay Annals'). Khoo's claim upset many Malaysian Chinese and it now seems he may well have been wrong. And it is Tomé Pires, the Portuguese chronicler, who gallops to the rescue of Hang Li Po – or someone very much like her.

In the *Suma Oriental*, Pires sets the record straight. Instead of a Chinese princess marrying Sultan Mansur Shah, he tells the story of an unnamed Chinese woman who gets hitched to the second ruler of Malacca, Sultan Megat Iskandar Shah (r. 1414–24), the son of Paramesvara aka Iskandar Shah. He also fleshes out the tale with some persuasive details. At the beginning of his reign, the sultan sailed to China to pay allegiance to Emperor Yong-le. In Beijing, he was received with great honour, and when he returned home he was entrusted to a 'Great Captain' to ensure his safety. Now this Chinese captain had, Pires tells us, a beautiful daughter, and when his ship arrived in Malacca, the sultan 'honoured his protector' by marrying his daughter, 'though she was not a woman of rank'. Later, she bore the sultan a son. The 'Great Captain' may well have been Zheng He who accompanied Sultan Megat Iskandar Shah to the Ming court in 1417. Since Zheng He was unlikely to have fathered any children, this suggestion further complicates the identity of the sultan's bride. Perhaps the admiral's 'Chinese daughter' was adopted and may well have been Muslim. This is speculation, but what we can say is that the story told in the *Suma* gallantly rescues Hang Li Po from oblivion.

In the fifteenth century, the Ming emperors guaranteed the security of Malacca, freeing Iskandar Shah and his successors from servitude to the Thai rulers of Ayutthaya and the Javanese. China had little influence on the customs and beliefs of the ruler's subjects and Malacca would always be a city of many different faiths. But as the Portuguese chronicler Tomé Pires tells us: 'The Moors were great favourites with the king and obtained whatever they wanted.' It was these deepening bonds with Muslim traders, Pires claims, that nourished trade and 'the king derived great pleasure and satisfaction from it.' In the next chapter, we will tell the story of how Islam revolutionised the lands below the winds.

CHAPTER 5

Faith on the Wings of Trade: The Coming of Islam to Southeast Asia

Ibn Battatu, Pilgrim, Scholar and Travel Writer

T he greatest travel writer of the pre-modern age, Abu Abdulla ibn Battuta strode, rode and sailed some 75,000 miles across forty countries and three continents. He journeyed to Constantinople, the capital of the Byzantine Empire, in the company of a Turkish princess. He travelled eastward through Transoxiana, Khurasan and Afghanistan to reach the banks of the Indus. And, yet, the great journey of Ibn Battuta had only just begun. His dream was to reach China, but to see for himself the realm of the Sons of Heaven he would have to sail through the Strait of Malacca.

Born in Tangier at the dawn of the fourteenth century, Ibn Battatu survived, by the skin of his teeth, all kinds of mishaps, tropical storms, shipwreck on a rocky shore and pirate attacks to eventually find his way home to write his celebrated *Rihla*, or 'Book of Travels'. As a devout Muslim and legal scholar, Ibn Battuta was fascinated by the customs, rulers and cities of the 'Dar al-Islam', the abode of the faith, which he explored and reported on. The *Rihla* is a vibrantly human, even quirky, panorama of a fast-changing world captured at the moment that the message of the Prophet was first beginning to be heard in Asia. Ibn Battuta was both pilgrim and scholar, a sharp-eyed adventurer driven by a passionate curiosity about the wider impact of his own faith. He was, it has been said, 'world-minded'.

Ibn Battuta was not a fanatic. One of the most gripping chapters in the *Rihla* describes his arrival in the Hindu kingdom of Jaffna in the northern part of Sri Lanka and his ascent of Adam's Peak, a mountain sacred to Muslims, Hindus and Buddhists. Pilgrims ascended to the summit where a depression in the rock resembled the imprint of an enormous foot. For Hindus, it was the trace of the Great God Shiva, for Buddhists the footprint of the Buddha, and for Muslims the place where Adam and Eve fell after their expulsion from the seventh heaven. When he reached the summit of the peak after a hazardous ascent, Ibn Battuta joined a brotherhood of fellow pilgrims, Muslim, Hindu and Buddhist.

After surviving storms, shipwreck and pirate attack, Ibn Battuta set sail on a commercial junk for the Strait of Malacca. He was now travelling into the unknown beyond the frontiers of the 'Dar al-Islam', where the Sacred Law of the Prophet and the rightly guided society had yet to set down roots. Arab and Iranian sailors and traders had voyaged from the Persian Gulf to the South China coast and back again since the eighth century. Muslim communities flourished in Quanzhou, Guangzhou and other southern Chinese ports, and their success led many Chinese to convert to this business-friendly faith. The allure of China for Muslims and other outsiders was deepened when Kublai Khan overthrew the Song. The new Mongol rulers, who distrusted the Confucian bureaucracy, opened China to outsiders, and in the thirteenth century many hundreds of Muslims from the Middle East and Central Asia took lucrative positions as tax collectors and bureaucrats. This open-door policy drew Muslim merchants to the booming ports and cities of southern China. Here, Muslims settled and built mosques, bazaars and hospitals in self-governing enclaves. This vibrant new world that seemed to extend the frontiers of the Dar al-Islam far to the east is what drew Ibn Battuta to China. But as his creaky old junk entered the Strait of Malacca, he would discover to his dismay that the word of the Prophet was as yet only dimly heard in the Malay world.

Ibn Battuta sailed into the Strait of Malacca in the autumn of 1345. After rounding the northern tip of Sumatra, he arrived in the port of Samudera-Pasai. As he would soon realise, Ibn Battuta had reached the last outpost of the Dar al-Islam, and as he travelled through the strait before veering north towards China, he would encounter few others of his own faith. In Samudera, he was warmly greeted by Sultan Al-Malik al-Zahir, who was third in a line of Mus-

Spread of Islam
in Southeast Asia
1500 – 1700

CHINA

Quanzhou
1010

BURMA

Thanglong

SIAM

Andaman
Sea

Ayutthaya
1540

Bangkok

Hue

Hoi An

Vijaya

Lozon

Manila
1500

PHILIPPINES

South China Sea

Pnompenh
1640

CHAMPA

Champa
1030

Saigon

Gulf of
Siam

Nakhon
Sithammarat

Patani
1520

Kedah

Pasai
1290

Samudra

ACEH
1400

Barus **BATAK**

**Malay
Peninsula**

Trengganu
1303

Melaka
1410

Pariaman

S u m a t r a

Palembang

Banten
525

Cirebon
1525

Sunda Strait

Demak
1480

Java

Pajang

Visayas

Cebu
1565

Palawan

Sulu Sea

Mindanao

Sulu
1460

Brunei
1500

Brunei

Celebes Sea

Borneo

Karimata Strait

Tanjungpura

Banjarmasin

Java Sea

Martapura

Makassar
Strait

Celebes

Makassar
1605

Buton
1580

Ternate
1460

Tidore

Maluccas

Seram

Ambon
1544

Bandaneira

Banda Sea

Gresik
1410

Tuban

Majapahit

Bali

Lombok

Sumbawa

Sumba

Flores Sea

Flores

Timor

Arafura Sea

INDIAN OCEAN

Timor Sea

AUSTRALIA

90° 95° 100° 105° 110° 115° 120° 125° 130° 135°

	Muslim by 1500		Christian by 1600
	Muslim by 1600		Christian by 1700
	Muslim by 1700		Christian minorities
	Muslim minorities	→	Islamic trade routes

lim rulers who had converted to Islam half a century earlier. Here in Samudera, Ibn Battuta was overjoyed to discover a truly Islamic culture. He attended Friday prayers at the mosque and was invited to the sultan's palace where the sultan presided over debates about the finer points of Islamic law with visiting Muslims.

The Chinese Connection

With the arrival of the southwest monsoon, Ibn Battuta bade farewell to Sultan Al-Malik al-Zahir and sailed south into the gullet of the strait, 'the country of the infidels'. When he eventually arrived in Guangzhou in southern China, Ibn Battuta was awed by the wealth and splendour of China. He described the beauty of Chinese silk and porcelain, admired its paper money, the size of its chickens and the quality of its plums. He also experienced culture shock: 'China was beautiful,' he recalled, 'but it did not please me. On the contrary, I was greatly troubled thinking about the way paganism dominated this country. Whenever I went out of my lodging, I saw many blameworthy things. That disturbed me so much that I stayed indoors most of the time.'

In the mid-fourteenth century, Islam had yet to conquer the islands of the Malay world. But Ibn Battuta was wrong about China. The story of the rise of Muslim kingdoms and cultures in the Malay Peninsula and across the Malay Archipelago was driven by a convergence of scholars, merchants and teachers who came from every corner of the Muslim world. Ibn Battuta may have been disappointed by his time in Guangzhou, but it would be Muslims from China who would first bring the faith of the Prophet to the worlds of the Nanyang, the 'Southern Ocean'. Here, Muslims encountered maritime kingdoms that were rich in older beliefs, customs and traditions. The island of Java was studded with innumerable shrines and temples of Hindu and Buddhist gods and spirits. In many regions of the Malay Archipelago, even older animist customs and beliefs still held sway. Islam would never completely unweave this intricate tapestry. Instead, the peoples of the Malay world would, in time, fuse the teachings of the Koran with much older customs and beliefs. Like the great Indic cultures of Buddhism and Hinduism, Islam revolutionised Southeast Asia not by conquest but through commerce and persuasion.

The Arab Conquests

It was a very different story in the Levant, North Africa and Central Asia. In the decades that followed the Prophet's death, Arab armies inspired by the new religion erupted out of the Arabian desert to carve out an Islamic empire centred on Baghdad, which would soon rival Imperial Rome at its zenith, that extended from the borders of Imperial China in the east to the Atlantic coast in the west. The lightning-fast Arab conquests of the seventh and eighth centuries were one of the greatest feats of arms in human history and changed the world forever. Many centuries after the Arab conquests, Islam came to Southeast Asia, not at the point of a sword but on the wings of trade.

So, Islam was a revolutionary faith. The Prophet preached, in the language of our own time, equality, human rights and the rule of law. The ideal Islamic state offers its people a universal code of guidance that applies equally to rulers and the ruled without discrimination based on descent, rank or wealth. Under Islam, at least in theory, a ruler who chooses the path of tyranny and causes hardships for his people forfeits the right to govern and can or must be deposed. Under Islam, government and commerce must be conducted by equals and according to strict codes. The lessons of Islam would have a deep attraction both for Asian rulers and their subjects and for ambitious merchants and traders who could share the same rules of commercial conduct.

Islam In China

Modern scholarship has shown that the story of Islam in Southeast Asia begins not in India and the Middle East but in Imperial China. According to Chinese Muslims, it was a diplomat and soldier called Sa'd ibn Abī Waqqās who, a thousand years ago, first preached the Koran in China. Revered as the maternal uncle of the Prophet, he was sent on diplomatic missions to the court of the Tang emperor in the seventh century. This was the first Chinese dynasty to allow all foreign religions freedom in the land of Confucius. Remarkably, Zoroastrianism, Judaism and Islam all flourished in China in the seventh century. It is said that when conflict erupted between rival

Muslim dynasties, Sa'd ibn Abī Waqqās fled Arabia and sought refuge in present-day Guangzhou. Muslim pilgrims come from all over the world to visit the 'Muslim Hero Tomb' where he is buried. Chinese sources tell us that many other Arab tributary missions arrived at the court of the Tang emperor. Some of these Muslim envoys took Chinese surnames such as *Li* or *Pu*, which were derived from *Ali* and *Abu*. The first mosque was built in Guangzhou for Arabs and Persians who traded across the Indian Ocean and the South China Sea. Then came the Mongol conquest of China and a new dynasty that overturned the old order and offered power and prosperity to Muslims from all over Central Asia.

In Chinese culture, foreigners are referred to as barbarians or, even less politely, 'foreign devils'. In Chinese script, part of the written character that refers to barbarians is the same as one used for animals. Yet, for two centuries China was ruled by barbarians. These barbarian emperors of China originated from nomadic tribes that roamed the steppes of the Mongolian plateau. Genghis or Chinggis Khan, which means 'Universal Ruler', forcibly united the Mongol clans under what came to be known as the 'Pax Mongolica'. In the course of the thirteenth and fourteenth centuries, the Mongol ruler and his sons and grandsons conquered the biggest land empire in world history. The Mongol Empire extended from Korea to Hungary, and from Iraq, Tibet, and Burma to Siberia. In the West, the Mongols were called the 'Golden Horde' after the colour of their tents. At the height of their power, the highly civilised Mongols established an international system of diplomacy and built trading networks on a globalised scale.

By the time Genghis's son Kublai Khan was born in 1215, the Mongols had seized the northern China capital of Yen-Ching, present-day Beijing, and the Song emperor and his family had fled south. His grandson would finish the job. Kublai began by conquering Yunnan and establishing a new capital which he called Shangdu, a name which Europeans would hear as Xanadu. After the death of his father, Kublai became the 'Great Khan' and set his sights on completing the conquest of China. By 1279, Kublai Khan had crushed the last of the Song rulers. He now ruled over all of present-day China, from Yunnan bordering Vietnam and Burma to Xinjiang stretching into Central Asia. To win over his new subjects, he took on the Chinese name of Yuan and established a new capital on the site of present-day Beijing. Kublai Khan's conquest of southern China threw open a gateway to the 'Silk Road of the Sea', trade routes and commercial networks that linked China to Southeast Asia and the Indian Ocean, and beyond to the Persian Gulf, the Red Sea, the Mediterranean and the shores of Africa.

But the Yuan emperor had a problem. The Mongol rulers were mighty conquerors but slapdash rulers. Even Kublai Khan himself, who was known as 'Setsen Khan', the 'Wise Khan', relied on hordes of foreign advisors who, it was said, slyly admonished the emperor: 'I have heard that one can conquer the empire on horseback, but one cannot govern it on horseback.' Kublai Khan was forced to govern through the old Song bureaucracy but distrusted the Han Chinese mandarin who controlled it. The solution was an open-door policy that lured 'Barbarian' talent. Under Mongol rule, China became a lucrative El Dorado for foreign advisors, or expats as we would say today. And the plan worked. The rule of the Yuan emperor saw grand infrastructure projects, including an efficient postal system and the extension of the Grand Canal from southern China to the new capital. This was the Mongol China that so impressed the Venetian merchant Marco Polo who visited the emperor's sumptuous summer palace at Shangdu. Kublai Khan lured Marco Polo into his service, probably as a tax collector, and sent him on missions to Hangzhou and perhaps as far as Burma. Marco Polo's ghost-written *The Description of the World*, later known as *The Travels of Marco Polo*, offered a distinctly reverential account of the emperor and his palaces. But Kublai Khan had unwittingly sown the seeds of decline and catastrophe.

Under the Yuan emperors, Mongols formed a privileged military caste who were exempt from taxation and lived at the expense of the Chinese peasantry, who worked the huge Mongol estates. It was the so-called 'Semuren', or privileged foreign auxiliaries, who administered the affairs of state and commerce. They, too, were exempt from taxation. Under the Yuan rulers, China resembled a huge Mongol colony and was blighted by extremes of inequality. The Song Dynasty had also favoured Muslim administrators but under the Mongols, hundreds of thousands of highly educated Muslims came to China from Persia and Central Asia to serve as administrators and tax collectors. A Muslim architect called Amir al-Din worked on the construction of the new 'Great Capital'. Muslims, who were known as Hui, had become the largest non-Chinese ethnic group in Yuan China by the end of the fourteenth century. Then in 1357, events took an unexpected turn. In China, rebellions had broken out against the Yuan rulers, and in Quanzhou a Shia Persian faction rose against the descendants of Muslim administrator Pu Shougeng and seized control of the port. At first, the rebels attacked Sunni graves, mosques and homes, but the violence escalated to threaten all Muslims in Quanzhou. Many fled into the mountains. Thousands escaped on boats for the refuge of the Southern Ocean. Javanese chroniclers describe Muslims flocking to Surabaya, Gresik and Cirebon, which would become early centres of Islamic culture. In many other regions of Southeast Asia, we find traces of the Muslim refugees in Barus on the west coast of Sumatra and in Trengganu [now Terengganu] on the east coast of the Malay Peninsula. On the island of Borneo, the kingdom of Brunei adopted Islam in the same period.

Kublai's dream of world domination would never be realised. He twice despatched huge armadas to conquer Japan, and twice the Mongol fleet was annihilated by ferocious typhoons that the Japanese called *kamikaze*, meaning 'divine wind'. The Mongol dream of world conquest foundered with Kublai's ships. The emperor became fat and ill. He suffered from gout. His wife and only son and heir died. He who had conquered China died in 1294. Kublai Khan's empire passed into less competent hands and was eaten away by war and rebellion. Eighty years after Kublai Khan's death, the Mongol warriors rode back into the windswept grasslands which had once nourished the dream of empire.

Light In The West

The great diaspora of Muslims from Mongol China seeded Islam in the worlds of the Nanyang, but it is only part of the story. Long before the Mongol invasion of China, the peoples of the Arabian Peninsula ventured on land and sea journeys that linked the fertile regions of the peninsula, such as Oman, Bahrain and the Hadramout in Yemen, with the Persian Gulf and the Indian Ocean. After the rise of Islam in the seventh century and the Arab conquest of Iran, Arab merchants would, over time, become masters of the Eastern maritime trade. Arabs settled on the Coromandel Coast of southern India and married local women. Many Hindu families adopted the new faith so that their sons could learn seamanship. We should be wary of the term 'Arab' in old texts, for the Muslim community was highly diverse. Much of the trade to and from Southeast Asia was likely handled by Indian Muslim middlemen who, in turn, traded with Arabs in the ports of southern India. A huge volume of trade was through 'middlemen' and thus point-to-point rather than end-to-end. South Asians had the great advantage of controlling the production of valuable textiles which were worn and prized by all Southeast Asians, especially the ruling classes. They transported these goods to ports in the Malay Peninsula, Sumatra and Java and exchanged them there for local spices and imported Chinese trade goods. Some European, Arab, Persian, Chinese and other traders and explorers undoubtedly travelled the entire maritime silk route that linked the Mediterranean to Chinese ports. But these travellers were the exception rather than the rule in earlier times.

From the Coromandel Coast, it was a short hop to Sri Lanka, and soon enterprising Muslim traders began venturing across the Indian Ocean and into the Strait of Malacca. By the ninth century, Arab written sources refer to the northwest and east coasts of Sumatra, the Malacca Strait as far as Palembang, Johor and the Riau-Lingga Archipelago. The majority of Arab traders, however, preferred the overland China routes, and there is scant evidence of any established Muslim communities. Some very old Muslim grave markers have been discovered in Kedah, but belonged to Persian traders, not local converts.

The rise of the Mongols had another remarkable consequence in western Asia. When Ibn Battuta arrived in the port of Samudera-Pasai at the edge of the Muslim world in Sumatra, the networks of trade that linked China with India and the Middle East had been disrupted when the Mongols swept away the Abbasid Caliphate and seized Baghdad. The Persian Gulf was effectively closed to shipping, forcing merchants to find alternative routes through the Red Sea to Alexandria. Since the caliph in Egypt permitted the only passage of Muslim shipping, the Muslim-dominated ports of the Gujerat region

of India, such as Cambay and Surat, now became import tranship-
ment centres for spices from the East. The Muslim Gujerati merchants were in the right place with the most lucrative products at
the most propitious time. Then in 1433, the Ming Dynasty, which
had ousted the last Mongol emperor, banned Chinese private trade.
Demand for spices in the Middle East and Europe was insatiable,
and so with the Chinese private traders out of the loop, the Gujeratis
soon dominated the flow of spices between the Indian Ocean and
the Spice Islands. Tomé Pires estimated that 4,000–5,000 Gujerati
merchants sailed into the Strait of Malacca every year. Many other
Muslim Indian traders from the Malabar and Coromandel coasts
plied the same sea routes, and many thousands settled in the monsoon ports. The brought with them not just trade goods but the
teachings of Islam – its values and ways of life.

For the ordinary people of Malacca, the faith of the Gujerati and
Muslim Chinese merchants who plied their trade in the port became inextricably bound up with an honourable way of doing good
business where everyone respected the rules. The Muslim scholars
who followed in the wake of the merchants preached a message of
equality: Allah was indifferent to rank or hierarchy. Everyone who
gathered for Jum'ah, the Friday Prayers, was equal to every other
Muslim worshipper who prostrated himself in the mosque: 'O you
who believe! When you are called to congregational (Friday) prayer,
hasten to the remembrance of God and leave off trade.' For the rulers of Malacca, Islam meant something altogether different. For
them, Islam was the faith of power.

The Conversion of the Ruler of Malacca

For the authors of the *Sejarah Melayu* ('Malay Annals'), the water-
shed moment in the history of Malacca, the foundational Malay
state, was the conversion of the ruler. The Annals tell the story as
follows. One night, the Prophet Muhammad appears to Raja Tengah, the grandson of the founder of Malacca, in a dream and offers
a crash course in the lessons of the Koran and the declaration of
faith, the *shahadah*. He gives him the Muslim name of Muhammad
and tells him that a ship will arrive from Jeddah the next morning:
'A man will land on the shore.... See that you do whatever he tells

you....' When Raja Tengah awakes, he discovers he has been circumcised. He begins reciting the *shahadah* and excitedly tells his ministers about his dream of the Prophet. The Bendahara, or chief minister, is sceptical. He is doubtful about the veracity of the raja's dream and the meaning of the miraculous circumcision. He is won over when the ship from Jeddah arrives on time as promised and a Makhdum, a teacher of Islam named Sayyid 'Abdul 'Aziz disembarks and begins to preach: 'There was such a disturbance that noise of it came to ears of the Raja ... who straightaway set forth on his elephant escorted by his ministers ... and he said to the Bendahara "That is exactly how it happened in my dream."' Now there could be no doubt: the Bendahara and the other ministers and chiefs become Muslims and escorted Sayyid 'Abdul 'Aziz to the palace ... 'and every citizen of Malacca, whether of high or low degree, was commanded by the Raja to do likewise'. Malacca was an Islamic state by decree.

To fully decipher the story told in the 'Malay Annals', it helps to know a little more about the history of Islam. The faith of Islam originated in the harsh world of the Arabian deserts. The Prophet preached the nobility of each individual as equal before Allah, but as the faith took root in other cultures it was taken up by powerful rulers who changed the message for their own purposes. In Persia, Muslim theologians began to preach that the ruler of Shah was the 'Shadow of God upon Earth'. Islam could, in other words, be used to bolster the ruler's right to rule since 'He who obeys the Sultan obeys God.' When Persian merchants and scholars entered the Malay world, this was the message they brought with them. Inscriptions begin to refer to the raja or sultan as the 'shadow of God, one who governed on earth in place of God'. In another famous 'Annal', the *Hikayat Hang Tuah*, we learn of a wealthy but ill-starred Indian merchant who suffers the misfortune to live in a land without a raja. So he 'expends his property' (i.e. sells land) to buy in such a ruler because 'the property of this world can have no use' in a ruler-less world. Subjects, we are being told, need rulers as much as rulers need subjects. It is better to be the poorer subject of a raja than a wealthy landowner without one. Like the Hindu and Buddhist faiths, Islam guaranteed the power of the powerful.

The Rise of Malay Malacca

Islam offered merchants a code of trusted practice and bolstered the status of rulers and nobles. They became sultans, semi-divine 'shadows of God'. But Islam alone does not explain the rise of medieval Malacca. The Ming Emperor Yong-le honoured and protected Malacca because it provided a secure and convenient hub 'below the winds'. Traders favoured Malacca because, like the rulers of Srivijaya, the sultan of Malacca forged allegiances with groups of Orang Laut (sea nomads) to protect the sea lanes and attack ships using rival ports. As a port, Malacca had a reputation for competence and offered safe warehouses for traders waiting for the northeast monsoon. Merchants who traded in Malacca had begun their journeys in the Gujerat and in southern India, China, Arabia, the Philippines and Java. This was a vibrantly diverse and competitive community where merchants sometimes came to blows. A book of rules, the *Undang-undang Malacca*, believed to have been compiled during the reign of the third Muslim ruler of Malacca, Muhammad Shah (r. 1442–44), contained laws and regulations to impose order in the Malacca sultanate. The ruler also appointed four harbour masters, or Shabandar, to act on behalf of the different ethnicities and help resolve disputes. So Malacca offered safe passage through the strait and an efficient rule-based business environment. It is little wonder that medieval Malacca flourished as a collecting centre for nutmeg, cloves and mace from the islands of the Nusantara, or Malay Archipelago, and for Indian textiles from Gujerat, Bengal and the Coromandel Coast. Malay traders came to Malacca with aromatic woods and products of the sea. As Pires put it, Malacca was a port 'where you could find what you want, and sometimes more than you are looking for'. When the sultan gazed out from his palace high above the port, he might see on any one day more than 2,000 boats lying at anchor and know that the royal coffers were bursting at the seams.

By the time of Sultan Muzaffar Shah (r. 1446–59), Malacca had become the most powerful and commercially successful port city in the Malay Peninsula. It provided the development model for other Malay states, and all became centres of Muslim learning. His successor, Sultan Mansur Shah (r. 1459–77), was a great ruler, Pires says, 'who built a mosque of surpassing beauty'. No wonder that Southeast Asia became known as the 'Muslim Lake'. According to the 'Malay Annals', the fame of Malacca 'spread throughout the world' and foreigners flocked to the port bringing their wealth and culture. This was the golden age of Malacca.

A Vulnerable Emporium

The Malay nationalist Dr Burhanuddin Al-Helmy proclaimed, 'On the ruins of Malacca Fort, we build the soul of independence.' But the Malacca of history was never powerful enough to stand and prosper alone. Its rulers depended on the patronage of the Ming emperors, and sometimes the Malaccan rulers had to buy off the Siamese threat by paying tribute in Chinese gold. The 'soul of independence' was never truly a sovereign power.

In short, Malacca was a small port city surrounded by enemies. The Siamese attacked the city in 1445 and 1456, and the raja was often forced to swallow his pride and pay tribute to Siam in Chinese gold. The sultans proclaimed their power by building an extravagant palace atop Bukit Melaka, the present-day St Paul's Hill, and indulging in elaborate court rituals. Ritual objects, such as the *keris* dagger, are mentioned frequently in the 'Malay Annals'. Many are described as being made of gold for 'Where there is sovereignty, there is gold.' The Annals refer obsessively to gold – there are bejewelled chairs of gold, golden caskets crammed with precious stones, gold bowls, gold plates, horses with gold trappings, even golden yachts. No one but the ruler is permitted to wear gold, unless it is a present from the ruler – and then he must wear it in perpetuity. Yellow, the imperial Chinese colour, could be worn only by members of the sultan's family. The power of the Malacca rulers was all about display. But all those gold objects and rituals could not protect Malacca from a determined and avaricious enemy power.

At the beginning of the sixteenth century, the Malay annalists tell us that 'there came a ship of the Franks from Goa, trading to Malacca and the Franks saw how populous and well-populated the port was.' The 'Franks' were the Portuguese, who envied the wealth of Malacca and, as Christians, feared and detested the faith of its rulers and peoples. They wanted, above all, to release the stranglehold Arab and Asian merchants had on global trade in the riches of the East. Now they would wage a crusade from their Iberian homelands to crush the infidels and control the wealth of the Indies. The first Europeans to seek a foothold in Asia would stop at nothing to overturn the old order of things in the lands of gold.

CHAPTER 6

Strangers from the West: The Portuguese Seize Malacca

Dawn, 25 July 1511.... The cacophonous din was overwhelming, like the thunder of heaven according to the authors of the *Sejarah Melayu* ('Malay Annals'). A succession of blasts from batteries of cannon and squealing trumpets shattered the early morning silence of the port of Malacca as it stirred into life. The firing of Portuguese muskets was like the rattling of dried peas. The infernal din drowned the morning call to prayer reverberating from the mosque. From the Istana, Sultan Mahmud Shah gazed out anxiously at the eighteen Portuguese galleons that had sailed imperiously into his kingdom. Few Asians had experienced the ear- and body-shattering power of modern artillery: shock and awe was just what the 'Great' Afonso d'Albuquerque, the Portuguese admiral, intended. The barrage of cannon fire that erupted in Malacca on that July morning in 1511 was the terrifying din of a new age.

Coveting the Riches of the East

The Portuguese had first spied on Malacca two years earlier, in 1509. Diego Lopes de Sequeira had sailed into the estuary with a squadron of galleons and demanded permission to build a fort close to the city. Sultan Mahmud seems to have grasped that these Bengali Putih, or 'white Bengalis', posed a serious threat and launched an attack. This time, the Portuguese were routed. They abandoned two ships and left behind some twenty of their shipmates who were taken captive. One of the men imprisoned by the sultan was Ferdinand Magellan who would circumnavigate the globe ten years later in search of the Spice Islands. The sultan's humiliation of Diego de Sequeira was one of the first acts of colonial resistance in Southeast Asian history. But there was more to the Portuguese assault on Malacca than mere revenge. In the great cities of Europe like Lisbon, London and Amsterdam, European merchants and monarchs had begun to covet the riches of the East. In the fire and fury of the Portuguese guns, a new era in world history was about to be born.

In the East, China was unchallenged as a regional power. But in the heartlands of Islam, tremendous changes reverberated across the ancient maritime silk roads. At the beginning of the sixteenth century, the Safavid Dynasty seized power in Persia. Just a decade or so later, the Mughals became dominant in India and in Central Asia, and the Ottoman rulers in Istanbul despatched conquering armies across Syria, the Arabian Peninsula and into Egypt and North Africa. They now controlled the sacred cities of Mecca and Medina. In the Muslim world, the spectacular rise of the Ottoman Empire unleashed a cultural revolution as Muslim teachers and scholars and their disciples were swept up in the wake of the Caliphate's all-conquering armies. The old Muslim trading networks were deepened and extended to encompass a vast market of lucrative commodities, as well as the latest weapons and the services of expert military personnel. Soon vast swathes of the known world were splitting into armed encampments of opposing faiths, not for the first or last time.

Iberian Crusaders

In Europe, it was the Catholic powers of the Iberian Peninsula that took on the role of defenders of Christendom. By the Treaty of Tordesillas in 1494, the kings of Spain and Portugal agreed to divide between them the entire world beyond European borders. The treaty had been endorsed by Pope Julius II in return for the Iberian rulers promising to impose their faith on any heathen peoples who were encountered in any newly 'discovered' lands. The Spanish and Portuguese royal families were enthusiastic backers of exploration and conquest. Historians often cite Prince Henry 'the Navigator'

(1394–1460) as the architect of Portuguese expansion, but in fact Henry did very little navigating and his ambitions were mainly focused on the other side of the Mediterranean, in North Africa. It was Manuel I (1469–1521), who inherited the Portuguese throne in 1495, who was obsessed with a coming apocalypse and waging a holy war on Islam who sent Vasco da Gama to venture round the Cape of Good Hope into the Indian Ocean in search of spices. When da Gama returned in triumph with enticing samples of pepper from Calicut, Manuel proclaimed himself 'king of Portugal, lord of Guinea, lord of the conquest and navigation and commerce of Ethiopia, Arabia, Persia and India'. From the very beginning of Portuguese expansion into Asia, European explorers wielded sword and gun to get their way. The foundations of the European maritime empires were laid by these Portuguese bullies. And let us not forget that it was Vasco da Gama's royal patron, King Manuel I of Portugal, who forced Portuguese Jews to convert to Christianity and expelled all his Muslim subjects. Portugal was the first European kingdom of the Iberian to create an exclusively Christian realm.

Royal patronage of new trading networks galvanised the port of Lisbon as 'the wharf between the seas', with busy enclaves of Genoese, Venetian, Florentine, Flemish, French and German merchants. The Portuguese planned to wrest the lucrative spice trade from Turkish control; Portuguese galleons would circumvent the Ottoman stranglehold on the Red Sea and the Persian Gulf, and explore and map new sea routes to the Spice Islands like Maluku to rake in profits from cargoes of pepper, cinnamon, and the holy trinity of clove, nutmeg and mace. As well as profit, there was another spur goading Portuguese ambitions. Spain and Portugal were Christian kingdoms that had defeated the armies of a Muslim caliphate that had once ruled the peninsula. Now the two Christian powers would wage a trade war against Muslim commercial networks in Asia and a holy war against Islam. Portugal's 'Glorious Enterprise' was driven by religious fervour, pride and commercial greed. The Portuguese kings managed a unique kind of state-directed capitalism: a Crown trade that sought a monopoly in its overseas territories by offering concessions to individuals who were charged with buying and selling commodities and returning a proportion of their profits to the Crown. And the architect of Portugal's Asian empire, the *Estado da India*, was Afonso d'Albuquerque, a veteran military and naval commander.

The Portuguese Conqueror

D'Albuquerque established his headquarters in Goa on India's southwest coast, ousting the local sultan and founding a colonial fiefdom that would endure for half a millennium. Here, in Velha Goa, d'Albuquerque conceived an ambitious scheme to capture the spice trade for Portugal and quash the power of Islam. He realised that his plan would mean taking control of the trading routes along the west coast of India, then seizing Hormuz at the mouth of the Persian Gulf and Aden at the entrance to the Red Sea. But d'Albuquerque faced a formidable rival. From his fiefdom in Malacca, Sultan Mahmud Shah controlled the flow of trade between the Spice Islands and the Indian Ocean, and the sultan had already humiliated Portugal by sending her galleons packing and capturing her intrepid sailors. There was little point seizing the ports of the Arabian Peninsula if Sultan Mahmud controlled the flow of trade through the Strait of Malacca.

D'Albuquerque outlines the plan in his *Commentaries*: 'The King of Portugal has often commanded me to go to the Straits, because ... this was the best place to intercept the trade which the Moslems ... carry on in these parts. So it was to do Our Lord's service that we were brought here; by taking Malacca, we would close the Straits so that never again would the Moslems be able to bring their spices by this route.... I am very sure that, if this Malacca trade is taken out of their hands, Cairo and Mecca will be completely lost.'

So it was that on 2 May 1511 d'Albuquerque set sail with 18 galleons and some 1,200 Portuguese and South Indian troops across the Bay of Bengal to teach the sultan of Malacca a lesson he would not forget. Once he had shown off the firepower of his cannons, d'Albuquerque demanded the return of de Sequeira's crew and permission to build a fort near the port. Once again, Sultan Mahmud refused. D'Albuquerque ordered his captains to bombard Malacca. Portuguese fire smashed ships in the harbour and set warehouses alight. Cowed, the sultan agreed to release his prisoners. But this was not enough for the Portuguese. D'Albuquerque redoubled the attack. He now ordered his troop commanders to take the city by storm. The key that would unlock the spice trade lay before him. In his *Suma Oriental*, Tomé Pires puts a Christian slant on the negotiations: '... the levity of the Malayans, and the reckless vanity and arrogant advice of the Javanese, and the king's presumption and obstinate, luxurious, tyrannical and haughty disposition – because our Lord had ordained that he should pay for the great treason he had committed against our People – all this together made him refuse the desire for peace.'

Sultan Mahmud threw everything he had against the 'Frangis' to defend his domains. His 20,000 strong army was a formidable force that mustered hard-bitten Javanese warriors as well as Persian and Turkish mercenaries. The sultan ordered his army to defend the bridge that led from the port to the Istana and the Royal Quarters. He sent his war elephants marching down to the all-important bridge, trumpeting and bellowing against the roar of the foreigners' guns. His soldiers wielded muskets, a few cannon but for the most part, spears and bows and arrows. These antiquated weapons were no match for the fearsome Portuguese cannon. Then, as the 'Malay Annals' tell us: 'The two armies met, and the battle began, the Malacca men closing up stoutly, playing their creeses and spears, and the Frangis again fell back. When Afonso d'Albuquerque perceived his men giving way, he quickly supported them with a thousand soldiers with their muskets, and set upon the Malacca men, and the sound of the muskets was like thunder, and their cannon-balls fell like peas on a sieve. This was a severe attack, and the whole array of the Malacca men was broken.' As the Portuguese galleons anchored in the harbour rained down cannon fire, the 'Frangis' fought street by street and lane by lane, inching uphill towards the Mosque and the Royal Quarters.

From the moment the Portuguese sailed, guns blazing, into the port of Malacca, many Indian and Chinese merchants had little doubt that a superior power had loudly and forcefully entered their world. They now faced a stark choice. To whom did they owe their loyalty? They paid the sultan taxes, not allegiance. Pires hints at this in the *Suma*: 'In trading-lands, where the people are of different nations, these cannot love their king as do natives without admixture of other nations.' The sultan and his nobles deliberately excluded foreign merchants from court circles. They had no sense of belonging and they acted accordingly by collaborating with the invaders. When the Portuguese attack began, Chinese merchants offered d'Albuquerque flat-bottomed junks so that soldiers and cannon could be landed closer to the town.

D'Albuquerque now launched his last and biggest assault. As his troops reached the Istana, he sent envoys to Sultan Mahmud, who had barricaded himself inside the royal mosque. Then he waited, and waited. Finally, d'Albuquerque ran out of patience and stormed the mosque. But he found it empty; his prey had fled and the royal cupboard was bare.

Sultan Mahmud Shah, his family and many of his noble courtiers, had fled with Malacca's finest treasures. As Pires laconically puts it: 'Finally the said Governor [Albuquerque] landed again, determined now to take the city and no longer to be friends with the said king. He took the city and occupied it. The king of Malacca fled with his daughters and all his sons-in-law....' Sultan Mahmud appealed to his overlord, the Ming emperor, who issued a stern rebuke to the Portuguese but did nothing more. So much for all those tribute missions to Beijing and imperial proclamations of protection.

The End of Malay Malacca

Now the Portuguese set about ridding Malacca of its history. The great Malay kingdom would be rendered into a Portuguese port. The Istana was torn apart as, Pires tells us: '... then they began demolishing the wooden one, and they made the famous fortress in the place where it now is, on the site of the great mosque, strong, with two wells of fresh water in the towers, and two or three more in the bulwarks. On one side the sea washes against it, and on the other the river.' With this act of brutish vandalism, the high days of Malacca came to a brutal and demeaning end. D'Albuquerque would ever afterwards be celebrated as 'Malaca Conquistada'. He would be the first of many European 'conquistadores' who sailed into the Strait of Malacca to wreak havoc in the Malay world.

Sultan Mahmud and his heirs fled south. The refugees finally settled in the upper reaches of the Johor River, where the sultan and his successors struggled to restore the glories of their lost em-

pire. Deprived of maritime revenues, the successor kingdom at Kota
Bharu was vulnerable to fresh attacks from the Portuguese and then
their rival powers. The sultan had no chance to compete with the
rising kingdoms of Pasai and Aceh in northern Sumatra that lured
the Chinese, Arab and Gujerati traders who had been driven from
Malacca. Soon Aceh, enriched by trade in black pepper, seized Pasai
and other port settlements strategically located at the north-western
mouth of the Strait of Malacca. Now it was the Achenese Sultan
Alauddin Ri'ayat Syah al-Kahar who was proclaimed, in a Portuguese chronicle, as 'Emperor of all the Malays'. Once again, power
had flowed back across the strait to Sumatra.

The Limits of Power

The ambitious and very well-informed Sultan Alauddin reached
out to the Ottoman ruler, Suleiman the Magnificent. He loaded his
ships with exotic gifts of bright green parrots, spices and aromatic
woods, not forgetting African slaves and eunuchs, destined for Istanbul to adorn Suleiman's Topkapi Palace. The Ottoman ruler sent
in exchange his most respected teachers of Islam, in addition to the
most sophisticated weapons. Soon the Acehnese sultan turned his
new ships, guns and poisoned arrows on the hated Portuguese. He
overreached. The problem was that the sultan was waging war on
Johor at the same time and, even with Javanese assistance, lacked
the firepower to dislodge the Portuguese. Only another European
power could achieve such a feat.

The Portuguese also soon discovered the limits of their power.
They failed to seize Aden, and in the Moluccas, the source of the
most lucrative of all spices, local Hindu rulers nimbly played the
Portuguese off against their Spanish rivals who had, by then, won
access to the Spice Islands and the Philippines. Fundamental weak-
nesses in the Portuguese mercantile system soon ate away at the
wobbly empire. The all-important Crown monopoly on trade was
undercut by freebooting Portuguese traders whose profits nibbled
away at the royal coffers. The first European colonial power, the
conquerors of Malacca, learnt the hard way that building an empire
in Southeast Asia was not a job for the faint of heart.

Writing History: The Origin of the Sejarah Melayu

It was during this time of defeat and humiliation for the Malay rulers of Malacca that the *Sejarah Melayu* ('Malay Annals') was composed or, to be more precise, distilled and edited from older royal genealogies such as the *Hikayat Melayu*, one of the treasures rescued by Sultan Mahmud when he fled the Istana. A century later, the regent of Johor, Raja Abdullah, commissioned Tun Sri Lanang, the Bendahara or chief minister of the court, to compose a new version of the old Malay stories. The 'Malay Annals' come from a time of crisis, uncertainty and fear. Just a year after the Bendahara and his scribes set to work, an Achenese army fell on the Johor capital and sacked the city. They seized Sultan Alauddin Riayat Shah, his regent Raja Abdullah and the Bendahara and sent them into captivity in Aceh. The sultan was executed but Tan Sri Lanang stubbornly continued working on the Annals. The sacking of Johor and the fate of its court adds pathos to the tales spun by the Malay chroniclers. Crushed and exiled, they needed these stories of mighty rulers, lions and underwater princesses, and to retell the story of the founding of the lost city of Malacca.

The Lion That Lost Its Roar

As Malacca fell, Singapura briefly flickers back onto the screen of history. In his *Commentaries*, Afonso d'Albuquerque reported that the Malacca Laksamana, or naval commander, fled to 'Çimquapura'. The Annals, which become a lot more factually reliable after 1511, refers to the port of Singapura crammed with ships and seafarers. Trade may still have been carried out in a string of villages along the southern coast, such as Tanah Merah and Sungei Bedok, names still in use today.

So Singapura, the city of the lion, had not completely lost its roar. Historian Peter Borschberg has drawn attention to the autobiography of Jacques de Courtre, a Flemish merchant born in 1577 who spied for the Portuguese. Dismayed by the rise of the Dutch in the East Indies and the decline of Portuguese colonies, de Coutre wrote a propagandist 'memorial' proposing the construction of 'castles and fortresses in the Strait of Singapore'. Based in Malacca, de Coutre

knew the Singapore Strait, which flows between the Strait of Malacca in the west and the South China Sea in the east, very well. He
refers to Singapore as the *Isla de la Sabandaria Vieja*, 'Isle of the Old
Shahbandar's Compound'. In Malay ports, the Shahbandar [harbour
master], supervised merchants, controlled the port, and collected
customs duties. This implies that Singapore was still an active port:
'Your Highness [the Portuguese king] should know that this port is
one of the best in all of the East Indies.' Long before Raffles sailed
into the Strait of Singapore two centuries later, de Coutre recognised the geo-strategic significance of Singapore. He writes: 'In the
Strait of Singapore, there is an island [Sentosa] which on the one
side features the New Strait and on the other the Old Strait. The
island is triangular in shape…. Your Majesty should mandate the
construction of a castle or fortress on this island and equip it with
good pieces of artillery. These two straits are well-frequented, and
no ship or vessel can pass through these straits without us being able
to sink them….' De Coutre's strikingly detailed narrative shows that
by the seventeenth century Singapore was firmly under the thumb
of the Sultan of Johor-Riau and a small outpost on the highway of
trade that flowed along the Johor River to its estuary. 'The river,'
reported the intrepid de Coutre, 'is very wide and beautiful; ships
laden with wares can enter and exit without any danger'. When de
Coutre sailed through the Strait, they encountered the island's first
inhabitants, the Orang Laut: 'They came on board with fresh fish
and many local fruits which are so different from the ones in Europe and which they pick in the hills. These fishermen also brought
us many *payones*, which are parasols made of palm leaves, and also
fresh water…. They carry as weapons poisoned daggers, which they
call krisses, and also saligas. These are spears made entirely without
iron, but are made [instead] from the palma brava. They cast these
with such a thrust that they can pierce through a steel chest harness.'

No one was much interested in de Coutre's proposal. No one
wanted to build a fort on Sentosa to protect the Singapore Strait. At
this point, the Lion City really does seem to fade into the margins
of history – a mere island in the estuary of the Johor River. But we
have one last glimpse of the island. In 1703, the sultan of Johor,
Abdul Jalil IV, offered to sell the island to an Englishman named
Alexander Hamilton: 'I called at Johor on my Way to China, and

he treated me very kindly, and made me a present of the Island of Singapura, but I told him it could be of no Use to a private person tho' a proper Place for a Company to settle a Colony on, lying in the Centre of Trade, and being accommodated with good Rivers and safe Harbours, so conveniently situated, that all Winds served Shipping both to go out and come into those rivers.' Hamilton was a 'private trader', not a grandee of the East India Company, and what he meant was he did not have sufficient capital to take advantage of the sultan's gift. Hamilton, perhaps out of politeness, agreed to tour the little island and reported that 'the soil is black and fat', beans grow wild in the woods and the forest 'abounds in good masts for shipping'. The island is eerily silent. It seems to be uninhabited. This may well explain the sultan's offer. He imagined perhaps that Hamilton would populate the island with productive Englishmen and women to restore Singapura to its former glory.

By the time Alexander Hamilton wandered through the thick rainforest that covered the island of Singapore at the beginning of the seventeenth century, a hurricane of change was sweeping across the monsoon sea. Now Dutch and English merchant companies, greedy for profit and armed to the teeth reached deep into the monsoon world to root out the riches of the Indies. By the mid-seventeenth century, the East India Company had grabbed huge swathes of territory from the Mughal rulers of India. The Company would soon rule dominions that stretched from Delhi in the west to Assam in the east and reach out across the Bay of Bengal and deep into the Strait of Malacca. The Company directors in the City of London had built a sophisticated 'state within a state' that dominated the national economy and would build the largest empire the world has ever seen.

CHAPTER 7

The Rise of the East India Company: Vanguard of Empire

T he early hours of 25 February 1603 … the Singapore Strait. Dutch Admiral Jacob van Heemskerck steps onto the deck of his flagship, the *White Lion*. He and his crew have been lying in wait for a Portuguese carrack to enter the Singapore Strait, laden to the gunwales with treasure. The *Santa Catarina*, he has been reliably informed by an emissary of the Sultan of Johor, carries a cargo of thousands of bales of silk, hundreds of barrels of camphor and sugar, chests of aloes, jewels, the highest quality Chinese porcelain, and bars of solid gold. For Admiral van Heemskerck, the wait has been a long one. He fears the Portuguese carrack may have slipped unnoticed through the strait. But when he wakes that February morning, he is astonished to discover that overnight the Portuguese treasure ship has anchored close by. There is no time to waste. Just after 8 o'clock, van Heemskerck orders his crew to open fire on the *Santa Catarina*, pointing their cannons upwards to prevent damage to the loot in the hold below. Dutch cannons rip the sails of the *Santa Catarina* to shreds. The fighting rages on most of the day, but at 6 o'clock, with his ship dangerously adrift, Portuguese captain Sebastiano Serrao agrees to terms. And soon the plundering of the *Santa Caterina* begins….

The Portuguese, conquerors of Malacca, had a brash new competitor. Admiral van Heemskerck urged his masters in Amsterdam: '… we ought to seize every opportunity and do our very best, in word and in deed, to settle our nation in the East Indies and establish a body politic, in the hope that it may grow and flourish, God willing.' As the Dutch fought with the Portuguese to seize the riches of the East, a third piratical nation entered the fray. To begin with, the English were bit-part players in Asia and the lands below the winds. They would eventually conquer the most extensive empire the world has ever seen.

The Empire-Builders

We have come to the point in our story when European interlopers begin to carve up the lands below the winds. They would transform a fluid world of kingdoms and sultanates, traders and merchants into a hard-edged jigsaw puzzle of colonies. The ancient ports of mainland Southeast Asia and Java, like Singapura and Surabaya, would become the hubs of British, Dutch and Spanish colonial administrations and globalised trading networks. Within the boundaries of the new colonial domains, the peoples of the Nanyang, the 'Southern Ocean', and the Nusantara, the 'outer islands' of the Malay Archipelago, would be forced to take on new roles and identities that shattered the ancient bonds and alliances that had tied together human landscapes for millennia. What drove merchants and soldiers from faraway European metropoles to become the masters of the lands below the winds? That is the question this chapter will try to answer. And to solve the puzzle, we need to take a close look at the giant corporation that employed the young Thomas Stamford Raffles.

The Portuguese had acted much like the Siamese or Chola rulers that had, long before the sacking of Malacca, attacked Srivijaya. They had upset the balance of power and seized a vital trade hub, but the repercussions across the region were hardly seismic. The Portuguese had merely joined all the other regional powers that had interacted with Southeast Asian states and empires for millennia. But in the course of the eighteenth century, three powerful new players sailed into the Strait of Malacca in the wake of the Portuguese. They arrived in the shape of corporations: the English East India Company, the Dutch Vereenigde Nederlandsche Oost Indische Compagnie, the VOC, and the French Compagnie des Indes. For over 200 years, the force and power of British, Dutch and French colonialism was imposed on Asians, not directly by the states or governments in London, Paris and Amsterdam but through competing private companies. These mighty commercial organisations became the makers and shakers of Asian history. Founded in London, the British East India Company, often referred to as 'John Company', would grow to become the most powerful corporation in human history. At the height of its power, the Company controlled half the world's trade. Few could have foreseen John Company's ascent to such heights when he was first brought into the world in the age of Queen Elizabeth I, the Virgin Queen.

The Birth of the Company

John Company's birthplace was Founders' Hall near Moorgate Fields in London, the date 24 September 1599. On this day, some of England's richest burghers, mariners, soldiers and other notables gathered together to send a petition to the ageing English queen to establish a company 'to venter in the pretended voyage to ye Est Indies ... abounding with greate welth and riches'. The notables who met that day feared that England was a Johnny Come Lately to the quest for the wealth and riches of the Indies.

For more than a century, the Spanish and Portuguese raked in massive profits from the New World of the Americas and the Spice Islands of the Indies. English privateers like Sir Francis Drake made fortunes plundering the Spanish galleons sailing home laden with gold. It was plain robbery on the high seas. It was an ambitious new European power on the other side of the North Sea, who hated the Spanish as much as the English, that stirred the English to think beyond mere piracy, however profitable. In 1568, the Dutch had begun a long and bloody struggle to throw off the yoke of the Spanish Crown, and political freedom fuelled an economic renaissance. In 1602, the government of the Dutch Republic merged several Dutch trading companies to found the Dutch East India Company, or VOC. Armadas of Dutch ships began venturing East and returning to Amsterdam loaded with eye-wateringly profitable cargoes of peppers, cloves, cinnamon and nutmeg. In London, English merchants looked on with envy. Most provoking was the arrival of a Dutch delegation sent to bulk-buy English ships to expand trade in the Far East. This was galling and the Dutch offer was snubbed. The English now insisted that 'we ourselves intend forthwith to have trade with the East Indies'.

A Risky Business

Jumping on the bandwagon of the spice trade was easier said than done. Trade in such expensive commodities on such a scale across the oceans of the world was not merely expensive but hazardous. Storms, pirates or treacherous reefs sent many a fine ship to the bottom of the sea along with its cargo and the hopes of its owners. This is why John Company came into the world as a joint stock venture. The idea of the joint stock company was not original; earlier examples are recorded in China under the Tang and Song dynasties and in medieval France. In essence, as the name suggests, a joint stock company pools the resources of passive shareholders or investors who have the means to buy and sell shares but without direct involvement in the running of the company. A joint stock company has a 'legal personality' that is distinct from its shareholders and directors and is therefore immortal. And so 'John Company' was born, clutching in his baby hands a birthright, a Royal Charter that granted the new company a monopoly lasting fifteen years over 'trade to the East Indies'. Although this provided the new company with powerful commercial muscle, the charter went much further. Queen Elizabeth granted the East India Company the right to seize territories and raise armies. These privileges are normally given only to states. This meant that the East India Company was a commercial organisation endowed with the power of a sovereign nation. John Company would, in the course of the next three centuries, take full advantage of its charter to act with impunity as an armed and sovereign power. John Company would, eventually, change the world. But before that happened, the company would need to contend with its clever Dutch rivals. For over two centuries, conflict and competition between the English and the Dutch would profoundly shape the story of the lands below the winds.

At the end of the sixteenth century, Dutch capitalism and the Dutch East India Company got off to a flying start. Amsterdam would become the wealthiest trading city in Europe and Dutch wages the highest in the world. This was the world's first 'miracle economy' and the VOC was the main engine of growth. Today, we would call 'Jan Compagnie' a 'national champion'. The VOC established the Amsterdam stock exchange, the Beurs, which was the first financial organisation to trade continuously. Its brokers invented short selling, option trading, debt equity swaps, unit trusts and many other all too familiar instruments of modern capitalism. How did Dutch merchants make all that money? The answer is not from cheese, beer or brickmaking, those traditional industries of the Low Countries. The engine of Dutch capitalism was, instead, located far away on its maritime frontiers where the VOC was busy mopping up the relics of the Portuguese Empire. By the 1620s, the VOC had a base in Batavia, and reached out to the island of Taiwan and Japan, where the shogunate ruler allowed the Dutch to trade from a tiny island in the harbour of Nagasaki. The Dutch purchased Chinese silk with Japanese silver and used the profits from silk to buy spices in bulk. By 1630, the VOC was clearing three million guilders worth of precious metals from Asian sources every year, and using this stream of treasure to finance yet more voyages to the Far East. [In 1680, 5,000 guilders had a purchasing power of 56,927.00 Euros.]

The English backed the Dutch revolt against the Catholic Habsburgs, but the rapid growth of the VOC and the rise of Amsterdam as the leading fulcrum of European commerce was a nasty surprise. Just as rattled, the Portuguese banned Dutch ships from using the port of Lisbon, and together with the Spanish looked for ways to keep Dutch companies out of the spice trade in the Indies. But the Dutch merchants refused to be blown off course by these competitive squalls. Jan Compagnie had powers beyond the wildest dream of even the biggest modern corporations like Apple or Amazon. The States General of the Republic authorised the VOC to wage war, to take and execute prisoners, to coin money, to negotiate treaties and to establish colonies. As part of its charter, the Stadholder urged the VOC to establish armed forts in southern Africa at the Cape and in the Indies. For the VOC directors and their admirals, the directive was a licence to assault Portuguese bases in the Spice Islands, and by the end of the first decade of the new century, the Dutch had seized Tidore and Ternate in the Moluccas as the new masters of the trade in cloves, nutmegs and spices. The rise of the

VOC meant that the new Dutch Republic could act like a European superpower, thanks to its overseas activities.

The First Multinational

The Dutch invented the modern multinational. The VOC raised money by issuing shares and invented the first instantly recognisable commercial logo. Its thousands of officials were interconnected by a system of reporting and accounting. In its overseas territories, production was rationalised in a system of plantations and processing 'factories'. The VOC business mantras were scale and efficiency. 'Customer feedback' was swiftly relayed to local managers: 'small nutmegs are of no value'. It was a model that the English would follow to found an empire.

Violence was integral to Dutch empire-building. In 1641, the VOC and its allies in the Johor sultanate seized Malacca from the Portuguese. In southern African, agents of the VOC fought a low-level war of attrition against the Khoikhoi people. In Southeast Asia, the Dutch fought three wars against a succession of resistant Javanese rulers to secure pliant successors who did the company's bidding. Jan Compagnie never hesitated to raise his fists and turn his guns on native peoples who stood in the way of profit. And that included English competitors. The Dutch successfully barred the English from the East indies and the profits of the spice trade. So the English turned instead to India. The 'Jewel in the Crown' had its origins in competitive frustration.

The Age of Empires

Imagine for a moment taking a stroll down Leadenhall Street in the City of London at the end of the eighteenth century. Here you will find the imposing London headquarters of the East India Company. Let us stop briefly to admire the ornate symbolism of the façade which the company directors designed to impress shareholders. If you are invited inside, you will be surprised by the depth of the building, which is stuffed with meeting rooms and the offices of the directors. Look up at the oval ceiling of the Revenue Committee Room. There is Britannia seated on a rocky footstool, receiving tributes of jewels, tea, and porcelain from her Asian children next to the *Ganges*. In the distance, a company ship, or East Indiaman, is setting sail.

We have come to a crossroads in our brief history. From the end of the seventeenth century and for the next 300 years, the story of the lands above and below the winds will be dominated by European empire-builders. Huge swathes of the surface of the earth will be carved up by competitive British, Dutch and French colonial administrators. Asians will become subjects of empires headquartered in faraway European capitals. There is a paradox here that will have a powerful bearing on our narrative. It was very well put by the British historian and East India Company employee Thomas Babington Macauley, who wrote that 'It is strange, very strange that a joint stock company of traders should be entrusted with the sovereignty of a larger population.' The economist Adam Smith called the company 'a strange absurdity'. The European empires that reached out to grasp huge Asia were built not by governments but giant corporations like the English and Dutch East India companies. This is important because empire was, above all, a business that reflected the ethics of business. We will see again and again that decisions made by colonial administrators had to make business sense. Empires were built and run on the cheap.

It may come as a surprise to discover that a good number of influential Englishmen reviled the East India Company and its works. They despised the greed and overweening ambitions of the company 'Nabobs', men like Robert Clive, the general, who in 1757 conquered Bengal and served as its first colonial governor. Its fiercest and most determined critic was the lawmaker and political philosopher Edmund Burke, who denounced the company as 'A state in the disguise of a merchant'. Burke was just one of a vocal chorus of critics of John Company who complained that 'mere merchants' were becoming 'umpires of Indostan', a 'cabinet of Asiatic princes'. In 1788, Burke launched a campaign to impeach Warren Hastings, the former governor-general of India for corruption. As prosecutor, Burke did not mince his words. Hastings was, he proclaimed, a 'spider of hell' and a 'ravenous vulture devouring the carcases of the dead' who showed 'an habitual depravity of mind'. For all Burke's vitriol, Hastings was, after a trial that lasted seven years, acquitted. John Company had won the duel to live another day.

The British government and the East India Company were bound together in a prickly and often fractious marriage. A decade before the young Thomas Stamford Raffles began work at India House, the government had imposed on the company a Board of Control as a condition of renewing its charter. The board was authorised to audit accounts and pick over the voluminous reports or 'narratives' generated by the legions of inky clerks employed in East India House. The British government reached deep into the affairs of the company and, likewise, the company men made sure they had access to the levers of state. Many used fortunes made in India to buy a seat in parliament. For the British government, the East India Company was too big to fail. It generated huge revenues from spices, tea and opium and employed tens of thousands of administrators, clerks, warehousemen, dockers and shipbuilders. At the end of the eighteenth century, the company was the biggest employer in the country. As we will discover, the British government wanted oversight of the company but at the lowest cost: an empire on the cheap. Parsimony informed every decision. So too did an obsession with data-gathering and the power of information.

By the end of the eighteenth century, when the young Raffles began toiling away in India House, the company's commercial and political independence had been steadily eroded by successive British governments. Six decades later, the catastrophe of the Indian Rebellion in 1857, known then as the 'Indian Mutiny', would provoke the government to abolish the company once and for all.

The Drug Trade

We have jumped ahead of our story. To understand the East India Company, there are two words that sum up its corporate identity: drugs and data, or opium and information. From the very beginning, the company men were fascinated by the commercial potential of the poppy, sometimes known as the 'Milk of Paradise'. In the 1580s, a London merchant called John Fitch travelled widely through India, Burma and Southeast Asia. It was Fitch who brought back to England the tale of the Siamese king's white elephants who, he claimed, were dressed in cloths of gold and lived in gilded stables. Fitch's tale fascinated the English who would associate a white elephant with a costly burden of dubious use. Fitch was not just interested in elephants. When he returned to London in 1597, he was full of enthusiasm for the opium trade. In Agra, Fitch had joined a trading fleet of 'one hundred and four score boats' laden with salt, lead, carpets – and opium. In London, he joined the fledgling East India Company as an adviser. By the time Raffles set sail for the Far East 200 years later, the company men had become the drug lords of Asia and China. The company's drug trade would be recorded in vast collections of data – known as 'narratives.'

The maze of offices inside East India House was the domain of the company clerks who, like the young Raffles, perched on high stools to toil on their 'narratives'. An elevated working position made taking a break more arduous. Company clerks were human data-processing machines. The writer Charles Lamb laboured for the company for thirty-three years among the clerks he called the 'quill-driving brethren'. His was a working life of 'captivity', 'daylight servitude' and 'slavery': 'I grow ominously tired of official confinement. Thirty years have I served the Philistines, and my neck is not subdued to the yoke....' Lamb was sometimes less restrained: 'Confusion blast all mercantile transactions, all traffick, exchange of commodities, intercourse between nations, all the consequent civilization and wealth and amity and link of society, and getting rid of prejudices, and knowledge of the face of the globe – and rot the very firs of the forest that look so romantic live, and die into desks.' Raffles' Malay secretary Munshi Abdullah noticed that his employer always 'walked with a slight stoop' – the physical inheritance of servitude in India House. Lamb's quill-driving brethren generated immense volumes of paper over the commercial lifetime of the Company that still occupied seven miles of shelving in the British Museum's India Office collections. The directors of the East India Company exploited the power of information long before the founders of Facebook and Amazon began monetising streams of our digitalised likes and life stories online.

So John Company was a data addict. But as the company expanded operations in Asia, the links between East India House in Leadenhall Street in the City of London and the company's emissaries in Asia were stretched to breaking point. Letters, orders, promotions and demotions, commercial reports and data despatched on board the fleets of East Indiamen could take between six and ten months to reach Bombay, Calcutta or Singapore. The directors of the company in London could be starved of news for up to eighteen months. For ambitious company men like Raffles, the sluggish network of company communications offered scope to daring and ambitious young men to strike out on their own.

John Company may have been confused about whether he was a state or a corporation, a merchant or a ruler, but in the course of a few hundred years the East India Company would fundamentally reshape the peoples and societies of Southeast Asia. Rivalry with the Dutch would lead to 'spheres of influence' that centuries later would become the moulds of new nations. But John Company would not make history on his own accord. Company men would be compelled to engage and negotiate with Asian powers like the Malay sultans and the rulers of Java. None would give in without a fight.

CHAPTER 8

'A very clever, able, active and judicious man': The story of Thomas Stamford Raffles

H e had, remembered 'Munshi' Abdullah bin Abdul Kadir, 'thick eyebrows, his left eye watered slightly from a cast, his nose was straight and his cheeks slightly hollow. His lips were thin, denoting his skill in speech, his tongue gentle and his mouth wide, his neck tapering; his complexion not very clear; his chest was full and his waist slender. He walked with a slight stoop.' 'Munshi' Abdullah was Stamford Raffles' Malay secretary; Munshi means 'teacher'. His graphic pen portrait is starkly different to the idealised marble statue of Raffles that still stands today on Boat Quay by the Singapore River. The plaque at the base reads, 'On this historic site, Sir Thomas Stamford Raffles first landed on 28 January 1819, and with genius and perception changed the destiny of an obscure fishing village to a great seaport and modern Metropolis.' For many Asians, this is an offensive fable. Raffles is shown as a visionary, an enlightened white man who alone possessed the power and insight to shape the future. Asians are merely invisible bystanders.

The irony is that Raffles himself knew very well that the 'obscure fishing village' had a deep and illustrious history. He had pored over the histories of Singapura told in the *Sejarah Melayu* ('Malay Annals'), translated by his friend John Leyden, and it was these stories that drew him to the island. Raffles built his official residence on the summit of the Forbidden Hill because, he wrote, 'the tombs of the Malay Kings are close at hand, and I have settled that if it is my fate to die here I shall take my place amongst them....' It was the British rulers of Singapore who came after Raffles who had no truck with such fantasies. They erased Singapore's Asian roots and sanctified Raffles as founder and visionary of a new, globalised metropolis. Singapore's clock began ticking in February 1819.

Yet, in modern, independent Singapore, Raffles still stands proud and defiant on Boat Quay. He survived by the skin of his marble teeth. In 1942, the Japanese ousted the British from Southeast Asia. Singapore became Syonan-to, the 'Light of the East'. The new Asian rulers toppled Raffles and stuffed him in a museum. After the Japanese surrender, the British returned to Singapore and Raffles was rescued and reconsecrated. When Singapore became independent in 1963, Singaporeans began to wonder whether Raffles should still be seen as such an important part of the national story. Should his statue be toppled and his myth forgotten? In 1961, the Dutch economist Albert Winsevius was sent to Singapore by the United Nations to serve as an economic advisor. In *From Third World to First*, Singapore's first prime minister, Lee Kuan Yew, reveals that the former cheese salesman turned development guru offered him two pieces of advice. The first was to destroy the communists who, he insisted, threatened Singapore's survival, and the second was to keep the Raffles statue. Why? Because its preservation was an unambiguous declaration that Singapore was open for foreign investment. Lee recalled: 'To keep Raffles statue was easy. My colleagues and I had no desire to rewrite the past....' And so Raffles stayed very firmly put. Singapore was, he seemed to say, open for business.

The True Founder of Singapore?

Like all legends, the founding myth of Singapore contains grains of truth. Archaeologists have unearthed the hard facts that show Singapura was a bustling commercial hub long before Raffles set foot on the island. From the Forbidden Hill, Malay rulers looked down on a harbour dotted with ships that came and went with the monsoon winds, loaded with expensive porcelain from China, nutmeg and pepper from the Spice Islands and textiles from the Coromandel

Coast. So Singapura had a rich history, but in the end it was a story of eclipse and decline from its medieval zenith. We should be careful not to throw the Raffles baby out with the historical bath water. It is not necessary to look as far back as Singapura's medieval heydays for, arguably, the true founder of Singapore was a descendant of Sultan Mahmud Shah III, Temenggong Abdul Rahman of Johor, who was ruling the Johor-Riau-Lingga sultanate at the time, which included the island of Singapore. In 1811, he invited Chinese farmers from Riau to develop plantations on the long-neglected island to grow pepper and gambier. He settled them in Kampong Glam, on the bank of the Singapore River. But Raffles, unlike the Temenggong, arrived in Singapore backed by a powerful British company. Even a royal Malay could not compete. So Raffles' arrival in 1819 may have been just one turning point in the story of Singapore, but a turning point nonetheless.

Raffles – Company Man

In every fibre of his mind and body, Thomas Stamford Raffles was an East India Company man. In the previous chapter, we discovered that 'John Company' was a merchant in the guise of a state. Company men like Raffles accrued wealth and prestige for a global corporation that could deploy its own army and fleets of East Indiamen to seize huge swathes of territory to compete with its commercial rivals. Asia was turned into a corporate battleground. Raffles' most recent biographer, Victoria Glendinning, claims that her subject was not greedy for money but wanted only fame and honours. This is rather generous. Like the giant company that took him under its wing at the age of fourteen, Raffles coveted wealth and power and used John Company's armed might to get his way. Like his masters in Leadenhall Street, Raffles was Janus-faced. Commerce drove his ambitions and career, but success meant taking on the French and Dutch who were just as determined to squeeze every last drop of profit from colonial fiefdoms in India and Southeast Asia. Cut-throat international rivalry turned merchants into empire-builders.

In 1800, the 19-year-old Stamford Raffles was toiling away in the bowels of East India House in London as a junior clerk. The streams of commercial data that hourly passed across young Raffles' lofty desk provided him with an education in company business, its operations, profits and losses on a global scale. The young Raffles' inky doings exposed the secretive inner workings of the company and its struggle with rival European powers.

At the dawn of a new century, Raffles was in the right place at the right time, for this was a time of enormous opportunity for John Company. The English and the Dutch had skirmished, waged inconclusive wars and signed and broken peace treaties for two centuries. After seizing Malacca in 1641, helped by the sultan of Johor, the Dutch had swept aside the Portuguese to become the biggest commercial power in Southeast Asia. The Dutch East Indian Company, the VOC, was firmly entrenched in Batavia, the Moluccas and Makassar. Preoccupied with managing its Indian territories and fighting the French, the British East India Company could do little to restrain Dutch dominance of trade and territory further east. But by the mid-seventeenth century, Dutch power was waning, and in January 1797 the English navy in the East Indies, based at Bencoolen in Sumatra, inflicted a bruising defeat on the French navy in the Strait of Bali. The British, or rather the East India Company, was now the dominant naval power in the Far East. The Prussian ruler Frederick II disparaged the Dutch Republic as a 'long boat trailing behind a British man-of-war'. But Anglo-Dutch friendship was strained and broken when the Dutch backed the rebels in Britain's American colonies. Yet another Anglo-Dutch war erupted in the 1780s and the Dutch 'Age of Decline' was quickened by the republic's struggle with the French. In the 1780s, France was convulsed by revolution and the new French Convention declared war on both Great Britain and the Dutch Republic. In the bitterly cold winter of 1794, French armies captured the Dutch fleet and rampaged towards Amsterdam. William of Orange fled to England on a fishing boat. As the republic fell into decay, the fortunes of Jan Compagnie spiralled towards catastrophe. By the end of the century, the once mighty VOC was a corporate basket case. In 1799, it vanished along with the Dutch Republic it had enriched for so long. The end of the century saw the rise of Napoleon Bonaparte as Emperor of France. For the next fifteen years, Napoleon and his allies waged war on all the other major European powers. In 1802, Napoleon imposed his younger brother, Louis Bonaparte, to rule over the Netherlands. The old Dutch Republic was now the kingdom of Holland, a vassal state of the French Empire. For the British, the long wars with Napoleon would have a very different outcome. Naval victories at Aboukir Bay and Trafalgar made Britain the most powerful maritime power in the world, and in Southeast Asia, the East India Company became bolder and more aggressive. Wars in Europe reverberated across Southeast Asia and offered ambitious company men like Raffles unprecedented new opportunities.

The Opportunity

For nearly five years, Raffles had toiled away on his lofty perch in the bowels of East India House on Leadenhall Street. Then, in 1804, the directors of the East India Company made a decision to reinforce their position in the Far East. The motivation was commercial and strategic. As an agent of the British government, the company and the Royal Navy would begin probing the defences of other European colonies in the region. The key to power would be finding the right staging post or base for future naval operations. At the turn of the century, the company had three 'presidencies', or bases, in India – in Bengal, Madras and Bombay. The governor-general of India was headquartered in Calcutta, and so the presidency of Bengal was the summit of company power in Asia. Where, then, should the company seek a new base on the other side of the Indian Ocean to extend its reach and secure the trade routes to China? The British had occupied Malacca in 1795 to keep it out of French hands after Napoleon's conquest of the Netherlands, but technically the old Malay port remained a Dutch possession. In Leadenhall Street, all eyes were on Penang. The English traveller Isabella Bird called the lush, green island 'a brilliant place under a brilliant sky'. Penang was chosen as the new company presidency, and so began British involvement in Malay affairs – and Penang would be the making of young Raffles.

Skullduggery in Penang

Penang had been leased for the British East India Company by a 'country trader' and sea captain, Sir Francis Light, from Sultan Muhammad Jiwa Zainal Adilin II (r. 1710–78) and his successor, Sultan Abdullah Mukarram Shah (r. 1778–97), the rulers of the Malay state of Kedah. Kedah was a reluctant vassal state of the Siamese and Light had promised that the company would provide military assistance to the sultan. He had no authorisation to make such an offer. Besides, he was supplying arms to the Thai kingdom of Thonburi. Light landed on Penang in 1786, claimed it for King and Company and renamed it Prince of Wales Island. He set about developing Georgetown, named after the prince regent, as a free port. As the new settlement prospered, Sultan Abdullah reminded Light of his promise to defend Kedah against Siamese incursions. The Englishman had been duplicitous for the East India Company. He had no interest in offending the Thais, who were important trading partners and allies, and the British governor-general based in India refused to offer the promised protection. The sultan went away empty handed. Abdullah made a futile attempt to retake Penang but the British swatted him away. It was a shabby betrayal of the Malay ruler, and would not be the last.

Promoting Penang as the company's fourth presidency would require an infusion of new company blood. And young, ambitious Tom Raffles leapt at the chance to make his name in the Far East. In British settlements in India and the Far East, the communities' company men and their families were relentlessly winnowed by sickness, alcohol and conflict with superiors. Raffles clambered up the rungs of any and every post that fell open: he was appointed acting first secretary, then permanent first secretary, then agent for the Navy, licensor of the press and official Malay translator. Thomas Stamford Raffles, as he now styled himself, showed himself to be a man of prodigious energy, a company man in a hurry, who was toughened by hard work and long hot days but regularly knocked back by ominously crippling headaches.

As Raffles prospered, the Dutch Empire fell ever deeper into torpid decay. Napoleon had completed the annexation of Holland in July 1810, and the momentous news reached Batavia in February the following year. At a grand ceremony attended by Dutch officials and, it was reported, thousands of 'Chinese, Moors, Malays and Javanese', the Dutch flag was lowered and a French tricolour raised to the crackle of a 45-gun salute. From that day on, all Dutch civil and military officials took an oath of loyalty to the emperor: Napoleon was now the direct ruler of Java.

For the British, it was time to act, and from Leadenhall Street the company's all-powerful 'Secret Committee' despatched an urgent memo to the new governor-general of India, Gilbert Elliot, First Earl of Minto, 'to proceed to the conquest of Java at the first possible opportunity'. In the monsoon months of that year, Raffles paid his first visit to Calcutta and was summoned to meet the governor-general. He was an up-and-coming company man and had an influential friend in the shape of John Leyden, Professor of Hindustani in Calcutta, who had the ear of Minto, a fellow Scot. Thanks to Leyden, Raffles soon had a new job. He was appointed 'Agent of the Governor-General with the Malay States', in other words, a spy. Raffles was loaned a cruiser called the *Ariel* and was soon on his way south from Penang to Malacca. Installed in a house on Bandar Hill, he haunted the quays and markets, digging up information from merchants, sailors and whoever else would talk to him. Raffles' Malay skills were basic, and so he took on a precociously intelligent and well-informed 14-year-old to serve as his clerk and go between. The young man's name was Abdullah Bin Abdul Kadir, and he would always be called Munshi, or 'Teacher' Abdullah. As well as Malay and English, Abdullah was fluent in Arabic and Tamil.

In Malacca, Munshi Abdullah could observe his new English employer's workaholic habits at close quarters. He refused visitors, Abdullah remembered, until he had completed the day's tasks and 'kept rigidly to his timetable of work'. Working late into the night, Raffles and Abdullah copied and edited reports to be sent to Lord Minto in Calcutta. On 14 March 1811, Raffles sent a 'Proclamation to the People of Java' which he had had translated into Dutch. 'The English are at hand!' Raffles declared, to liberate the Dutch colonists from oppression and tyranny, meaning, of course, *French* despotism. He built up a network of informers and tried to curry favour with the Javanese rulers in Yogyakarta and Palembang, as well as other Javanese chieftains. He hit a brick wall. The sultans had signed treaties with the Dutch and were reluctant to believe that the British could defeat the French.

Conflict with William Farquhar

Raffles also ruffled English feathers during his time in Malacca, especially those of one of the most intriguing minor characters in our story, namely Captain William Farquhar, who was appointed British Resident and Commandant of Malacca in 1813. Like so many other 'British' members of the colonial elite, Farquhar was a Scot. He had begun his company career as an engineer in Madras, and it was as chief engineer that he joined the British expeditionary force sent to seize Malacca from the Dutch in 1795. He became acting Resident a few years later. As soon as he settled in Malacca, Farquhar had taken a mistress who was the daughter of a French officer called Clement and a Malay mother, whose name was never recorded. Antoinette Clement bore Farquhar some six children. One, recorded as 'Baby Farquhar', died in infancy. (In 2018, the *Straits Times* revealed that the Canadian Prime Minister Justin Trudeau is descended from one of Farquhar's daughters with Antoinette – Esther Farquhar Bernard, his great-great-great-great grandmother.) Raffles often made fun of Farquhar's 'Malay' family although such relationships between Europeans and mixed-race women were common. Farquhar enjoyed a lifestyle pretty typical for his time and may well have been less intolerant than his peers of local peoples and customs. Munshi Abdullah said he was generous 'to all the servants of Allah'.

When Raffles first met Farquhar in Malacca, the more experienced and knowledgeable older man was in every way his superior. But when he was appointed 'Agent of the Governor-General', Raffles seems to have treated Farquhar as if he was a subordinate employee. Farquhar was very well informed about Malay and Javanese matters, as well as the doings of the Dutch and French in Batavia, and came to resent the way Raffles deviously took ownership of his expertise. Farquhar built up a head of resentful steam about the uppity younger man who seemed to want to hoard any credit. Raffles tactlessly snubbed Farquhar when he turned to another engineer and surveyor, Lieutenant-Colonel Colin Mackenzie, to pick his brains about Dutch military and naval resources on Java as well as the island's network of roads, canals and ports. Raffles may simply have not realised he was rubbing the Resident up the wrong way, but in any event, any chance of a real friendship was holed below the waterline.

Taking on the Dutch

During the monsoon months in Malacca, Raffles harvested every scrap of information he had wrung out of his informants in voluminous reports sent to Government House in Calcutta. Raffles' intelligence-gathering confirmed that the British were right to be concerned about French intentions. Napoleon himself had appointed a new governor-general and despatched him to Java. Marshall Herman Willem Daendels was irascible, hard-driving and widely loathed. Soon after he arrived in Batavia, he demolished the city's dilapidated old fort and replaced it with a spanking new fortress called Meester Cornelis. He began laying out plans for a new and airy city outside the dilapidated walls of the squalid old colonial town. Most troubling to the company men in Calcutta poring over Raffles' reports from Malacca, Napoleon had ordered Daendels to begin construction of a massively ambitious new highway, the Grote Postweg, the Great Post Road, that would link Batavia to all the other Dutch outposts on Java and extend some 900 miles. The Dutch were digging in for the long term.

Early in 1811, Lord Minto informed Raffles that the British government had formally approved his plan to solve the Java problem: a naval expedition would be launched to forcibly expel the Dutch and destroy their fortifications. But Lord Minto's letter went further. He warned that the 'ancient and populous' Java colony would be at risk from 'the vindictive sway of the Malay chiefs'. Once the British had thrown out the Dutch, who or what was to stop the natives falling on hard-working European settlers? Raffles clearly understood what Minto was suggesting. It was not the British way to hit and run and in Raffles' mind a tantalising thought took shape that Java might become a jewel in the British colonial Crown, whether or not the Crown wanted such a prize. Lord Minto offered Raffles the chance to turn merchant-conqueror. Minto made it clear that high office would be Raffles' for the asking if the Java expedition was a success. He had a 'strong desire', his Lordship wrote, that 'the utmost will be done to make the *best attainable situation* worthy of your services....' For Raffles, Java had become, he wrote, 'the land of promise'.

In June 1811, a rising storm of British armed might swept towards Java. Some 12,000 company troops, at least half of them

Asian, embarked on a fleet of a hundred vessels led by Lord Minto's flagship, the *Modeste*, including four battleships, frigates, sloops and company cruisers, transports and gunboats mustered in the port of Madras, and set sail for Malacca. The flagship carried Lord Minto himself and Raffles' friend John Leyden. From Malacca, the invasion fleet sailed south through the Singapore Strait and across the Java Sea. For more than a year, Raffles had been consuming great gobs of information and news about this alluring island, and on 4 August, from the deck of the *Modeste* and in the company of Lord Minto, he had his first sight of Java. The company troops, as well as ordnance, horses and supplies were disembarked on the beach at Cilincing, a few miles east of Batavia, the Dutch capital.

As the British approached Batavia, they discovered that the much-feared Daendels was long gone. He had been summoned home a few months before the British arrived, a vital piece of information that Raffles seems to have missed, and had been replaced by Dutch aristocrat Jan Willen Janssens, an equally fervent admirer of Napoleon. The East India Company got down to work. Commanded by Colonel Robert Rollo Gillespie, the British captured Meester Cornelis, the mighty redoubt built by Daendels outside Weltevreden, in a bloody battle on 26 August. The company lost some 500 men but routed Janssens' force of Franco-Dutch troops and Javanese auxiliaries. Six weeks after the British landed at Cilincing, the Dutch territories in Java fell into British hands.

The Sack of Yogjakarta

The question for the British conquerors was, what now? For the governors in Calcutta, it was job done. The Dutch had been expelled and Java was safe from the machinations of Napoleon. But Lord Minto had grander ambitions. And it was Stamford Raffles he chose to fulfil his plan. On 11 September 1811, Lord Minto swaggered into the forlorn wreck of the Dutch headquarters in Ryswick where he proclaimed that Java was securely in British hands and, more specifically, the eager hands of the new Lieutenant-General Stamford Raffles. Java, he urged the members of the Secret Committee in London, should be transformed by English colonists and English capital into an English colony. Distracted by military campaigns in Spain and Portugal, the British parliament raised no urgent or immediate objections. Relations between parliament and the East India Company were rarely harmonious, and adding yet more territory to the company's Asian realm would be expensive. Minto and Raffles both understood that a reckoning would come when Napoleon was eventually defeated and a peace treaty signed with the French. 'All I fear is a general peace,' confessed Minto. He urged Raffles, 'While we are here let us do as much good as we can.'

The company had ousted the Dutch but Java was not simply there for the taking. Raffles would need to take on the Javanese rulers. His campaign began in Yogjakarta. He sacked the Dutch Resident and replaced him with John Crawfurd, whom we met exploring the Forbidden Hill in Singapore. Like Raffles, Crawfurd had scholarly pretensions and spoke good Javanese. He enjoyed hobnobbing with Javanese royalty in the Kraton, or palace, but reported to Raffles that Sultan Hamengkubuwano was 'unsafe' and would not easily give in to the British. The Yogyakarta court was by this time bitterly divided between rival factions, and the sultan may have underestimated the force and power that Raffles could unleash. He would soon be disabused.

As a Javanese source, the *Chronicle of the Fall of Yogyakarta*, tells us that shells rained down on the Kraton and many princes made their escape to local villages. Two hours later, red-coated soldiers tramped out from the old Dutch stronghold, the Vredeburg Fort, along the ceremonial avenue towards the huge royal compound. With brutal despatch, Raffles' men penetrated the Kraton walls and swept aside the Javanese troops, who flung down their lances and swords and fled. In a wild frenzy, officers and men tore the palace apart, broke into the women's quarters and tore jewels from the bodies of terrified royal princesses and concubines. In a wild hunt for the legendary treasures of the sultanate, they tore up floors, smashed apart cabinets and even descended wells. In the midst of this, one Lieutenant Hector Maclean of the 14th Rifle Company, inflamed with lust and intent on rape, had been stabbed to death by his intended victim who had concealed a *keris*, or Malay dagger, in her robes. The looting continued for four days. As soon as the Kraton had been stripped bare of its treasures, British officers humiliated princes and members of the sultan's court by forcing them to carry the booty in heavy chests back to the Vredeburg Fort.

Historian Peter Carey writes in The Power of Prophecy: 'The foundation of Crawfurd's own private collection of Indonesian manuscripts appears to have been laid at this time with a personal haul of at least 45 Javanese manuscripts from the Kraton library, most of which he subsequently sold to the British Museum in 1842. A slightly larger group of 55 manuscripts was claimed by Raffles for the British government and formed the core of his own personal collection of Javanese and Indonesian MSS, the bulk of which were presented by Lady Raffles to the Royal Asiatic Society in 1830 after his death. In this fashion, the private and public archives of Great Britain were swelled by the plunder of its soldiers and colonial administrators; intellectual booty capitalism in its purest form, invaluable for subsequent Western scholars, but deeply impoverishing for those non-European societies who fell victim to its depredations.'

Raffles rampaged across Java bending Javanese rulers to the company will. He imposed a punitive treaty on the once-powerful ruler of Surakarta who was forced to give up huge swathes of his kingdom. In the meantime, Crawfurd was busy deepening the humiliation of the Yogyakarta court by drafting a new treaty that enshrined the 'utter extinction' and 'unconditional submission' of the old sultanate. At the signing ceremony, Crawfurd seized the sultan by the neck and forced him to kneel before Raffles and kiss his mighty knees. Raffles reported to his patron Lord Minto: 'The European power is for the first time paramount in Java. We never till this moment could call ourselves masters of the more valuable provinces in the interior, nay, our possessions on the sea coasts would always have been precarious and, had our military force been materially reduced, much eventual danger was to be apprehended.' Raffles and his family installed themselves with due pomp and circumstance in the majestic Buitenzorg Palace in Bogor, the former residence of the Dutch governor-general.

The Cabal

The historian Peter Carey has revealed a very surprising facet of British rule in Java. The East India Company was ruled by a secretive cabal of Freemasons. There were numerous Masonic lodges in Calcutta and Lord Minto was a 'brother' of long standing. Freemasonry had emerged in its modern form in England in the seventeenth century and spread to the American colonies and the Continent. For all its arcane rituals and mystique, Masonry is just a system of elite networking. The governors of the British East India Company and the Dutch VOC were all Masons. During the brief period Lord Minto was in Java, he initiated Raffles into a small Masonic lodge called the *Virtutis et Artis Amici* located on Pondok Gedeh, a coffee estate that belonged to Dutch Mason Nicholas Engelhard. Lord Minto had long been a brother, and all of Raffles' associates in Java were Masons, including Colonel Rollo Gillespie, who would become his arch enemy. At the ceremony, Raffles was referred to as an 'Entered Apprentice', and the records reveal something very surprising. Another 'Apprentice' was entered at the same ceremony. His name was Harman Warner Muntinghe and he was Dutch. A few years later, in July 1813, both Muntinghe and Raffles were 'elevated' as Master Masons at the Lodge De Vriendschap in Surabaya. And three years after that, Raffles and a number of British and Dutch Masons were granted 'Perfection in the Rose Croix Chapter' at the Lodge La Vertueuse in Batavia. Raffles was now the Worshipful Brother Raffles and seems to have devoted a lot of time to his Masonic duties. Lord Minto had a very good reason for initiating Raffles alongside the Dutch administrator Harman Muntinghe at the same ceremony. He was reaching out to the network of Dutch Masons to help govern Java. In 1812, the British were heavily overstretched in numerous theatres of war and so it was vital to enlist experienced Dutch administrators like Muntinghe. To secure their loyalty, Minto played the Masonic card. As Raffles admitted: 'Muntinghe and Cranssen were both selected by the Earl of Minto to be members of the Java Council. Of the wisdom and benevolence which determined the late Earl of Minto to place two members of the Dutch nation at the Board of the British Council in Java, it is unnecessary to speak.' For Minto's plan to work, Raffles had be initiated as a Mason.

Raffles under Attack

In Calcutta, a new British governor-general was making waves. Francis Rawdon-Hastings, 1st Marquess of Hastings, later Lord

Moira, was a scion of the Anglo-Irish aristocracy and, unlike his predecessor, a battle-scarred veteran of colonial wars. He was an ambitious politician, a friend of the bibulous Prince Regent and a Master Mason. In 1814, Raffles had sent a voluminous 'Minute' to Lord Moira explaining his ambitions for land reform in Java. But his fellow Mason was unimpressed. He mocked Java as a 'drain', sucking out not just treasure but troops desperately needed in rebellious Bengal. There were other voices raised against Raffles. Most poisonous was that of Major-General Rollo Gillespie, who insinuated that Raffles had exploited his land reform scheme to enrich himself. As if one accuser was not enough, Raffles soon faced another. Major William Robison accused Raffles of profiteering from his spending money on 'perfectly useless' cavalry and heavy artillery, all in the interests, Robison ranted, of self-promotion. And there was worse to come. Raffles' enemies had the ear of Lord Moira and he acted decisively. He requested that the East India Company Court of Directors in London sack Raffles as governor of Java. Soon, a formal notice of dismissal was on its way to the Buitenzorg Palace. Four years after conquering Java and bringing its rulers to heel, Raffles was sick, broken, defeated and humiliated. As Lord Minto warned, the defeat of Napoleon Bonaparte and his exile to the remote East India Company outpost of St Helena forced the British government to hand Java back to its Dutch proprietors.

Meeting the Emperor

On 25 March 1816, Raffles boarded the *Ganges*, taking with him some 200 chests and cases stuffed with Javanese treasures. After rounding the Cape of Good Hope in May, the *Ganges* anchored in the harbour at St Helena to take on water. Raffles was thrilled. He asked for a meeting with the remarkable Corsican Napoleon Bonaparte, who had changed the course of his life. The former emperor, Raffles recalled, was a 'clumsy looking man, who walked with a very awkward gait'. Bonaparte was mortally ill and resented being treated as an exhibit. 'Boney', the soldier who had shredded the political map of Europe and invaded the nightmares of English children, turned out to be rude, abrupt and ungentlemanly. Raffles wrote to a friend that 'this man is a monster ... determined and vindictive....' It seemed, he said in a memorable phrase, 'as if the despotism of Europe were concentrated in him'.

Back in London, Raffles recovered his health, met and swiftly married the accomplished and notably 'affectionate' Sophia Hull, the daughter of a company grandee, and, in short, dragged fame and honour from the jaws of ignominious defeat. He toiled away on a two-volume *History of Java*, which he cunningly dedicated to the Prince Regent. He supplied the priapic and bibulous ruler with copious supplies of *arak*, which he praised as 'the strongest spirit in the world'. For his work on the *History*, he was admitted to the hallowed ranks of the Royal Society. His tireless self-promotion paid off handsomely. On 29 May 1817, Raffles was summoned to Carlton House in London to be knighted by the Prince Regent. His cousin Thomas described Raffles' disappointment: he had hoped for a baronetcy.

Raffles' crafty management of his battered reputation caused difficulties for his critics in East India House. In February 1817, the Court of Directors pronounced on charges brought against Raffles of incompetence and corruption. Their verdict was, in short, a fudge. The directors were 'decidedly convinced' that Raffles' critics had not provided enough evidence that impugned his moral character. Raffles' honour had been restored. Sir Stamford Raffles, FRS had successfully relaunched his glittering career.

At the end of 1818, the *Edinburgh Review* published a review of *The History of Java*. While the map included in the book was 'the best ever compiled', the text was 'hastily written', 'fluent but diffuse and a little careless'. The reviewer haughtily surmised that the author 'blots too little' and failed dismally to present an account of Javanese history and religion. The author of this sour essay was none other than John Crawfurd.

Raffles in the White Man's Graveyard

There was a sting in the tail of the company's rehabilitation of Raffles. The former ruler of Java was now offered a demeaning new post as governor of Bencoolen on the south-western coast of Sumatra. Long reputed to be a 'white man's graveyard', this feverish and dilapidated settlement, officially known as 'Fort Marlborough', that festered in the shadow of the Barisan Mountains was now the sole British outpost south of Penang. Bencoolen was, Raffles told a friend, 'the most wretched place I have ever beheld'. The company's governors had, it seems, found a way to rebuke Raffles by sending him to this sickly hellhole. His enemies must have gloated. Yet, Sir Stamford Raffles now stood on the brink of a remarkable new chapter in his career.

CHAPTER 9

Thwarting the Dutch: How Raffles Seized Singapore

O n 22 March 1818, Sir Thomas Stamford Raffles, accompanied by his wife Sophia and their growing family, landed at Fort Marlborough on the southwest coast of Sumatra. Lying directly above the Sunda fault, Bencoolen is frequently wreaked by earthquakes. Lady Raffles was dismayed to discover that Government House was in a very poor state of repair and temporarily uninhabitable. Polecats ran wild through its rooms and grounds. The streets of the town were overgrown with weeds and infested by feral dogs. 'The state of society,' Raffles reported, 'even among Europeans, was very bad.' Undismayed, Raffles set out, often accompanied by Sophia, to explore the Sumatran hinterland. His most important official task was promoting the cultivation of pepper.

Confronting the Dutch

Raffles kept himself very busy in Bencoolen, but what obsessed him was the resurgent power of the Dutch in Southeast Asia and the dire threat this posed to the fortunes of the East India Company and the British treasury. But loyalty to Company and Crown was never his sole spur. Raffles wanted revenge for his ignominious expulsion from Java, the land of promise. From his ramshackle new base in Bencoolen, Raffles took it upon himself to thwart the Dutch phoenix that had risen from the wreckage of Napoleon's empire. To wage this undeclared war, Raffles defied not only the Dutch but his masters in

East India House. He would flout fundamental principles of international law. In the aftermath of the Napoleonic Wars, the British and
the other victorious powers who had defeated Napoleon, installed
the last Dutch 'stadhouder', William Frederick, as sovereign ruler
of the United Netherlands. The plan was to counterbalance against
any rekindling of French belligerence. To restore Dutch power in
Europe, it was necessary to return Dutch overseas possessions. Since
the British had decided to cling to Dutch colonies in southern Africa and Ceylon, that left only the East Indies as bargaining chips.

Raffles was thoroughly dismayed. Handing back Java, Riau, Malacca as well as other ports on the east coast of Sumatra was a dire
threat to British power, prestige and prosperity. By the time Raffles
arrived in Bencoolen, the Dutch had already banned British ships
from all the ports they controlled with the exception of Batavia.
Raffles was convinced that only drastic, unilateral action could fend
off a restored Dutch monopoly. That meant he had to take the risk
of provoking an important British ally. And provoke he did – for
when Raffles took possession of the island of Singapore a year after
he took up his post at Bencoolen, he was acting *illegally*, and the
legal mess he created would take years to disentangle.

In the meantime, Raffles and his British friends in Bencoolen occupied their time trying to make improvements to the shabby British
outpost. They had a hill cleared and built a new official residence,
and they tried to find out more about the rather cowed peoples of
the settlement. Chinese and Bugis had settled in Bencoolen as well
as hundreds of convict labourers deported from Bengal by the East
India Company. The Bugis or Buginese people who originated in
south Sulawesi played a significant and influential role as traders,
mariners and power brokers throughout Southeast Asia. The company had also imported slaves from Africa. Bondage of some sort
defined the experience of many of Raffles' new subjects. For several decades, former British governors of Bencoolen had struggled
to make a profit from growing pepper using a system of forced cultivation and so-called 'free gardens' which depended on bonded
labour. Before he left London, the East India Company directors
had ordered Raffles to be frugal and not repeat the mistakes they
alleged he had made in Java. Instead, he freed slaves and tried to
reduce the tax burden on the pepper growers. These were worthy

efforts, tinged with puritan zeal. He also banned cockfighting and gaming. Hoping to attract more trade, he declared Bencoolen a free port. Raffles had little success. A frustrating year later, all he could show for his efforts was a mounting deficit. In the autumn of 1818, Raffles set out for Bengal hoping to interest the governor-general, Francis Rawdon-Hastings, the Earl of Moira in a new plan for a free port in the Eastern seas. His advocacy must have been persuasive. Hastings agreed to back Raffles' plan provided he did nothing to aggravate the Dutch. As he sailed back to Sumatra on 12 December 1818, Raffles wrote to a friend that he was likely to be sending his next letter from the ancient Malay port of Singapore.

The Opium Factor

To understand why the governor-general agreed to Raffles' plan, we need to understand how John Company made his money. A quartet of commodities powered trade with the Indies. Spices had once been top of the list, but by the mid-eighteenth century the company was raking in bigger profits from saltpetre and tea. Saltpetre was used to make gunpowder, and so the company happily profited from the wars that so frequently erupted on the European continent. At the time Raffles was scouting out a new base in the Malacca Strait, the company was becoming ever more dependent on another high-paying commodity. This was opium.

Opium was the fuel of empire-building. For five centuries, the British, French and Dutch invested heavily in the sap of the poppy plant to reap vast profits and cast a pall of addiction and despair over millions of Asian lives. The huge edifice of European colonial empires was erected on the emaciated bodies of multitudes of wretched addicts. Profits from the sale of opium filled the pockets of European merchants and cascaded into the coffers of European governments. On European-owned plantations, the opium pipe eased the pain of hunger and blurred the rigours of hard labour for the armies of 'coolies' toiling from dawn to dusk in scorching sun and drenching rain on European-owned plantations and mines. An addicted 'coolie' was, for at least part of his abbreviated life, a more productive worker.

The East India Company sought to understand how to control the production of these natural commodities, and amassed infor-

The Sultanate Palace in Malacca is a modern replica of the Istana burned by the Portuguese in 1511. When rebuilding the palace, designers referred to the description of the Istana in the *Sejarah Melayu* or Malay Annals.

Chinese vessels like this one – known to Europeans as junks – used the monsoon winds of the Indian and China Oceans to enrich the 'Maritime Silk Road'.

The port of Malaka is pictured here in a French print from 1750. The great
Malay entrepot was razed by the Portuguese in the 16th century and occupied

successively by the British and the Dutch. (Photo: Tavarius, Shutterstock)

In the 12th Century, the area now known as Fort Canning Park, Singapore, was called Forbidden Hill (*Bukit Larangang*). In 1819, the remains of a palace and a 'Malay' Wall fascinated the British. Archaeologists have discovered a rich array of artefacts here revealing the history of medieval Singapura.

A statue of the Chinese admiral Zheng He stands in Malacca. A Muslim eunuch, Zheng He was a diplomat and commander of the Chinese 'Treasure Fleets' dispatched by the Ming Emperor Yong Le in the 15th century. After Zheng He's arrival in Malacca, the Sultan paid tribute to the Chinese emperor.

In 1786, Sir Francis Light acquired the island of Penang from the rulers of Kedah and established Georgetown. Penang would become one of the Straits Settlements along with Malacca and Singapore.

In this photograph from March, 1890, Malay chiefs in all their finery gather in Singapore. From left to right: Tunku Besar Pahang, Sultan Abdul Samad of Selangor, Sultan Idris of Perak, and Yam Tuan Muhammad of Negeri Sembilan.

Sir Thomas Stamford Raffles was employed by the British East India Company. He took part in the British invasion of Java and established a trading base in Singapore in 1819.

Raffles' rival, William Farquhar was the first Resident of Singapore. Farquhar played a vital role in establishing Singapore as an East India Company base.

In 1818, Raffles was appointed Lieutenant-Governor of Bencoolen (*Bengkulu*) on the west coast of Sumatra. It was from here that he launched a search for an East India Company base to thwart the Dutch.

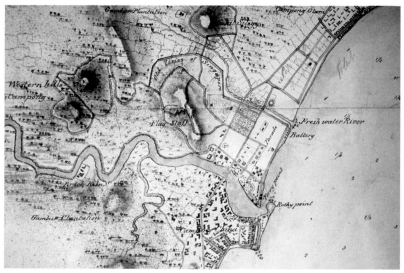

Shown here is a survey map of Singapore made in 1825 shortly after the final agreement between the British and the Dutch. The map shows the Singapore River, 'Forbidden Hill' (Fort Canning) in the centre and the 'Old Lines of Singapore'.

One of the last surviving Chinese burial places in Singapore, the tombs at Chua Chu Kang Cemetery resemble small theatres designed for commemorative rituals during the Qingming festival and the Seventh Lunar month.

From very early times, Chinese culture flourished on the Malay Peninsula. The Cheng Hoon Teng Temple in Malacca, also known as Temple of the Green Cloud, was founded by three 'Kapitans China' in 1645 under Dutch rule.

From 1819, Hindu Indian peoples have played a vital role in the development of Singapore. The Sri Thendayuthapani Temple, also known as the 'Chettiars' Temple' (Indian money exchangers), is dedicated to Lord Subramaniam.

Brought from Japan in 1880, rickshaws were ubiquitous in Singapore and Malaya in the 19th century. *The Straits Times* called rickshaw pulling 'the deadliest occupation in the East (and) the most degrading for human beings to pursue'.

Designed by a British architect and completed in 1932, the Masjid Sultan
Mosque in Kampong Glam symbolises the long history of Islam in Singapore,

introduced hundreds of years ago by Indian and Arabic-speaking Muslims.

In the 1850s, Kuala Lumpur began its life as a feverish mining settlement at the confluence of the Gombak and Klang Rivers. The booming tin mines in Ampang drove the growth of the city under 'Kapitan China' Yap Ah Loy and the British resident Frank Swettenham.

The raw materials that powered the growth of British Malaya were tin, rubber and gutta percha. Gutta percha was used to make a natural plastic to coat under-sea cables but so voracious was the industry that the supply of gutta percha trees was exhausted by the end of the 19th century.

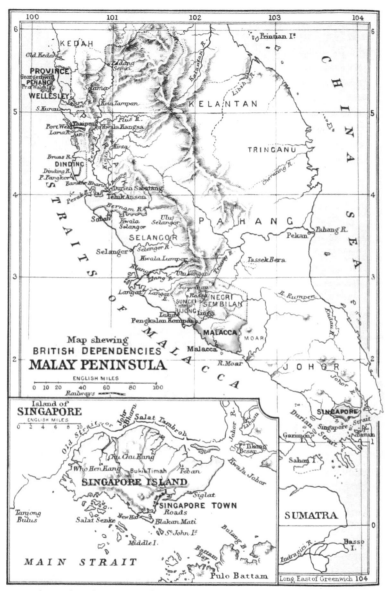

From the mid-19th century, the British began extending their control across
the Malay Peninsula by appointing 'Residents' to the Malay courts. Complete control of the Malay states was achieved by the end of the 1920s.

One of the oldest mosques in Malaysia, the Masjid Jamek Sultan Abdul Samad or 'Friday Mosque' is located at the confluence of the Klang and Gombak Rivers. Designed by a British architect, the mosque is typical of the Indo-Saracenic colonial style.

A statue of a *sepoy* – an Indian soldier in the British Indian Army – stands guard over a Chinese grave in Bukit Brown Cemetery in Singapore. Indian prisoners built much of colonial Singapore and Indian soldiers guarded the city.

mation, designed experiments and drew on the expert knowledge of people in the settlements and of individuals and institutions in London. Frequent collaborators included the Royal Society and the Society of Apothecaries. In 1773, James Kerr, an assistant surgeon stationed in Bengal, reported on opium manufacture in India. He described the cultivation of huge fields of poppy plants and how incisions made in the ripe capsules of the plant yield a thick 'juice' that is scaped off to make small globular opium cakes. Kerr complained to the company directors that the opium was often adulterated by producers with cow dung, and urged the East India Company to monopolise opium production to improve quality. He observed that the consumption of the drug 'emaciates the person' and induces a 'languid stupefaction' that 'allays the Cravings of Hunger'. In Britian, opium was not illegal; indeed, doctors prescribed huge quantities of liquid opium or laudanum for a variety of real or imagined ailments.

It was the British obsession with tea drinking that forced the East India Company into the opium trade. By the early eighteenth century, the custom of drinking tea with sugar had taken hold among the upper and middle classes. By mid-century, a nice cuppa sweetened with a dose of sugar was a working-class staple and tea imports accounted for one-tenth of overall tax income. By the 1760s, annual duties on sugar imports, buoyed by demand for tea, was enough to maintain every ship in the British navy. The demand for cheap sugar-sweetened tea powered the Industrial Revolution: it provided a caffeine hit to endure the slog of the working day and plentiful calories. Coffee, too, cleared the head and improved spirits, but prices wildly fluctuated. Coffee was imported from countries such as the Yemen and Eritrea and was out of reach of European control. Rising demand led to higher prices. Tea, on the other hand, was imported from China where tea production was highly sophisticated and responsive to demand from the British and Dutch East India companies that had long experience of buying spices, silks and other goods. For Europeans, the dominance of Chinese tea led to a nasty fiscal headache. The structure of the Western trade with China was based on silver; thus colonial products from India and the Malay Archipelago, like silver, cotton, pepper and lead, were exchanged for Chinese tea, silk and porcelain. As long as the trade structure was kept in balance, the European companies were able to make large profits. By the end of the eighteenth century, however, the British government realised that the tea trade was draining its silver reserves. Between 1821 and 1830, the East India Company's investment in Chinese goods totalled over £19,000,000, more than 90 per cent of which was payment for Chinese tea. The solution was to increase exports to China to halt or reverse the silver deficit. At the beginning of the nineteenth century, the trade imbalance was reversed by a rapid increase of trade goods from the company's plantations in India. By far the most important in value and bulk was opium. For the first time, silver began flowing from China to Britain. An anti-opium campaigner in the late eighteenth century wrote that 'every ball of opium filled in the Government factories was intended to transfer a certain amount of solid silver from the pockets of citizens of China into the Indian treasury'.

In 1800, the Chinese government banned imports of opium, and in 1813 outlawed its consumption. The company had to find ways to get around the Chinese ban on opium. Company agents began auctioning off whole opium crops to speculators and merchants in Calcutta, who would then contract with British traders and smuggle the opium on their ships to China. By doing so, the company was able to distance itself morally from the destructive trade while still reaping its benefits. So the British sold the drug to private trading companies such as Jardine, Matheson and Co., David Sassoon and Co. and Dent and Co. in Calcutta for export to China. James Matheson and other British traders were the opium barons of the age of empire. Every year, some 900 tonnes of illegal opium passed through the Strait of Malacca on the way to Chinese ports. From the beginning, the British trade in opium was illicit, secretive and highly profitable, but it kept British teapots flowing and lubricated an empire. So a base at the southern end of the Malacca Strait that would protect the flow of opium now looked a lot more feasible.

The Search for a British Base

The problem was the Dutch. The East India Company could not afford to let the monopolistic Dutch block the arteries of the drug trade. The problem for the company was the London Convention signed in 1814 by the British Foreign Secretary Robert Stewart, Viscount Castlereagh, and the Dutch Ambassador Baron Fagel. The convention was a legally binding agreement to return almost all former colonies to the Netherlands, including Malacca. This angered English traders who had freely used the old Malay port since the end of the last century. The loss of Malacca infuriated Raffles and concentrated company minds on the future security of the strait. Raffles had vehemently opposed letting the Dutch back into Malacca. The British government could not afford to antagonise the kingdom of the Netherlands and upset the new balance of power in Europe. It was a tricky dilemma. The solution offered itself on a plate. The company would use the ambitious Raffles as an expendable asset. He could do the dirty work in the field, but if he made too much of a diplomatic mess, the British government could explain it all away as a maverick bull inadvertently let loose in a political china shop.

By the end of 1818, Raffles had persuaded Lord Moira, the governor-general, to find a new base, as he put it, to 'secure the free passage of the Strait of Malacca'. Although Raffles was already intrigued by the island of Singapore which he had read about in the *Sejarah Melayu* ('Malay Annals'), there were other options on the table. Moira asked him to explore the possibility of forging an alliance with a claimant to the sultanate of Aceh at the northern end of the strait. Much to Raffles' relief, the 'Aceh option' soon fizzled out. He was convinced that the new base had to be found at the southern end of the strait. But where? It would be a mistake to assume that Raffles and the governor-general had fully made up their minds by the end of 1818. Moira next proposed that Raffles 'establish a presence' in the port the governor-general referred to as 'Rhio' on the island of Bintan, some 13 miles southeast of Singapore at the extreme southern end of the Malacca Strait in the territory of the Johor-Riau sultanate. The 'Rhio option' was risky because it was well known that the Dutch had a long-standing interest there, so the governor-general insisted that establishing a trading post or factory must not be carried out as 'the extension of any territorial interest' and that he must avoid any 'negotiation and collision with the Dutch'. Raffles' task was to find an advantageous position, not capture territory – a fine distinction to be sure. As it turned out, the Dutch already had rights to the entire territory of the sultanate. In diplomatic jargon, these rights were 'suzerain' rights of influence rather than 'sovereign' ones of control, but were nevertheless rights. In the mid-eighteenth century, Sultan Sulaiman Badrul Alam Shah (r. 1722–60) of Johor-Riau-Lingga had allied with the Dutch to crush the Bugis faction that had come to dominate the sultanate. In return, the sultan was forced to accept Dutch control of the Riau Archipelago. On the Malay Peninsula, the Dutch also seized Johor, Selangor, Perak and Trengganu. Riau was the sultanate's main port in the south. It was here that the Dutch had built a formidable fort at Tanjung Pinang. They had no intention of giving up such valuable real estate. At the very moment Raffles was preparing to launch his search for a new base, Adrian Koek, a Dutch merchant, had begun negotiations with the squabbling but still powerful Bugis factions to secure the port and block any British incursion. In other words, the 'Rhio' door was closing fast.

It is at this point in our story that we once again meet the affable Major William Farquhar, the former 'Raja of Malacca' and once the butt of Raffles' malicious jokes. Farquhar was older and more experienced and, unlike Raffles, widely liked and admired. He had good friends in the Penang administration who disliked Raffles just as much as he did. One was John Palmer, who scorned Raffles as 'our Knight' or 'Sir Knight' and talked of 'spiking a too rapidly revolving wheel'. When Malacca was returned to the Dutch, Farquhar made plans to return to England. Before he could make his escape, a letter landed on his desk in Government House, signed by none other than the arrogant company agent he had fallen out with a decade before and who now stepped back into his life garlanded with a knighthood. Sir Thomas Stamford Raffles commanded Major Farquhar to 'embark on the brig *Ganges* and proceed to the Straits of Singapore'.

On the last day of 1818, Raffles and Sophia sailed into Georgetown harbour in Penang. A few days later, Raffles met with Major Farquhar to flesh out his brusque order. In the meantime, Palmer had procured a ship for Raffles, the *Indiana*, skippered by Captain James Pearl. He sent a final barbed message to Farquhar: 'I do hope, my dear friend, that you will be employed to complete and perfect the only substantial measures which have been attempted since the peace with Holland … and that even Sir Stamford may not be used to diminish the value of your previous services.' Palmer warned Farquhar in a flurry of capitalised nouns that the impulsive Raffles might provoke the 'Terror and Hatred and Hostility' of the Dutch.

It would seem that Lord Moira, the governor-general, saw Farquhar as an almost equal partner to Raffles. His instructions were clear. Once 'Rhio' had been secured, Raffles should 'leave that officer [Farquhar]' and return to Bencoolen 'where your presence will be required'. Farquhar was ordered to 'remain in the local charge of the British interest in that quarter, under the general superintendence of the Lieutenant Governor of Bencoolen'. Raffles would be in charge of the new base but would exercise his authority from Bencoolen. It made sense to give Farquhar such an important role. He had learnt a lot about Malay rulers and how to bend the rules of the diplomatic game without causing dire offence. His experience would be vital if the British stood any chance of forging alliances with local rulers and so outmanoeuvring the Dutch. He was well aware that the key to the 'southern base' lay in the hands of the rulers of the Johor-Riau sultanate. Farquhar was well acquainted with rival factions in the sultan's court, and how to play one against the other.

As Raffles and Farquhar made preparations to sail south to 'Rhio', they received bad news. The Dutch had finally concluded a deal with the Bugis and so the Riau option was off the table. This setback cast a deepening shadow over British plans. The Dutch now controlled both Malacca and the southern entrance to the Strait of Malacca. Farquhar now proposed a new solution. Captain J. G. F. Crawford, who would command the expedition's survey ship, *Investigator*, recalled that 'Sir Stamford, at the instigation of Major Farquhar, picks on the Carimons.' There was no mention of Singapore. The expedition had a new destination: the two islands situated off the east coast of Sumatra and bang in the middle of the strait – Karimun and its bigger neighbour Kundur. The islands were eight days sailing from Penang. There was no time to waste.

On the early morning of 18 January 1819, as the sun punched above the eastern hills overlooking Penang, Major Farquhar set sail for the 'Carimons'. He led a small fleet of ships captained by Crawford and Daniel Ross. Ross was an experienced hydrographer and surveyor. In the meantime, Raffles ordered that the *Indiana* and its escort schooner, the *Enterprise*, be readied for an early departure the next morning. There would be tough negotiations ahead and so he insisted on bringing on board a vital tool of diplomacy – a tightly rolled red carpet. A few days later, on 27 January, Raffles sighted Farquhar's fleet close to the island of Karimun. Captain Ross had already gone ashore with his hydrographical and survey tools. As soon as the *Indiana* had dropped anchor, Raffles summoned Captain Farquhar on board to find out what Ross had discovered. Yes, the 'Carimons' were in the perfect place to protect British trade in the strait but, as Ross explained, the main island was tiny and had no natural harbour. Despite a prime location, the 'Carimons' would be difficult to settle and well-nigh impossible to develop. It would end up a rocky minnow in a sea of Dutch whales. It was Captain Ross who then pointed out that there was another island, just a day's sail away that had, in his expert view, an excellent and deep harbour. The British fleet weighed anchor the following day. As the little island of Karimun disappeared below the horizon, Raffles set sail for Singapore.

The Arrival

On the evening of 28 January 1819, the *Indiana* and the flock of frigates and schooners in its wake anchored off the tiny island now known as St John's to the south of the main island. In the waning light before the sun set, Raffles contemplated a faraway strip of white sand and low green hills of the place that would make him one of the most celebrated and detested figures in British colonial history.

And Singapore gazed back. It has been estimated that some 1,500 or so native 'Singaporeans' were living on the island in 1819. A good number were recent arrivals. It was hardly a 'sleepy fishing village', as the British claimed. A few weeks before Raffles sailed into the strait, one of the passengers on a ship sailing close to the south coast made a sketch that shows numerous dwellings clustered on the estuary of the Singapore River. Another map made in the same year marks the location of two villages, one at the seaward edge of the Padang, the other, a 'Ryat Village' in the area now called Kampong Glam. 'Ryat' (today's *rakyat*) means 'commoner' or 'royal dependent'. Further inland, Ross discovered forest clearings where Chinese plantation workers were growing and processing gambier, a plant used for tanning.

That day in 1819, Raffles barely noticed the ordinary people of

Singapore. All British eyes were on the local ruler, Temenggong Abdul Rahman. His presence was living testimony that Singapore had a long, complex history and was not merely the 'little fishing village' that Raffles and his successors turned into myth. Abdul Rahman himself had already spotted the potential of the island, and years before Raffles and Farquhar turned up it was he who brought Chinese workers to develop plantations in Kampong Glam.

Like all Malay chiefs, Temenggong Abdul Rahman was a sea lord. His influence reached across the ring of islands in the north-western part of the Riau Archipelago, including Singapore and the estuary of the Johor River. He commanded the allegiance of thousands of Orang Laut, or sea peoples. Since the time of the Malacca sultanate, the two most important offices of a Malay state were the Bendahara, or prime minister, and the Temenggong, who were, respectively, second and third to the Sultan. The Laksamana, or naval commander, came fourth in the line of precedence. We can imagine the Temenggong as a kind of maritime mayor, who was in charge of police, defence and running local markets. He received all import and export duties charged in the ports in his domain and the position was a lucrative one. Remember that Malay ports were not free ports.

Temenggong Abdul Rahman was vulnerable to internecine and often violent feuds between Bugis and Malay factions, and in this volatile culture depended on the support of the Orang Laut in his territories. Europeans reviled these 'sea peoples' or 'sea gypsies' as pirates. They were nothing of the sort. We should imagine the Orang Laut as formidable local naval forces or coastguards who acted on behalf of Malay rulers and chiefs. In 1819, Abdul Rahman's following may have numbered as many as 10,000 Orang Laut who sailed between a chain of strategically located bases like the one at Kampong Glam. So it would be a mistake to regard Temenggong Abdul Rahman as a mere pawn in the colonial game. The arrival of the British was a godsend for Abdul Rahman as he had the chance to enter into an alliance with some powerful foreigners.

As it happened, when Raffles anchored off St John's Island that morning in February 1819, the Temenggong was in need of new allies. Before settling in Singapore, Abdul Rahman had lived in Bulang, not far from the port of Riau. He was a powerful and wealthy man, but in 1818 the machinations of the Dutch knocked him off his perch. In 1812, Sultan Mahmud Shah III had died, setting off a battle for succession. The Temenggong had backed Sultan Mahmud's eldest son, Hussein Shah (Tengku Long). But the powerful Bugis Raja Muda favoured a younger son, Abdul Rahman Muazzam Shah, as did the Dutch. Tengku Long did not stand a chance. Dynastic squabbles after a ruler's death were frequent, if not customary, in Malay courts and Europeans took advantage of the squabbling rivals to put in place a new ruler who would toe the colonial line. So the younger son prevailed and Tengku Long and his backer, the Temenggong, lost.

For the Temenggong, defeat was bitter. He lost both power and income. Denied a share of revenues, the Temenggong fled to Singapore with hundreds of his followers. The new Sultan Abdul Rahman Muazzam Shah (r. 1812–19) offered the Dutch rights to set up trading posts throughout the territory of the sultanate, *including the island of Singapore*, where the Temenggong was busy plotting revenge. Tengku Hussein (Tengku Long) fled to a nearby island, where he devoted his time to praying and fishing. As it would turn out, all the elements of a conspiracy to outwit the Dutch and claim Singapore for King and Company were now in place.

The three conspirators, Raffles, Farquhar and the Temenggong, wasted little time. On 28 January, the Temenggong was rowed out to the *Indiana*. He asked Raffles why he had come to the island, and in turn Raffles enquired about the Dutch. Had they authority on the island? Remember that Raffles was under orders not to provoke the Dutch, so a lot hung on the Temenggong's reply. No, he said, only he and Tengku Hussein (Tengku Long) had any authority to negotiate with his English visitors. Raffles had shown due diligence and must have breathed a sigh of the relief that the Dutch, according to the Temenggong, had no claim to Singapore. That evening, Raffles and Farquhar went ashore to continue discussions and agreed to meet again the following day.

An eye-witness, a young man named Wa Hakim, whose memories were recorded years after, remembered 'Tuan Farquhar' and 'Tuan Raffles' coming ashore one morning, accompanied by a sepoy. He observed that Raffles was 'a short man'; Farquhar was taller and 'wore a helmet'. They entered the Temenggong's house and were plied with 'rambutans and other kinds of fruit'. Then the three men disappeared inside the house and negotiations began. The meeting lasted until four o'clock when the two British men left. The Tuans were very pleased with the negotiations.

A Treaty of Alliance and Friendship

Two days later, Tengku Hussein (Tengku Long), the eldest son of the late Sultan Mahmud Shah III, arrived in Singapore. Now the British would become king-makers. As Chinese plantation workers cleared the field now known as the Padang, the British erected a tent of bright red cloth and installed a table and five chairs inside. The red carpet Raffles had brought on board the *Indiana* in Penang was rolled out as far as the riverbank. Then a detachment of East India Company officers and their Indian sepoys was rowed ashore and assembled close to the tent. Here was the theatre of conquest masquerading as diplomacy. On board the *Indiana*, the ship's gunners primed their weapons and waited for orders.

It was 6 February 1819. As the sun ascended into a brilliant blue sky, Raffles and Farquhar waited at the entrance to the tent. A small crowd of curious Malay and Chinese onlookers had gathered at a respectful distance. Tengku Long arrived an hour or so later. He was escorted from the beach, as befits a man about to become sultan, to proceed along Raffles' blood red carpet as company soldiers presented arms. On board the *Indiana*, gunners ran out the ship's cannon and yanked lanyards to set off a barrage of fire.

Our second eye-witness, Captain Crawford, who commanded the *Investigator*, now takes up the story. Tengku Long, he condescendingly noted, wore a 'gaudy' costume that seemed 'inelegantly put on' thereby exposing 'a disgusting breast and stomach'. During the ceremony that now unfolded, Tengku Long sweated profusely and inspired in spectators 'a horrible and disgusting loathing'. He seemed cowed. Sitting on stiff-backed chairs in the shade of the red British tent, a 'Treaty of Friendship and Alliance between Sir Stamford Raffles and Sultan Hussein and Temenggong Abdul Rahman' was signed by all parties. Tengku Long was now Sultan Hussein Shah of Singapore and was awarded an annual salary of 5,000 Spanish dollars. Naturally, his vassal, Temenggong Abdul Rahman, was also rewarded; he would receive a salary of 3,000 dollars. In

return, the Malay power brokers resolved to 'aid and assist the English against all enemies'.

As soon as the treaty had been signed by all parties, the Union
Jack was raised and the guns of the *Indiana* thundered out once
again. Captain Crawford watched, 'revolted', as the new Sultan and
Temenggong Abdul Rahman 'promiscuously' sat down to quaff
some kind of libation with their British friends. The celebrations
finally ended in the late afternoon.

Crawford reported: 'A Raja as if dropped from the clouds, made
his appearance … declaring himself the lawful sovereign of the
lands extending from Lingga and Johor to Mount Muar near Malacca….' The ceremony that took place that day was a political ruse
that all parties both Malay and British hoped would offer spectacular
rewards in the future. At the same time, it was another chapter in
the story told long ago by the scribes of the 'Malay Annals'. Power
was yet again being passed on … but the sacred chain of descent
from Alexander the Great and Iskandar Shah had been broken by
a stooped Englishman with a splitting headache. Raffles, like Francis Light before him, had cleverly exploited a Malay weakness to
get his way.

The Dutch React

Following to the letter the orders he had received from the British governor-general in Calcutta, Raffles sailed out of Singapore
on 7 February and returned to Bencoolen to resume his duties. As
agreed, he had appointed William Farquhar as the first Resident of
Singapore, and it would be Farquhar who would bear the brunt of
the storm that was about to break.

Raffles' act of king-making was an audacious provocation. And
it did not take long for the Dutch governor-general, Baron Van der
Capellen, to launch a blistering fusillade of diplomatic outrage. He
despatched a furious letter to the British governor-general in Calcutta insisting that the sultanate was a 'lawful and perpetual fief of
the Netherlands'. Raffles had raised the British flag on Singapore but
the British grip on the island was shaky. In fact, it was unlawful.
The treaty Raffles and Sultan Hussain had signed was quite limited
in scope. It granted the East India Company the right to 'maintain

a factory or factories on any part of His Highness's hereditary Dominions'. John Crawfurd, who would become the second Resident of Singapore, pithily summed up the problem. 'The treaty,' he said, 'amounted to little more than permission for the formation of a British factory. There was in reality no territorial cession giving a legal right of legislation. The native chief was considered to be the proprietor of the land, even within the bounds of the British factory.' Crawfurd understood that Singapore belonged not to the British East India Company but remained the domain of Sultan Hussein Shah. For Crawfurd, such a state of affairs was intolerable. How he solved the problem will be told in a later chapter. In 1819, the future of Singapore as a British base hung precariously in the balance.

CHAPTER 10

Singapore Secured: The Age of Pioneers

I n the last decades of the nineteenth century, Singapore would emerge alongside Bombay and Hong Kong as one of the great port cities of the Asian world. The story of how that happened will be told in the next chapters. By the time Raffles sailed into Singapore in January 1819, the British East India Company had used its formidable military power to carry out a political revolution that smashed Indian commerce and turned the subcontinent into a 'Company Raj'. British power was exercised across a kind of double arc that hinged on the island of Ceylon, with its western tip at Aden in the mouth of the Red Sea, and its eastern extremities reaching through Burma to the vital new base in Singapore. In 1826, following the resolution of the dispute with the Netherlands which divided the Malay archipelago into zones of influence, the East India Company had established the Straits Settlements comprising Penang, Malacca and Singapore. Later the Dindings in the present-day Manjung district of Malaysia, Christmas Island, Labuan in north Borneo and Christmas Island were added to the Straits 'collection'. For the company, the Straits Settlements were both strategic acquisitions and useful dumping grounds for many thousands of Indians who agitated against company rule. The Straits were known as the 'Botany Bays of India' after the notorious penal settlement in Australia.

It was the governors of the 'Honourable Company' in Leadenhall Street, in fractious partnership with the British government, who built the British Empire. In 1857, the Indian Rebellion brought company rule in India to an ignominious end. The British government abolished the company and the Crown seized its territorial possessions and armed forces. So began a long period of direct British rule over India which continued until independence in 1947. The fall of John Company would send shock waves rippling through the Malay Peninsula.

The Impact of Empire

The nineteenth century would become the age of empires as Europeans tightened their grip on the lands and peoples of Africa and Asia. It was also an era of conflict, insecurity and traumatic change. We should keep in mind that huge volumes of trade between India and the rest of Asia were controlled by smugglers. The East India Company and the government it served depended on British merchants like Jardine Matheson, known as the 'Iron Headed Old Rat', who made fortunes illegally selling tens of thousands of chests of opium into China. Opium fuelled misery and bruising wars with China. It was the merchant lords of the opium trade who founded Hong Kong and provoked a succession of wars to force open the Chinese markets.

To secure trade and profit, the European powers frequently resorted to violence. Her Majesty's opium trade and the wars it provoked was only one source of uncertainty and conflict in the lands below the winds. The British waged wars against China and the Burmese Empire. Dutch armies crushed the Javanese Prince Diponegoro, who dared oppose colonial rule. By the 1860s, French armies seized territory in Cambodia and Vietnam. In the course of the nineteenth century, Europeans tore apart the old orders of rule in every region of Asia. The Opium Wars not only humiliated the Qing Dynasty in China but prepared the way for one of the cruellest catastrophes in human history. In 1850, Hong Xiuquan, a fanatical Hakka Chinese convert to Christianity who believed he was the second God, led a huge peasant uprising against the Qing and declared a new dynasty, the 'Heavenly Kingdom of Peace'. Hong led a huge army of chaste peasant warriors to capture the city of Nanjing, which he renamed the 'Heavenly Capital'. The Taiping rampaged across China, consuming the great cities of the lower Yangtze, like Yangzhou, Ningbo and Hangzhou, which were then among the richest in the world. Backed by French and British forces, the Qing eventually crushed the rebel armies in a campaign of exceptional ferocity. The scale of violence during the Taiping Rebellion was unprecedented, with terrible atrocities committed on all sides by the rebels, Qing soldiers, foreign troops and other opportunist militias. China was transformed into a vast human pump as millions fled for their lives to the world of the Nanyang, the 'Southern Ocean'.

The Diplomatic Battle for Singapore

It was against this unpredictable backdrop of war, conflagration, social fragility and refugee flight that the new rulers and peoples of Singapore would confront the challenges of the age of empire. To reiterate, in February 1819, Raffles had returned to Bencoolen in south-western Sumatra, leaving William Farquhar in charge as Singapore's first Resident and Commandant. The two men later fell out badly and much ink has flowed picking at the bones of the quarrel. Even today, there are historians ready to take up cudgels on behalf of Major Farquhar, to proclaim him the 'real founder of Singapore', thus brushing aside not only Raffles but also the prince of Srivijaya and Temenggong Abdul Rahman. What was the squabble all about? When Raffles first returned to his post in Bencoolen, he had left instructions that Singapore should be treated as a 'military post', not a 'fixed settlement'. This meant that there could be no ownership of land or issue of titles. Raffles knew very well that the British East India Company still had only tenuous claims to the island and that any sign of permanent settlement would anger the Dutch. He also instructed Farquhar to retain the land between the Singapore River and Rochor Street for public use. Commercial warehouses should be restricted to the shore at Kampong Glam. These restrictions put Farquhar in a very difficult position. The ban on issuing and selling land titles cut off a revenue stream to pay for the defence of Singapore. He was harassed by merchants who complained that the shallow coastline at Kampong Glam made loading and unloading cargoes hazardous. The upshot was that Farquhar capitulated: he began selling land, licensed gambling and gave permission for new warehouses in reserved parts of the settlement.

Raffles returned to Singapore for a few weeks in May 1819 and then for a much longer stay between October 1822 and June 1823.

He was horrified to see new warehouses crammed higgledy-piggledy on the banks of the Singapore River and he was even more appalled when he discovered that Farquhar had agreed to legalise gambling and had turned a blind eye to the sale of slaves. Farquhar was given his marching orders and Raffles took control of town planning. On 4 November, Raffles formed a Town Committee to assist him in planning and appointed Lieutenant Jackson, the officer in charge of the Bengal Artillery, as assistant engineer. The offending warehouses were swiftly demolished: Raffles was the puritanical originator of that Singaporean passion for tidying up and manicuring. For many of the first Singaporeans, scrabbling to make a living, Raffles' high-mindedness was a vexing, loss-making development. It is surely telling that, according to Raffles' Malay teacher, Munshi Abdullah, when Farquhar sailed home in June 1823 thousands came to bid farewell and 'people of all races put out in their boats.'

Even as Raffles was hatching up his masterplan, the battle for Singapore was heating up. The Dutch clung obstinately to their claim to the island. The diplomatic campaign was led by Raffles' old foe and Masonic brother, Herman Mutinghe, and the Dutch ambassador in London, Baron Hendrik Fagel. Raffles had created a legal quagmire, and for some time the Dutch had few doubts that in the words of one minister 'Singapore will be restored to us!' On the British side, there was hesitancy. Europe was at last at peace and no one wanted another war with the Dutch. Raffles feared that the East India Company's many and vocal critics in parliament would take umbrage about another land grab. The government prevaricated; the Dutch huffed and puffed. The final showdown came five years after Raffles had landed on the estuary of the Singapore River.

In the end it was the enormous value of trade with China that finally convinced the British government to throw its weight behind Singapore. All those opium clippers sailing from Bengal through the Strait of Malacca and across the South China Sea had to be protected. In short, Britain's prosperity depended on securing Singapore. At the southern end of the Strait of Malacca, Singapore was better sited than Penang and by the early 1820s its free trade policy was already drawing trade away from Batavia. The Dutch had re-imposed tariff restrictions in 1816. Besides, the power of the Netherlands was much diminished. The Dutch East India Company had rotted to nothing and the power and prestige of Britain had begun to eclipse all other European powers. From the point of view of the British government, Singapore now looked very desirable.

Then, quite suddenly the Dutch changed their minds. Yes, the British could have Singapore, and they would even throw in Malacca. In return, the British would give up Bencoolen and any interests in Sumatra. And so it was that on 17 March 1824, the Dutch Ambassador Anton Reinhard Falck and the British Foreign Secretary George Canning signed the Treaty of London. After four years of wrangling, Singapore was officially the property of the British East India Company.

Research by historian Peter Borschberg shows that the Dutch gave up their claim to Singapore for a very simple reason. They were not convinced that the island was worth the fight. Falck considered Singapore worthless as a 'produce-yielding territory' and its value as a naval station 'appraised far too high'. It would be no great loss. It would be far better to grab the huge island of Sumatra than squabble over Singapore. Falck's appraisal of Singapore as 'of little value' might raise a smile today. But in 1824, few could have been certain he was wrong.

Spheres of Influence

Not a single Malay representative took part in the negotiations. Yet, the Treaty of London had momentous and far-reaching consequences for all the peoples of the lands below the winds and generations of their descendants. In 1824, British and Dutch negotiators in London did much more than settle their squabble over Singapore. They went much further by agreeing on the boundaries of spheres of influence that would shape the future of Southeast Asia. The Dutch took possession of the Malay Archipelago from Aceh in the north to Bali and the chain of islands in the east. The British cast a net across the Malay Peninsula and the Straits Settlements. Singapore and the Strait of Malacca would become a territorial marker. The Treaty of London had enormous implications for the Malay rulers of Johor-Riau. None were consulted. And soon enough Raffles and Crawfurd would ruthlessly extinguish any legal rights they had to the island.

In 1823, as the British and Dutch wrangled over the future of Sin-

gapore, Raffles appointed Dr John Crawfurd to replace William Farquhar as Resident. Readers will recall Crawfurd rampaging through
Java in 1811 and laying siege to the sultan's Kraton in Yogjakarta.
Raffles left Singapore the same year, never to return. His final act, in
June 1823, had been to force Sultan Hussein Shah (Tengku Long)
and Temenggong Abdul Rahman to sign a new treaty. First, he
stripped both rulers of any right to customary taxation. This was, of
course, a crucial part of his plan to make Singapore a free port. Secondly, Raffles demanded that the territory of Singapore and its adjacent islands pass into the hands of the British East India Company.
The sultan and his subjects would, excepting marriage ceremonies
and the rule of inheritance, be subject to British law. The treaty
struck a hard blow at the deepest roots of Malay political culture.

Five months after the British and Dutch signed the Treaty of
London, making Singapore a British territory in law, Crawfurd compelled Sultan Hussein and Temenggong Abdul Rahman to sign a
final 'Treaty of Friendship and Alliance' on 2 August. Rarely has
a treaty been so inaptly named. Singapore was now unequivocally
a British possession, and to celebrate the fact a proclamation was
publicly read, cannons boomed out from Government Hill, gongs
clanged and Crawfurd embarked on a triumphant sightseeing trip
on HMS *Malabar* around the coasts of the new British settlement.

Why had the Sultan and Temenggong given in to the British
demands? One answer is obvious. The East India Company that
employed Crawfurd was an *armed* corporation. It held the most
powerful card of all – guns. But there was another pressure. Money
now meant more to the sultan than territory and he had become
dependent on his monthly allowance to maintain his court. Impov-
erishment did not suit a ruler of Singapore. So Malay rulers could be
bought. British power and money were impossible to resist. Crawfurd cut the Malay rulers down to size. Sultan Hussain retreated to
the palace he had built in Kampong Glam, and in 1825 left Singapore for good. He died in Malacca. The Temenggong's palace was
moved from its traditional place overlooking the Singapore River
to a less prestigious site in Teluk Blangah. He died there in 1825.
As Raffles' secretary Munshi Abdullah wrote in that fateful year, 'I
am astonished to see how markedly our world is changing. A new
world is being created, the old world destroyed.'

The New World

The new Singapore soon began to fascinate European visitors. This is the English seaman George Windsor Earl writing in 1833: 'Ships from all parts of the world are constantly arriving,' Earl wrote 'and the flags of Great Britain, Holland, France and America may often be seen intermingled with the streamers of the Chinese junks and the fanciful colours of the native perahus.' Singapore was, Earl exclaimed, the 'epitome of the whole Archipelago' as well as India, Arabia and North Africa. The sheer spectacle of so many thousands of different kinds of vessel and ship from every corner of Europe, Asia and China jostling in the harbour astonished newcomers. And when visitors ventured beyond the quays on the Singapore River and into the town, they encountered Chinese, Bugis and Malay traders, natives of Bengal and Madras, Parsis, Arabs and Africans. The naturalist Alfred Russel Wallace was a meticulous and attentive observer of the natural world. In The Malay Archipelago, he turned the same naturalist's eye on the peoples of Singapore: 'The native Malays are usually fishermen and boatmen, and they form the main body of the police. The Portuguese of Malacca supply a large number of the clerks and smaller merchants. The Klings of Western India are a numerous body of Mahometans, and, with many Arabs, are petty merchants and shopkeepers. The grooms and washermen are all Bengalees, and there is a small but highly respectable class of Parsee merchants. Besides these, there are numbers of Javanese sailors and domestic servants, as well as traders from Celebes, Bali, and many other islands of the Archipelago.... The town comprises handsome public buildings and churches, Mahometan mosques, Hindu temples, Chinese joss-houses, good European houses, massive warehouses, queer old Kling and China bazaars, and long suburbs of Chinese and Malay cottages.'

The Segregated City

A visitor to medieval Singapura in the fourteenth century might have plunged into the same teeming world of bustling streets, warehouses, wharfs and temples and glimpsed the palace of the Malay sultan on the Forbidden Hill. Now a British governor resided on the Forbidden Hill where Raffles had built a bungalow and the new world of Singapore was rigidly segregated. All those fine government buildings, temples, mosques, warehouses and bazaars were fitted into the framework of a masterplan. As soon as he had sacked Major Farquhar, Raffles set up a Town Committee under Captain Edward Davis, who was Farquhar's brother-in-law, S. G. Bonham (superintendent of lands and later governor of Singapore and governor of Hong Kong), and the merchant A. L. Johnston. The committee invited the Arab, Malay, Bugis, Javanese and Chinese communities to send representatives. Raffles instructed Lieutenant Philip Jackson to work on the town plan to reflect his vision of a 'place of considerable magnitude and importance'.

Raffles' plan was not original. It was inspired by his experience living in Penang where Indian and Chinese communities were strictly separated from European quarters, as well as visits to Calcutta, the jewel of the East India Company's overseas trading stations. The colonial city that grew up on the silt banks of the Hoogly was dominated by the ramparts of Fort William and imposing new 'Grecian' buildings set back from the waterfront. These grand, airy edifices could not disguise an utter disregard for the most basic precepts of town planning. It was remarked that in Calcutta, one of the wickedest places in the universe in the words of Robert Clive, appeared as if its dwelling had been 'thrown up in the air and fallen down again by accident.' Raffles wanted to do better. Singapore, he believed, could be both prosperous and planned.

In the 'Jackson Plan', Singapore Hill, later Fort Canning, was Singapore's defensive core. Like the colonial planners of Calcutta, Raffles punctuated Singapore with swathes of tamed and cultivated foliage such as the Botanic Gardens and the Padang to advertise Singapore's civilised prosperity. Raffles' insistence that each new house should 'have a veranda of a certain depth' seems to have made the famous 'five-foot way' a ubiquitous feature of Singapore.

Pragmatism soon prevailed over utopian master-planning and, over time, the Jackson Plan was quietly forgotten as the city grew. And yet the traces of Raffles' unrealised plan are visible to any visitor to Singapore today. This is a city-state proud of its obsessively manicured green spaces, parks and gardens. This is a city still compartmentalised by ethnic identity in Chinatown, Little India, Geylang and European 'ex-pat' enclaves like Holland Village.

Raffles' masterplan distilled one of the most powerful ideas of his time. For Europeans like Raffles, the 'races of man', keenly studied by the philosophers and scientists in Paris and London, stood at different stages of development. White-skinned Europeans occupied the top rungs of the ladder of civilisation. Darker-skinned natives clustered on the lower rungs. Certain native populations were more civilised than others and were offered hope of climbing upwards. Raffles' plan for Singapore literally embodied this rigid hierarchy. Grand government buildings, banks, hotels and offices formed the core of the European quarter. A commercial quarter stretched along the southwest bank of the Singapore River earmarked for what we would now call 'high-value' merchants. To the west of the river was the Chinese quarter. On the furthest outskirts of the settlement, close to the sultan's new palace in Kampong Glam, were the Arab and Bugis quarters that Raffles and his planners insisted should be 'as far as practicable' from the European dwellings.

The Men Who Built Singapore

Singaporeans of Indian ancestry are, of course, an important minority. They are one of the main 'races' of modern Singapore and comprise some 9.2 per cent of the resident population. Tamil is one of the four official languages of Singapore, while Bengali, Guajarati, Hindi, Punjabi and Urdu are recognized second languages in the school curriculum. The Indian festivals Deepavali and Thaipusam are national holidays. 'We had brought a kind of India with us,' in the words of novelist V. S. Naipaul, 'which we could unroll like a carpet on a flat land'. The vibrancy of South Asian cultures in Singapore today reflects the fact that, after 1819, Indians came to Singapore in many different roles as merchants, soldiers, convicts and labourers. Indians built nineteenth-century Singapore. As we saw in earlier chapters, long before the British East India Company subjugated India and secured control of the Straits Settlements, South Asian conquerors, merchants and priests had sailed across the Bay of Bengal to profoundly influence Southeast Asian trade, faith and culture. Traders from the Coromandel Coast were ubiquitous. In the 1820s, Singapore and the other Straits Settlements came under the direct control of the East India Company and its governors in Calcutta. As the British became ever more dependent on trade with China, it was Indian merchants, notably Parsis, who took on ownership of the 'country ships' that, commanded by European captains, smuggled opium into China.

As Singapore rapidly overtook the other Indian government ports in volume of trade, the port city lured tens of thousands of Tamil-speaking merchants who thronged its quays and bazaars. Singapore sucked in armies of labourers. Since Singapore was controlled from Calcutta, Indian troops provided the bulk of the military garrison. The very first Indians recorded in modern Singapore were the lascars and sepoys of the 2nd Battalion 20th (Marine) Regiment of the Bengal Native Infantry, who had first arrived with Raffles. Singapore's military garrison reflected the tremendous diversity of native peoples drafted by the British. The East India Company established permanent recruiting centres in Bhojpur, Patna and Buxhar in Bihar and Jaunpur and Ghazipur in Benares. Recruits, it was reported, were 'Mohamedans, Brahmins, Rajpoots and Hindoos of inferior description', in other words, from lower castes. High-caste Hindus dominated the Bengal Army. After 1827, various regiments of the Madras Army held the garrison in Singapore. They comprised a mix of soldiers mainly recruited in the Carnatic region, Trichinopoly, the Northern Circars and Mysore. Muslims made up between 30 and 40 per cent of the Madras units as well as upper-caste Telugus and Tamils, and a few Marathas, Rajputs and Brahmins from northern India.

Then there was the 'bazaar contingent', a kind of shadow army of domestic servants, chaiwallahs or tea-makers, grooms and dhobis, the Hindi term for washermen. The majority of dhobis would have been lower-caste Hindus or Muslims since their occupations were considered 'polluting' for upper-caste sepoys. Soldiering and trade defined Indian identity. In this new Singapore, the Indian garrison had to double as policemen. This was a raw, fractious world where many overlapping communities lived cheek by jowl, elbow to elbow, pushing and shoving for profit, influence and living space. Under British rule, Singapore became a hot, wet battleground. When Chinese clans or 'secret societies' clashed, as they often did, Indian troops stationed on Singapore Hill were ordered to raise their cannons, aimed not out to sea but in the direction of Chinatown.

Many Indian soldiers stayed in Singapore for the length of their tour of duty, then sailed away never to return. Many others chose to stay. Colonial records describe the flourishing settlement of dhobi washermen that grew up in the shadow of Singapore Hill. The garrison itself moved to Pearls Hill in 1828, but the dhobi community stayed put and prospered. They had access to the narrow stream known to Malays as Sungei Beras Basah, or 'wet rice river'. Long before the dhobis came here, Malays had brought rice to dry on the banks of the stream. There was a unique rhythm to the dhobi experience. Indian men would travel to Singapore to find work in the laundry business, returning to India once every three or four years to support their families. Before they returned to India for good, dhobis would return to Singapore with a son or a relative to carry on the dhobi business. Writing in the 1860s, John Cameron remembered taking a detour from Orchard Road 'along the windings of a small stream' and finding the dhobis at work. He observed the washermen, busy from morning till nightfall, grabbing pieces of clothing, dipping them into the stream, then swinging the cloth pieces over their heads and slapping them down on stone slabs: 'It undoubtedly secures a matchless whiteness.' Cameron calls the 'strong, stalwart' dhobis 'Klings', a term now regarded as derogatory, that referred to Tamil-speaking Muslims.

The Indian Pioneers

For Cameron, the dhobis were a mass of hard-working brown men. The Indian community in Singapore to begin with was fragile, shifting, and impermanent. It was predominantly male. Few flesh-and-blood individuals step out from the rather sparse records of early Singapore. The great exception is Naraina Pillai, sometimes spelled Narayana Pillay. We first encounter Pillai in Penang. He was an ambitious young Tamil speaker, who accompanied Raffles on his second visit to Singapore in May 1819. He liked the look of the place and sensed an opportunity, and so stayed on. Pillai was first employed as a clerk in the Treasury, weeding out counterfeit coins. When a more experienced clerk from Malacca joined the Treasury, Pillai was asked to leave. Had he not been sacked by a long-forgotten

Treasury clerk, we might never have heard of Naraina Pillai.

As Pilai haunted the streets of Singapore town looking for work, he noticed the frenzy of building work and set up a brick kiln at Mount Vincent, now Tanjong Pagar. He sent for bricklayers, carpenters and cloth merchants he knew in Penang to come to Singapore. Pillai's business as the first Indian building contractor swiftly prospered. He also began selling cotton goods and his bazaar at Cross Street became the largest and best known in Singapore. When the bazaar was destroyed in a fire, Pillai wrote directly to Raffles to grant him land for a new godown at Commercial Square, now Raffles Place.

There was a lot more to Naraina Pillai than bricks and cloth. His commercial success and connections with the British elite made him a natural choice as a community leader. Pillai lobbied Singapore's first Resident, William Farquhar, for a site to build a temple. This proved rather difficult since a Hindu shrine required plenty of water and many sources of water lay in areas already allocated for other uses. Despite these setbacks, by 1827 Pillai and his Tamil craftsmen had succeeded in building a simple wood and thatched roof structure on South Bridge Road in the Chinatown area. Inside, he installed a Sinna Amman, representing the goddess Mariamman who is worshipped in southern India to protect against disease. The beautiful Sri Mariamman Temple, which still stands as a national monument on South Bridge Road, offered refuge for new immigrants and shelter while they looked from work.

Indians settling in Singapore chipped away at Raffles' famous plan. Communal barriers were ignored or their edges blurred. In 1823, Secretary L. N. Hull had ordered the removal of the Chuliah Indians from Tamil Nadu, and the evacuation of the dhobi encampment 'up the Singapore River'. His plans were thwarted. The Chuliah and dhobis stayed put. Many Tamil migrants from southern India clustered very close to Chinatown in Cross Street and Market Street. This is where Naraina Pillai set up shop to sell cotton. By 1836, when the first comprehensive town map was drawn up, southern Indians were firmly established in this part of Singapore between the Stamford Canal and the location of the modern Cathay Cinema, along Kling (later Chulia) Street. Many Chettiars, the all-important Tamil moneylenders, opened offices in Market Street.

And not far from there, Tamil Muslims had aggressively won a monopoly ferrying goods and people across the Singapore River. In the Muslim district of Kampong Glam, George Windsor Earl noticed in addition to Malays and Arabs 'Bengali washermen hanging out clothes to dry, and dairymen of the same nation milking their cows'.

History Road

The story of Serangoon Road that runs through present-day 'Little India' as far as Punggol, tells the same story of migrant communities spilling over boundaries and defining their own worlds. In the map Lieutenant Jackson drew up for Raffles in 1823, we can see a pathway that is named the 'road leading across the island' that connects the Rochor and Kallang rivers in the south to the Serangoon River in the north. Take a walk along Serangoon Road today and you will notice many street names (Cuff, Desker, Norris....) that testify to early English settlers. In the nineteenth century, the plentiful water and grass found close to Serangoon Road drew Indian buffalo herdsmen. A police report from 1835 describes a Chinese gang attacking the house of a 'Bengalee' in a new kampong called Buffalo Village. As Singapore grew and became richer, edges and borders were fraying. Identities were shifting.

Serangoon Road was one of Singapore's earliest roads, linking the town to Serangoon harbour in the northeast of the island. The story of Serangoon Road is the story of Singapore. In the early decades of the nineteenth century, along this muddy artery, rickety bullock carts heaved granite blocks hewed from quarries on the little island of Pulau Ubin. Early maps show many hundreds of brick kilns dotted along the same route. Every red hot kiln supported a miniature working community, locked behind high brick walls, where Tamil workmen toiled in sheds, pug mills and moulded tens of thousands of bricks standing at long wooden tables in the broiling sun. When it was dark, the brickmakers were herded into huge dormitory buildings. Who were the nameless and forgotten brickmakers of Serangoon Road? The answer to that question tells us a lot about who built Singapore. Many of the brickmakers were convicts.

The British rulers of the Straits Settlements, like their present-day counterparts, had little difficulty attracting merchants and traders. They struggled to find the legions of workers needed to clear land and throw up a new city on this swampy, equatorial frontier. Indian soldiers (sepoys) or sailors (known as lascars) might set up temporary military camps but baulked at menial hard labour. Slavery was outlawed in 1823 and few Malays or Chinese could be persuaded to toil on the new roads, bridges and public buildings.

The British found a solution inside the overcrowded and verminous prisons of colonial Bengal. From the seventeenth century onward, penal transportation was a key strategy of British imperial rule, exemplified by deportations first to the Americas and later to Australia. The blood of convicts ran through the arteries of the British Empire. You may remember Magwitch, the escaped convict in Charles Dickens' *Great Expectations*, who terrifies young Pip and many years later becomes his mysterious benefactor. After 1820, a quarter of a million convicts were shipped across the world's oceans to colonise Australia, New Caledonia, French Guiana – and Singapore. India dispatched 4,000–6,000 convicts to Bencoolen between 1787 and 1825 and 15,000 to the Straits Settlements of Penang, Malacca and Singapore between 1790 and 1860. Another 1,000–1,500 were transported from Ceylon to Malacca between 1849 and 1873, and several thousand more were sent to Burma, Mauritius and the Andaman Islands.

Driving this forgotten migration was race. The British could not tolerate importing 'white'- skinned felons to Singapore. Law and order depended on upholding the moral superiority of the European race. The sight of white convicts in clanking chains could only harm the reputation of Singapore's rulers. For British officials in Calcutta, transportation solved the problem of overcrowding and seething unrest in the hellhole prisons of the Raj – and could be used a deterrent. Hindu convicts learnt to fear transportation across the 'Black Water' of the Bay of Bengal in ships they called *jeta junaza*, 'living tombs'. For higher-caste Indians, transportation was defilement.

In April 1825, the brig *Horatio* sailed into Singapore Harbour carrying a human cargo of 80 prisoners sent from Madras. A week later, they were joined by 122 convicted men sent from Bengal ... and so the passage of human bodies sentenced to hard labour went on year after year. During this period, between 15,000 and 25,000 convicts were sent from India to the Straits Settlements. The majority ended up in Singapore. The convict armies provide a panoramic human portrait of India's lower depths. Some had been convicted of violent crimes such as murder, dacoity and so called 'Thuggee', a colonial term for armed natives. Many others were political prisoners whose only crime was to challenge British rule, and Adivasi groups who boycotted revenue collection by the East India Company. Among the prisoners sent to Singapore was a tiny number of women.

Major J. F. A. McNair wrote a first-hand account of the convict labour system in Singapore which he called *Prisoners Their Own Warders*. He described a convict population of 'Seikhs, Dogras, Pallis, or a shepherd race; thugs and dacoits from different parts of the Bengal presidency, and mostly from round about Delhi and Agra; felons from all parts of the Madras and Bombay presidencies, and a few from Assam and Burmah,... and a sprinkling of Cingalese....' At first, the convicts were locked up in a huge godown on the eastern bank of the Singapore River. As numbers increased, the prisoners were forced to build their own prison on the edge of the Bras Basah canal. Escape attempts were rare. After all, where could you escape to? As Edmund Blundell, a governor of Singapore, put it: 'Generally a dense jungle, where, if they escape from tigers, they are pretty sure of falling into the hands of the Malays, who, for the reward always paid, are ready to make a seizure of them.' Besides, many prisoners were either tattooed or badly scarred by ankle irons or whippings. An escaped man could never slip away unnoticed.

For many Indian convicts, Singapore was an island hell. They served out their time locked up in dank, rat-infested cells overlooking the Bras Basah canal, or working soaked to the skin for days on end on waterlogged building sites. Many succumbed to malaria, cholera, dysentery and, if they were injured, gangrene. Even colonial officials admitted that convicts suffered the 'most wretched conditions'. Some took their own lives. Major McNair cited a Dr Rose who explained: 'The love of their native country is very great with them, and the idea of never again seeing their homes, their old and sacred places ... and loss of caste, act powerfully both on mind and body ... some obstinately refuse to eat at all.'

In the nineteenth century, the new Singapore was built by slaves. Convict labour is a form of slavery. Major McNair describes convict labourers clearing and filling swampland and jungle. They reclaimed land from the sea and pushed roads deep into the island interior. And the convicts did much more than shovel, chop and hack. These were the nameless builders of St Andrews Cathedral, Government House, now the Istana, and the Horsburgh Lighthouse. If you seek their monuments, even today, look around. Governor Blundell effusively paid tribute: 'The whole of the existing Roads throughout the Island, more than 150 miles in extent, every Bridge in both Town and Country, Jetties, piers, etc. have been constructed by Convict Labour. A Church has been erected every brick and every measure of lime in which has been made and laid by Convicts and which in Architectural beauty is second to no Church in India.' Blundell admitted: 'Powerful batteries have been erected at various points and fortifications are now in progress by Convict Labour which would have been too expensive for sanction if executed by free labour.' Yes, Governor Blundell – it is called slavery.

Greasing the Oils of Trade

Indian labour built Singapore and Indian business expertise fuelled its prosperity. Since the golden age of Malacca in the fifteenth century, Tamil Muslims played important roles in the flow of trade along the 'Silk Road of the Sea'. European merchants took advantage of their expertise and connections with the Malay ports and courts. After 1819 and the establishment of Singapore as a free port, opportunities for Tamil Muslims, often called Chulia, rapidly expanded. As early as 1822, Tamil community leaders petitioned the first Resident, William Farquhar, to appoint a headman or 'Captain' for Chulia 'mercantile and labouring classes'. The following year, Raffles instructed Crawfurd, who had replaced Farquhar, to take measures to stop pirate attacks on Chulia square-rigged vessels in the Strait of Malacca. In Singapore, Tamil Muslims traded in gems, cattle, leather, tobacco and tin; many were ship owners. On shore, Tamil Muslims set up money exchanges and sold textiles and hardware. When he visited Singapore, Alfred Russel Wallace observed: 'If you buy a few things from [an Indian trader], he will speak to you afterwards every time you pass his shop, asking you to walk in and sit down, or take a cup of tea; and you wonder how he can get a living where so many sell the same trifling articles.'

As well as Tamil Muslims, Singapore drew wealthy Parsi merchants, described by Wallace as 'highly respectable', who dominated the cotton and opium trades, and Nattukottai 'Chettiars'. Chettiars were a tight-knit caste-based community that first emerged in a cluster of villages known as the Chettinad in Tamil Nadu. In the Madras Presidency, many Chettiars had made fortunes loaning money to Indian landowners forced to pay taxes to the East India Company. Since British banks in the Straits Settlements refused to offer loans to non-European clients, Chettiars found a lucrative niche market offering financial services.

The Rise of the Towkay

Long relegated to the margins of history, Indians made distinctive contributions to early Singapore. They crossed oceans as merchants, traders and convicts; they prayed as Hindus, Muslims and Zoroastrians. They worked with money or brick, with shovel and abacus. But for many visitors, and Wallace was no exception, the overriding impression of Singapore was of a Chinese town. He wrote: 'By far the most conspicuous of the various kinds of people in Singapore, and those which most attract the stranger's attention, are the Chinese, whose numbers and incessant activity give the place very much the appearance of a town in China.' Wallace portrays a successful Chinese merchant, known as a tawkay [towkay], meaning literally the head of a Chinese household: 'The Chinese merchant is generally a fat round-faced man with an important and business-like look. He wears the same style of clothing (loose white smock, and blue or black trousers) as the meanest coolie, but of finer materials, and is always clean and neat; and his long tail tipped with red silk hangs down to his heels. He has a handsome warehouse or shop in town and a good house in the country. He keeps a fine horse and gig, and every evening may be seen taking a drive bareheaded to enjoy the cool breeze. He is rich – he owns several retail shops and trading schooners, he lends money at high interest and on good security, he makes hard bargains, and gets fatter and richer every year.'

There was, in fact, no single 'Chinese' identity. The majority of Chinese who arrived in Singapore were crushingly poor refugees who faced a lifetime of struggle and not infrequently life-sapping addiction. The bulk of these new arrivals, or sinkeh ('new guests'), had fled different regions of southern China, driven by famine or war, and belonged to distinct dialect groups – Hokkien, Teochew, Cantonese and a smaller number of Hakka speakers. Others, like Tan Tock Seng who we will meet properly very soon, had been born in one of the Straits Settlements. These 'Baba', 'Peranakan' or 'Straits Chinese' conventionally spoke Malay at home but did business in a rather mangled dialect.

The commercial power and prominence of the Chinese towkay was a consequence of close bonds with British merchants. The growth of Singapore was fuelled by this alliance. The majority of Europeans preferred to do business with Chinese rather than Malays or Bugis. Once again, the shadow of race falls across the story of Singapore. Europeans believed that the Chinese represented a superior civilisation and were blessed with singular business acumen. The success of the Chinese was, of course, the gift of history and the deep, wide web of connections that had defined towkay commercial culture for many hundreds of years.

The Real World of Tan Tock Seng

The story of Tan Tock Seng is familiar to many Singaporeans. Every day, thousands of Singaporeans come for state-of-the art medical treatment in the impressive modern hospital named after him. Who was the real person behind the iconic name? Tan was born in Malacca in 1798 into the hybrid Peranakan world that blended Malay, Chinese, Indian and even European ingredients. His father was from Fujian Province in China; his mother a local Peranakan. Baba Malay, that Tan grew up speaking, was a patois of Malay and the Hokkien dialect. After 1819, many ambitious young Peranakan men moved south spurred by news of Singapore's early success. They were lured by the very familiar figure of the genial Resident, William Farquhar, the former 'Raja Malacca'. Farquhar governed Singapore much as he had ruled Malacca. He got on well with Sultan Hussein and Temenggong Abdul Rahman and happily tolerated gambling and the sale of liquor and opium, just as he had in Malacca. Raffles was infuriated when he returned to Singapore and discovered that Farquhar had all but ignored his instructions, but

he had Farquhar to thank for enticing skilled Peranakan networkers to the new settlement.

China-born migrants such as Seah Eu Chin, known as the 'Gambier King', had to learn the same skills from scratch. The word often used to describe these networkers or middlemen is *Comprador*.
Today, the word, from the Portuguese *Compradore*, which simply
means 'buyer', has pejorative overtones. Compradors are scorned
as 'collaborators' who greased the wheels of European empires and
exploited their own kin. As previous chapters have shown, networkers, many of them Chinese emigrants, wove together the many
threads making up the tapestry of Asian commerce. From the end
of the eighteenth century, Europeans merchants, acting on behalf of
faraway states, entered this intricate web. The newcomers relied on
compradors as go-betweens. The Portuguese set the pattern in Malacca. They worked with the Chinese community through a Kapitan,
a wealthy and influential local merchant. In Java, a century later,
Chinese merchants served the Dutch as contractors and tax farmers. They recruited labourers and craftsmen, and supplied the bricks
and timber needed to build the new colonial city. When the British
won control of Singapore after 1824, Raffles and his successors followed the Portuguese and Dutch example, luring wealthy Chinese
merchants from Penang and Malacca and opened Singapore to the
tidal waves of Chinese migrants that swept across the Nanyang.

The most successful towkays made spectacular fortunes and few
hesitated to put wealth on display. For the tight-fisted British rulers
of the Straits Settlements, Chinese wealth was a godsend. The great
towkays of the Straits Settlements oiled the networks of communal
exchange and, at the same time, allowed the British to run their empire on the cheap. In Singapore, it would be wealthy towkays who
paid for the new roads, bridges and reservoirs.

In the oft-told 'rags-to-riches' tale, Tan Tock Seng arrived in Singapore, aged twenty-one, and began buying fowl, fruit and vegetables from smallholders in the countryside, which he sold from a stall
on Boat Quay. It was an astute business plan because fresh produce
was in short supply in the new settlement. He soon accumulated
capital, and this opened the door to a business partnership. Tan
went into business with an English merchant, Mr J. H. Whitehead of
Shaw, Whitehead and Co. Like other Straits-born Chinese, Tan pos-

sessed another priceless networking asset, a common language. It is unlikely, although not impossible, that Mr Whitehead knew much 'Baba Malay', the lingua franca of the Straits Chinese, and even less, or any, Hokkien. Tan himself was probably an imperfect speaker of Hokkien. So, Tan and Whitehead would have conversed in English and, more subtly, shared manners, habits and ways of doing business. Tan and Whitehead plunged into land speculation, and it was property that made Tan Tock Seng a very rich man. By the time of his death, Tan's empire included 50 acres in Tanjong Pagar as well as substantial tracts of land stretching from the Padang all the way to High Street and Tank Road. This was indeed shrewd speculation.

The partnership with Whitehead was important for Tan Tock Seng. But he and other Straits Chinese forged equally vital bonds with Chinese migrants, or sinkeh. Hokkien-speaking Peranakan would reach out to Hokkien families arriving in Singapore to provide business advice and all important contacts. They also offered more intimate connections; business partnership were lubricated by marriage. Most new arrivals were men and the Baba community enjoyed a surplus of eligible young women. When the first junks of the season sailed into the Singapore River, Baba Chinese rushed to Boat Quay to size up the latest batch of young bachelors. Tan Tock Seng married one of his daughters to the China-born Chan Koo Chan, who would make a fortune of his own.

Marriage was one way of bonding the old Straits Chinese with the new guests from the mainland. Another was philanthropy. And once more, Tan Tock Seng showed the way forward by founding a hospital for Chinese paupers. As the port developed into a colonial metropolis, Malacca Baba like Tan and other Straits Chinese sponsored a spate of temple building. Temples like the ones that sprang up across Singapore in the decades after 1819 offered more than spiritual solace. Temples were vehicles of development for the different dialect communities. Tan was the most generous benefactor of the beautiful Thian Hock Keng Chinese temple on Telok Ayer Street, the most important religious site for Singapore's Hokkien community. He was the first chairman of the temple's board of directors and contributed 3,000 dollars in gold towards its construction, an eighth of its cost.

It is hard to imagine today but at the time it was built, in 1842, the Thian Hock Keng temple lay very close to the sea in the Telok Ayer basin. Land reclamation has since pushed the shoreline miles to the south. But in the 1840s, the splendid roofline of the temple would have been visible to sinkeh stepping unsteadily onto the quay and, as its reputation spread, many immigrants headed straight to the temple gates to give thanks for safe passage and light joss sticks to honour Tianhou or Mazu, a Chinese sea goddess. Mazu, who was also called the Dragon Lady or simply the Goddess, was a kind of supernatural networker. The new temple in Singapore was just one of many temples dedicated to Mazu in the ports of the Southern Ocean. When the goddess was installed inside Thian Hock Keng in Singapore, an English journalist commented that Mazu 'is supposed to be the especial protectress of those who navigate the deep: at least, it is to her shrine as the Goddess of the Sea that the Chinese sailors pay the most fervent adoration, there being an altar dedicated to her in every junk that goes to sea.'

As soon as he had given thanks to Mazu for safe passage, our sinkeh would have discovered that behind its walls, the Thian Hock Keng temple was a refuge in a frightening new world. Here he could meet other Hokkien speakers who shared the same ancestral home; he could look for work, take language lessons and be entertained. In the grounds of the temple, Chinese associations like the kongsi and Hui Guan were formed based on dialect or clan that glued the community together. Clans provided vital community services, resolved disputes, and organised the performance of sacred rites at festivals and funerals.

Temple festivals were glorious spectacles. And they cost the towkay who endowed the new temples of Singapore huge sums of money. The rewards for such extravagant patronage in terms of social prestige were enormous: one British resident aptly compared a temple festival in Singapore to a Lord Mayor's Show in London. The *Singapore Free Press* reported that Mazu was carried on a palanquin decorated with yellow silk and crepe, protected by a bodyguard of Celestials, at the head of a procession that stretched for a third of a mile. Gongs were banged; celebrants held aloft gaudy banners of 'every colour, form and dimension'. British officials who saw and heard the lavish welcome put on for the Sea Goddess were impressed. The colonial administration, starved of funds, was run on a shoe-string. To make up the administrative deficit, the British turned to men like Tan Tock Seng to help govern the new settlement. In 1844, Tan was appointed the first Asian Justice of the Peace, a post he held until his death.

The Gambier King

The life of Seah Eu Chin followed a very different path. He was born in Chenghai county, Guangdong Province, and as the son of a petty bureaucrat, was relatively well off, but Seah had none of the privileges of a Straits-born Baba. He arrived In Singapore in 1823, a Teochew-speaking youth of eighteen. By the early 1840s, Seah was crowned Singapore's 'Gambiah King' and founder of the Teochew temple Wak Hei Cheng Bio on Phillip Street and the first Teochew association, the Ngee Ann Kongsi. In China, young Seah Eu would have been expected to follow his father's privileged career as a Qing official, but for reasons we will never know he decided to flee China and seek his fortune in the grubby world of commerce. He may have failed an all-important examination; perhaps he was caught up in a village scandal. In any event, Seah fled Chenghai, never to return, with the clothes on his back and one rare advantage. His father Seah Keng Liat had given his son a traditional education in the Chinese classics. Because he could read and write with such proficiency, he was taken on as ship's clerk and accountant on a junk sailing for Singapore. He must have done well. Instead of settling in Singapore, Seah set off again, and for five years worked on junks that plied the Strait of Malacca from Palembang in Sumatra to Penang. Seah's life as a rover was an education in the risky and roustabout lore of maritime commerce. For Seah, five years was enough. And his mind was crammed with an insider's hard-won knowledge of the top merchants and tricks of the trade. This time, when he disembarked in Singapore, he stayed put. Seah set himself up as Eu Chi and Co., selling supplies to Chinese traders and buying their cargoes to sell on in the markets of Singapore. He knew what could be bought cheap from regional traders and sold on at a handsome profit to European buyers. Like Tan Tock Seng, he began investing in real estate. Unlike Tan, he was not content merely to own land and profit from rents.

In 1835, Seah bought an eight-mile tract of land stretching from what is now the western end of River Valley Road to Bukit Timah. Like many other Chinese in Singapore, he began growing pepper and gambier, and to begin with results on the plantation were dismal. Gambier is an astringent plant extract that had traditionally been used as a medicine or food additive in confectionary. Gambier and pepper are always grown together as gambier waste provides fertiliser for pepper plants. For a few years, Seah struggled with Singapore's acid soils. His other businesses were thriving, and he made plans to sell up. Then his fortunes changed. European leather manufacturers discovered that gambier could be used to tan and preserve high-value goods and demand set off a boom. Seah's gamble on gambier had paid off. Profits from his huge plantations skyrocketed. His other businesses prospered too, and soon he was one of the wealthiest sinkeh in Singapore and a dominant figure in the Teochew community. Like Tan Tock Seng, he founded social welfare organisations and a temple. Such was the Gambier King's commercial muscle and status that in 1838 he married the daughter of the Kapitan China, or community leader, of Perak, and in 1842 Seah was admitted into the exclusive Singapore Chamber of Commerce.

British and Chinese Alliances

The rags-to-riches stories of Tan Tock Seng and Seah Eu Chin are archetypal 'pioneering' narratives of early Singapore. The important point is that the rebirth of Singapore was driven by alliances struck between British and Chinese or Baba entrepreneurs. That is another way to explain why Raffles is still standing on Boat Quay. He understood very clearly that the rise of Singapore would depend on Chinese capital and Chinese mercantile energy. The stories of the pioneers brings us to another point. These rags-to-riches legends of Singapore cloak the poverty that afflicted so many of the migrants who fled to the Straits Settlements and the indifference of the British colonial administrators who defray the costs of running a colony. For every Tan Tock Seng, there were many thousands of other sinkeh who endured back-breaking toil and grinding poverty. The streets of Singapore were paved with gold and soiled by the filth of humiliation. Anger simmered in the streets and markets.

European visitors brought home stories of Singapore's humming harbour and waterfront and beyond a townscape of imposing neo-classical government buildings that gleamed in the equatorial sun and clusters of reassuring church spires, minarets, and pagodas. The ever-changing panorama was thrilling, enticing and deceptive. Trade, free trade, was Singapore's lifeblood. Raffles envisioned Singapore as a commercial hinge linking trade in the Indian Ocean, the South China Sea and the Java Sea. But for many decades after 1819, the future of Singapore as a commercial power was blighted by uncertainty. In the European merchant community, there was mutinous talk about the stranglehold of the East India Company.

Throwing off the Chains of Company Rule

By the middle of the nineteenth century, Britain was approaching an apogee of imperial pomp and was the most prosperous manufacturing and trading nation in Europe. But in Singapore, the city's commercial and governing community was frustrated. The focus of their ire was the India Office and the East India Company. John Company still ruled the Asian waves from Government House in Calcutta, and in Singapore the great and the good commercial elite felt neglected and disgruntled. Business leader W. H. Read complained that 'the rich and fertile countries of the Malay Peninsula are as little known as they were at the time of settlement of Singapore....' The Straits Settlements, the Malay Peninsula and the entire region of Southeast Asia was, Read concluded, viewed from Calcutta as a kind of unappreciated appendage to British India.

Read and his fellow merchants had good reason to complain. Between 1830 and 1834, the main British merchant firms in Calcutta collapsed. This deepened a financial crisis that had begun when the company fought, at huge cost, the Anglo-Burmese War between 1824 and 1826. Then in 1833, pressure from British merchants persuaded the government in London to end the company's monopoly of trade with China and pare down its commercial activities to bare bones. John Company ceased to be a merchant and became an administrator. The consequences for the Straits Settlements were dire. The company savagely wielded the axe of fiscal prudence, slashing jobs and budgets. For the merchants of the Straits, the message from

Calcutta was loud and clear. You do not matter.

The challenge from the Straits to the East India Company was sharpened by the emergence of newspapers like the *Singapore Free Press* and the *Straits Times* which promoted the mercantile case for reform. The Straits merchants had important allies in Britain. Backed by John Crawfurd, the Orientalist and second Resident of Singapore, powerful commercial groups like the Glasgow East India Association and the London East India and China Association fought hard against the company. All agreed that the Straits Settlements must be freed from the dead hand of the company and become a Crown Colony. They had no idea that the days of John Company would soon come to a crashing end.

In 1857, India was engulfed by insurrection. The Indian Rebellion shattered British India and wrecked the East India Company. In August 1858, an act of parliament transferred the government of India to the Crown. The era of company rule was ended and a new age of empire was born from the ruins. The demise of John Company was celebrated in the clubs and merchant houses of Penang, Malacca and Singapore. The Straits rejoiced. In London, *The Times* newspaper enquired: 'What has Singapore to do with India? It carried on a larger trade with China than with India….' Singapore should, the grand organ declared, become the centre and citadel of British power in the Eastern Seas to defeat the 'ceaseless intrigues of the Dutch to exclude us from the Indian archipelago'. The stage was set for the next chapter in the history of Singapore.

At the mid-point of the nineteenth century, Singapore was an Asian emporium that lagged behind the other great port cities such as Bombay and Sydney. The reason is that there was a brake on prosperity. Singapore lacked the connections to an inland interior, a hinterland like the ones that had enriched its rivals. Singapore lacked staples like the cotton and opium that enriched Bombay and Calcutta or the vast sheep farming stations that drove the rise of Sydney. By 1838, Australia was challenging Spain and Germany as the largest supplier of wool to England. The Straits Settlements were enclaves without backyards.

In a fast-changing and ever more globalised world, change, enormous change, was just over the horizon. War in mainland China opened the floodgates of a vast new human exodus that would surge across the Nanyang, the 'Southern Ocean'. New technologies like the steam engine and electric telegraph and the construction of the Suez Canal in Egypt would shrink the distances between the European metropoles, India and Asia. These revolutionary developments would transform the commercial fortunes of Singapore as the port city threw off the chains of company rule for good and tapped the wealth of its hinterland in the Malay Peninsula.

CHAPTER 11

The White Rajahs: The Conquest of North Borneo

The Decline of the Malay States

F or the Malay rulers, the rise of Singapore as a free port controlled by Europeans augered the decline of the Malay entrepôt states. Beyond the coast, there was a pervasive weakening of the old Malay states. By the mid-nineteenth century, the British exploited fractures in Malay society to begin exploiting the natural resources of the Malay Peninsula which would become Singapore's lucrative hinterland. Historians date the beginning of decline to the assassination of Sultan Mahmud Shah III, ruler of the most powerful Malay state of Johor. He was stabbed to death by court nobles as he was carried to the mosque on the back of a servant. The conspirators justified regicide on the grounds that Sultan Mahmud had acted in cruel and unpredictable ways and neglected his duties by allowing rival powers like the Bugis to damage trade in the Straits. The assassination of Sultan Mahmud was momentous and traumatising. He was supposedly the last direct descendant of the medieval ruler of Srivijaya, Sri Tri Buana, and with his death the Malay genealogical line that began with Alexander the Great came to an abrupt and violent end. Sultan Mahmud had no direct heirs and his murder set in motion events that led to the decline of Johor as rivals exploited its fragility. Power passed into the hands of Minangkabau peoples from Sumatra and Bugis from Sulawesi. Malacca was blighted by succession disputes and when the British briefly occupied the city in 1809, they destroyed the old fort. Raffles' Malay teacher Munshi Abdullah lamented: 'After its destruction, Malacca lost its glory like a woman bereaved of her husband, the lustre gone from her face.' Not all the Malay states suffered such precipitous decline. In the eighteenth century, Trengganu and Selangor were formally established as independent kingdoms and the rulers of Kedah and Perak seized on new opportunities in international trade.

Founding a Dynasty in the Jungles of Borneo

On Borneo, the giant rugged island situated to the southeast of the Malay Peninsula, a freelance British adventurer would exploit fissiparous rivalries that blighted the Malay kingdom of Brunei to seize his own kingdom in the jungles of Sarawak and keep it by force. The story of Sir James Brooke has been encrusted with romantic myths. 'I am supreme! Whatever I require I can procure. If I desire I might have a dozen rivers besides Sarawak.' For a few years in the 1840s, Brooke was a legend, his reputation raised aloft on the flimsy paper wings of a promotional extravaganza funded by devoted admirers. He seemed to be the real life hero of a Victorian adventure story who had fought dastardly pirates and founded a dynasty in the jungles of Borneo. He was feted by the great and the good and invited to Windsor Castle as a guest of Queen Victoria and her consort Prince Albert. Brooke was wined and dined, awarded the Freedom of the City of London and made a knight of the realm. His fame would come crashing down all too soon.

Brooke was not an East India Company man like his hero Sir Stamford Raffles. He was a freelance imperialist, a heroic English swashbuckler in the tradition of Drake and Raleigh. Sylvia Brooke, the wife of the third and last member of the Brooke dynasty, Rajah Vyner, reported meeting the Hollywood star Errol Flyn: 'He said that he had always imagined that the first White Rajah was like him and I agreed that he was perfect for the part.' Well, not quite perfect.... Flynn wanted to inject a strong dose of romance into the story of the White Rajah. Sylvia interrupted: Was Mr Flynn 'aware of the fact that James Brooke had been severely wounded in India, and deprived of his manhood'? Flynn laughed and shrugged. 'You can't have a motion picture without love,' he said. 'And you cannot have James Brooke with it,' Sylvia replied. The real story of James

Brooke was even darker than the Hollywood movie star imagined.

The Violent Underpinnings of British Power

The story of James Brooke exposes the violent underpinnings of British power. The British East India Company seized the island of Singapore using guile and deception. Raffles and Farquhar exploited the human cracks and fissures that lay behind the ceremonial splendour of the Malay courts. But the crackle of cannonades fired by the sailors of the *Indiana* and the line of red-clad sepoys that greeted Sultan Hussain Shah (Tengku Long) were not very subtle reminders of the iron fist barely hidden in a velvet glove. The company, after all, was an armed corporation that bristled with firepower. The wealth of its holdings in India meant that the company could spend lavishly on its army and fleet of East Indiamen. Its legions of sepoys were supported by a well-oiled war machine. When, in 1787, an Indian minister visited Calcutta he was astonished by armouries of Fort William where he counted 3,000 muskets 'hung up in good order' and ammunition factories hard at work. The acquisition of Singapore was a peaceful affair but in the Malay Peninsula and on the island of Borneo, British empire-builders like Brooke deployed the full force of British fire power.

The Lure of Borneo

In 1812, an English merchant and traveller called John Hunt returned to London with tales of an island 'indented with safe and capacious harbours' and 'boasting commercial products that have in all ages excited the avarice and stimulated the desires of mankind'. Hunt was over optimistic. In the annals of Europeans, Borneo appears as a land of treachery, violence and sudden death. Its oldest inhabitants are nomadic peoples of the seas and rainforest, such as the Iban and Sea and Land Dyaks. These are merely broad-brush terms. Borneo is home to at least forty distinct aboriginal peoples. From the ninth century, migrants from China and the islands of the Malay Archipelago took root in coastal areas and river valleys, Malays from the west, Javanese from the south, Bugis and Sulus from the east. Settlements evolved into mercantile states of seafaring peoples under the sway of the Srivijaya and Majapahit empires. In the fifteenth century, Islam arrived in Borneo and Muslim dynasties were founded at Sambas, Soekadana and Landok on the west coast and Bandjermasin on the south. Anthony Pigafetta, one of the companions of Ferdinand Magellan, visited the Muslim sultanate of Brunei in 1521 and was astonished by the opulence of the sultan's palace and the size of the town. The Spanish government of the Philippines later sent naval expeditions to seize Brunei – and failed.

Early in the seventeenth century, merchants of the British East India Company reported that the island of Borneo 'abounded in great riches' and was unspoilt by any Spanish or Portuguese 'castle, fort, blockhouse or commandment'. But English adventurers in Borneo, like the merchant captain Alexander Hamilton, were thwarted by fierce competition from both Dutch and Chinese merchants who reaped huge profits from pepper, gold, and diamonds, which were the chief attractions for European traders, but also camphor, rattans, wax, resin, timber, and table delicacies like agar-agar (seaweed), sea cucumbers, sharks' fins and edible bird's nests.

By the end of the eighteenth century, the British had become preoccupied with protecting the all-important opium and cotton trade between Bengal and China. This meant that from the British point of view, northern Borneo took on increasing strategic importance as a staging post on the shipping highway that led across the South China Sea. In 1763, British East India Company man Alexander Dalrymple, a Scottish geographer and the first hydrographer of the British Admiralty, persuaded the sultan of Sulu, Muhammad Muizzuddin, who ruled the long chain of islands between Borneo and Mindanao in present-day Philippines, to set up a factory, or base, at Balambangan, just off the northern coast. The factory was a dismal failure and the company had the island evacuated in 1805.

During the nineteenth century, British interest in Borneo was focused on the northern part of the island, while the Dutch, who thought of Borneo as an adjunct of Java, sought to extend their influence in the south. Here we can find the deep roots of the present-day division of the island between Indonesian Kalimantan and the Malaysian states of Sabah and Sarawak in the north. This was the volatile and uncertain situation that prevailed in Borneo when James Brooke sailed into the Sarawak estuary forty years later.

Born with a Silver Spoon

Born in 1803, James Brooke was a child of the Honourable Company and grew up in the Indian city of Benares, also known as Varanasi, in northern India. The Brooke family home was in the European quarter of Secrore. The European settlement had been built upwind of the great tiers of ghats, temples and shrines where the dead are still consumed in hissing and spitting pyres to escape the cycle of rebirth in the ashy waters of the sacred Ganges. James's father Thomas Brooke was an official of the British East India Company with a lucrative practice as a judge. His wealth ensured that his children, whether legitimate or not, were 'above pecuniary excitement', meaning that his brood would never have to worry about money. Thomas Brooke firmly lodged a silver spoon between the infant gums of young James. In 1819, as Raffles and Farquhar sailed into Singapore harbour, Brooke followed his brothers into the Bengal Army as an ensign in the 6th Native Infantry. He was an indolent soldier, devoted to japes and games of 'pig sticking'. That all ended in 1824 when the British East India Company went to war with Burma.

The First Anglo-Burmese War (1824–26) was nasty, brutish and short but it made heroes of military commanders Lord Amherst and Sir Archibald Campbell. In a book written many decades later about the British 'Rulers of India', Anne Thackeray Ritchie bluntly explained to her readers why the 'Honourable' East India Company had gone to war in Burma: 'In the light of experience the policy of the Burmese war needs no justification. Arakan and Tenasserim in due course became valuable possessions. Arakan is one of the great rice-fields of the world. The superb timber forests of Tenasserim were especially a gain. Assam was destined to become more than the rival of China in the production of its tea. It was as a first step which led of necessity to the complete absorption of Burma in the Empire, that Lord Amherst's policy became a landmark in history.' Such were the heroes of the age of empire.

In January 1825, young Lieutenant James Brooke led a charge, galloping up against Burmese lines at Rungpore in Assam. In the words of his first biographer, secretary and friend Spencer St John, he 'foremost, fighting, fell.' Brooke fell so hard, he was assumed to be dead until his commanding officer noticed signs of life and removed the wounded man to camp. Young Brooke's soldiering days were over. He had a new ambition. He would follow the road to glory of his hero Sir Thomas Stamford Raffles.

The New Raffles

Brooke had advantages denied to Raffles. He was a dreamer of means. In 1830, he had resigned from the British East India Company. For the next few years, he drifted, flitting between grand plans hatched up with like-minded friends who had vague ideas about breaking the company monopoly or looking for adventure. For Brooke, the turning point came in 1835. His father Thomas Brooke died and his children each inherited £30,000 (the equivalent of £3,836,775.37 in 2022). At the age of thirty-two James Brooke was a multi-millionaire. He purchased a 142-ton and heavily armed schooner, the *Royalist*, from the Royal Yacht Squadron: ownership came bundled with the same privileges accorded to a British warship. Brooke was permitted to wear a semi-official uniform and hoist the white ensign. Brooke recruited a crew of like-minded British adventurers and sailed the *Royalist* to Singapore.

It was here that he got wind of an opportunity in Borneo. By then, Singapore traders were using a number of sea routes to China. One followed the west coast of Borneo northwards past the sultanate of Brunei. The Singapore trade with China had stimulated local enterprises – and local miners had discovered antimony close to the village of Kuching in the Sarawak region. Brooke was intrigued and sailed the *Royalist* to Kuching. Here he discovered that the sultan of Brunei, Omar Ali Saifuddin II (r. 1828–52), was embroiled in conflict with local Malay barons who hoped to profit from the antimony mines. Brooke offered support to the sultan's party, insinuating that he represented the British government. After routing the rebels, Brooke persuaded the grateful sultan to grant him the vaguely defined Sarawak region as a gift. He wrote later: 'I was declared rajah and governor of Sarawak amidst the roar of cannon, and a general display of flags and banners from the shore and river.' To crush the Sarawak rebels, Brooke had called on the firepower of the British Royal Navy – and he had been able to secure this favour because Britain had declared war on piracy in the South China Sea.

Land of Headhunters and Pirates

In a prospectus titled 'Expedition to Borneo' published in the *Athaneum*, a magazine known as the 'mirror of Victorian culture', Brooke openly proclaimed his ambition to rid Borneo of 'Paganism and the horrors of the eastern-slave trade'. It must always be born in mind, he continued, that while the Dutch are masters of the Archipelago, this was '*only* because no other nation is willing to compete with them'. The Dutch, he lamented, 'had reduced the "Eden of the Eastern Wave" to a state of anarchy and confusion'.

There were two powerful words that shaped European perceptions of Borneo and its peoples, which underpinned how Europeans treated the peoples of Borneo. Piracy was one, headhunting the other. Both words proved to be potent weapons for Europeans like Brooke who sought influence and control in the Malay world. The practice of headhunting was, for the Western mind, a sign of brute savagery that affronted Christian values. Only by eliminating headhunting might the savage hope to become civilised. Piracy was a legal term, defined in European law, that provided Brooke with the excuse to call on the full might of the British Royal Navy.

Borneo was a complex patchwork of very different peoples. The coastal regions and riverine settlements were dominated by a mobile population of Malays, Arabs and Chinese. The latter were mainly involved in mining. A labyrinth of rivers connected the coast to the mountainous and ridge-backed interior. This was the rainforest that so fascinated naturalists like Alfred Russel Wallace. The jungle was the realm of numerous tribal peoples like the Iban and Bidayuh who Western anthropologists tended to lump together as Dyaks, further subdivided as 'Sea' and 'Land' Dyaks. The human landscape of Borneo was in continuous flux and tribal groups often identified themselves using rivers and regions: 'We of Skrang' or 'We of Undup', and even 'We of this area.'

The lives of the peoples of Borneo revolved around the longhouse. These were truly remarkable structures, built close to rivers, that housed entire communities, often as many as a hundred families. The interior of the longhouse was divided between family rooms and a communal interior 'street' and meeting place. The most impressive longhouses extended more than 1,200 feet and were raised some 12 feet off the ground. The imposing height of the longhouse was practical. It protected against floods, and in time of war against poison-tipped darts and spears. The peoples of the interior were highly mobile, migrating along river courses, and for this reason were warlike. The main goal of war was to kill and decapitate the enemy. Heads were brought back to the longhouse, smoked, dried (or mummified) and hung from the roof beams. Capturing heads empowered warriors since it represented capture of the enemy's 'soul matter' which would contribute to the well-being of the community, its people, livestock and crops. For Iban men, the possession of dried heads was an essential social accoutrement. No Iban woman would marry a man without heads. Since palaeolithic times, and well into the twentieth century in some parts of the world, headhunting was widely practised in Europe and Africa as well as Asia and Oceania. Rather than excoriating headhunting as savagery, it is better seen as a funereal practice based on a spiritual understanding of the head as the seat of the soul and 'soul matter' as the life force of a community. Headhunting was seen as a way to restore cosmic balance. And it should be remembered that in some tribal wars, taking a few heads, while unfortunate for their owners, might avert prolonged bloodshed. Headhunting may not have been very 'nice' but it was never merely savagery.

Headhunting was tied to another Iban activity. This was maritime raiding, which brings us to that second powerful word, piracy. Brooke, taking his cue from Raffles, missed few opportunities to go on about the dire menace of piracy that, he claimed, blighted lives and livelihoods in the Eastern Seas and, worse, endangered British vessels plying the South China Sea. Brooke, unlike his father, was not employed by the British East India Company, nor was he a government agent. The *Royalist* was a maritime minnow alongside the formidable East India Company ships of the line. To stand any chance of imposing his will on Borneo's rivers and estuaries and quashing the Iban and Malay fleets, he had to find a way to cajole the Royal Navy to bring its massive firepower to bear on the fragile craft of his piratical enemies. The solution was in that word, piracy.

The key point is that piracy was not merely a way of describing the wicked actions of gnarled, one-legged men forever exclaiming *Aaaaaahhhh!* Piracy was, and is, a legal concept that in English law refers, in the words of Sir Charles Hedges of the High Court of the Admiralty in 1696, to 'a robbery committed within the jurisdiction of the Admiralty'. Piracy as a crime of the high seas was set in legal stone just as the English began searching for new markets and commodities in the East: 'The Act for punysshement of Pyrotes and Robbers of the See' was passed during the reign of Henry VIII. The menace of the 'Pyrote' would become vital to the arsenal of English merchants as they flexed their trading muscles in the Eastern Seas. Piracy law was used to stigmatise Asian traders who refused to comply with the rising new powers of the sea lanes and their riches.

Remember that English national heroes like Francis Drake and Walter Raleigh attacked and plundered treasure ships of the Spanish Empire. But because they acted with royal approval, in the form of a 'letter of marque', Drake and his kind were, according to the law, not pirates but *privateers,* in other words, adventurers, not criminals. Colonialism was legalised plunder but Europeans used international law to brand their Asian competitors as criminals. In 1846, a magazine article about Brooke, who was then at the height of his fame, described the 'corsair system', meaning Asian piracy, as 'so satanic in its influence' that once beautiful islands had become the 'abode of misery and want'.

According to Brooke's first and most deferential biographers, when he sailed into Kuching for the first time in 1839, piracy was rampant. Fleets of pirates in swift-pulling war boats known as *prahu,* cruised among the smaller islands spreading terror wherever they landed. These reports of 'pirate infestation' can, in fact, be put to the test. Ships' logs of the same period, which can be studied in the UK National Archives in Kew, diligently report any sightings of both *prahu* and the vessels used by the Dyaks, known as *bangkong.* HMS *Samarang* voyaged from Singapore to Sarawak and then on to Hong Kong between June and September 1843. During that time, the ship's log records the sighting of just three *prahu.* When the captain changed course to search for a fleet of 100 pirate *prahu* reported near Palawan, just a single vessel was found, which escaped. The hard data of these ships' logs do not support alarmist stories of pirate infestation. But for Brooke, the dread myth of the Bornean pirate won him the backing of the Royal Navy and a reputation as a pirate hunter.

Brooke's War on Piracy

Raffles haunted Brooke's plans and dreams. He wrote of making
Sarawak a 'new Java'. From his base in Kuching, Brooke set up a
regional principality on classical Malay lines. He was the 'White
Rajah'. The upriver hill tribes, known as Land Dyaks, were obliged
to buy salt and rice in Kuching at exorbitant prices from Malay and
Chinese merchants, and were forced to provide labour services to
make up any deficit. Brooke called on the more belligerent coastal
peoples, or Sea Dyaks, to crush rebellions in the interior. In exchange, Brooke allowed them to take away women and heads. Again
following Malay custom, Brooke built forts at strategic points along
Sarawak's major rivers which were commanded by various young
relatives and sons of family friends.

Brooke's masterplan depended on winning two very different
battles. He needed to persuade the British government to recognise his Borneo fiefdom and this, in turn, depended on crushing
any opposition to his rule in Sarawak. Dyaks who accepted his rule
would be offered the gift of becoming civilised, with the assistance
of missionaries. 'Bad Dyaks' would, as Brooke made clear, be ruthlessly 'extirpated'.

Brooke launched his campaign by targeting tribal settlements
along the Saribas and Sekrang rivers in Batang Lupar about 60 miles
east of Kuching. These were, in fact, mixed communities of Malays
and Dyaks, seasoned with a few Arab 'sharifs', who joined forces to
organise raiding expeditions from their river strongholds along the
west coast of Borneo as far as Bandjarmasin and the Celebes. These
were hierarchical communities. Dyaks served as oarsmen for Malay or Arab captains. When a trading ship was captured, the Malays
rewarded the Dyaks with heads of captured sailors. The missionary Harriette McDougal described a pirate fleet: 'Prahus were about
ninety feet long; they carried a large gun in the bow and three or
four lelahs, small brass guns, in each broadside, besides twenty or
thirty muskets. Each prahu was rowed by sixty or eighty oars in two
tiers. Over the rowers, and extending the whole length of the vessel,
was a light flat roof, made of split bamboo, and covered with mats
on which they mounted to fight, from which they fired their muskets and hurled their spears. The Dyaks of Sarebas and Sakarran,

a brave and noble people, were taught piracy by the Malays who dwelt among them … in course of time, the Dyaks became expert seamen. They built boats which they called bangkongs, and went out with the Malays, devastating the coast and killing Malays, Chinese, Dyaks, whoever they met with. The Dyak bangkong draws very little water and is both lighter and faster than the Malay prahu; it is a hundred feet long, and nine or ten broad. Sixty or eighty men with paddles make her skim through the water as swiftly as a London race-boat. She moves without noise and surprises her victims with showers of spears at dead of night....'

The Dyak chief on the Saribas hung a basket on a high tree and boasted that it would soon contain the head of Brooke, and the White Rajah would become as fearsome a warrior as his tribal enemies.

In 1843, Brooke had returned to Singapore for a brief visit and made the acquaintance of Captain Henry Keppel who commanded HMS *Dido*, a three-masted sloop carrying eighteen 32-pounder cannons. The red-headed and impulsive Keppel would become an important ally. At the time he met Brooke, he was under orders to sail to Sulu to weed out local dens of pirates. Keppel was thrilled to meet a fellow warrior who shared the same passions, and offered Brooke passage back to Sarawak on the *Dido*. During the voyage, Brooke urged Keppel to strike at the Dyaks in Sarawak.

In May 1843, an oddly assorted squadron of Brooke's launch, the *Jolly Batchelor*, a pinnace, two cutters, a gig from the *Dido* as well as numerous craft belonging to Brooke's Dyak allies Patinggi Gapoor and Patinggi Ali, set off upriver from Kuching to carry out the plan the English pirate hunters had hatched up to crush the pirate strongholds. The Dyaks who joined Brooke were, Keppel claimed, 'eager for heads and plunder'. Brooke called it 'Setting a Dyak to catch a Dyak'.

The expedition fell on the Dyak communities at Padeh, Paku and Rimbas on the Saribas with savage enthusiasm. His men brushed aside the Dyak's river barriers, set fire to villages and fortifications, and destroyed guns and war boats. For the Dyak, such material losses could be replaced. It was the shock and awe of British weapons that shattered the Dyak communities. It was said, Keppel recalled, that a 'common signal rocket' fired in the course of a night-time battle provoked horror and consternation among the Dyak warriors. The story was repeated all over the expanding European empires from Cape Town to Canton. Superior arms were the making of empires. Few aboriginal peoples stood a chance against well aimed rifles, cannons and signal rockets.

Keppel's popular narrative *The Expedition to Borneo of HMS Dido for the Suppression of Piracy*, published in 1846, shows off the 'Boys Own' adventure he and Brooke enjoyed. 'I had some difficulty,' Keppel told his readers 'in getting my long gig round; but while my friend Brooke steered the boat, my coxswain and myself kept up a fire, with tolerable aim…. That evening the county was illuminated for miles by the burning of the capital Padi, and adjacent villages; at which work, and plundering, our native followers were most expert.' Brooke was appalled by the Dyak passion for collecting the heads of enemies slain in combat, but he and Keppel happily indulged Dyak headhunting if it made them fight harder.

In the course of the next decade, the Royal Navy frequently lent its firepower to Brooke and the scale of his war escalated. Early in 1846, the sultan of Brunei, Omar Ali Saifuddin II, had murdered Brooke's friend and ally Pengiran (or Raja) Muda Hashim in a Malay version of the 'Night of the Long Knives'. Brooke swore revenge. Six months later, the Admiralty despatched Admiral Thomas Cochrane and a squadron of ships led by the flagship *Agincourt* to Borneo to bring the sultan to heel. Brooke joined the expedition on the *Royalist*. As the British fleet steamed into the Brunei estuary, the sultan's batteries obligingly opened fire, leaving Cochrane with an excuse to bombard the town. The captain of HMS *Iris*, which had remained downriver, reported that the sound of guns could be heard for several days. A pall of thick, black smoke rose over the town.

The British established a provisional government under a compliant Malay noble and Cochrane sailed his squadron back down the Brunei River to Labuan and then set off north in relentless pursuit of sea raiders. The British fleet attacked and burned coastal villages in a ring of fire from Brunei to Pandassan. As the acrid smoke of burning villages rose into the hot skies along the northeast coast, the sultan returned, tail between his legs, to Brunei where he submitted an abject apology and Brooke extracted yet another piece of paper that affirmed, again, his rights to Sarawak. Brooke wrote, 'I made him renew my title to Sarawak and make over the right of working the

coal that it might be useful to the Government some of these days.'
He ordered the sultan to publicly pray at Hashim's grave. Brooke
collected the remaining members of Hashim's family and took them
back to Sarawak. There was little more that Brooke and his allies in
the Royal Navy could do to further humiliate Sultan Omar Ali. The
tales of Brooke's righteous campaign against the 'dastardly' sultan
were soon on the tongues of patriotic Englishmen and women and
when he returned to London in October 1847, Brooke, like Raffles
before him, rode a cresting wave of public adulation.

A Heroic and Glamorous Hero?

For large numbers of Victorian Englishmen and women, Brooke was
a heroic and even glamorous hero. His reputation was spun from
tales of battling pirates and headhunters by his canny agent Henry
Wise and devoted supporters like Captain Keppel. When Brooke returned briefly to England in October 1847, his journal was already
in its third edition. Reviewers praised it as a 'delightful narrative'
and assumed its readers would be 'anxious' for news of its hero. He
was happy to satisfy a voracious public appetite for heroism.

By mid-century, the strategic significance of Borneo was increasingly clear. At the end of August 1842, the tectonic plates of global
power shuddered. A humiliated Qing emperor, defeated in the First
Opium War, abjectly signed the Treaty of Nanking, the first treaty to
be photocopied, on board HMS *Cornwallis*. The agreement obliged
the emperor to open Shanghai and other Chinese ports to international trade and ceded the island of Hong Kong to Britain. Now, at
last, the strategic significance of the north-west coast of Borneo,
on the other side of the China Sea, seized the full attention of British strategic minds. The rise of the China 'treaty ports' meant that
naval bases and coaling stations would be urgently needed east of
the Strait of Malacca. As Brooke and his supporters in London frequently reminded the British government, Sarawak was in the right
place at the right time. Brooke had longed for official recognition
of both himself and his Borneo fiefdom. The government had dithered and fussed but finally, in 1847, Queen Victoria confirmed his
appointment as Governor of Labuan and Consul-General in Borneo
and made him a Knight Commander of the Bath, a matter of great

pride for Brooke. He was now Sir James Brooke. He was disappointed that the government refused to consider making Sarawak a Crown Colony, but he had status and a salary: his father's inheritance was by then near exhausted.

Brooke under Fire

Not every Victorian Englishman was impressed by Brooke and his escapades in Borneo. As the gallant Englishman set sail for Kuching, a consortium of British businessmen with interests in the Far East complained to the Board of Trade that Brooke's new position of governor of Labuan was unethical. They reminded the board that Henry Wise, Brooke's agent, had set up the Eastern Archipelago Company to exploit the coal seams on Labuan with the Treasury's blessing. The merchants argued that by appointing Brooke as governor, he and Wise would enjoy a commercial monopoly which flouted the hallowed principles of free trade. Over the next few years, voices speaking against Brooke became ever louder. To begin with, criticism was commercial. Brooke's position as governor was, it was claimed, not only unethical but, worse, too costly. He had been given an annual budget of £6,327 (worth more than £600,000 today) on the assumption that the coal seams would eventually make a profit. Why was the government propping up Brooke's equatorial folly with such a profligate sum?

The squalls besetting Brook's reputation took on the force of a storm when the critics were joined by the redoubtable Richard Cobden (1804–65), the radical founder of the Anti-Corn Law League, which had brought down the government of Sir Robert Peel, and an outspoken critic of British imperialism. Cobden was a successful businessman and a devout Christian who feared that the ideal of a world shaped by divine providence was threatened by imperial hubris. Seizing territory, forcibly opening overseas markets and establishing spheres of influence – achieved at huge cost – should have no part in a world order founded on peaceful cooperation. It is well worth tracking down one of Cobden's lesser known polemical pamphlets, 'How Wars are Got Up in India', which describes in impressive detail how British nabobs like Lord Dalhousie had manufactured justifications to wage war against the Burmese. Cobden soon had Brooke in his gunsights. He told his friend, the peace campaigner Henry Richard: 'It shocks me to think what fiendish atrocities may be committed by English arms without rousing any conscientious resistance at home, provided they be only far off enough, and victims too feeble to trouble us with their remonstrances and groans.' Cobden and his liberal campaigners were sickened by the way Brooke had used the guns of the Royal Navy to carve out a private empire. 'Sir James Brooke seized on a territory as large as Yorkshire,' Cobden wrote 'and then drove out the natives and subsequently sent for our fleet and men to massacre them.'

The Legacy

Brooke took no notice of his critics. He carried on waging war against rebellious Dyaks and pirates. Today, Sarawak is a Malaysian state and the dynasty of the three 'White Rajahs' – James, Charles and Vyner – has long gone. The temptation to remember Sir James Brooke as a romantic adventurer and even philanthropist who founded a kingdom in the land of savage headhunters and rapacious pirates remains, as a recent blockbuster movie demonstrated, surprisingly potent.

The temptation should be resisted. Brooke may have posed as a buccaneering, freelance imperialist, but he longed for recognition by his government. His persistent stigmatising of the indigenous peoples of Borneo as piratical headhunters legitimised violent and ruthless campaigns waged against the indigenous peoples of Borneo. Brooke's rule was frequently challenged by Malay and Iban leaders, but he and his successors could always invoke the 'war on piracy' to persuade the Royal Navy to sail in and quash any rivals for power.

Brooke and his successor, Charles, created a model for colonial rule in colonial Southeast Asia. Government was based on strict racial segregation. Chinese immigrants were encouraged to stimulate economic growth while the Ibans and Bidayuhs provided jungle produce for export and the Melanaus grew sago. Malays were offered roles in administrative services as civil servants and policemen. The Brookes recruited former enemies, the fearsome Dyak headhunters, as warriors. The 'White Rajahs' of Sarawak cobbled together a model colonial state on racial lines that would eventually be adopted throughout 'British Malaya'.

CHAPTER 12

The Making of British Malaya: The Rise of the Men of Tin

Singapore Finds a Hinterland

I n the decades after 1867, as Singapore shed the burden of rule from Calcutta, its growth was spectacular. The opening of the Suez Canal in November 1869 shortened the voyage from Europe to Singapore by a third, from 12,000 miles to 8,300. It was possible to take an express train from London to a Mediterranean port, board a steamer and reach Singapore in twenty-three days. Steamships in ever greater numbers raced from Europe to Asia via the Bay of Bengal, through Colombo to the Strait of Malacca and Singapore, which became a vital coaling station en route to China and Japan. Steam power ended the old dependence on the monsoon timetable but the fast, new steamships had prodigious appetites for water, coal and a human reservoir of seamen and engineers. Steamship owners and trading companies began demanding ever faster turnaround times to load and unload in port. That required new skills and new technologies like steam cranes. Singapore offered all these and more. At the same time, new telegraph cables connected Europe to Singapore, Hong Kong and the ports of southern China. In the second half of the nineteenth century, the old networks of the Silk Road of the Sea were transformed by steam and electrical power. For Singapore, the rewards would be astounding. Between 1870 and 1885, the tonnage of shipping in Singapore's harbour rose from 1.3 million to 5 million tons. By the beginning of World War I, the world's ocean-going tonnage had multiplied three times. Singapore's had grown tenfold.

Singapore had for some time lagged behind other port cities like Bombay and Sydney that were enriched by the flow of staple products like cotton, opium and wool harvested from their enormous regional hinterlands. The colonial authorities in London and Singapore realised that they could not compete by exploiting the meagre natural resources of the island. Instead, they reached out across the Strait of Singapore to the huge, barely tapped riches of the Malayan Peninsula. The ambition of colonial Singapore to compete with the other ocean ports of Asia drove British and Chinese expansion into Peninsular Malaya and a new phase of colonial expansion. And two commodities above all would drive the conquest of 'British Malaya'. Global demand for tin and then rubber, the white gold of Asia, would turn Malaya into one of the most lucrative colonial possessions in the British Empire. It will come as no surprise to learn that the making of British Malaya was a tale of skulduggery and deceit.

Resistance to British Rule

Early on the morning of 2 November 1875, James Wheeler Woodford Birch, the first British Resident of the Malayan state of Perak, accompanied by a small company of sepoys, a Lieutenant T. F. Abbott and his interpreter Mat Arshad, moored his boat, the *Naga*, at Pasir Salak on the Perak River. For more than a year, Birch, an abrupt cantankerous man, had been struggling to impose his authority on the young state ruler Sultan Abdullah Muhammad Shah II (r. 1874–76). Birch was under tremendous pressure. Recently widowed and with four young children to support, he was heavily in debt. Birch and the sultan had clashed repeatedly. 'We are unfortunate in the Sultan,' he wrote to colleagues in Singapore. 'He riles me awfully. He is so childish.' Birch deplored Abdullah's use of opium and his refusal to release his slaves. By the beginning of November, during the Muslim festival of Hari Raya Puasa, rumours began to reach Birch that trouble was brewing. This was the reason for Birch's expedition – and the cause of his demise. Early the next day, while it was still cool, Birch moved the *Naga* to the other side of the river and tied up alongside a riverside bath house owned by a Chinese goldsmith. The bath house was a modest affair: a wooden frame sheathed in braided palm leaves. While Lt. Abbott set off to do some hunting, Birch sent Arshad to post proclamations declaring in no uncertain terms that he was determined to 'administer the Government of Perak in the name of the Sultan...'.

It was now very hot and Birch, after posting a sepoy to stand guard, disappeared inside the little riverside bath house. He should not have been so complacent. A group of armed men sent by the sultan surrounded the bath house and thrust spears through its thin palm leaf walls. Birch, taken by surprise, naked and vulnerable, died instantly. The other sepoys managed to reach the boats and make their escape as Birch's bloodied corpse floated past. A few days later, Birch's mutilated corpse was recovered and sent to Bandar Bahru where he was buried with full military honours. When his son Ernest Birch visited Pasir Salak ten years later, he met many Malay villagers who claimed they had known his father. An elderly man returned the murdered Resident's gold watch and gun to his astonished son.

The killing of James Birch makes two important points about the British expansion into the Malay Peninsula. The main agents of colonisation were so called 'Residents', or advisers, appointed like Birch to seize control of the Malay courts backed by armed force. Secondly, British expansion was frequently and violently resisted by the Malay rulers. And yet the Resident system slowly but surely brought Malaya under the yoke of British rule. Residents, who usually survived longer than the unfortunate Birch, were the makers of British Malaya.

A New Colonial Strategy for Malaya

Before 1857, the grandees of the British East India Company, headquartered on the far side of the Bay of Bengal, had taken scant interest in the interior of the Malayan Peninsula. The maxim of the company was trade, not territory. The Straits Settlements of Penang, Malacca and Singapore functioned as outward-looking maritime power bases that guaranteed and protected the lucrative flow of commodities to and from India and the great Chinese emporiums. But by the end of 1875, when J. W. W. Birch took that fatal bath in the Perak River, a more activist strategy was beginning to edge out the traditional 'hands-off' *ad hoc* style of colonial rule.

The shock of the Indian Rebellion led to the humiliating demise of the much-decayed British East India Company. 'The Company' was, it turned out, not too big to fail. Benjamin Disraeli's 'India Act' of 1868 ushered in a new era of imperial government. The Act created two executive posts: the Secretary of State for India, who answered to parliament, and the Viceroy, who presided over a cabinet in Calcutta. This was the dawn of the age of imperialism and the British now talked about bringing the gift of civilisation to the many millions of savage peoples ruled from London. The influential *Edinburgh Review* proclaimed that the 'glorious destiny of England was to govern, to civilise, to educate and to improve the innumerable tribes and races whom Providence had placed beneath her Sceptre'. As the British embarked on this mission, the other European powers rattled competitive imperial sabres and a new power joined the great game. In the 1870s, the German Chancellor Otto von Bismarck had unified the German states into a single nation and German nationalists began playing imperial catch-up with the French, Dutch and British. Just as there was a scramble for Africa, the European powers vied for territory and power in Southeast Asia, China and the Pacific.

The British Colonial Office which had replaced the East India Company headquarters in London kept a beady eye on the activities of European rivals. The French were busy empire- building in North Africa and Cochin China. Rumours of suspicious German activities in Siam focused British minds on the northern Malay states like Kedah that had for centuries paid tribute to the Thai kings. Could these fragile vassal states become weak links in the imperial chain? The British feared that the Malay Peninsula might offer a wide open back door to Singapore. And they were right to be worried.

The problem for the British was that Malaya was not a single unitary state. It comprised a number of Malay states ruled by sultans. 'Malaya', in short, did not exist. The London Treaty, signed with the Dutch in 1824 to settle the legal ownership of Singapore, split Southeast Asia into British and Dutch 'spheres of influence'. The Dutch grabbed Sumatra and the islands of the Malay Archipelago while the Malayan Peninsula fell within the British sphere. Four decades later, the question on the minds of anxious Colonial Office mandarins in London was how a 'sphere of influence' could be ruled – and exploited. And how rival powers could be kept out. The solution the British discovered was to exploit the weakness of the Malay rulers.

The Fragility of the Malay Sultanates

The British often vilified the Malay states as 'decayed'. The word dripped with contempt for native peoples and their rulers and reflected an even deeper contempt for the faith of Muslims. It was the coming of Islam, Raffles had claimed, that had diminished the ancient Hindu and Buddhist empires. There is no doubt that the Malay kingdoms had been weakened since the glory days of Malacca. And it was not only Europeans who lamented the decline of the Malay states. In 1837, Abdullah bin Abdul Kadir, known as 'Munshi' Abdullah, set off on a journey through the Malay Peninsula and wrote a report called the *Hikayat Abdullah* ('The Account of Abdullah'). It will be recalled that Abdullah was Raffles' translator, secretary and teacher, and he remains a controversial figure. Many despise him for complicity with his British masters. Abdullah had few illusions about British rule, but his sharp eyes and words spared no one. Sultan Hussein Shah (Tengku Long), who signed the notorious treaty with Raffles and Farquhar, grew 'plumper and plumper as time went on...,' remembered Abdullah. He had 'never seen a fatter man'. This is not a very generous observation. What Abdullah meant was that the sultan had grown fat on his British pension.

As he toured the Malay states of the peninsula, Abdullah scorned 'ignorant', 'uneducated' Malay rulers, and sneered at their shabby, dilapidated palaces. When he reached Trengganu, he reported that the sultan's palace was 'in the Chinese style' with crumbling walls of 'dirt, spittle, betel juice and moss'. The ruler's subjects occupied meaner dwellings that 'emitted foul odours'. Everywhere he went, Abdullah deplored the miserable condition of Malay peasants, and blamed their plight squarely on 'the tyranny and injustice of the government of the rajas ... to live close to a raja is like making friends with a poisonous snake'. The sultans were obsessed only with revenues, custom and ritual. They cared little for the well-being of the people, the *rakyat*. Abdullah did not pull his punches: 'Whenever a common man meets his ruler he is obliged to squat on the ground in the mud and filth.... The laws and subjects which he imposes on his subjects depend solely on his own private whim.'

The Sultan's Dilemma

The sultan was in many respects a master of ceremonies, a curator of ritual. Real power was vested in district chiefs (*dato*) and village headmen (*penghulu*). Each dato was obligated to pay obeisance to the sultan but could, if he possessed the means to do so, exercise near despotic power within his own fiefdom. Many sultans wielded symbolic rather than real, hard-edged power and were frequently outmanoeuvred by other power brokers.

In the Malay state of Perak, the various datos controlled swathes of territory from armed riverside stockades. They administered local justice and had the right to demand free corvée labour (*kerah*) from the peasantry, the *rakyat*. Malay peasants worked the fields, mines and plantations and were also obligated to defend the dato's domain. The power and wealth of a dato came from monetising the natural resources of the territory he controlled. Traditionally, in a riverine state like Perak, the datos made their money from taxes on river traffic. They used these revenues to support extended families as well as an entourage of servants, agents and bodyguards who served as emblems of the dato's prestige. They also owned slaves. All slaves were, of course, non-Malays since Sharia law permits only the enslavement of non-Muslims.

The sultan may have stood at the apex of the Malay state, but he needed to build and maintain alliances with the datos and their headmen who were often wealthier than the sultan. But if a Malay chief 'struck it rich', he might even defy the sultan and set himself up as a rival ruler. Not only that, but the Malay rulers faced dissent from within their own families. Malay writers used a phrase about these recurrent family squabbles – *raja dua, negeri sebuah*, or 'two captains in one ship'. Sultanates were socially rigid but inherently unstable. It was this fragility of the Malay sultanates that James Brooke exploited to seize the province of Sarawak from Sultan Omar Ali Saifuddin II of Brunei, by helping him defeat a rebellion. States like Brunei or Perak on the Malay Peninsula only remained stable if the sultan played off and so kept in check both his quarrelsome kin and the district chiefs. In the mid-nineteenth century, these delicate balances would be smashed asunder. This violent upheaval began in Perak, and it was all to do with tin.

Tin, the Metal of Empire

Today tin, along with tungsten, tantalum and gold is classified as a 'conflict mineral'. The reason is that in some regions of the world, profits made from exploiting these rare metals is used to fund the purchase of deadly weapons and civil wars. Most people have heard of so-called 'blood diamonds' but there are also 'blood metals' and many of them are in your mobile phone. In British Malaya, tin would become one of the world's first 'conflict minerals' with consequences that would last more than a century.

Tin was the metal of empire. In the cold summer of 1813, Queen Charlotte, wife and consort of King George III, and other members of the British royal family cautiously tasted the contents of a tin of canned beef manufactured by inventor Bryan Donkin in a factory in Bermondsey on the outskirts of London. Soon after this momentous tasting, Donkin received a letter: 'I am commanded by the Duke of Kent to acquaint you that his Royal Highness, having procured introduction of some of your patent beef on the Duke of York's table, where it was tasted by the Queen, the Prince Regent and several distinguished personages and *highly approved....*' Donkin's groundbreaking tinned beef won more plaudits from Arthur Wellesley, the 'Iron' Duke of Wellington, and he was soon supplying tinned beef to the British Army and the Royal Navy. Donkin's cans rescued Britain's soldiers and sailors from the monotony of rotten, weevil-infested salted meat, and soon he was sending handmade tins of beef, mutton, carrots, parsnips and soup to the furthest corners of the empire. Donkin had taken the first faltering steps in the growth of a multi-billion pound global business. When the United States was convulsed by civil war in the 1860s, soldiers in blue and grey marched to war armed with rifles and can openers.

The tin can would make the Malayan Peninsula one of the most lucrative possessions of the British Empire. After World War II, it would be the huge profits that could still be made from the tin mines of Perak that forced a bankrupt Britain to cling onto Malaya as the empire crumbled. Tin mining had yet another impact in the Malay Peninsula that reverberates long after the last British flag was lowered, and the sun set on the empire. The ore washed down from the Main Range fundamentally changed the ethnic landscape of Malaya and the balance of power between Malays, entitled 'sons of the soil', and Chinese who came to the peninsula as sinkeh, or 'guest workers'. In the nineteenth century, Chinese sojourners would dominate the tin mines and plantations of 'British Malaya', sowing the seeds of a conflict that still divides the peoples of modern Malaysia.

The Chinese Tin Men

Since the founding of Singapore, Chinese involvement in both plantation agriculture and mining had also been expanding, sucking in huge numbers of new immigrant workers fleeing poverty and violent unrest in southern China. Most of these new men, or sinkeh, came to Singapore and Malaya under the credit ticket system, which tied them to Chinese employers for very long periods of time. This very diverse community did not yet think of itself as 'Chinese'. Dialect shaped identity and so you belonged to the group that spoke Hokkien, Cantonese, Hakka, Teochew or Hainanese. Celebrated Baba Chinese entrepreneurs like Tan Tock Seng and pioneer immigrants like Seah Eu Chin became community leaders but enjoyed a lifestyle that was barred to less prosperous kinsmen. For many sinkeh, a 'new life' in one of the British territories in the Straits Settlements – Penang, Singapore, Malacca and the Dindings – meant decades of back-breaking, badly paid hard labour alleviated by the sweet sap of the opium poppy. In some Chinese immigrant communities, the death toll from disease and sheer exhaustion could be above 50 per cent. It was these toiling Chinese legions that would make British Malaya rich.

By mid-century, the global tin boom had exhausted the older Malay-owned mines that had used the same extraction techniques for centuries. This was known as dulang, the washing of the alluvial ore panned in shallow wooden bowls. To dig deeper, new technologies were needed, and innovation fired up a demand for new sources of capital investment. Since Malay rulers and chiefs habitually frittered away any reserve capital on ceremonial displays, many were forced to turn to wealthy Straits oligarchs such as Chee Yam Chuan and See Boon Tiong. In the early part of the century, these Baba merchants outnumbered British and European financiers who began to invest in tin mines. ('Engaged in the native trade' was the formula used at the time.) The Baba entrepreneurs were themselves local-born. Their ancestors, who were mainly Hokkien speakers from the south-eastern province of Fukien, had first come to Malacca in the fourteenth century. Many had close ties to the Malay royal families. Chee Yam Chuan, for example, was one of the major creditors of Sultan Shahabuddin Riayat Shah (1830–1851) whose debts amounted to an eye-watering 169,000 Straits Dollars. But even with Baba backing, by the 1840s the Malay chiefs faced fierce competition from a fast-rising new breed of Chinese entrepreneurs who had made their piles in Singapore and were often allied with British or European merchant houses. This new breed of tin men introduced new technology, such as the wooden chain pump that sucked water out of the mines. The British Resident of Perak, Hugh Low, persuaded the Chinese to adopt steam-powered centrifugal pumps which had been invented in Cornwall in south-west England. Controlling water and preventing floods was the key to digging deeper. In a matter of decades, steam-powered sluicing and pumping machines were sucking more tin from ever-deeper deposits. By the end of the century, British Malaya was the world's biggest tin producer. The alliance between Chinese and British entrepreneurs was transforming Singapore's backyard into a lucrative hinterland. New technology and new ways of investing capital brewed up a storm that soon broke across the Malay Peninsula.

The Kongsi Business System

Chinese entrepreneurs brought with them a particular way of doing business. This was the 'kongsi' system, which first emerged among Hakka copper miners in Yunnan and had been refined over many centuries. Kongsi literally means 'meeting hall', but in practice referred to a group of individuals from the same region of China and speaking the same dialect who held shares in cooperative ventures. In the next chapter, we shall dig a lot deeper into kongsis and other Chinese societies which the British tended to pigeonhole as 'secret

societies', inferring that members were up to no good. Chinese societies in colonial Singapore and Malaya had some pretty arcane rituals but were never secret. A kongsi was, in essence, an association
of risk-takers, who shared both profit and loss and was not much
different from a British or Dutch joint stock company. Kongsis were
profit-making machines, a brotherhood of shareholders. For even
the rawest sinkeh, joining a kongsi might offer a way out of crushing
poverty. Like all immigrants, the Chinese who fled war and famine in
their homeland were aspirational. They bent every sinew to prosper.
Not all succeeded but the ambitious and hopeful could find plenty of
inspiration in the oft-told tales of the pioneers. Many sinkeh came to
revere the Cantonese merchant called Mr Whampoa after his birthplace in China (now known as Huangpu district, Guangzhou city).
Hoo Ah Kay arrived in Singapore in 1830 aged fifteen to join his father's provisions company, Whampoa & Co. He was not poor, but
when his father died and he inherited the family business, Whampoa made an impressive fortune in land speculation. He was one of
the few Chinese businessmen who spoke fluent English and was on
very good terms with the colonial government. He was appointed the
first Chinese member of the Legislative Council in 1869 and later the
honorary consul for China in Singapore. He also had a hand in establishing the Singapore Botanic Gardens. For Chinese immigrants,
Whampoa was a shining success, and he was not shy about showing
off his wealth. He led a glamorous lifestyle and hosted elaborate dinner parties. He was painted by the English artist Edward Cree and
attended by numerous servants fluttering fans. He owned racehorses
and opened his opulent home to visitors. The life and times of Mr
Whampoa were, in short, a lure for striving sinkeh who relished his
success. A European observer remarked that he 'always looked upon
a Sinkheh [newcomer] as a Towkay Labur [financier], Towkay Bantu
[advancer], or a Capitan China in embryo and respected him accordingly'. In other words, the humble put-upon Chinese labourer might
be the wealthy and influential towkay of the future.

　　Chinese miners were soon digging deeper and wider, opening
up highly profitable new seams and deposits. In the southern state
of Johor, the Malay rulers and datos had developed bonds with
Chinese entrepreneurs through land grants. But this was unusual.
In most other states, the Malay chiefs could not compete with the

deluge of new Chinese capital. As the power of the chiefs eroded, the kongsis tightened their grip on the tin mines and plantations, to the dismay of many Malays. Tin would make fortunes for some and crush the lives of others. In the early 1830s, there were just 500 Chinese miners scattered throughout the Malay Peninsula. A few decades later, there were some 10,000 miners in Sungai Ujung, Negeri Sembilan, alone. Few women emigrated to the peninsula and the miners often took wives from among the Orang Asli, the indigenous communities, paying their families or acquiring slaves from Malays. A visitor to North Borneo encountered tribal groups who spoke fluent Hokkien and talked proudly of their Chinese descent. Most sinkeh faced many years, if not a lifetime, of back-breakingly hard work in ferocious temperatures and frequent soaking downpours. But in the Malay Peninsula, on the edge of the rainforest, the rigours of work were harsh. Tropical diseases, above all malaria, often rampaged through the mining villages. No wonder so many came to depend on opium, which invariably led tin miners into a crushing spiral of addiction, debt and exploitation. Yet, those who survived the rigours of Malaya's tin mines showed a competitive spirit and will to succeed that reverberated across the Malay world.

Tin Transforms Malaya

Tin shaped the human spirit, but it also transformed the landscape of the Malay Peninsula. The quest for tin left in its wake vast deltas of gravel wastes and, as the new dredgers got to work, clawed out huge scars in the earth. The tin lands became pitted and disfigured. The tin men would throw up brash, rough-edged new towns and cities like Kuala Lumpur and Ipoh, the 'city of millionaires'. In the vicinity of the mines, hastily built rough-and-ready settlements sprang up to accommodate Chinese mine workers and cater to their needs. These ramshackle settlements were controlled by 'headmen', who lived in separate, often quite grand houses. Further south in Selangor, close to tin mines at Ampang and Pudu, now part of greater Kuala Lumpur, a few score Chinese traders set up a cluster of shophouses selling general provisions on marshy land where the sluggish, brown waters of the Klang and Gombok rivers converged.

The ramshackle settlement soon had a name of sorts – Kuala Lumpur – which simply means 'muddy confluence'. The cluster of huts, stores and little temples grew into a town, then a city. Today, the capital of Malaysia is a richly storied metropolis but in the mid-nineteenth century it was a place without a history. There were no relics here, as there were in Singapore, of a royal palace or even a riverside port. Kuala Lumpur was the upstart, cuckoo child of the tin-mining industry and the men who vied to control its profits. It was ravaged by disease and vulnerable to floods and fires. It was the quintessential town of the wild east.

The Kapitan China

In June 1869, the powerful administrator of the Klang Valley, Raja Mahdi bin Raja, appointed an ambitious young man called Yap Ah Loy as the headman, or Kapitan China, of this brash, fast-swelling new settlement. Yap Ah Loy is often called the founder of Kuala Lumpur, and it is true he played important roles in the rise of the city. But the term is rather misleading, for in the 1860s and 1870s he was one of many Chinese towkays who competed for control of the city and its hinterland of mines and plantations. In the end, Yap Ah Loy would be outmanoeuvred by the British who would make Kuala Lumpur the administrative hub of British Malaya.

In the Malay world, the role of the Kapitan China was well established. The sultans and their datos used the kapitans to manage their relationship with Chinese communities. He was usually a man of standing among both Malays and his own people and the Chinese recognised the right of the sultan to consult with the kapitan to adjudicate disputes. But as numbers of Chinese in the Malay Peninsula soared, the old system began to fray. Hostilities between different Chinese dialect and clan groups were imported from China and unsettled the old bonds with Malays who found that they could no longer rely on a kapitan to referee so many quarrelsome factions. He would owe allegiance to one or other dialect group or clan. By the 1870s, in Sungei Ujung there were at least five different Chinese headmen. At the same time, princes in the Malay courts sought the backing of Chinese clans to oust their rivals. Local politics became ever more volatile.

Among the Chinese, the dialect you spoke was often bound up with how you made a living. Hakka, for example, came from the mountains of southern China and were traditionally miners, often ridiculed by other Chinese for their rough manners and speech. In the mines, Hakka competed with Cantonese who had the same skills, while the Hokkien and Teochew were likely to be farmers, small shopkeepers or boatmen. Local politics in the Nanyang, or 'Southern Ocean', could be baffling to an outsider. In Sarawak, the Hakka Chinese controlled the mines while most Chinese in Kuching were Hokkien or Cantonese. In the Malay Peninsula, natural affinities between the Hokkien and Teochew were muddied by older links between the Hokkien Baba Chinese and Europeans. These fissures were deepened by the Chinese clans, or *hui*. For Europeans, the hui and the kongsi were difficult to tell apart and were lumped together as 'secret societies'.

The Rise of the Chinese Clans

According to historian Heng Pek Koon, the hui originated in China at least 2,000 years ago among bands of dispossessed peasants who had been driven from their homes and villages by war, flood, famine or the whim of a warlord. These vulnerable, displaced peoples sought out charismatic leaders to organise mutual aid and resist authority. The members of this early kind of hui were bonded together by esoteric rituals of initiation and secret oaths of loyalty that fused, Heng tells us, shamanism, Taoism, Buddhism and Confucianism. Secret society rituals alarmed and fascinated Europeans in equal measure. From early on in the nineteenth century, the hui dominated the social and political life of the new Chinese communities in the other Straits Settlements and the Malay Peninsula and had developed close ties with the kongsis. Thanks to the power of the wealthier members, some secret societies controlled major tax farms such as opium and *arak*, a rice wine. Others profited from gambling, extortion and prostitution. Secret societies, which were rarely secret, were not criminal organisations but often acted as umbrellas for criminal activities. There is one further and very important point to make. Sinkeh who came to the Nanyang had little choice about joining a secret society whether they wanted to or not.

The societies offered help in a strange land far from home. Even if a sinkeh wanted to rely on his own resources, he would soon find out that he really had little choice in the matter. The Chinese societies were aggressive and very determined recruiters. Once a sinkeh had joined the Ghee Hin, Ho Seng or Hai San, he belonged to the society, hand, heart and soul. The society could demand his services in almost any capacity. He was obligated to defend his fellow clansmen in disputes about matters as different as women or watercourses with which he had no direct involvement.

The Clans Go to War

In the Malay interior, far from the older cities of the Straits Settlements, the kongsi and the hui secret societies soon ruled the fast-growing tin-mining communities in Perak and Selangor. Tin could be a fickle commodity, with its price wildly fluctuating on world markets, but in good years the flow of revenue to the kongsi could be spectacular. So too were the taxes that ended up in the coffers of Malay rulers and nobles. But where there is profit, there is envy, and where there is envy, there is conflict. And in Malaya conflicts erupted in many different directions at once. The kongsis and their followers fought one another bitterly to maximise their rights and revenues. At the same time, tensions between the Chinese societies coincided with a fresh bout of dynastic squabbling among Malay rulers. In the Malay world, as we saw in Borneo, it was traditional for embattled rivals to seek out allies with the most lethal firepower. In the past, many Malay rulers had turned to Bugis mercenaries or European powers – the Dutch or the British. Like James Brooke in Borneo, mercenary Europeans took full advantage of their Malay patrons. In the aftermath of the tin boom in the Malay Peninsula, Chinese clans emerged as power brokers. Contenders for power in the Malay courts turned to one or another clan to support their claim to the succession. In Selangor, Kapitan China Yap Ah Loy, who was a member of the Hai San, backed one royal claimant while the Kang Yeng Chew clan allied with a rival. In Perak, the tin boom amplified these overlapping, interwoven conflicts between rival Malay princes and their Chinese allies.

The Forward Policy

As the Chinese and their Malay allies squabbled, the mines were neglected and profits began to tumble. In Singapore, hard-nosed British businessmen and their Baba Chinese partners became thoroughly alarmed. William Henry Macleod Read of A. L. Jonston & Co., Freemason, former policeman, founder of the Singapore Turf Club and leading member of the Legislative Council of the Straits Settlements, began lobbying the Colonial Office in London for support. Read's wealthy business associate, the Straits Chinese towkay Tan Kim Cheng, kept his British partners well informed about the deteriorating situation in Perak. Read and his Chinese associates feared that anarchy would erode profits. British businessmen bombarded London with a stream of petitions and memoranda demanding the government act and take control. They began to call it the 'Forward Policy'. But Colonial Secretary John Wodehouse was adamant. London could not afford to get involved in Malaya. It was too complicated and too costly. Loss of revenue worried London for certain, but not enough. There were many in the British establishment who shared Disraeli's view that colonies were a 'millstone round our necks'. But the Forward party had another card to play. They knew that even more than pecuniary loss, the Colonial Office feared foreign interference. So, Read and his British and Chinese partners in the Straits changed tack. They stopped lamenting their losses and sent reports of mysterious Germans who seemed to have become rather too interested in the British sphere of influence. British diplomats also noted German interest in Siam. Something was afoot. The Forward plan was beginning to look a lot more interesting.

The Residential System

As in Singapore in 1819, the British seized control of the Malay Peninsula through an act of outrageous skulduggery. This was the Pangkor Treaty that was imposed on Malay rulers in 1874. The story of the British game of deception begins in September 1873. As the Malay rulers and their Chinese allies brawled, and the tin wars showed no sign of abating, Lord Kimberley ordered the new governor of the Straits Settlements, Sir Andrew Clarke, to find out more about the baffling conflicts in the Malay states and send a report to London. Like many other 'men on the spot' in the British Empire, Clarke was, like Stamford Raffles before him, used to thinking, and in many cases acting, independently of his chiefs in London. Clarke turned to the shrewd Mr W. H. Read to get a grip on what was happening in Perak.

Read explained that for some time Perak had been plagued by increasingly acrimonious wrangles between rival princes and their Chinese allies. In 1871, the elderly Sultan Ali Muhammad Shah had died. Both his son Yusuf and the regent, Raja Muda Abdullah, were widely detested. Yusuf was overly fond of violence and Abdullah was, so it was rumoured, promiscuous, addicted to opium, fond of gambling and cockfighting, and, unsurprisingly, virtually bankrupt. When Abdullah churlishly refused to attend Sultan Ali's funeral, the Perak chiefs retaliated by handing power to a court minister, the Raja Bendahara, Raja Ismail Mu'abidin Riayat Shah (r. 1871–74). Abdullah was infuriated. Now, Ismail's most powerful backer was the chief of the Larut River valley, Ngah Ibrahim, who had made a fortune by taxing the tin mines in his fiefdom and had close ties to the Chinese Hai San clan. Ibrahim also had designs on the throne. Not to be outdone, Abdullah turned to the bitter rivals of the Hai San and Ghee Hin to back *his* claim. Perak was now ruled in effect by two sultans, both backed by competing Chinese secret societies. Read had no hesitation urging Clarke to cut the Gordian Knot. Intervention was the only answer and the 'Forward Policy' must prevail.

Read took the first steps. He prompted, or rather persuaded the regent, Raja Muda Abdullah, to write to Clarke proposing that in return for the British supporting him as sultan he, Abdullah, would permit the appointment of 'a man of sufficient abilities to show us a good system of government'. Here, in a nutshell, we have the device that would become the main instrument of British rule in Malaya – the Residential System. With Abdullah's agreement, Clarke called a conference to settle matters in Perak. The various warring parties met at the beginning of 1874 aboard the British steamer *Pluto* moored just off Pangkor Island, guarded by a platoon of Indian sepoys. A young man called Frank Swettenham, who spoke good Malay, joined Clarke's team as a translator.

Clarke conducted negotiations at a rattling pace. He was accompanied by Chinese expert William Pickering, who spoke Cantonese, Hakka, Hokkien, Foochew, Teochew and Mandarin fluently, and would be appointed the 'Chinese Protector' of the Straits Settlements a few years later. Pickering had already warmed up the Chinese delegates, and all twenty-six of them quickly agreed to a truce. They were all weary of fighting. Since the other claimants were no shows, Clarke formally recognised Abdullah as the legitimate ruler of Perak.

And so the Pangkor Agreement was drawn up on 19 January 1874 and signed by all parties the next day. The rise of the British Empire, it has been said, was advanced as much by the pen as the sword and British imperial history is littered with long-forgotten treaties that paid mere lip service to the honour of native rulers. Clarke had taken the law into his own hands and reversed the election that had made Ismail Mu'abidin Riayat Shah the sultan in 1871. It was an act of arrogant duplicity that rode roughshod over the claims of Abdullah's rivals and their subjects. It was Sultan Abdullah and his successors who would pay the highest price. The nub of deceit was contained in a single word. According to the terms of the treaty, both Ibrahim and Sultan Abdullah Muhammad Shah II (r. 1874–76) were obliged to accept the appointment of a British Resident. Here are the crucial words in the treaty: 'That the Sultan receive and provide a suitable residence for a British Officer to be called Resident, who shall be accredited to his Court, and whose advice must be asked and acted upon on all questions other than those touching Malay Religion and Custom.'

When the young Frank Swettenham translated the text into Malay, he duplicitously softened the peremptory language of the English text. To describe the role of the Resident, he used the word *muafakat*, which means or strongly implies *consultation* between equal parties. The all-important phrase 'whose advice must be asked and acted upon' was deliberately watered down. Swettenham's use of *muafakat* misled the Malay negotiators who were led to understand that that the Resident would take part as an equal or advisory partner in the traditional court, *mesyuarat bicara*, or 'meetings for discussions'. These usually took place over several days and participants were obligated to reach consensus decisions. Arguably, too, the qualifying phrase 'in all questions other than those touching Malay Religion and Custom' was meaningless in a Muslim culture.

Every aspect of life touched on Malay religion and custom. The sultan, after all, was 'the shadow of God'.

Clarke later admitted that he had indeed compelled the Malay rulers to come to an agreement. If he had not, he claimed, nothing would have been achieved. The truth was that the Pangkor conference was negotiation by diktat. The British imposed a solution by recognising Sultan Abdullah because they believed he would do their bidding. The former lieutenant governor of Penang, Colonel Archibald Anson, had no doubt that 'these chiefs did not fully realise what they were asked to agree to; or if they did had no intention of acting up to it....' What the British meant by advice was *control*. And to mollify the cheapskate empire-builders in the Colonial Office, Clarke promised that the residential system would be cheap to run. A lot depended on the Residents. James Birch, the first British Resident of Perak, turned out to be the wrong man in the wrong place at the wrong time.

Birch was choleric and short-tempered. He spoke, it was said, to the sultan 'peremptorily'. He was also known to berate Malays for dilatoriness and 'shilly-shallying'. Birch insisted that 'Easterners' were incapable of 'good government' and so it was his job to enforce it. Two years later, his mutilated corpse would be floating down the Perak River. Above all, Birch failed to get on with the new sultan. He harboured an intense and personalised dislike of Abdullah whom he called a 'young fool'. 'We are unfortunate in the Sultan...,' he concluded. Two years after the signing of the treaty, Birch had made little progress in bringing the fickle Abdullah to heel and his job was on the line. Clarke's anxiety that Birch was not up to the job was shared by his successor, the new Straits Governor Sir William Jervois, who concluded that 'there is not the "holy calm" reigning in the Peninsula which the Pangkor treaty is supposed to have inaugurated....' Many of the Malay chiefs had fiercely opposed the terms of the treaty, and one warned Abdullah: 'I think bye and bye that Mr Birch will bring many more Europeans to take charge of the country.... It is improper for your majesty to follow the Resident for his rank is only that of a Datuk....'

In October, Birch was warned that plans were afoot to do him harm. He said: 'I will take good care ... if one Mr Birch is killed, ten Mr Birches will take his place.' On 1 November, Birch arrived in Pasir Selak on the Perak River, which happened to be the home village of one of the Malay plotters. He spent the day posting official proclamations. When he had finished the job, Birch walked down to the river's edge and the little attap bath house. As the first Resident of Perak relaxed in the tepid, brown waters of the Perak River, armed Malays rushed the bath house and speared the first Resident of Perak to death.

Enforcing the System

Now British blood was up. Rumours of a Muslim uprising led by 'ferocious and fanatical Malays' spread like wildfire. Colonial administrators were haunted by the shock of the Morant Bay Rebellion in Jamaica and the Indian Mutiny which had brought down the East India Company. Jervois demanded reinforcements, and soon 2,000 troops were on their way from India and Hong Kong to be unleashed in Perak.

It is most advisable, Jervois declared, 'to make a show of power'. Like Raffles in Java and Brooke and his navy friends in Sarawak, he waged what historians like to call a 'Small War'. Jervois ordered Royal Navy ships to blockade the Perak coast and banned the sale of gunpowder and arms. Commander Stirling, who led a brigade of navy soldiers, was said to be 'spoiling for a fight'. Some of his men were enraged when they marched along the Perak River and found Birch's boat, the *Naga*, abandoned near Pasir Salak. Vengeance came swiftly. Stirling boasted that 'the village was fired, and the banks were for a mile and half ablaze.' It was, Stirling reported to Jervois, a most satisfying act of vengeance carried out with no loss of life on the British side. Stirling's commanding officer, Major General Francis Colbourne, now led troops north of Pasir Salak in pursuit of the Malay ringleaders who had murdered Birch. Village after village was razed to the ground. Private James George was thrilled by the 'pretty sight of Rockets flying over the village…. The Malays were frightened to death very near for they all ran out of the village. Our men saw them running and fired into them, and killed a good number.' Jervois used the word pacification, and this is what he meant. Another soldier described 'killing another lot of Malays' and burning another village to the ground. As the British soldiers burned and killed, the blockade began to bite. Rice supplies dried up. Pacification fell heavily on Malay villagers. Their homes were destroyed and their bellies emptied.

The Times of London gleefully reported on the British campaign. The blockade, British readers learnt at breakfast, had 'prevented supplies being thrown into Perak' and 'contributed greatly to the success'. A force of 1,600 Indian sepoys, backed by an artillery regiment and a company of Bengal sappers, exacted revenge and made it abundantly clear that the Resident system would be ruthlessly enforced. The conspirators who had murdered Birch were all hanged. Abdullah and the other claimants to the succession were deported to Johor or the Seychelles. And Jervois appointed Yusuf Sharifuddin Muzuffar Shah (r. 1874–77), the outsider, as the new sultan of Perak. Later, Swettenham called the Perak War a 'duty forced upon England as the Dominant power'. The Malays, he wrote 'needed saving from themselves'.

Extending British Rule

The creation of British Malaya was not a gentlemanly affair of appointing a few Residents to the Malay states and expecting the sultans to do what they were told. The residential system was frequently resisted and, if necessary, imposed on Malay rulers by force of arms. As the British tightened their grip on the Malaya Peninsula, the Dutch were busy crushing the old Malay kingdom of Aceh in northern Sumatra. For many in the Colonial Office in London who had opposed the 'Forward Policy', the troubles in Perak proved their point. Direct intervention merely led to expensive wars. Jervois was accused of reckless sabre-rattling. The Forward movement went into reverse. Then in the 1880s, another bout of great power anxiety swept through the Colonial Office in London. The French now had their perfidious hands on Indochina (Laos, Cochin China, Vietnam and Cambodia), and the busy Germans grabbed a few islands in the Pacific which they christened the Bismarcks. After three wars, Burma was at last under British control, but in Siam the new Thai king Chulalongkorn was importing European 'specialists' to help modernise his kingdom. To the dismay of the Colonial Secretary, not all of these specialists were British. Fears about the potential vulnerability of the northern Malay states bubbled up once again. The nightmare scenario for the British was a Germanised Siam pushing decisively into Kedah, Kelantan and Trengganu. More than a decade after Clarke had cobbled together the residential system at Pangkor, the status of the Malay states remained vulnerable. The Forward movement was again resurgent.

Lord Curzon, who became viceroy of India at the turn of the century, put it like this: 'India is like a fortress ... with mountains for her walls ... beyond these walls extends a glacis of varying breadth and dimension.' That 'glacis' was formed by Malaya and Singapore. He went on: 'We do not want to occupy it, but we cannot afford to see it occupied by our foes. We are quite content to let it remain in the hands of our allies and friends, but if rivals and unfriendly influences creep up on it ... we are compelled to intervene.' From Singapore a new governor, Frederick Weld, saw his mission as pushing British power and control right up to the border with Siam. He was persuasively backed by Swettenham, who believed himself the new Raffles, bringing civilisation and good government to Malays who would, he believed, benefit as much as the British.

After the signing of the Pangkor Treaty in 1874, it took over half a century for the British to erect that curious and ramshackle edifice of Crown Colonies and protectorates that came to be known as 'British Malaya'. By the end of World War I, British Malaya comprised the old Straits Settlements and a Federation of Malay states governed from Kuala Lumpur. Ever closer federation had been punctuated by rebellions and petty wars. Over time, the British stripped more powers from the sultans. Federation left open the status of the troublesome but resource-rich northern states. The final push to complete incorporation was yet again inspired by 'Germanophobia'. Fearful that mysterious German engineers had been reported infiltrating into Kelantan, the British clinched a deal with the Thai government in 1909. All the northern states, with the exception of Patani, now became an integral part of British Malaya as the 'Unfederated Malay States'. Only Sultan Zainal Abidin III of Trengganu (r. 1881–1918) held out. In 1914, the Turkish government allied itself with Germany and declared a global Jihad against France and Great Britain. Convinced that the infidel British would lose the war with the Kaiser and the Caliph, the devout sultan refused to comply with British demands. It was only in 1918, with the defeat of Germany and the collapse of the Ottoman Empire, that the new Sultan Muhammed Shah II (r. 1918–20) capitulated and accepted a Resident, who then forced him to abdicate. The Trengganu court, in any event, was bankrupt.

For its British residents, Malaya was a 'magical world'. After Malayan independence, memories of this equatorial paradise tugged at retired hearts and minds in the English Home Counties. 'It was enough for me to fall for everything,' wrote larger-than-life adventurer John Sjovald Cunyngham-Brown: '… for the mountains and plains and the streams and the empty coasts of sand so golden in the dusk; for the charm of the inhabitants, the elegance of their gestures, and, when young, the ineffable grace of their physique….'

For the coolies toiling in the mines and plantations that fed the coffers of empire, the reality had always been very different.

CHAPTER 13

Singapore:
The Golden Age

As the British tightened their grip on Malaya, the Crown Colony of Singapore was spun into the fast lane of history. English visitors struggled to find ways to capture the raw sights and sounds of a tidewater port city and its peoples caught up in a tidal wave of development. It was a city of splendour and squalor. A city of comfortable bankers, merchants and colonial administrators. A city of rickshaw pullers, coal coolies, stevedores and hawkers. Letters home were awash with clichés. Singapore was for its English visitors the 'Liverpool of the East', the 'Clapham Junction of the East', the 'Charing Cross of the East' and, for one homesick Scotsman, the 'Oban of the East'. Singapore always slipped the moorings of any banal comparison. It was gentrified and ramshackle; prosperous and blighted with poverty. Here, lives were led high on the hog or on the razor's edge of poverty. It was a city of much-haves and have-nots. It was a melting pot that, thanks to Stamford Raffles' segregated town planning, never melted.

Booming Singapore

As the world shrank, Singapore boomed. Between the 1870s and the beginning of World War II, its port recorded an eightfold increase in the volume of trade. The port city pulsed ever faster as the pent-up energies of global trade were released after the opening of the Suez Canal in 1869 and by the brisk development of steamship technology and the laying of a worldwide web of undersea cables. Telegraphy transformed time and space. Capital and market information sped between the European metropoles and the cities of Asia to revolutionise the old world of international banking. International behemoths like the Hongkong and Shanghai Banking Corporation put down roots in Singapore. Connecting Singapore and its flows of capital to the world made the rich richer. It also benefitted ordinary folk who could send a letter home in a few weeks. Steamships brought the migrants who toiled in shophouses and go-downs and sweated on plantations. Steam took Muslim pilgrims to Mecca and Medina. And through the arteries of the imperial postal system flowed hard-won remittances back to families in the homeland. Connectivity was enabling, even egalitarian. For the British administrator with his pith hat and stick and the coolie alike, home was suddenly much closer. For Europeans, the world that revolved around cricket on the Padang and high tea at a splendid new hotel was both thrillingly exotic and comfortably genteel. For the delicate Memsahib, all the comforts of an English suburban home were within reach. Servants were plentiful and cheap.

Experiencing Singapore

Isabella Bird, the intrepid English traveller, arrived in Singapore in 1879. She exclaimed, 'It is hot – so hot....' She was immediately dazzled by 'all the rich-flavoured coloured fruits of the tropics'. She was thrilled as 'Big canoes, manned by dark-skinned men in white turbans and loin-cloths, floated round our ship, or lay poised on the clear depths of aquamarine water....' Bird arrived in Singapore just a year too early to experience the rickshaw revolution, and as soon as she had disembarked hired a pony-drawn carriage, known as a gharry, for the two-mile journey from pier to town. She was driven past mangrove swamps and banana groves; a profusion of cocoa-palms, tree ferns, mango, custard apple, jack fruit, durian, pineapples and orchids: 'vegetation rich, profuse, endless, rapid, smothering, in all shades of vivid green, from the pea-green of spring and the dark, velvety green of endless summer....' A 'world of wonders' opened at every turn. She spotted monkeys and bright-winged birds. For her first night in Singapore, Bird stayed in a downmarket hotel, 'a shady, straggling building, much infested by ants....' She was rescued the following day by 'Mr Cecil Smith, the Colonial

Secretary, and his wife, full of kind thoughts and plans of further-
ance; and a little later a resident, to whom I had not even a letter of
introduction, took me and my luggage to his bungalow.' For all her
privileges, Bird was a sharp-eyed observer of colonial Singapore: 'As
Singapore is a military station, and ships of war hang about constantly, there is a great deal of fluctuating society, and the officials of
the Straits Settlements Government are numerous enough to form a
large society of their own. Then there is the merchant class, English,
German, French, and American; and there is the usual round of gay-
ety, and of the amusements which make life intolerable. I think that
in most of these tropical colonies the ladies exist only on the hope
of going 'home!' It is a dreary, aimless life for them – scarcely life,
only existence. The greatest sign of vitality in Singapore Europeans
that I can see is the furious hurry in writing for the mail.'

American zoologist William Hornaday was a lot less impressed.
On the way into town, he was jolted through a 'muddy and dismal
mangrove swamp' past 'dingy and weather beaten Malay houses
standing on posts over the soft and slimy mud' or lakes of 'slimy water'. Many visitors to Singapore were directed to the city's best hotel,
the London, which had been opened by French artist and photogra-
pher Gaston Dutronquoy close to the Esplanade. He promoted his
hotel as a kind of health spa catering to invalids and convalescents
and supported by a team of well-qualified doctors. Dutronquoy
was evidently a confidence trickster. A nineteenth-century version
of Tripadvisor would have soon filled with a barrage of negative
reviews of the London. It was, complained American businessman George Francis Train, 'a labyrinth of passages, show cases and
rooms which required a man to have a compass, if he does not wish
to lose his bearings.' For guests who found their rooms, worse was
to come: 'Your food looks uninviting … your boots get mildewed
and your brown leather trunk resembles the skin of a Maltese cat
it has become so mouldy.' Charles Walter Kinloch, a guest from
Bengal, grumbled that his search for a bathroom ended at 'a range
of buildings altogether distinct from the hotel'. Back in his room,
Kinloch retired for the night. Any hope he had entertained of a good
night's sleep was soon dashed. To make extra cash, Dutronquoy
had installed a bowling alley just outside the hotel, underneath the
windows of the hotel's best rooms. Every night, Kinloch was driven

half-mad by the thunder of rolled balls, clashing skittles and the shrieks of inebriated revellers.

World City

By the end of the 1870s, as Singapore was being transformed into a world city and a favourite destination for adventurous tourists, things were looking up. The Hôtel de l'Europe, the Adelphi and the Raffles were admired as 'first-class houses' and pleased the most fastidious globetrotters. Americans praised the 'Boston Arctic soda-water fountain' and billiard room at the Hôtel de l'Europe, and the British officer R. V. K. Applin recalled arriving at the Raffles 'hot and inflamed' and finding relief in an 'Indian bath'. By the end of the century, downtown Singapore was crammed full of clubs, theatres, reading rooms, public libraries, museums and churches. Constructed by Indian labourers, St Andrews was a landmark. A year before Isabella Bird visited Singapore, Manasseh Mayer opened a beautiful new synagogue on Waterloo Street in the Jewish quarter that had grown up around South Canal Road.

Singapore's elite was thoroughly spoilt. Ethel Colquhoun noted that 'The servant question is not so pressing in the Far East because there are always plenty of "boys", as Chinese domestics are called in pidgin English.' C. D. MacKellar, a tourist who booked into the Raffles Hotel, had high praise for the 'way of things' in Singapore: 'I could not get on without attention,' he admitted, 'so said to the hotel people: I must have boys to wait on me, and "put them on the bill". They all look the same – if I want attention I pull the nearest passing bell rope – I mean pigtail....' Soon, Mr MacKellar was getting whatever he wished for 'without my pointing'. Such flippant racism was endemic.

New Men from China

These young Chinese men had crossed a frontier between two worlds to find work. It divided the colonial district, its wide streets, hotels, banks and department stores, from the gaudy, jam-packed and chaotic worlds of Chinatown, Bugis Street, Kampong Glam and the upper reaches of Serangoon Road. Europeans liked to imagine that an invisible wall divided their world from the Asian city. The reality was more complicated. Elites prospered on both sides of the wall. Chinese traveller Li Chung Chu talked about a 'Greater Town', that included both the European colonial district *and* Chinatown, and a 'Lesser Town', which was spilling out to the north of the Singapore River and was the domain of 'natives'. Li Chung Chu was implying that elites flourished on both sides of the ethnic frontier. Origin and identity counted less than wealth and influence. The rise of Singapore as a world city was driven by a tight web of partnerships forged between Chinese and European entrepreneurs.

For many, Chinatown was a realm of poverty, refuse, disease and crime. Between 1840 and the end of the century, some two and a half million people emigrated from Chinese ports like Nanking and Canton to destinations in the Pacific, Europe, Australia and the United States. Singapore was both a destination and a gateway. Many tens of thousands of migrants flowed through Singapore to the mines and plantations of Malaya. The wealth they created in the Malay Peninsula flowed back through Singapore to voracious world markets for tin and then rubber. It was once conventional to explain this great migratory wave as a consequence of wars and upheavals in southern China, such as the calamitous Taiping Rebellion that ravaged central and southern China in the 1850s and 1860s. While vast numbers of Chinese were driven out of China, the movement was not one way. Imagine an immense human whirlpool, in which huge numbers make their way back and forth between their villages in China and the cities of the Nanyang, or 'Southern Ocean'. And if many Chinese were pushed out of their homeland, others were pulled in by the promise of a better life in Singapore and beyond. By the end of the century, Qing officials were referring to a category of Chinese they called Huaqiao, 'the Chinese who sojourn overseas'. Sojourn, of course, implies a temporary stay. Many Chinese migrants, in fact, maintained two families, one in their ancestral village and a second in the Nanyang. Like the ocean itself, the migratory whirlpool was always in flux.

As steamships and telegraphy revolutionised world trade in the second half of the nineteenth century, Singapore grew richer. The flow of raw materials sucked from the plantations and tin mines of Malaya pushed Singapore into the wealthy global club of port cities like Mumbai, Hong Kong and Sydney. The 'Clapham Junction of the East' was fast becoming the 'Chicago of Asia'. Entrepreneurial energies transformed lives at every level of society. For millions of immigrants, Singapore was a beacon of hope and betterment. In the last decades of the century, its working-class population boomed. The multitudes of sinkeh who fled Fukien and Kwangtung provinces in south-eastern China to sail from Swatow, Amoy and Hong Kong were indigent, barely literate but driven by will and burning ambition. For many tens of thousands, dreams of betterment hung on a new invention imported from Japan.

The Rickshaw Revolution

In 1868, an out-of-work samurai and Tokyo restaurant owner called Yousouke Tzumi invented a light, hooded cart he called a *jin-riki-shaw*, which means 'man power carriage'. Refined and mass-produced by other Japanese inventors, who added springs to the wheels, the rickshaw was rapidly adopted all over Asia. By 1872, some 40,000 rickshaws were operating in Tokyo. The first rickshaws appeared on the streets of Singapore in 1880 and were an immediate success. Rickshaws offered a new system of fast, comfortable mass transport, at least for passengers, and created thousands of new jobs as pullers. In short, the rickshaw revolution yoked together a new technology and cheap Asian labour. An army of pullers, anonymous for the most part, their lives lost to history, revolutionised the daily life of Singapore.

From the beginning, rickshaws were an astonishing success. They were an inexpensive and convenient way to get around town for people from every walk of life. From before dawn to the early hours of the next morning, colonial officials, hawkers, prostitutes, children on the way to and from school, servants shopping for groceries, sailors and soldiers, the temple priest and the gambler, the inebriated and the sober – the rickshaw puller served them all. When the Duke and Duchess of Cornwall visited Singapore in 1901, hundreds of rickshaw pullers joined a celebratory procession clad in specially made scarlet outfits. 'The Duke looked quite at home in his rickshaw,' reported Edwin Brown, 'the Duchess sat very stiffly, and seemed most uncomfortable, as if she expected to be thrown out at any moment.' In blazing heat or torrential downpour, the beetle black hood of the rickshaw sheltered and shaded all human life in Singapore.

Pulling demanded muscle and stamina. Over the years, the job was ruinous to bodies and health. There were very few elderly rickshaw pullers. Most sinkeh who came to Singapore after the 1880s on rickety junks or tramp steamers came from the lower strata of Chinese society. They came to Singapore with few skills and fragile hopes and dreams. They had heard tales from a father or uncle, kinsman or clansmen of the rickshaw trade. Money could be made by strong young men willing to bend their backs, seize the shafts of a rickshaw and pound the streets of Singapore. By 1920, 50,000 rickshaws were registered in Singapore. Ten years later, that figure had doubled. In 1917, a twelve-hour survey of the main bridges in Singapore recorded 72,772 crossings by rickshaws.

The burden that fell on the shoulders of the men who tugged and pulled their human loads for over a century along its streets and through markets and narrow alleyways became ever heavier as the city swelled and its population multiplied. In 1871, the Straits government counted some 97,000 inhabitants. Three decades later, the city was home to 200,000 people, and numbers would not stop rising until World War II. Population growth pushed city limits outwards, to the west towards New Harbour; east towards Geylang, Tanjong Katong and the East Coast Road; northwest along River Valley Road to wealthy Tanglin; and far to the north along Serangoon Road. Singapore, like any modern city, sprouted suburbs and a flight of the better-off from the grubby inner city to the green and pleasant land of the Burbs. And as Singapore expanded, so too did the rigours of the rickshaw puller's life. They were mute beasts of burden. Writing in 1926, Richard Sydney remembered: 'It is difficult to recapture the early thrill. I have got into a rickshaw somewhere near the top of a hill and then have felt quite thrilled by the fast moving puller who has made the rickshaw travel at a pace at least equal to that of a smartly stepping horse.' Sydney went on: 'Believe me, pullers were pullers in those days.'

A puller's day might start at Johnston Pier, where new arrivals to Singapore stepped ashore. Here, a seething multitude of rickshaws competed fiercely for business as the ride into town paid well. Most pullers wore a pair of shorts and a straw fibre hat. Many ran naked from the waist up until new laws were passed after 1900 forcing rickshaw drivers to dress decently and respect the refined sensibilities of European clients. Other pullers clustered outside luxury hotels and railways stations like the one at Tank Road. And so the puller's day began. To make a decent wage, he would endure up to twelve hours hauling several hundred pounds of human weight across town. Pullers would take very few breaks to escape the scalding sun or seek refreshment with a hasty opium pipe.

By the beginning of the twentieth century, entire districts of rickshawmen and their families had sprung up in the nooks and crannies of Chinatown. Cheek by jowl, they were densely packed in dim, damp and dusty cubicles lacking windows and ventilation linked by narrow, gloomy passages.

On a hot day, the puller would soon be thickly crusted with the dry, red dust of Singapore's laterite roads. In drenching equatorial downpours, dust became thick mud, forcing pullers to lug their blithely comfortable passengers through viscous sludge and floods. Each puller rented his rickshaw from an owner who might have a fleet of up to twenty vehicles. They charged pullers at a rate between 8 to 10 cents a day and took 25 per cent of their earnings. Owners usually hired from their own district and dialect group. Before the turn of the century, the rickshaw business was dominated by Cantonese and Hokkien owners. After 1900, Hockchew and Hengwah speakers muscled into the trade. For fleet owners, this was a profitable business. Few pullers could save enough to buy even one rickshaw and most had to take second jobs. This was the gig economy of its era.

Our rickshaw puller has left his fare at the Adelphi Hotel and hauled his rickshaw, wheels clattering, to another competitive pick-up spot outside the Railway Station. From here, he may get a fare to the markets of Beach Road or, later in the day, to the red light districts of Bugis Street and Chinatown. Over the course of his working day, he would haul every kind of Singaporean, from pith-hatted European bankers and office workers to silk and satin-clad towkays to every part of town and into far-flung new neighbourhoods in Bukit Timah or along the East Coast. The rickshaw puller saw life in the raw. He would convey ruddy-faced British husbands to brothels and then home to their wives. He would take Memsa-hibs to department stores and clubs. The puller was indispensable to bibulous pub crawlers. Captain A. H. Tilly described a boozy day that began 'at the Rendezvous Club, opposite to the Chinese burial ground. Then I went to Smith Street to a spirits shop, as I know a Chinaman who is an interpreter in the Police Court, and had a whiskey and tonic. After finishing the same, I went to the Prince of Wales Hotel and had two glasses of beer there. Then I proceeded home by the Tanjong Pagar Road.'

> Tug and pull, tug and pull,
> Life is short, life is cruel.
> Sob and wheeze, sob and wheeze,
> Finish up, lung disease.
> Nights spent in filthy rooms,
> Dreaming dreams in opium fumes.

City of Opium

Opium – the solace of the rickshaw puller, tin miner and plantation worker and the lifeblood of imperial commerce. The British Empire was the world's most lucrative drug cartel. When social campaigners spoke out against the ills of opium, the British belligerently defended a vital source of revenue and ridiculed do-gooders who spoke against the trade. In 1916, the American nurse, journalist and anti-drugs crusader Ellen La Motte reported from Singapore that opium shops in the city were 'established under government auspices' and received supplies of the drug from government sources. She discovered 'a thorough and complete establishment of the opium traffic, run by the government, as a monopoly.' In her book *The Opium Monopoly*, La Motte denounced the British government for distributing 'thousands of pounds of opium, which are thus turned loose upon the world, to bring destruction and ruin to the human race'. The governors of the East India Company were the drug lords of Asia, and when the company fell from grace after 1857, the drug habit was maintained by pious colonial mandarins from their offices in London, Calcutta and the Straits.

The sweet stench of opium saturated Singapore's colonial era.

The first British Resident, William Farquhar, established the system of 'farming' licences to sell opium to Chinese towkays in return for 'rents'. By the 1880s, Farquhar's system had become too big to fail. Opium farming benefitted both the colonial government, which depended on revenues, and the local merchants who held government licences. Fortunes made from opium laid the foundations of business dynasties that diversified into banking or shipping. Between 1898 and 1904, historians have estimated that opium accounted for between 43.3 and 59.1 per cent of revenue pouring into the coffers of the British Straits Settlements.

The consumers lived in a very different world. Inside dimly lit opium dens in neighbourhoods like Tanjong Pagar, men with vacant eyes and gaunt faces lay on raised beds sucking in the sweet-smelling fumes from pipes or lamps to find escape from the punishing exertions of daily life. During her visit to Singapore, La Motte describes staying at the Hotel de l'Europe and being waited on by a handsome young Malay waiter. Surly and indifferent, he seemed incapable of doing anything right. Asked for tea and fruit, he brought only coffee. Eventually, she writes, she and her companions realised the waiter was as high as a kite: 'It was the same thing every day.' After breakfast, La Motte set off to visit the government-licensed opium shops and dens. 'So we went on', she remembered 'down the long street. There was a dreadful monotony about it all. House after house of feeble, emaciated, ill wrecks.' La Motte was shocked by what she discovered:

'We three got into rickshaws and went down to the Chinese quarter, where there are several hundred of these places, all doing a flourishing business. It was early in the afternoon, but even then, trade was brisk. The divans were rooms with wide wooden benches running round the sides, on which benches, in pairs, sharing a lamp between them, lay the smokers. They purchased their opium on entering, and then lay down to smoke it. The packages are little, triangular packets, each containing enough for about six smokes. Each packet bears a label, red letters on a white ground, "Monopoly Opium"'.

In the British tabloid press, the 'Opium Wreck', a person ruined by a drug habit, was a stock character. British readers were fascinated by illustrations of the murky dens and hollow-eyed and emaciated 'Orientals' reclining on pallets, pipe in hand. It was pure hypocrisy. The thousands of Chinese coolies who 'chased the dragon' in search of oblivion indulged their habit courtesy of the British government. Outside Singapore, in British-owned mines and plantations, the local 'Opium Shop' was never far away. Who can blame the men toiling in furnace-like temperatures and drenching downpours who sought respite? The average coolie was said to consume about 35 grams of *chandu*, or refined opium, every day. Rickshaw pullers, it was said, smoked twice that amount. Opium eroded livelihoods as well as bodies. A British surgeon, Dr Robert Little, published a short pamphlet in 1850 'On the Habitual Use of Opium in Singapore' which denounced 'a most expensive habit, the gratification of which plunges the poorest classes into the direst poverty'. The addict's poverty was another man's fortune.

The Battle against Opium

By the last decade of the nineteenth century, Singapore was becoming a hub for a new abolitionist movement. On April 9 1891, a petition of 11,000 signatures was presented to the parliament decrying the 'the terrible evils of opium-smoking among so many thousands of Chinese'. The most important leader of the movement was the respected Peranakan doctor Lee Boon Keng who was a founder of the Singapore Anti Opium Society. Lim was an impressive person, and a stubborn thorn in the side of Singapore's colonial government. He was highly educated in both Chinese and Western schools and was founder of the first English language periodical published by Malayans, *The Straits Chinese Magazine*, which was read very widely across Southeast Asia as well as in France and the United States. Lim excoriated the 'baneful habit' and its destruction of health. It was the duty of any government, he proclaimed, to repress sources of vice and crime not, as the Straits government did, profit from helpless victims.

Dr Lim's campaign soon spread across Asia. In 1895, Japan prohibited opium imports across its borders and those of its then colony Taiwan. The Japanese ban finally made the British colonial authorities sit up. Faced with reputational damage on an international scale, the British responded in the way all governments do when under pressure to act. In the same year, the government appointed a Royal Commission chaired by the politician and writer Thomas Brassey. Some of its members, like Arthur Pease, were anti-opium, but a number of others came from Indian civil service backgrounds and opposed any kind of prohibition. They would do all they could to defend a vital source of revenue. Outnumbered and outmanoeuvred, Pease complained of 'misleading circulars, prescribed questions, suggestions in a particular direction, examination and filtration of evidence, and withholding of certain witnesses'. The Commission finally concluded, in a 2,000-page report, that opium was not harmful for Asians and was enjoyed in much the same way alcohol was in Western cultures. Prohibition, pronounced Earl Brassey, was motivated by commercial jealousy, not medical evidence. Like so many other commissions or enquiries before and since, the report silenced any further discussion of the opium problem.

It would be the Japanese, who occupied Malaya and Singapore after 1942, who enforced a complete ban. Opium had a very long life in Singapore. In the 1970s, it was still possible to find illicit dens in Duxton Street and Amoy Street in Tanjong Pagar. The sweet odour of the drug that fuelled the British Empire took many decades to fade.

For over a hundred years, the colonial government of the Straits Settlement was funded by revenues from opium. And yet British residents liked to complain loudly and frequently that the world beyond the Padang was filthy, overcrowded and ridden with vice. The spectre of crime stalked the markets, shophouses and alleyways of Chinatown. Streets were potholed, strewn with sodden rubbish and menaced by stray dogs. There was no fire brigade, few hospitals and no sewage system. Singapore was smelly, dirty and for many of its people dangerous. The state of the city's 'native quarters' provoked disgust and fear, but any talk among Europeans of stepping in to make improvements clashed with the doggedly laissez faire attitude of the governor and his administrators. Welfare was taboo, or rather it was pushed out of sight and out of mind as the duty of high-minded Chinese philanthropists with spare cash.

The Battle for Chinatown

By the first decade of the twentieth century, the old hands-off mentality of the Straits government was coming under severe strain. Singapore had become a showpiece port city of the British Empire and the poverty and squalor behind the gleaming waterfront facades was impossible to mask. Fear of disease was one powerful changer of minds. In the 1890s, an old enemy of our species went on the rampage. Bubonic plague erupted in China and was spread on the ill wind of trade from Hong Kong to Karachi, Calcutta and the Straits Settlements. Plague and other infectious diseases did not respect the borders between the High City and the native quarters. Everyone on the island was at risk. Another kind of contagion kept colonial minds awake through the warm, equatorial nights. Crime and its noisy attendants, riot and disorder. Chinatown, it was feared, was becoming ungovernable. And the colonial government had a ready explanation for this troubling state of affairs: the notorious Chinese clans or secret societies.

The battle for control of Chinatown sputtered into life in 1876. That year, the government opened a post office in Chinatown. For many decades, Chinese sinkeh had sent money home to their families using the remittance system. The business was dominated by Teochew towkays who used Chinese junks and charged heft fees. The traditional remittance system was a ramshackle business, and the idea behind the new post office was to provide a more reliable service. But the colonial authorities had blundered. They farmed out the reformed system to Straits Chinese from Penang, enraging the towkays. 'We hear that lately one or two rascals have established a post office ... to oppress the Chinese in their private gains.' The aggrieved towkays sent young men all over Chinatown with placards threatening dire retribution for anyone who took a job in the post office. Their daughters and wives would be raped, their heads cut off. As the placards multiplied, a riot erupted. Eventually, the post office prospered, but not before another riot swept through Chinatown when the government insisted on clearing the five-foot ways of shopkeepers to alleviate chronic congestion. Riots were a symptom of the fact that in Chinatown the British faced a rival power, and it was time to despatch the urban equivalent of a gunboat.

For many decades, the British authorities had skirmished with the Chinese clans for control of Chinatown. Legislation introduced in 1869 to compel the clan organisations to register had failed miserably. A different strategy was needed, and it was a gifted Englishman the Chinese called Pi-ki-ling who would confront the clans and transform the local headmen into government agents. William Pickering's plan was daring, and it very nearly succeeded.

The Pickering Plan

What is remarkable about the story of William Pickering, the first Protector of the Chinese in Singapore, is that when he arrived in the Straits in 1872, he was the first European official to speak and write Chinese. He had leant Mandarin and most of the dialects working as a commercial agent in Quanzhou in the Hokkien-speaking Fujian Province of south-eastern China and in Taiwan, then known as Formosa. In Singapore, Pickering found work as a government interpreter. This involved translating official documents into Chinese and attending trials to translate witness testimonies. These duties were normally undertaken by local translators. Pickering was astonished to discover that the humble art of official translation was being used to undermine the hallowed status of pompous British officials. Pickering informed his employers that when government proclamations were translated by locals, colonial officials were called Ang Moh, meaning 'red-haired barbarians', and in court documents the judges, barristers and members of the jury were 'barbarians' or 'devils'. They called the police 'big dogs'. These were all profoundly insulting terms. Until Pickering pointed out this embarrassing fact, not a single British official had the competence to understand that Chinese translators were poking seditious fun at their colonial masters. Translation was a form of rebellion. It was derogatory and insulting. Now the Ang Moh really did have red faces. Pickering also suspected that the official translators were members of Chinese clans who, naturally, had an interest in undermining colonial justice. And William Pickering knew a great deal about secret societies. It was, in fact, an obsession.

The roots of Pickering's fascination can be traced to his experiences in the Malay Peninsula. In 1873, Pickering was a member of the British party that negotiated with the Malay and Chinese delegates at Pangkor. Soon after the treaty was signed, Major Samuel Dunlop, the inspector general of police for the Straits Settlements, sent Pickering to the mining town of Larut to negotiate with warring Chinese clans. During his time in Formosa, Pickering made an unusual discovery. He had somehow acquired a set of bagpipes and found that many Chinese were instantly captivated by the sound. In Perak, Pickering used the same trick. It was said, by a British eyewitness of Pickering's antics, that he 'quite won their hearts like Orpheus of old' – and 'became quite tractable'. The story is rather patronising, but the same observer adds an interesting detail. He describes the British party approaching a Chinese stockade and 'Mr Pickering would strike up on his pipes. The Chinese would flock out of their strongholds by the hundreds and regard the player with wonder', entranced by a sound they believed was Chinese music. In any event, the Pied Piper of Perak acquired legendary status among Chinese and British official circles as a cunning and effective negotiator. And his skills would soon be put to the test when he returned to Singapore.

Early in 1877, angry crowds gathered in Market Street and Major Dunlop and Pickering rushed to find out what was going on. It turned out that members of a Chinese clan were rounding up large numbers of migrants who had been promised work in Singapore and driving them onto ships bound for Sumatra where they would, they found out, be put to work in tin mines. The sinkeh had vigorously resisted, and the clan men had begun dragging them towards the wharf where the transports were tied up. All hell had broken loose. Dunlop arrested some of the kidnappers and took them to the Chinatown police station. Here, Pickering discovered that a number of terrified sinkeh had taken refuge. They were bruised and battered. But they were lucky. The attempted kidnapping had taken place in broad daylight and the uproar brought powerful British officials running to aid the desperate young men. Many sinkeh were not so lucky. Imported under the credit-ticket system, they were at the mercy of unscrupulous 'coolie brokers' who treated migrants like cattle, in fact they were called *chui tsai*, or 'piglets'. The brokers hired gangs of *samseng*, or 'rowdies' to herd the sinkeh from port to depot and then back to ships to Sumatra. This happened all the time, but Pickering made a report about the incident in Market Street, and it outraged the government. And this time the governor acted. A few months later, in May 1877, the British established a Chinese Protectorate and appointed Pickering as Protector of Immigrants and Emigrants. To begin with, Pickering and a tiny staff worked out of an office in a shophouse on North Canal Road, but as the first protector of Chinese in Singapore, he had a grand vision of his new mission.

By the 1880s, the Chinese Protectorate, which now occupied an imposing building on Havelock Road, could report to the colonial government that abuses suffered by migrant workers had been curtailed. But Pickering had a much grander ambition. He would take on the headmen of the Chinese clans and transform them from rivals for power into agents of the Straits government or, as he put it, make dangerous secret societies into friendly societies. First, he had to dig deep into the world of secret societies and find out how they commanded such fervent loyalty from their members.

So it was that in 1879, Pickering accompanied by Major Dunlop and the new Colonial Secretary Sir Cecil Clementi Smith, who also spoke good Mandarin, paid a few dollars to attend an initiation ceremony of the Ghee Hin sworn brotherhood. The Ghee Hin, or Heaven and Earth, was one of the most combative, wealthy and powerful clans in the Straits, and had taken a leading part in the tin wars in the Malay Peninsula. In Singapore, the Ghee Hin had fought the Ghee Hok for control of the city in pitched battles that in the course of ten days in 1854 led to the violent deaths of at least 400 Chinese.

In a report to the Royal Asiatic Society, Pickering wrote in impressive detail about the astonishingly complex initiation ritual and its mythological significance that he and his friends witnessed that evening. It lasted five hours, from ten at night to three in the morning. At the climax of the ritual, candidates knelt in pairs before an alter ornamented with symbolic numbers, candles, rice, tea and wine and flags that commemorated notable events in clan history. The master of the lodge asked a series of questions and the new brothers swore oaths to the society. They drank deep from cups of wine mixed with their own blood. They now belonged to the Ghee Hin. Pickering and his friends were, like Raffles, all Freemasons, but the Chinese initiation ceremony they had witnessed that night was so much more splendid and powerful than the arcane rituals of a Masonic lodge. The British could offer nothing to compete with the ties of allegiance and loyalty that bound together the members of the Ghee Hing. Pickering saw with his own eyes that secret societies offered a sophisticated form of government quite independent of the colonial authorities. Pickering's insight was that the British would have to work through the headmen of the clans and recruit clansmen as loyal servants of the Crown.

Pickering's grand plan had some success. His staff took on resolving quarrels, financial disputes and even domestic squabbles. They threatened uppity rebels with deportation back to China. Pickering became a respected community arbitrator. But over time, the clans found they had been stripped of their old powers and chaffed at the rules and regulations imposed by the Protectorate. The threat of banishment began to lose its force because, by the end of the 1880s, many of the clan leaders were Straits-born and so could not be deported. When Pickering discovered that some clans refused to give up gaming and prostitution rackets, he pressed the Straits government to give him legal clout to strike hard at the syndicates.

On the morning of 18 July 1887, Pickering's crusade was brought to a shattering end. The *Straits Times* reported that 'A Chinese Tew Chew [Teochew] carpenter came to the office.... He went up to Mr Pickering's desk and threw at his face the iron-head of a carpenter's axe, which he carried in his hand.' The carpenter's name was Chua Ah Siok. Pickering, we discover from the *Straits Times* report, had noticed Ah Siok 'gnashing his teeth' and asked him what he wanted. He said he had come to the Protectorate to present a petition, but seconds later 'the chopper came flying straight at him, like a cannonball'. Pickering leapt to his feet, clutching his head and bleeding profusely. Rage cancelled out pain. He chased Ah Siok into the street where he was pinned down by Protectorate staff. It turned out that Pickering's assailant had been sent by the leader of the Ghee Hok society who was running a gambling syndicate. Here was an example of ferocious clan loyalty. The young man who came to Pickering's office clutching an axe head was doing his duty.

Pickering never recovered. He suffered from what would now be diagnosed as post-traumatic stress disorder. He could no longer concentrate, his memory deteriorated and he was often 'over excited'. Pickering was eventually retired. He had seen his master-plan destroyed by his friend Sir Cecil Clementi Smith, who became the governor of the Straits. Clementi Smith introduced a Societies Ordinance that abolished the secret societies and made it illegal for any Chinese to belong to one. It was a draconian measure that merely drove the clans underground. They became truly secretive. The British, in short, never really understood the Chinese brother-hoods. Few British administrators could empathise with the masses of homeless sinkeh who arrived alone in Singapore and sought out the warm embrace of the Chinese brotherhoods.

Muslim Singapore

Migrants from southern China dominated the human flood across the Southern Ocean to Singapore and other port cities. Many other migrant streams flowed through Singapore that profoundly shaped its story and character. Despite his disdain for their faith, Raffles, it seems, made a pragmatic bet that Arabic-speaking merchants would also invest in the growth of Singapore. After all, traders from the Arabian Peninsula had been weaving an intricate network of trading links across the oceans of the world for many centuries. Betting on Arab prosperity was shrewd. A Dutch scholar, L. W. C. Van den Berg, called Singapore the 'most flourishing Arab colony in all the Indian Ocean'. If there was a founding father of Arab Sin-gapore it was Syed Omar Aljunied, a wealthy merchant, who was a contemporary of Tan Tock Seng and Seah Eu Chin. His ances-tors, like so many other Arab traders, came from the Hadramawt region in Yemen and had traded across Southeast Asia in Sumatra and Java since the eighteenth century. Aljunied was born in Palem-bang, the old capital of the Srivijaya Empire. When the British be-gan developing Singapore, he and his uncle moved their business and networks across the Strait of Malacca. Aljunied rapidly pros-pered. As a Muslim, he easily won the trust of Malay sultans who let him trade without charging him duties. Like his Straits Chinese counterparts, Aljunied turned to philanthropy to make his mark in the fast-changing new city and showed himself to be impressively cosmopolitan and broad-minded. He donated land and built Singa-pore's first mosque as a *wakaf* (public property), the Masjid Omar

Kampong Malacca, which is still standing on Omar Street, and the Benggali Mosque on Bencoolen Street.

Successful Arab merchants like Aljunied were clever risk-takers. They embraced new opportunities and new technologies. And in the mid-nineteenth century, it was the steamship, along with the marine telegraph cable that powered a revolution in trade and the movement of peoples. Steam power dethroned that fickle deity of the Indian Ocean, the monsoon, and for Muslims from all over Asia, steam propelled the Hajj, the annual pilgrimage to the House of God, the Kaaba in Mecca. Every year, during the Hajj season, many thousands of Muslim pilgrims from all over Malaya, Borneo and the Dutch East Indies gathered in the Arab quarter in Singapore to wait for a passage west across the Indian Ocean. Pilgrimage was expensive, and many poorer Hajjis were forced to stay on in Singapore to pay off the exorbitant costs. They all needed somewhere to stay, clothing, food and currency, and for local merchants in Singapore, every Hajj season meant good business.

Who Is a Singaporean?

Even as it prospered, Singapore stubbornly remained a port city that was defined by flux and movement. It was a place of diaspora, not permanence. But at the beginning of the twentieth century, many Asians began to ask challenging new questions about allegiance and identity. Who were they? Was their identity defined by residence in a British Crown Colony. The British certainly believed so, but an identity as a subject of a foreign empire hardly fitted with the new nationalist ideas that had seized the imaginations of Asians in every corner of the world. The consequence of globalisation, of connectivity, was not just wealth-creating. New ideas spread on the wings of trade. About nationhood. About identity. About freedom from colonial rule. Globalisation meant that the peoples of Southeast Asia began asking big new questions. Were they loyal British subjects or in some way Asian? And what kind of Asian? Were they Chinese or Hokkien or Teochew? Malay? Indian? How should Chinese in Singapore respond to the turmoil that was engulfing the Qing Dynasty and promising a Chinese Republic? As Indian nationalists demanded ever more loudly that the British get out of India, how should South Asians, who had come to Singapore as convicts and plantation workers to prosper and put down roots define their allegiances? And most tricky of all, what did it mean to be a Malay in the Straits settlements? That puzzle was addressed most eloquently by the son of a Sumatran merchant, Mohammed Eunos Abdullah.

Born in 1876, Eunos was one of the few Malays to attend the Raffles Institution, which had been established by Raffles to educate a native elite. But for much of the nineteenth century, the British rulers of Singapore showed very little interest in such high-minded ideals. Singapore was, in their view, a commercial emporium, not an educational charity. The Raffles Institution provided secondary education mainly for the sons of wealthy businessmen who realised that an English education unlocked the tightly guarded doors of the more elevated social and business circles. Only a tiny trickle of the best and the brightest Asians won places at the Raffles Institution and future membership of the elite. This fundamental inequality was deepened by the basic mindset of the British rulers. They segregated Singapore into distinct quarters for Chinese, Malays, Indians and Arabs, and typecast the peoples who grew up, lived and worked inside these separate communities. These stereotypes are all too familiar: Chinese enterprising but treacherous; Malays loyal but lazy; Indians best suited for hard labour. Only at the end of the nineteenth century did the British begin to take education seriously as a public duty and to feed the ever more complex bureaucracies that sustained the prosperity of the Straits. Eunos was fortunate, and what he did with his privileged education was ground-breaking.

When he graduated from the Raffles Institution, Eunos, as his teachers expected, entered government service as a harbour master across the Strait of Singapore in Johor. A few years later, he returned to Singapore to edit a Malay language newspaper, the *Utusan Melayu,* or 'Malay Messenger'. It was as a journalist, a Malay man of letters, that Eunos would set off a revolution in how Malays in the Straits imagined their identity and destiny.

Until Eunos founded the *Utusan Melayu,* Muslims in Singapore had looked for leadership to wealthy Arab businessmen like Syed Omar Aljunied and members of the elite Jawi Peranakan community, locally born Malay-speaking Muslims of mixed South Indian and Malay ancestry. Eunos and his friends challenged the old leadership so effectively that in 1924 he was appointed to the Straits Settlements Legislative Council. At the time, Eunos was the single Malay Muslim representative. Based in the Empress Place Building, now the Asian Civilisations Museum, the council was a tame talking shop. When he stood up to make his maiden speech in a cramped and airless meeting room in June 1924, Eunos raged against the 'imperfect education' of Malay youth. He expressed the problem vividly: 'Being unable to swim, a young Malay boy is lost in the swelling sea of unemployment.' It was what he said next that showed just how radical was his thinking: 'Surely, sir, this is not a thing to be desired among the original sons of the soil.'

Here we have one of the first expressions of the idea that Malays could claim natural rights as Bumiputera, 'sons of the soil', and so had a unique identity. In his writing, Eunos often used anther important word. He described Malays as a 'Bangsa,' a Malay word meaning 'race' or 'nation'. By calling Malays a Bangsa, Eunos broke with Malay tradition and with the colonial idea that Malays or any other Asian was merely a subject of Empire. Today, Bumiputera privilege is in disrepute, but in the 1920s colonial subjects were feeling their way into new identities and imagining different futures.

CHAPTER 14

The Empire Strikes Back: Singapore at War

2 2 March 1915. Pearl's Hill, Singapore…. Crowds gather outside the walls of the Outram Road Prison. Something shocking and extraordinary is about to happen. Reporters from the *Straits Times* and a few photographers grab the best positions. The crowds fall silent as Subedar Dunde Khan, Jemadar Christi Khan, Havildar Rahmat Ali, Sepoy Hakim Ali and Havildar Abdul Ghani are marched under heavy guard and tied to posts outside the prison walls where a twenty-five man firing squad is waiting. Their feet and hands are tied. Cameras click loudly. Seconds later, rifles crackle and the five mutineers slump forward, dead or dying. For a few moments, the crowd is dazed by the brutal reality of lives ending in front of their eyes. There is another flurry of camera clicks. Why had the men of the 5th mutinied and why did the British punish the ringleaders so harshly? The 'Singapore Mutiny' of 1915 was dismissed by the colonial administrator Sir Richard Winstedt as 'the merest pustule in the world's upheaval'. Less complacent observers understood that the Singapore Mutiny was a harsh shock, a hammer blow that exposed, in the words of a Japanese reporter, 'the pitiful state of a colony without effective power'. The world was changing and yet for the British rulers of Singapore and Malaya the new century seemed to have brought the best of times. What few realised was that the prosperity of the British Empire would be the root of its undoing.

In the twentieth century, two global wars would send powerful tremors across Southeast Asia that would throw the European rulers of the Straits Settlements, Malaya and the Dutch East Indies from their colonial perches. Bloody turmoil and carnage on faraway battlefields would fatally weaken the old empires in India and Southeast Asia. A brash new Asian power would take on European empire-builders and take them on at their own game. The Japanese generals who ousted the British and Dutch from Malaya and the East Indies in 1942 were rival empire-builders. Like the Portuguese, the British and the Dutch needed cheap raw materials to power new industries: raw materials like rubber.

Empire of Rubber

At the beginning of the twentieth century, the end of empire was simply unimaginable. As the English Queen Victoria, the gloomy Empress of India, was laid to rest in the Royal Mausoleum in Windsor Grand Park in February 1901, the empire she had ruled for sixty years had rarely seemed so secure and prosperous. Huge areas of the globe were tinted vermilion red and British Malaya was becoming ever more profitable. The sticky source of all this new wealth was a substance known as the 'devil's milk' – rubber. At the end of the nineteenth century, the bicycle and the automobile transformed the viscous sap of the Pará rubber tree, *Hevea braziliensis*, into a globally desired raw material. If the Indian Raj was the 'Jewel in the Imperial Crown', Malaya was now the backyard factory of Empire.

Some 3,000 years ago, the Olmec and Maya peoples extracted primitive rubber from the *Hevea* trees to make balls to play games. Jump forward to 1839 and the discovery of 'vulcanisation' by Thomas Hancock and Thomas Goodyear. Vulcanisation revolutionised the potential of wild *Hevea*. It binds together the long polymer chains of natural rubber, making vulcanised rubber less sticky and more elastic. Hancock began to manufacture waterproof mackintoshes by rubberising leather. The demand for Hancock's revolutionary new macs led to a wild rubber boom in Amazonia. Overnight, the 'devil's milk' enriched the cities of Belem, Santarem and Manaus in Brazil and Iquitos in Peru. The British government took envious note. How could Brazil's monopoly be broken? A plot was hatched by the India Office in London and the eminent botanist Joseph Hooker, director of the Royal Botanic Gardens at Kew in Surrey, to smash the Brazilian rubber monopoly. In 1859, the English geographer and explorer Sir Clements Markham led a mission to the South American Andes to acquire seeds of the cinchona plant. Cinchona bark was a source of quinine, the only available treatment (not a cure) for malaria. Malaria is a parasite that kills half a million people, mainly children, every year and it blighted European empire-builders. The British East India Company used its military might and money to conquer India. But the swamps of India were breeding grounds for mosquitos that carried the parasite. As a consequence, the number of British soldiers in India who succumbed to malaria exceeded the numbers killed in combat. In South America, Spanish 'Conquistadores' discovered that drinking a concoction made from the bark of the cinchona tree significantly reduced the deadliness of malarial fevers. Markham's plan was to transplant the cinchona trees to plantations in India, Burma and Ceylon. Markham's scheme was a spectacular success. The mass production of natural quinine vastly improved the lives of tens of thousands of British servants of empire.

Rewarded with a knighthood, Sir Clements began looking around for other potentially lucrative botanical treasures and soon focused his attention on the para rubber tree and its sticky sap. Markham got his hands on a handful of *Hevea* seeds from the British consul in Para, the port of entry to the vast rubber lands of the Amazon basin. He despatched them to Hooker who did some experiments but failed to make the *Hevea* seeds germinate. It was at this point that the frustrated Hooker contacted the maverick explorer Sir Henry Wickham, who was eking out a precarious livelihood in Santarem in Brazil. Most of his family had perished in this disease-infested Amazonian backwater. Wickham then secretly acquired 70,000 *Hevea* seeds which he despatched to Liverpool, where a Customs Office Bill of Entry noted the arrival of a cargo of '171 cases of rubber'.

Soon afterwards, Hooker sent some 2,000 seedlings to Ceylon and the Straits. H. J. Murton, director of the Singapore Botanic Garden, planted his 22 seedlings, and every one of them survived. In Perak, the British Resident Hugh Low planted *Hevea* seeds in the garden of his residency in Kuala Kangsar, also with great success. In 1888, a decade after the *Hevea* seeds had first been planted in Singapore, the new director of the Botanic Gardens, Henry Ridley, became obsessed with the unfulfilled commercial potential of wild rubber, so much so that he was known as 'Rubber Ridley' or, less politely, 'Mad Ridley'. The problem was that a *Hevea* tree takes six years to reach 'profitable maturity' and for the next decade or so, no one was willing to invest in scaling up production.

Then, in the last decade of the nineteenth century, blight ravaged the coffee and tea plantations of Sumatra and Malaya. At the same time, Asian sugar planters were hit by intense competition from the European beet industry. Rubber production began to look very attractive. Ridley turned to merchant and philanthropist Tan Chay Yan, the Peranakan grandson of Tan Tock Seng. Fired up by Ridley's passion, in 1896 Tan began developing an experimental rubber estate on 43 acres of land at Bukit Lintang, a hill in Malacca, using seedlings of the *Hevea brasiliensis*. It was the first rubber plantation in Malaya.

In the meantime, John Lloyd Dunlop, the Scottish inventor, had patented the pneumatic rubber tyre, commercially produced by the Dunlop Company from 1898. That year, 'Rubber Ridley' reported requests for one million *Hevea* seeds on a single day. The bicycle and then the automobile pushed demand for rubber to astronomical levels. By 1908, rubber was being planted and tapped in every Malayan state.

The triumph of rubber can be illustrated by the fortunes of the Ramsden family, who controlled numerous plantation businesses at the turn of the century in northern Malaya. The family owned the Penang Sugar Estates, which began planting rubber rather half-heartedly in 1900 but were reluctant to give up sugar. The correspondence of a company executive called E. L. Hamilton shows that he was worried about possible labour shortages, a fickle market and the vulnerability of the *Hevea* trees to white ants and root disease. Hamilton changed his mind when a plague of rats attacked not the rubber trees but the sugar beet: they had sharp teeth and a sweet tooth. Five years later, Sir John Ramsden had switched entirely to rubber planting. Penang Sugar became Penang Rubber.

Mr Hamilton was right in one respect at least. The global rubber market was chronically unstable. But by 1915 rubber had overtaken tin as Malaya's most valuable export and was worth 40 per cent of the colony's total export value. Rubber accounted for four-fifths by volume of all agricultural output. The first rubber estates were small-scale affairs run by owner-operators, but as production boomed, bigger conglomerates began to dominate the industry. At the beginning of the twentieth century, Asian producers, who could draw on huge reservoirs of 'native' labour in Malaya and French Indochina, overtook the Amazonian growers for the first time. By 1914, Asian rubber conglomerates dominated the global market: the Brazilian industry would never recover.

The Natural Plastic

During the nineteenth and early twentieth centuries, a handful of European powers (later joined by Japan and the United States) carved up the globe to create the biggest empires the world has ever seen. The rulers of these sprawling, often unruly empires confronted unprecedented administrative challenges. In the early decades of the nineteenth century, communication between imperial capitals and colonial territories was slow and unreliable. Letters, messages, instructions and replies – all had to be sent by ships that took several months to complete a round trip. Even the fastest clipper ship took a hundred days or more to sail from London to Hong Kong via the Cape of Good Hope. So the speed of imperial communications was restricted to the pace of physical transportation. News could take weeks, months, even years to travel from Batavia, Singapore or Penang to London or Amsterdam. The 'tyranny of distance' or 'imperial stretch' threatened the integrity of the European empires.

The maintenance of overstretched empires was a spur to technological innovation. The tyranny of distance was solved by a quantum leap in communications which was as globally transformative as the development of the modern worldwide web. The invention of the electric telegraph was the engine of high imperialism. For the first time, just about every faraway outpost of empire, however insignificant, could be in near simultaneous communication with Whitehall in London, the rue de Brederode in Brussels, the Reichskolonialamt in Berlin or the Quai d'Orsay in Paris. The creation of the telegraph network in the mid-nineteenth century was a huge industrial undertaking. It required the manufacture and installation of hundreds of thousands of miles of cable, much of it laid across deep ocean beds. These networks of cables would become the indispensable electrical sinews of far-flung empires. One revolution spurred another, for every inch of these submarine cables had to be insulated to protect the stream of electrical pulses from the continuous ravages of the ocean floor. The solution was found in a natural plastic that is almost forgotten today.

Gutta-percha is a gum extracted from the rainforests of Southeast Asia. In fact, the source of this vital substance, the tree Malays call the *taban*, grew only within a region comprising Malaya and Sarawak, Dutch Java, Sumatra, and Borneo, Cambodia, the Mekong delta in French Indochina and the southern Philippines. The gum is in technical terms a 'stereoisomer' of rubber and shares a similar chemical composition. European travellers had known about gutta-percha for some time, but as one commentator put it 'only its defects were seen'. It resembled rubber but lacked elasticity and bounce. Malays fashioned gutta-percha into canes, whip handles and knives, but for Europeans it was a curiosity. In 1835, William Montgomerie, a Scottish physician, was appointed head of the medical department in Singapore. Earlier in his career, the newly qualified surgeon had attended both Raffles and William Farquhar, who was stabbed by a would-be assassin in 1823. He established the first 'lunatic' asylum in Singapore. As well as attending to the medical needs of Singapore's administrators, Montgomerie was an enthusiastic farmer and owned a large estate on Duxton Hill. It was here that he learned of the remarkable qualities of gutta-percha from a Malay gardener who worked on his estate and used the gum to make hard-wearing handles for *parang*, large slashing knives. The anonymous Malay craftsman showed Montgomerie how gutta-percha hardens on exposure to air, but could be moulded to a new shape after boiling in water. As it cooled, gutta-percha hardened. Montgomerie was so impressed by the malleability and resilience of gutta-percha that he sent samples to the Medical Board in Calcutta and recommended using gutta-percha to make surgical appliances.

In a few years, gutta-percha was near ubiquitous. If the twentieth century was the plastic age, the nineteenth was the era of gutta-percha. The Malay gardener's tip launched a global industry that generated insatiable demand for a raw material that was used much as we use plastics and synthetics today – in the manufacture of furniture, boats, boots and shoes, surgical appliances and dental fillings. Gutta-percha was a vital raw material for hatters and fuse makers, and because it was water and acid resistant, it was in demand in laboratories and photographic studios.

The most remarkable and far-reaching quality of gutta-percha was first discovered in Germany. In 1847, the engineer and industrialist Werner von Siemens began developing a telegraph network running parallel to his new railway system. To insulate the cable, Siemens experimented with gutta-percha coated with a special dye. The success of Siemens' innovation impressed competitive British engineers who set about creating a network of telegraphic cables both above and underground. It was swiftly realised that gutta-percha was ideal for cables laid underwater and in the early 1850s, British and French engineers laid submarine cables across the Channel. Then in 1857, the Indian rebellion, known then as the Indian Mutiny, provoked an empire-wide panic and urgent demands to expand the telegraphic network and forge links with London. Communications were instruments of warning and control. By 1865, messages could be sent by gutta-percha insulated cables from Karachi to London.

By the end of the century, the world was interconnected by cable. In 1907, the cable network had grown to some 200,000 nautical miles laid at a cost of between £150 and £200 a mile. Altogether, the cost of connecting the imperial world with gutta-percha insulated cabling cost between £97.5 and £130 million – equivalent to between £7 billion and £9.5 billion in today's values. The first internet, as the cable network has been called, was funded initially by private companies. Governments with costly colonial territories such as Britain and France heavily subsidised the construction of these gutta-percha clad tentacles of progress and pushed for its expansion. Imperialists realised that if London, Paris or Brussels were the brains of empire, the telegraph cables were its nervous system that sent a continuous stream of vital messages from the furthest corners of the imperial domain. Had Dr Montgomerie not met that Malay gardener on Duxton Hill, the global network of submarine cables might not have revolutionised the world of high imperialism.

Why then is gutta-percha forgotten? One reason is that wireless supplanted the telegraph and the invention of synthetic plastics made gutta-percha obsolete. There was a much darker and more powerful force driving its decline and fall. The gluttonous Western demand for gutta-percha led to an environmental catastrophe.

It is remarkable that high-tech nineteenth-century industries such as cable manufacture was entirely dependent on a low-tech extractive industry in the forests of Southeast Asia. To satisfy Western demand, groups of Chinese, Dyak or Malay woodsmen trekked deep into forests, armed with *parangs*, to find groves of *Isonandra* trees, often reaching sixty feet into the forest canopy, which they would fell. The woodsmen would cut incisions into the soft wood of the trees to extract and drain the latex within into bamboo or coconut bowls. It was an inefficient process and the yield from each *Isonandra* tree was quite small – and a lot was wasted. The relentless demand for gutta-percha from industries that knew little about its origins and how it was extracted led inexorably to an ever more ruthless felling of an ever rarer resource. By 1890, the cable industry was consuming four million pounds of gutta-percha every year. In just two years between 1845 and 1847, some 70,000 *Isonandra* trees were hacked down in the rainforests of Singapore. By 1857, the tree had disappeared from Singapore – and had vanished from Malacca, Selangor and Perak by 1884. Five million trees were felled on the island of Borneo. In 1902, an American diplomat reported to the *New York Times* that not a single *Isonandra* tree could be found growing wild in the Dutch Indies. It is not surprising that the extraction of gutta-percha became known as 'slaughter cropping'. Experts warned of the dire consequences, and in 1883 the British authorities of the Straits Settlements banned logging. But it was too late. By the end of the century, the manufacturers of submarine cables began to panic. The world had run out of gutta-percha. It was a Victorian ecological disaster.

The Planters' World

For the British or French or Dutch planter, the rubber estate was a world within a world. 'He hadn't much to talk about but rubber and games, tennis, you know, and golf and shooting.' The novelist Somerset Maugham described a planter he met in Malaya: 'He had the mind of a boy of eighteen. You know how many fellows when they come out east seem to stop growing.' Many of the young Europeans employed on the rubber estates of Southeast Asia started as assistant planters or 'creepers'. They were the backbone of estate operations simply because a colour bar stopped Asian coolies, however bright, rising about the level of clerks.

The 'creepers' were an odd bunch. It was said that the main purpose of Empire was to 'provide outdoor relief for the British upper
classes'. Many planters were social misfits or black sheep exiled by
their families. Others were restless fellows who had fled dreary office
jobs in the City of London. Many were Scots. The Ramsden Company archive is chockfull of reports of assistants sacked because they
drank, or were prone to violence, or were mentally ill or just bone
idle time-wasters. A surprising number of planters ended up desti-
tute on the streets of Singapore, waiting, or begging, for money to
buy a passage home. But for many others, the life of a planter was
a step up. In the world of the plantation, even wet-behind-the-ear
newcomers had, for the first time in their lives, power. These 'Tuan
Besars' and 'Tuan Kechils' – the 'great gentlemen' and 'junior masters'
– who strutted about in stained khakis, tropical whites and pith hel-
mets (solar topis), periodically lunging at coiled snakes with a stick,
were the petty lords of all they surveyed. A good number were brazen
racists who fervently believed in the natural inferiority of coolies.

Many of the French planters in Indochina were veterans of the
Foreign Legion, and some were distinctly unsavoury types. The
British recruited their planters from the 'great' public schools like
Eton and Rugby, or 'lesser' public schools and elite state grammar
schools (many of the Scots had been educated at Fettes School near
Edinburgh). A handful became decent linguists, learning the rudi-
ments of Tamil, Malay, Javanese and the Chinese dialects, often with
the assistance of Asian 'wives' known as 'sleeping dictionaries'. The
working day was tough, and most of the Tuans endured recurrent
bouts of debilitating malaria. After a day on the estate, checking and
rechecking the work of the tappers, they fled to their bungalows to
sip whiskey *stengahs* and bitter English beer. Who can blame them?
The Dutch, too, were 'tremendous soaks', who could, as one memoir
admitted, 'put away an incredible amount of beer at an incredible
pace'. 'Beer, Boy!' was the distinctive cry of the planting species.

For the pale-skinned Englishman, a working life in the tropics
was, as Noel Coward wittily sang, beastly. It was often lonely. Ian
Matheson described living in a leaking bungalow with no running
water or electricity and a 'thunder box which needs no description'.
Leopold Ainsworth, who was sent to an estate near Penang, could not

forget the 'miserable dreary light' of the single oil lamp in his quarters, and a malodorous mildew-ridden mattress and rotting 'Dutch Widow' pillow. The monsoon delivered a 'solid, streaming, crashing wall of water' through the roof. Matheson's employer was a cantankerous Scot who relished whipping his servants. Supper was a 'disgusting meal' of tinned soup with ants floating on its greasy surface, accompanied by coffee strained through an old sock. Every morning Matheson was woken by a barrage of hammering on his bedroom door: 'Get up you lazy bastard!' In the harsh world of the planters, strong drink was a refuge. Not a few sodden, prematurely aged and alcohol-pickled Tuans lost their wits and ended up in the Singapore Lunatic Asylum before being shipped back home, if they were lucky.

The planter elite was a predominantly male enclave. The rubber companies discouraged marriage and 'creepers' were forbidden to tie the knot until the fourth year of their contracts. Lonely, and far from hearth and home, many young Tuans found relief and solace in Malay 'kip shops', or in the arms of concubines known as 'keeps' (short for 'housekeeper') in Malaya. A few planters treated their Asian mistresses with respect, fathered families and sent their children to school. A tiny minority of European planters married their 'keeps', but the hypocritical Victorian values of the colonial elite that informed the poisonous gossip of the Club and English tea party disdained the Eurasian children of these unions. Most 'keeps' were sent packing with their light-skinned children when a respectable 'Memsahib' finally turned up to share the planters' world.

The Lives of Coolies

The privations of the planter elite were trifling compared to the suffering of the coolie labourers who toiled in their thousands on their estates. Only a tiny minority who came to French Indochina, British Malaya and the Dutch East Indies were native to Southeast Asia, which by the end of the nineteenth century was a great emporium of labour. In ports all over Asia, rickety ships disgorged armies of men who were herded into a 'coolie ghat', where officials logged names (as they heard them), place of origin and date of arrival in a register. Each person was photographed and then held in sweltering sheds before being selected by plantation owners, just as in

the Antebellum American South. The 'ghat' was not much different
from a slave market.

Coolies enriched European plantation owners and transformed
the human landscape of Southeast Asia. By 1911, Malays made up
a mere 7 per cent of the workforce on the rubber plantations in
Malaya. The hunger for coolie labour was insatiable, but since the
prices of rubber and tin fluctuated, often wildly, plantation labour
was disposable. The colonial economy thus acted like a vast bellows sucking them in during times of plenty and spewing them out
when prices dropped.

By 1941, on the eve of the Japanese invasion, 350,000 coolies
worked in the rubber plantations in Malaya – over 220,000 from India and 86,000 from China. British Malaya, the world's largest producer of rubber, sucked in these enormous human reserves and also
acted as a distribution centre, funnelling the great coolie streams
to Java and Sumatra. The coolie supply business was managed by
rapacious Asian middlemen known as 'crimps', who sold Chinese
labourers, or 'kongsi men', to plantation owners at Straits $10 a
head. Like the European slavers, these labour contractors held new
recruits in 'pig stations' in the ports of southern China until sufficient numbers had been recruited to make up a cargo for shipment
south. This was, strictly speaking, a system of indentured labour,
for the 'kongsi men' owed money to the 'crimps' for transportation
costs and sundry expenses. These debts could take years to pay off.
According to British planter Leopold Ainsworth, the kongsis had
joined a labour force that was 'to all intents and purposes comprised
of slaves'. The colonial authorities made some efforts to reform these
practices but with only limited success. They were creating a new
working class, a plantation proletariat that from early on showed
signs of resisting their new masters. This was why the British came
to prefer the supposedly more tractable Indian coolies from the Madras region, the Tamil districts and the Coromandel Coast to the
better organised but often defiant and frequently rebellious Chinese.
A governor of the Straits Settlements, Sir Frederick Weld, believed
that the 'peccable and easily governed' Indians would be a counter-
poise to the Chinese.

The coolie found himself in a foreign country surrounded by
wild animals and malicious insects. The drab and dusty *Hevea* 'lines'

stretched monotonously to the distant horizon. It was a world of dirt, poor hygiene, foul food and disease. Malaria and dengue fever were endemic as were tropical ulcers, anaemia and beri-beri, and the plantations were periodically ravaged by water-transmitted diseases like dysentery and cholera. Harder to quantify was the psychological toll of depression and other mental illnesses that blighted the coolie's world. In 1919, a Dutch writer wrote about conditions in the rubber district of Asahan in Sumatra: 'At the point of destination [for the labourers], there was no accommodation whatsoever. Mud and dirt were their mattress. Many were starving because they had sold their rice rations to some sly Malay.... There were no permanent houses.' Mortality was high, reaching as much as 30 per cent because of the appallingly poor washing facilities.

Many coolies suffered injuries from falling trees or were bitten by poisonous snakes and insects. Sharp slivers of bamboo that lay strewn on paths and tracks lacerated feet. Wounds turned septic very quickly. Festering bamboo injuries must have been common, for the Dutch came to call all their plantation workers 'stinkers'. Conditions were not much better on the 'coolie lines' in Malaya. In 1890, as the rubber boom was just taking off, Dr S. Patrao, the acting civil surgeon in Negapatam in India, complained about the 'deplorable' death rate on rubber plantations in Malaya. He blamed the 'unhealthy conditions of most of the estates, and the climatic influence, overwork.' A British manager complained about 'weaklings from India ... who build up our hospital bill', but the Ramsden Company archives show that the Indian doctor was not exaggerating. Conditions on the British estates could be just as lethal as those on the notorious Dutch plantations, and in some cases the mortality rate was higher than 30 per cent.

Asian plantations were a realm of violence. Leopold Ainsworth witnessed numerous cruel punishments, and came to enjoy administering retribution himself as 'a new and rather amusing form of sport'. On one occasion, he witnessed a manager 'quivering with rage' while confronting a group of coolies who had refused to continue working because their pay day had been postponed. As the estate 'creepers' brandished Schneider rifles, he 'beat the stuffing out of them'. The colonial administration did not turn a blind eye to the arbitrary violence that festered on Malayan estates. Tuans who assaulted workers could be fined, sacked and arrested. But they had to step a long way over the line. On a Malayan estate in 1910, a creeper called R. C. Gray beat two Javanese women to within an inch of their lives, and the police were forced to step in. His boss, general manager William Duncan, refused to sack Gray because he 'got on so well with the natives', so he was fined and quietly packed off to another estate.

Like the slaves of the American plantations, the coolies resisted through the cultural weapons of religion and song. One folksong lamented the life of the bonded labourer with these eloquent words:

I hoe all day and cannot sleep at night
Today my whole body aches, Damnation to you arkatis. [recruit-
ers]
I have toiled day and night
from the moment I entered your house.
The skin of my body has dried
And happiness has become but a dream.

In the 1950s, the plantations would be one of the main battle-fields of the Malayan Emergency. The seeds of revolution had been sowed like the mythical dragon's teeth by the cruelties of the coolie diaspora.

The Fragile Empires

Rubber and other raw materials enriched the European empires. In August 1914, those empires went to war, tearing apart an intricate skein of alliances. The bloodiest battles were fought in Northern Europe and on the frontiers of the Russian Empire. But in the domains of the European empires, millions of young Asian and African men were called up to fight and die for the imperial powers. The war exposed the brutish cruelty of the European empires – and their underlying weakness. Across Asia, politically conscious young men and women began to question how long the old empires could last – and how they might be hurried to their demise. In China, a nationalist movement led by Sun Yat-Sen had vanquished the last imperial dynasty. For many Asians, the question was – when would the European empires suffer the same fate? As French, British and German armies dug into muddy trenches to fight a faraway war of attrition, on the streets of Singapore the chatter was all about world politics. Genteel strollers in the People's Park were astonished to encounter huge, animated crowds of Chinese who had gathered to hear the latest impassioned speech about people and events in China. It may surprise Singaporeans today to know that under British rule a century ago, the city ran fiercely conducted arguments on the pages of multilingual newspapers, and on street corners and in coffee shops. The future was up for grabs and everyone it seemed had an opinion. The great Asian port cities of Shanghai, Bombay, Hong Kong and Singapore were choke points of human activity. The global networks of Western powers collided with the energies of highly mobile Asians and a lot went on behind the backs of colonial administrators. Singapore was a funnel and echo chamber. After 1870, millions travelled into and out of the port city from China and India. By the first decade of the twentieth century, Singapore was a beacon of modernity that outshone London, Paris or Berlin. Its glittering surface disguised another world of darkness, danger and crushing poverty. In this anti-city of lodging houses, dormitories, food stalls and kopitiams (coffee shops), locals rubbed shoulders with 'new men' who had just arrived on a steamer from India or China. This was a realm of turbulence and conflict. Coroners' reports expose a catalogue of everyday death and injury, where many died without known names or kin and a young man could stagger into Telok Ayer police station with his throat cut, incapable of uttering his name. This was a world blighted by recurrent bouts of malaria, dysentery, tuberculosis, suicide and exhaustion. But it was a world where people could learn to read in coffee shops, and where the shared dialects of Hindustani, of *pasar Melayu* (bazaar Malay) and Cantonese were the vociferous medium of new identities and hopes, or despair and destitution.

The European community was just as diverse. It would be a mistake to see Singapore and the other Straits Settlements as distinctly British. In 1911, of the 5,711 Europeans resident in Singapore, 209 were Dutch, 181 German and 128 French. There were also many Russians, Austrians, Italians and Americans. The Teutonia Club had been founded by an enterprising German in 1856 and was en-

vied by the British establishment. Many Chinese merchants preferred dealing with Germans as they gave longer credit terms and,
it was said, dealt with Asians 'men to men'. In Malaya, there was
a German community of traders, doctors, journalists, bandlead-
ers and missionaries. In the Straits, 'British' identity was claimed
by Peranakan Chinese and Arab merchants as well as Indian and
Eurasian civil servants. No one was a 'Singaporean' or 'Malayan'.
Identity was volatile.

The slaughter on the battlefields of France and Belgium shattered
the rough-and-ready harmony of the Straits Settlements. World War
I tore apart the European communities as the new Alien Enemies
(Winding Up) Ordinance of December 1914 sanctioned official
raids on German-owned businesses. Even Britons suspected of pro-
German sympathies were hounded out of jobs. Employees who were
'noticeably' Eurasian often suffered the same fate. In wartime, any
kind of difference in accent or skin tone provoked fear and loathing. The racial barriers of British Singapore deepened and ossified.

Mutiny!

Then, on 15 February 1915, the Chinese New Year holiday, the
shooting war erupted on the streets of Singapore. At around 3 p.m.,
the Indian 5th Light Infantry mutinied at Alexandra Barracks. Soldiers, all Muslims, broke open the magazine, cut the military phone
lines and headed out of the barracks towards Chinatown. On the
way, they shot and killed any Britons they encountered. The Singapore Mutiny had begun. When it was all over, the *New York Times*
described the events of 1915 as the greatest threat to British power
in Asia since the Indian Mutiny of 1857. For a week, terror stalked
the streets of Singapore. The mutiny naturally led to an official enquiry. The records of the enquiry offer a day-by-day account of what
happened and why. The story begins on board a German cruiser in
the Indian Ocean.

For several months, the German light cruiser SMS *Emden*, commanded by Lieutenant Commander Karl von Müller, wreaked havoc
in the Indian Ocean. It preyed on Allied shipping and attacked the
coaling stations and 'all red' telegraph routes that were the vital sinews connecting British Asian and Pacific colonies. In September,

Müller raided Madras and blew up oil tanks of the British Burmah Oil Company. The *Emden* then steamed southeast across the Bay of Bengal, threatening the British penal colony on the Andaman Islands, and at the end of October the German raider approached Penang flying Japanese flags and displaying a dummy funnel. Here, Müller and his crew torpedoed a Russian cruiser and bombarded a French destroyer, then slipped away.

The *Emden* stalked the Strait of Malacca like a malevolent phantom, terrifying the British and their Japanese allies. If a single German cruiser could disrupt imperial shipping and communications in imperial waters, what might an entire German fleet achieve? In the Straits Settlements, from Penang to Singapore, the British began interning all German and Austrian nationals.

The *Emden*'s maritime reign of terror was at last ended in early November. The Australian light cruiser HMAS *Sydney* cornered the German raider close to the Cocos (Keeling) Islands where Müller had attacked the wireless station. The heavily armed *Sydney* pounded the *Emden*, causing catastrophic damage and forcing Müller to beach his ship. Hundreds of his crew were killed. A few survivors escaped to Sumatra. The others were captured, taken on board the *Sydney* and transported to Singapore. For the *Emden*'s boisterous navigator, Julius Lauterbach, a braggart and lover of strong liquor, the war was far from over as the British rulers of Singapore were soon to discover. The British had always boasted that Singapore was a fortress, but the truth was that the island was only lightly defended. By February 1915, most troops had been withdrawn to serve on the Western Front and the 5th Light Infantry was the mainstay of the Singapore garrison. It was known as the 'Loyal Fifth'. So, Singapore was hardly prepared for a shooting war.

In the early years of the war, it was by no means certain which of the great European powers would prevail. On 14 November 1914, the Ottoman Caliph allied with Germany, and in Istanbul the Sheik-ul-Islam proclaimed a Jihad against the Allied powers. For the European rulers of Asian colonies, this was profoundly troubling. Muslim elites in North Africa and Asia were often the bedrock of indirect rule and Muslims were the backbone of many colonial armies. The echoes of the Ottoman Jihad reverberated across India and Southeast Asia and the mood among the soldiers of the 'Loyal

Fifth' was febrile.

Trouble had been simmering for weeks. Letters intercepted by the British censor should have set off louder alarms: one soldier wrote that 'Germany had become Mohammedan.' There was a rumour that the daughter of 'Haji Mohammed William Kaiser', as the German emperor was called in Muslim countries, had married a Turkish prince. Kassim bin Ismail Mansoor, a local Gujerati merchant and rubber plantation owner, had taken to visiting the Alexander Road barracks where he was mobbed by sepoys who exhibited, in the words of an English officer, 'an undue amount of praying'. Mansoor invited some of the Indian sepoys to spend time on his plantation in Pasir Panjang.

The British knew that both Mansoor and Shah had connections to the Ghadar movement. This was a revolutionary anti-imperialist association that had been founded in San Francisco in 1913 and which published a journal, *Ghadar,* meaning 'mutiny'. Published in Gurumukhi, Urdu, Hindi and English, *Ghadar* had a global readership. Its message was simple and direct: 'A new epoch in the history of India opens today, the 1st November, 1913, because today there begins in foreign lands but in our country's language a war against the English Raj … what is our name? Mutiny. What is our work? Mutiny. Where will the mutiny break out? In India. When? In a few years. Why? Because the people can no longer bear the oppression and tyranny practised under British rule and are ready to fight and die for freedom.' Copies of *Ghadar* were sent on mail steamers across the Pacific Ocean to Manila, the treaty ports of China and then despatched through the ports of Singapore and Penang to India. Har Dayal, the founder of the Ghadar movement, urged his followers to act. And his message was heard loud and clear at the barracks in Alexandra Road.

The British authorities feared insurrection but they showed gross inattention when it came to the 'Loyal Fifth', and this brings us back to those German POWs incarcerated at Tanglin camp. They were guarded to begin with by Malay States Guides. The officers and men of the *Emden* were hostile prisoners who seized the chance to incite discontent among the Guides, with so much success that in December the army authorities complained to the governor-general that the Malays had been 'tampered with' by the German prisoners and insisted that only 'white' soldiers should be assigned to guard duties at Tanglin. But soldiers of the right colour were in short supply and so the 5th Regiment were assigned to take over from the Guides for guard duty. The German POWs were only too happy to laud the Kaiser and celebrate his victories: 'Lauterbach said Belgium is taken, France is taken.... The Germans will invade England.' The Germans spoke favourably of the Islamic faith and pretended to say prayers in the Muslim fashion at sunset and recite the Koran. A number of Sepoys were, it was said, 'thick with the Germans.'

The German POWs can hardly be blamed for sowing dissent among the British sepoys. The British officers of the 5th Regiment deserve less sympathy. The commanding officer of the 5th, Lieutenant-Colonel Edward Martin, was widely disliked by his fellow British officers and the Indian sepoys. He was, the Court of Inquiry concluded, a 'hopeless C.O.' The court noted that a symptom of Martin's poor leadership was his tolerance of poisonous squabbling among Indian officers over promotions.

In early February, Martin informed the Indian soldiers that they would be transferred to Hong Kong. No other information was offered and soon a rumour spread through the barracks that the 5th would be sent into battle against fellow Muslims. The soldiers were frightened and angry. On the morning of 15 February, Martin ordered the regiment to assemble for a final inspection. They would be addressed by the commanding officer in Singapore, Major-General Dudley Ridout. In the Alexandra Road Barracks, the mood among the sepoys was tense. Now, Major General Ridout threw petrol on the blaze. He told the sepoys that it was 'not their good fortune to go to Europe.' No, it was their duty to go *anywhere where they are ordered.* The Empire, he proclaimed, is vast, and the duty of guarding it great! There was no mention of Hong Kong. Lieutenant-Colonel Martin translated Ridout's remarks into Hindustani for the Indian officers, NCOs and rank-and-file sepoys who all leapt to a single, frightening conclusion. Khan and others had been right. Hong Kong was a lie. By the time Martin finished translating RIdout's speech, the 'Loyal 5th' was ablaze.

Martin and the other British officers seemed indifferent to the dangerous mood of the sepoys and many rushed off to splash around on local beaches or play a round of golf. They returned to the barracks around teatime. Soon afterwards, shots were heard; the sentry, it seemed, had 'run amok'. Shouting 'Ali! Ali!' the sepoys smashed open the ammunition store with pickaxes and cut telephone lines and broke out of the camp. One party headed towards Chinatown, shooting any British persons they ran into. Another party of sepoys rushed to a nearby gun battery manned by Malay States Guides. Here they killed a British officer and tried, without success, to persuade the Malays to join the uprising.

The rebel soldiers next broke into the POW camp at Tanglin. They shot the British and Malay guards and dragged the German prisoners out of their cells. They all shook their hands and shouted 'Islam! Islam!' By now, rumours had begun spreading that the city of Kuala Lumpur was aflame and all English people in the town had been killed. Lauterbach and about seventeen other prisoners made their escape.

In Singapore, the fighting was far from over. Over the next several days, the mutineers shot dead forty-seven soldiers and civilians, including a few unfortunate Chinese and Malays who got in the way. Government officials ordered English women and children to assemble in an enclave close to the Raffles Hotel for transfer to British-owned ships in the harbour. In an ugly foreshadowing of the catastrophe of 1942, the English women barred any Eurasian family or local women boarding. As it turned out, the refugees were forced to stay at sea for two weeks with no washing or bathing facilities.

They were at least alive. Since the 'Loyal 5th' was the first line of defence, the British were forced to call on a ragtag militia to defend 'Fortress Singapore'. Parsons and church officials, beachcombers and bankers rallied in the hour of need, many still togged up for the golf course or tennis court. It was Singapore's foreign community that put up the staunchest defence. The Japanese Consul met with Governor-General Young to seek permission to raise a volunteer force from among Japanese nationals resident in Singapore and from crews of Japanese ships in the harbour. Remember that Japan was a British ally in World War I. The Japanese were joined by a few hundred seamen from the French cruiser *Montcalm* and a Russian ship. The Sultan Ibrahim Abu Bakar of Johor sent some of his private militia to cut off the mutineers who were trying to flee across the Causeway. It was this ad hoc international brigade that eventually crushed the mutiny. Soon, nearly 700 rebels were in custody, though many others fled, some getting as far as Siam. When, a few days later, the inevitable victory parade took place on the Padang, pride of place was offered to the Japanese volunteers. A Japanese journalist reported that the flag of the Rising Sun was fluttering over Singapore for the first time.

Fortress Singapore was saved, but British confidence was shaken and retribution was swift and savage. No one in Government House doubted that the rebel Indian sepoys had humiliated them in the eyes of the world. National dishonour demanded the harshest punishment. The alleged ringleaders were executed on the afternoon of 21 April in front of a large crowd that gathered outside the gates of the prison in Outram Road. A British eyewitness reported: 'The condemned men Subedar Dunde Khan and Jamadar Chisti Khan dressed in plain native clothes in step with the escort marched erect and steadily to the execution posts, to which they were tied by the ankles. Facing the firing party at eight paces their bearing never faltered. The condemned men stood rigidly to attention. They were not blindfolded. Whatever their crimes, their calm and dignity at the end was impressive.'

Aftermaths

In March, a gathering of some 3,000 Muslims affirmed loyalty to the British King and Empire: 'The King is considered the shadow of the Most High...', proclaimed an Imam. In private, officials admitted it had been a close run thing. The official report into the causes of the Singapore Mutiny was never made public. It both exposed the vulnerability of the British in Singapore and upset the delicate balance of communal harmony. Many young Chinese sympathised with the Indian rebels and were dismayed by the prominent role played by the Japanese volunteers: just weeks before the mutiny, the Japanese government published its 'Twenty One Demands' for special privileges in China. On 25 May, the beleaguered Chinese president Yuan Shikai signed a series of humiliating Sino-Japanese agreements that conceded Japan's claims to railway construction and mining claims in Shandong and Manchuria and access to ports and islands on the Chinese coast. Fear and hatred of Japan swelled in China and the diaspora communities of the Nanyang. For Singapore's Chinese communities, the sight of the imperial Japanese flag was a shock. For the Japanese government in Tokyo, the question would soon become whether to continue cooperating with the Western powers or to support anti-colonial nationalists. In 1915, the Japanese chose to back the British rulers of Singapore and help crush the sepoy mutiny. Two decades later, Singapore and the Malay States would face an even greater test and a mighty new Asian enemy dedicated to 'Asia for Asians'.

CHAPTER 15

The Fortress: Defending Singapore between the Wars

I n the aftermath of the Singapore Mutiny, the British rulers of the Straits Settlements and the Malay States reluctantly admitted that the violent events of February 1915 had caught them napping. Violence had exploded in their midst like a tropical storm. There, they concluded, was an intelligence black hole that threatened to make one of the pivotal bastions of the British Empire vulnerable. Something had to be done. Singapore would become a surveillance state; the watchword would be vigilance.

Establishing the Special Branch

It would be a gruff, puritanical young Scot who rectified this hopeless state of affairs. Born and educated in granite Aberdeen, David Petrie joined the Indian Police and Criminal Intelligence Department after leaving university in 1900. He was tough, stern and cunning. In November 1918, Petrie was dispatched to Singapore to begin a root-and-branch reform of intelligence operations. His most far-reaching proposal was to create a dedicated intelligence department that could devote all its resources to ferreting out enemies of the colonial state. The new Criminal Intelligence Department (later renamed the Special Branch) began work in 1918. Its director was René Henry de Solminihac Onraet, a former police officer and an alumnus of Stonyhurst College in Lancashire. At Stonyhurst, the young Onraet was taught by Jesuits who drummed into his young mind the moral virtues of hard work and convinced him of the power of sect-like organisations. When Onraet was appointed to lead the new Special Branch in Singapore, he was very clear that his mission was to defend the Straits Settlements from the deadly infection of Communism. And he had no doubts that this deadly virus had its origins in China.

Onraet had first made his mark in Penang, where he had successfully taken on a Chinese gambling syndicate. His success in Penang distorted his view of the 'enemy': he became obsessed with Chinese criminals and subversives. It is true that the Japanese '21 Demands' radicalised many Chinese in the Nanyang, the 'southern ocean', who feared the rise of an Asian rival. In Singapore, the first truly mass political movement was spearheaded by Chinese rickshaw pullers who, in 1919–20, led a mass boycott of Japanese goods to protest Japan's refusal to hand over Shandong Province. But this emerging Asian underworld was transnational. As Indian nationalists challenged the British Raj, Vietnamese radicals based in Siam set out to overthrow the French in Indochina. Behind the backs of its British administrators, anti-colonial radicals often passed through Singapore or spent time in the city. Singapore was one of the most globalised cities on earth. The wealth of its many minorities – Chinese, Arab, Armenian and Jewish – rivalled and sometimes eclipsed the fortunes of its European residents. And it was not only huge volumes of capital that flowed through its banks. This free port was also a market place of ideas. Here, as the Indonesian radical Tan Malaka put it, 'ideas were leaping about, hiding, turning, left and right, and breaking through like damned up water.'

The Chinese Enemy

By the early 1920s, the European empires in Southeast Asia were under threat from many different directions and could not be defended from every side. The threat posed by Japanese aggression did not go unnoticed, but after the Russian Revolution in 1917 and the founding of the Chinese Communist Party (CPP) in 1921, the 'red peril' seemed the biggest menace to colonial rule in Southeast Asia. Certainly, generations of Chinese migrants and their descendants formed the most numerous and vocal of the Asian communities in

Singapore, and young Chinese radicals spoke out loudly against Western imperialism. In 1919, Chinese students led protests in Beijing against the decision by the Allied powers at the Paris Peace Conference to cede Chinese territory to Japan, and the 'May Fourth Movement' soon spilled across the Nanyang. Chinese activists in Singapore led demonstrations that sometimes ended in violence and the looting of Japanese businesses. The British responded by clamping down on Chinese schools and colleges where, it was believed, emotions ran highest, and, it was feared, quite rightly, that teachers preached subversion. The Chinese passion for education, which found expression in night classes and labour organisations as well as schools and colleges, meant that new ideas found a receptive audience.

Special Branch reports show that Onraet and his agents were fixated on migrants from Hainan Island, known as Hailams, who often seemed to take prominent roles in Singapore's radical netherworld. Onraet knew that the CCP had won many converts on Hainan Island, which, as one agent put it, had 'gone red'. In the Straits Settlements, the Hainanese were latecomers in the great waves of Chinese migrations and tended to find work as coolies on plantations or as domestic servants. The more established Chinese in Singapore looked down on Hailams who were welcomed in Singapore's flourishing political underground. To counter the communist threat, Onraet appointed Alex Dixon as Singapore's first immigration officer to ferret out any suspicious Chinese immigrants. Dixon's methods were oddly intimate. As new arrivals lined up to be checked by a quarantine doctor, Dixon roamed the arrival hall grabbing hands. He described his method as follows: 'Nine out ten of the hands I touched were hard and calloused. The tenth – a coolie with the soft hands of a cook – were invariably detained for further examination.' Why? Dixon was on the lookout for 'wandering intellectuals' who had evidently not performed hard manual labour. He also reported that 'Hailams' tended to be 'foppishly dressed' and had a liking for 'gents' boaters' – which he seemed to imagine was the tell-tale garb of the subversive radical

The Bob Haired Woman

Newspapers in Singapore and Malaya fed the public fascination with stories of dangerous young radicals at loose in the cities of the Straits and Malaya. Take, for example, the story of the 'Bob Haired Woman'. The story begins at the end of January 1926, on the eve of the New Year of the Ox. A young Chinese woman walked unnoticed through Market Square in Kuala Lumpur and turned left into the High Street. It was late morning, and the banks and businesses of Market Square were bustling despite a fall in the price of rubber. She was elegantly dressed in a white jacket, with matching white shoes, and a black skirt, and strode through the densely packed crowds hatless, revealing a severely modern hairstyle. She tightly clutched a briefcase. She was a striking sight in colonial Kuala Lumpur. Most European women dressed in long skirts and veils and usually avoided the downtown area that was dominated by Asian prostitutes and their very aggressive pimps. The protector of Chinese, Daniel Richards, who had an office in Kuala Lumpur, knew of at least forty Chinese or Japanese brothels and sometimes sent young women to find refuge in the 'Federal Home for Women and Girls'.

Richards' office was halfway along High Street, opposite the police station. The young woman briefly halted, then entered the office where Richards and his assistant Wilfred Blythe were working. Blythe recalled that the mysterious woman announced loudly in Cantonese, 'There is someone threatening me!' then placed the briefcase on the table. Someone, she said, had asked her to give it to Richards. Moments later, there was a loud explosion that ripped through the office and scattered papers across High Street. The young woman had thrown herself beneath one of the tables. Now she staggered into the street bleeding profusely and collapsed. Both she and Richards were rushed unconscious to the European hospital. Both recovered, although Richards lost the use of his left hand.

Two months later, on 23 March, the 'Bob Haired Woman' appeared before the Kuala Lumpur Assizes. Her name was Wong Sang. Standing before the judge, this notorious 'modern woman' carried her right arm in a sling and showed 'unnatural calm'. She smiled, it was reported, 'eternally'. The proceedings were in English, hastily translated into Cantonese for the accused. Wong Sang refused to plead but admitted she had brought the bomb to the protectorate office. The public prosecutor informed the judge that she had 'some political reasons' for her action and 'some weird notions about the brotherhood of man.' She had made, he claimed, 'wild, anarchical statements'. In the end, Wong Sang was sentenced to ten years 'rigorous imprisonment'. There was public outrage that this dangerous female had received such a lenient sentence. In short, why hadn't she been hanged?

In prison, the 'Bob Haired Woman' spilled the beans. Cantonese speakers will have realised that her name was not really Wong Sang, which means 'Life's Victim'. Her real name was Wong Sau Ying. When she walked into the protectorate office in Kuala Lumpur, she was just twenty-six. She had been born in Beijing and had spent some time in Shanghai. In prison, Wong revealed she had been after much bigger game. Her target had been Laurence Guillemard, the British governor of the Straits Settlements and high commissioner of the Malay States. She had acquired the bomb materials from China and an electric battery for the primitive detonator in Singapore. In a somewhat comic chain of events, Wong had pursued Guillemard for some time. When the governor visited Penang, she had waited for him on a golf course, but at the wrong tee. She then followed him onto a train to Kuala Lumpur but was foiled when he got off early at Kuala Kangsar for a meeting with the sultan of Perak. So it was that on 23 January, she had come to High Street in Kuala Lumpur in search of lesser prey. Poor Daniel Richards!

The 'Bob Haired Woman' was a rich source of fascination and terror. A modern young woman with ideas about the 'Brotherhood of Man'. Two years later, all hell broke loose in Kreta Ayer in Singapore.

The Kreta Ayer Incident

Prior to World War II, the spider's web of streets and alleyways around Tanjong Pagar station had a notorious reputation. This was the beating heart of Chinatown. The shophouses lining Smith Street, Sago Street and Spring Street were crammed with brothels, gambling houses and opium dens, all jam-packed with clients. The local police station was well known to be the busiest in Singapore.

In early March, a number of Chinese organisations applied for permission to celebrate the second anniversary of the death of Sun Yat Sen on 12 March. Sun was one of the founders of the Chinese Republic. He had spent many years exiled in Penang and Singapore. The British granted the requests, but almost immediately regretted the decision and issued bans on any speeches, parades and 'slogan shouting': only 'quiet and peaceful' observance of the anniversary would be permitted. The plan was to hold a public meeting at the Happy Valley Amusement Park on Anson Road on 12 March. As the date approached, Onraet's agents reported troubling signs of 'agitators' making preparations to cause trouble. The Special Branch was, as ever, most vexed about the Hainanese, and some Hailams had provocatively hung big Kuomintang banners from their windows. The Teochew and Hokkien community leaders, who shared Onraet's fears about the Hainanese, had deviously instructed Hailam leaders to assemble in Happy Valley one and a half hours *after* the time agreed with the police. They had made a grave tactical error.

At noon, some 20,000 Chinese from dialect, clan and workers associations as well as hundreds of schoolchildren gathered in Happy Valley and then marched off past a huge poster of Sun Yat Sen. The humid air was filled with the sounds of thousands of quietly shuffling feet and murmured homage to the Kuomintang founder. As a sign of respect, the British had sent just a handful of policemen. Special Branch agents mingled with the crowds, listening and noting.

A few streets away, Special Branch officer Alec Dixon was sitting on the veranda of his house catching up with paperwork. At precisely 1.30 p.m., he was startled to see 'several long processions of Hailam schoolchildren' making their way towards Happy Valley, boisterously playing drums and trumpets. Dixon noticed 'gawky adolescents' and even 'tots of five or six'. At the head of the children's march he noticed 'grim faced' Chinese teachers gripping Kuomintang flags. In the rear, Dixon recalled, was an incongruous party of laughing Hailam cooks and houseboys.

As they approached Happy Valley, the Hailam leaders were dismayed to discover that the memorial ceremony was already in full swing. As they unhappily joined the huge crowd assembled, a number of speakers began eulogising Sun Yat Sen, ignoring the police ban on speeches. Some of the conservative Hokkien and Teochew speakers warned about the dangers of Communism. In the crowd, some Hailams became increasingly agitated and a few of the teachers who had led the procession leapt up to denounce the other speakers. There were shouts of 'Down with imperialism!' A pulse of anger surged through the crowds.

Dixon tells us what happened next. When he heard loud excited shouting, he took his car and drove to the Kreta Ayer police station. Here he saw 'white coated Chinese', the Hainanese teachers, surging around the entrance. A few Indian constables struggled to hold the crowds at bay. Then Dixon heard shots, and the crowd fell silent. As the demonstrators pulled back, Dixon saw 'torn banners, poles and burst drums' in the road. Five or six Chinese lay prone nearby. Others had taken shelter behind an abandoned rickshaw. A wounded man was crawling across the street. Pools of blood glinted in the hot sun.

The Kreta Ayer incident happened because of successive miscalculations by both British and Chinese community leaders. But it was a gift for Onraet. He seized the moment to demand better pay for his agents and more funding for new equipment and training. He cleverly used the Singapore press to let loose the forces of communal anxieties that focused on the menace of Chinese revolutionaries. In the streets of Chinatown, Onraet launched a campaign of arrests, mainly targeted at the Hainanese community, that Dixon described as an 'orgy of raiding'. Hailams aged from six to sixty were rounded up and interrogated. Special Branch agents closed night schools and broke printing machines.

For many Chinese, the Kreta Ayer killings reinforced distrust of Singapore's colonial masters. Even conservative Chinese leaders denounced the murder of the 'Kreta Ayer Martyrs'. The Chinese community began to see itself as under attack and the old bonds with the British began to fray.

On the Eve of War

The ferment in Chinatown slowly abated, and for the European communities in Singapore life went on much as before. A Japanese journalist, Fuji Tatsuki, who visited Singapore in 1939, described 'white buildings gleaming in the sun' and a city that seemed 'quietly asleep'. Singapore in the 1930s showed, as the port city always had, many contrasting faces. Merchants, traders and bankers did business as they had since the time of Raffles and Farquhar. Talk was of profit and loss, not politics. New arterial roads rippled outwards as the city expanded, but if you followed the Serangoon and Bukit Timah roads into the countryside, those gleaming buildings and villas soon gave way to a world of plantations, impoverished kampongs, swamps and jungle. On the way, you would have passed through 'Little India' and noticed new residences, temples and shophouses that had sprung up in the latticework of streets. But even in vibrant Little India, signs of change coexisted with deep continuities. Here, you could still find the traditional dhobi men taking in laundry and Chettiar moneylenders laying mats outside their shophouses, known as *kittangi*, to wait for customers, or rushing off to pursue the repayment of loans on the steps of government offices in Empress Place.

Few European residents of Singapore took much notice of the storm that was brewing on apparently distant horizons in Tokyo and Berlin. The tectonic plates of world history were in violent motion once again. An aggressive new power was rising in the East.

Japan Takes on the World

Today, China is a superpower, an Asian giant that competes with the United States of America for global influence. Eighty years ago, China was impoverished and at war with another Asian power. The notional rulers of China, the successors of Sun Yat Sen, controlled a shrinking area of central and south-west China fighting the Japanese and a communist army ensconced in a remote region in the northwest. During the terrible Second Sino-Japanese War that had begun in 1931 with the Japanese invasion of Manchuria and had escalated after 1937 into a full-scale conflict, between 15 million and 20 million Chinese died and 90 million fled their homes and villages to become refugees in their own country.

World War II began not in Poland in 1939, but at the Marco Polo Bridge, the Lugouqiao, in July 1937. General Chiang Kai-Shek had contemptuously dismissed the Japanese as 'dwarf bandits'. To begin with, he had compromised with the Japanese Imperial Army so that he could focus on fighting the Chinese communists. Even when some of his own generals forced him to compromise with the CCP in December 1936 and Japan launched a full-scale invasion of China the following year, Chinese resistance was crippled by civil wars.

Few in the United States or the West rated Chiang Kai-Shek's chances. Nor did Western commentators foresee the way Japanese armies would utterly transform Southeast Asia. What is fascinating about the rise of Japan and the emperor's proclamation of a 'Great East Asia Co-prosperity Sphere' is that so much was learnt from the West. The Japanese understood that state-building required empire-building. In 1868, Japan's first prime minister, Ito Hirobumi, the main architect of the Meiji Restoration that restored Imperial rule to Japan, turned to Imperial Germany to learn statecraft and to build from scratch a military and industrial power. Meiji emissaries rushed to Berlin to study how to build battleships and siege guns in order to conquer an empire in the East. The might of new Japan stunned the world when Japanese armies and battleships crushed Imperial Russian forces in the Russo-Japanese war in 1905. Japan was now a world power, and world powers need empires.

Now, at the end of the 1930s, as the Japanese emperor's armies rampaged across the Chinese mainland, his warlords in Tokyo were forced to seek out new ways to oil the wheels of war. They looked covetously at the riches of the rubber plantations of British Malaya and the oilfields of the Dutch East Indies.

CHAPTER 16

The Japanese Conquest of Malaya and Singapore: Light in the South

Prelude

Take a map of the Malay Peninsula and the islands of the Indonesian archipelago. Stretching eastwards is the great archipelago of islands of the Nusantara, the Dutch East Indies, modern Indonesia. Now imagine the thoughts and emotions of a Japanese soldier on the early morning of 8 December 1941 as he struggles, burdened with rifle, life jacket and kit, through heavy surf onto the beach of Kota Bharu, Kelantan, in northern Malaya. Shells from British guns roar overhead, and even if this soldier of the Imperial Japanese Army makes it off the beach, ahead of him stretches more than 300 miles of hard marching and savage fighting along heavily defended jungle roads to reach Johor Bahru and gaze across the Causeway at the mighty fortress of Singapore. And yet Lieutenant General Tomoyuki Yamashita, the commander of the Japanese invaders, had good reason to be confident that his attack would prevail and that Singapore would fall.

The Fortress That Never Was

As Britain confronted the German armies in Europe, the new prime minister, Winston Churchill, took comfort that in the Far East, at the furthest reaches of the empire he loved, Singapore was an impregnable fortress. No Asian army could possibly hope to conquer this island outpost. Singapore and British Malaya would stand firm.

Nothing could be further from the truth. Malaya was, in fact, like a door without hinges – and the Japanese knew it.

In early November 1940, the Blue Funnel Line steamer, the *Automedon*, was steaming for Singapore with a cargo of aircraft parts, alcohol and cigarettes and a consignment of mailbags, locked in the ship's storeroom. For reasons that have never been explained, the planning division of the British War Cabinet in London had decided to use the battered merchant ship to send 'highly confidential' reports to the commander-in-chief of the British Far East Command, Robert Brooke Popham. Prepared by the joint chiefs of staff, one of the reports, 'The Situation in the Far East in the Event of Japanese Intervention Against Us', not only provided detailed information about British defences but bluntly concluded that resistance to a Japanese attack would fail because of Britain's commitment to the war against Germany. On board the *Automedon* was an intelligence goldmine.

Early on the morning of 11 November, the lookout on the German surface raider *Atlantis* spotted the British merchantman some 200 nautical miles north-west of the coast of Sumatra. Surface raiders were converted cargo vessels, bristling with hidden weapons, that targeted enemy shipping. As the *Atlantis* swiftly closed in on the British merchantman, Captain Bernhard Rogge ordered his crew to raise the German ensign and uncover the ship's formidable array of guns. On board the British ship, the master, William Ewan, ordered full steam ahead, but his wheezy old ship stood little chance of escaping. Four salvoes scored direct hits on the bridge. The captain and most of his officers died instantly. Rogge ordered First Lieutenant Ulrich Mohr to board the crippled steamer and carry out a thorough search.

Once on board, Mohr began scavenging the wrecked chart room of the *Automedon*. As he recalled, 'Our prize was just a long narrow envelope enclosed in a green bag equipped with brass eyelets to let water in to facilitate its sinking. The bag was marked "Highly Confidential.... To be destroyed", and contained the latest appreciation of the military strength of the British Empire in the Far East.... What the devil were the British about, sending such material by a slow, old tub like *Automedon*, I puzzled? Surely a warship would have been a worthier repository? We could not understand it.' By early

December, the secret British materials had been sent to Tokyo and were being closely studied. Colonel Masanobo Tsuji, who planned the attack on British Malaya, said of the *Automedon* cache: 'Such a significant weakening of the British Empire could not have been identified from outward appearances.' The Japanese awarded Captain Rogge a ceremonial sword known as a *katana*. They had every reason to be very grateful to the German captain.

The Worst Disaster

British wartime prime minister, Winston Churchill, fought the war as a champion of Empire. Britain fought to defeat the menace of Nazism and to defend its empire. After the Germans had broken through the French defences in May 1940, the prime minister spoke on the radio of 'a solemn hour for the life of our country, of our Empire, of our Allies and, above all, the cause of freedom'. It was remarked once that 'If talking about a chip shop in Salford, Churchill would find a way to mention how important its chips were to the Empire'. But in 1941, as Japan prepared its assault on Southeast Asia, Churchill was much less interested in the possible fate of Singapore than the vexing problem of stubborn American neutrality. Churchill's military assistants, Sir Ian Jacob, admitted that 'Winston has never really understood the Far East problem and had deliberately starved Singapore in favour of home and the Middle East.' The reason for Churchill's neglect is that he knew Britain depended on American backing to win the war against the Axis Powers of Nazi Germany, Italy and Japan. From the moment the war began in September 1939, Churchill ardently wooed American President Franklin Roosevelt. But Roosevelt was hamstrung by powerful Americans who doggedly resisted joining the war. When the two leaders met in Placentia Bay, Newfoundland in August 1941, Churchill bit his tongue when Roosevelt lambasted British imperialism. He made it clear that the price of ending American neutrality would be winding down the British Empire and giving the rights of self-determination to its millions of subject peoples. It was a bitter pill for Churchill to swallow.

In February 1915, Indian Muslims of the 5th Light Infantry mutinied in Singapore. They were influenced by Indian nationalists and contact with German prisoners-of-war held in Tanglin. Fifteen thousand people watched the executions of the ring leaders outside Outram Road Prison. *(Photo: Imperial War Museum)*

The statue of Thomas Raffles, first erected on the Padang, has its own history. Here it is after a move to Empress Place in 1919. When the Japanese occupied Singapore in 1942, they moved the statue inside a museum. It would not be there for long.

Boat Quay on the lower reaches of the Singapore River was the site of the ancient port of Singapura. After the arrival of the British, Chinese traders built warehouses and jetties serviced by an armada of *tangkang*, or 'bumboats', imported from India.

Completed by the Singapore Improvement Trust (SIT) in the 1930s to cope with a housing shortage, Tiong Bahru is the oldest public housing estate in Singapore. Once known as the 'den of beauties' because wealthy men kept their mistresses or 'pipa girls' in apartments there, Tiong Bahru properties are now very costly.

Lee Kuan Yew was born on 16 September 1923 into a prosperous yet unstable family. Life was dominated by his mother, Chua Jim Neo, who was of Peranakan heritage.

Known as 'Harry', Lee was educated at the Raffles Institution and Raffles College where he met his future wife Kwa Geok Choo. Both were precocious students who, after the war, won scholarships to Cambridge University to study law.

On 8 December 1941, the Japanese 25th Army commanded by Lieutenant General Tomoyuki Yamashita landed on the north coast of Malaya. The Japanese 'driving charge' crushed British opposition and by February, Singapore had fallen.

Winston Churchill called the fall of Singapore the 'greatest disaster', the surrender of the largest number of British-led troops in history. In this photograph, General Yamashita can be seen thumping the table insisting that General Arthur Percival agree to unconditional surrender. He did.

Commonly known as Tunku Abdul Rahman ('Tunku' is a Malay royal title), the 'Father of Independence' studied law in Britain like Lee and after the war, rose to power in the United Malay National Organisation (UMNO) which had been founded by Dato' Onn Bin Jaafar.

In 1948, Chin Peng (Ong Boon Hua), chairman of the Malayan Communist Party, launched a guerrilla war against the British in Malaya. The 'Emergency' would dominate Malayan society in the 1950s as the leaders of the UMNO pushed for independence.

David Marshall was imprisoned by the Japanese during the war and led Singapore's struggle for independence in the 1950s. Marshall was Singapore's first Chief Minister and steered the 'London Negotiations' with the British but would later be outmanoeuvred by Lee Kuan Yew. Here Marshall speaks with journalists in New Delhi before meeting with the British in 1955. *(Photo: Mary Evans Picture Library)*

By the mid-1950s, the streets of Singapore were ablaze. Many on the left, especially in the Chinese Middle Schools, demanded independence and social equality. On 26 October 1956, police entered the schools and cleared the students with tear gas but the spirit of rebellion would not be quelled. Rioting lasted seven days and thirteen people were killed.

OPPOSITE: Behind the grand facades of colonial Singapore was a world of poverty and substandard housing. Today the old shop houses of Tanjong Pagar are a picturesque world of hipster cafes and media companies. Before independence, this was a realm of grinding poverty.

On Saturday, 31 August 1957, Malaya became an independent nation. The 'Emergency' was close to an end and UMNO leader Tunku Abdul Rahman pro-claimed Merdeka! ('Freedom!') in a stadium before thousands of Malayan citizens. The British held onto Singapore – it was too valuable a base during the Cold War.

The urban landscape of Singapore is dominated by government-built housing blocks. These blocks first sprang up in the 1960s as the Housing & Development Board (HDB) launched a campaign to resettle Singapore's *kampong* (village) residents into high-rise towers.

The People's Action Party (PAP) has played a major role in the politics of Singapore since its founding in 1954. Successive PAP governments have governed Singapore since independence, winning between 60% and 80% of the vote in elections. In the early 1960s, Lee purged the leftists in the PAP and the party is today socially conservative but economically liberal.

Twice prime minister of Malaysia, Dr Mahathir Mohamad was born in Kedah and became a physician before turning to politics. He would dominate Malaysian politics in the 1990s, winning five consecutive general elections and presiding over a period of rapid industrialisation and growth which transformed Malaysia into a 'Tiger Economy'.

The scion of a notable Malaysian political family, Najib Razak's tenure as prime minister has been controversial. Scandal swirled around his time in office and in 2015, he was implicated in a major corruption scheme linked to the 1Malaysia Development Berhad, the infamous IMDB. In 2020, he stood trial for corruption, was convicted and sentenced to 12 years in prison.

As prime minister, Lee Kuan Yew governed Singapore for twenty-five years. He astutely seized the commercial opportunities of the Cold War to stoke Singapore's developing economy and deftly balanced the interests of Singapore against the United States and the rising power of communist China. Lee Kuan Yew stepped down in 2011 and died in 2015, aged 91.

Singapore appears to be the quintessential 21st century city and yet it has a rich 700-year history that links it to a medieval past as a trading port.

Marina Bay Sands and Gardens by the Bay are two contrasting representations of Singapore's past, present and future. These showcase structures represent Singapore's commercial success and its commitment to a green future – with more than a nod to the botanical treasures of its history. *(Photo: Sean Pavone, Shutterstock)*

Singapore first gained independence as a member of the Federation of Malaysia in 1963. Twenty-three months later, the Tunku expelled Singapore, forcing Lee's government to go it alone. The trauma of separation was a prelude to spectacular growth that has made Singapore one of the world's richest countries.

The Twin Petronas Towers in Kuala Lumpur are among the world's tallest buildings. Opened by Prime Minister Mahathir Mohamad in 1999, the iconic towers

were inspired by the Islamic Star, or Rub-al-Hizb, and use many Islamic motifs in its powerful modernist design.

During Singapore's Bicentennial Year of 2019, the statue of Sir Thomas Stamford Raffles at Boat Quay was joined by a diverse group of founders and builders of the city-state – the Malay prince Sang Nila Utama, the Peranakan merchant Tan Tock Seng, Raffles' Malay teacher 'Munshi' Abdullah and the Indian pioneer Naraina Pillai. Many Singaporeans will offer different opinions about the true founders of Singapore but for many, the history of the island now stretches back 700 years.

The Japanese Rampage

The Japanese onslaught on Malaya began on 8 December 1941 with simultaneous landings in neutral Thailand at Songkhla (Singora) and Patani, and at Kota Bharu in the northern Malay state of Kelantan. Three huge transport ships anchored off the Malayan coast at Kota Bharu. They carried a 6,000-strong brigade of the 18th Chrysanthemum Division, led by Major-General Hiroshi Takumi. His task was to secure the airfield at Pengkalan Chapa and, more importantly, divert British attention from the main Japanese landings to the north in Thailand. It is a myth that the British did not defend Malaya – and for Takumi the first wave of landings on the Kota Bharu beaches was touch and go. As the heaving boats filled up, British Hudsons suddenly roared low across the waves hurling 250-pounders at the now vulnerable Japanese invasion fleet. They scored direct hits on the *Awagisan Maru*. Fire erupted from the superstructure and thick, oily smoke billowed across the sea. When Takumi's men finally reached the beaches, they were hit by withering fire from behind a labyrinth of entangled barbed wire. The Japanese soldiers were forced to dig their way under the wire with spoons.

Just over an hour after Yamashita's armies stormed onto the beaches of Kota Bharu on the north-east coast of the Malay Peninsula, Japanese air and naval forces launched a surprise attack on the American naval base of Pearl Harbour on the island of Hawaii. The following day, the United States Congress declared war on the Empire of Japan. Churchill brushed aside the news from Malaya, and rejoiced. He was, he admitted, 'saturated and satiated with emotion … England would live; Britain would live; the Commonwealth of Nations and the Empire would live.' That night, as Japanese soldiers fought their way off the beach and into the town of Kota Bharu, Churchill slept 'the sleep of the saved and thankful'. Roosevelt called 7 December 1941 as a 'date that will live in infamy'. For Churchill, the attack on Pearl Harbour was a godsend. As Churchill slept, Japanese soldiers began marching south from Patani and Kota Bharu.

Lieutenant General Tomoyuki Yamashita called his strategy *kiramoni sakusen* (the 'driving charge'). In a matter of weeks, Japanese forces punched through every defensive line that the retreating British threw across the peninsula. On 12 December, Japanese troops marched into Alor Star, the capital of Kedah. In the meantime, the US Pacific Fleet had been crippled, and half the American air force destroyed at Clark Field in the Philippines. On 10 December, Japanese aircraft sank the British capital warships HMS *Repulse* and HMS *Prince of Wales* off the coast of Kuantan in Pahang. Japanese bombers rained fire and terror on Pahang. The British fled, leaving their Asian subjects to fend for themselves. By 28 December they had seized Ipoh in Perak. Kuala Lumpur, the colonial capital of the Federated Malay States, fell on 11 January. At the end of January, the Japanese marched into Johor. Here General Yamashita was warmly welcomed by Sultan Ibrahim Abu Bakar. From the comfortable vantage point of the Bukit Serene Palace, Yamashita could look out across the Causeway towards the great prize of Singapore.

The back door to Singapore now swung precariously on its hinges. Soon Japanese soldiers would kick it wide open. The Malayan campaign would be the prelude to the shaming of Singapore's colonial masters by soldiers who had been belittled by General Sir Archibald Wavell as 'highly trained gangsters'. Historians continue to fret over who was to blame for this humiliating rout, but for the peoples of Malaya and Singapore, the consequences of defeat are not in doubt.

Singapore Falls

The end came quickly. On 15 February 1942, the British commander, Lieutenant General Arthur Percival, abjectly surrendered to General Yamashita in the boardroom of the Ford Factory. At the end of a campaign of just 68 days, the British rulers of Malaya had been vanquished. By then, Japanese troops had captured Manila and Cavite in the Philippines. From Thailand, Japanese troops struck at Burma, but General Yamashita, the 'Tiger of Malaya', had not yet fulfilled his solemn promise to Emperor Hirohito. The Japanese swept into Sumatra and on to Java, seizing Batavia, the capital of the Dutch East Indies, on 6 March. By early May, the Japanese had captured the vast archipelago of the East Indies. The old colonial map had been torn apart and the new Japanese empire stood complete. Singapore had been officially renamed Syonan-to, the 'Light of the South'. Malaya became Malai. The rising sun had reached its zenith.

In the days following the surrender, Singapore was a surreal maelstrom of chaos and despair. British and Commonwealth troops raided liquor stores and brawled drunkenly on the streets. An order was issued to destroy all supplies of alcohol to prevent them from falling into Japanese mouths, and on the Padang members of the Singapore Cricket Club organised bacchanalian parties to drink cellars dry. The Cathay Building had been turned into an improvised air raid shelter. As the Japanese came ever closer, Singapore's elite sheltered in its air-conditioned restaurants, while the poor and desperate sought refuge in the sweltering basement. On the waterfront, crowds of frenzied Europeans laid siege to the docks, clutching evacuation passes as hundreds of British deserters, brandishing tommy guns, forced their way along the quays to clamber on board departing ships. Australian commander, Major General Henry Gordon Bennett, who later accused British troops of cowardice, was observed fleeing on a *sampan*, screaming blue murder at a desperate soldier who had leapt on board stark naked. As the former masters of Singapore fled in confusion, Japanese aircraft strafed the docks, teeming with desperate men, women and children, and rained down a tornado of shells on streets, setting off warehouses stuffed with Chinese New Year fireworks in fiery blazes. As cars and rickshaws burned, oil spewed into the Singapore River. Everywhere, blackening corpses lay scattered, bloating in the heat, and the torpid air filled with the stench of death. On 11 February, Japanese soldiers rampaged through the Alexandra Hospital bayoneting helpless patients and staff.

Then, suddenly, Singapore fell deathly quiet. The city, a journalist wrote, 'had the stillness of the grave'. At noon, the silence was shattered as Japanese military trucks roared into the hallowed European centre of the city, horns blaring. Roadblocks were set up and Japanese military police fired into crowds of looters as General Yamashita handed out medals to his officers. While the Japanese soldiers showed mercy to Indians and Malays, they dragged scores of Chinese aside and peremptorily lopped off their heads. Outside the Cathay Cinema, the Japanese set up a macabre display of severed heads in cages. The fly-ridden remains were a foreshadowing of the catastrophe that would soon engulf the Chinese communities in Singapore and Malaya.

Now Singapore was Syonan-to, the 'Light of the South', caught in the python-like embrace of the Japanese 'Co-Prosperity Sphere'. When Hokkien speakers heard the new name of their city, the word made them think of the word for birdcage. In Mandarin, Syonan echoed the phrase *shou nan dao*, 'island of suffering'.

The Asian Experience of Occupation

The Japanese conquest of Singapore has too often been told as a British tragedy. For Asians, the conquest by the Japanese of British, Dutch, French and American colonial territories in Southeast Asia in 1941–42 was an event more decisive than the fall of Malacca to the Portuguese in 1511. The conquest of Malaya and the fall of Singapore altered for ever the balance of power, both political and emotional, between the European powers and Asians. The Japanese electrified Asian nationalists and held up the beacon of self-determination to the oppressed peoples of Asia. The Japanese had no intention of granting such freedoms to other Asians, but the conquest of British Malaya and the Dutch East Indies released long bottled-up energies. Even if we consider the weakness of the other imperial powers, France and the Netherlands, which had been occupied by Nazi Germany, and the beleaguered position of Great Britain, the speed and territorial reach of the Japanese advance was astonishing. In a matter of months, the Japanese seized a Southeast Asian empire which had taken Europeans five centuries to conquer. The Japanese dealt a savage and lasting blow to French, British and Dutch imperial prestige. As the Japanese army raced through the Malay Peninsula and British troops retreated across the Causeway that linked Johor with Singapore, students gathered at Raffles College heard a tremendous explosion. The British had mined the Causeway. A young man called Lee Kuan Yew explained to a fellow student: 'That is the end of the British Empire.' As historian Brian Farrell concludes, '… the manner of this defeat was its worst consequence.'

The Consequences of Occupation

From the moment the 25th Army landed in Thailand and northern Malaya, Japanese soldiers looted and raped with ferocious abandon.

The architect of the campaign, the abstemious Masonobu Tsuji, raged against the larcenous behaviour of his men, but in the heat of battle no one listened. Officers turned a blind eye to rape as it seemed to heighten their men's determination to win. In a memoir, *This Singapore: Our City of Dreadful Night* written by N. I. Low and H. M. Cheng after the war, we discover that 'some [Japanese soldiers] did it [raped] sadistically and brutally, booted and belted as they were; some did it indifferently as men answering calls of nature…. The victims steeled themselves to accept the inevitable.' Most at risk were paler-skinned Chinese girls. Some dressed in Malay style and artificially darkened their appearance. As the Imperial Army marched south, they left in their wake a gruesome trail of severed heads, often displayed on pikes with placards inscribed with homilies such as 'This is an example for those who disobey the Japanese Imperial Army.'

The Japanese military police, the Kempeitai (Military Police Corps), deservedly acquired the same kind of notoriety as the German Gestapo (part of the Secret Service), but was, in fact, modelled on the French gendarmerie, a branch of the armed forces. Founded in 1881, the Kempeitai was deployed as a semi-colonial force in Korea and Manchuria, where it was commanded by future wartime prime minister Hideki Tōjō and answered to the minister of war. Like the German SS, the Kempeitai was an elite paramilitary organisation of volunteers that strictly controlled admission to its ranks. According to an American military report, 'This policy of selection and education has produced in the Jap MP [*sic*] an individual of much higher caliber than the average Japanese soldier. But though the I.Q. of Kempei men is higher than that of the rest of the Jap Army, it in no way has decreased their cruelty, or their devotion to the Emperor, as the residents of Jap-occupied territory will certify.' In Malaya, Kempeitai units recruited local spies and informers to track down stolen goods and dispense summary lethal punishment.

After the British surrender, General Yamashita set up temporary headquarters at Raffles College, the quintessential symbol of enlightened colonial rule. Yamashita had no intention of staying there long as he had much bigger fish to fry. The bulk of the 25th Army would soon cross the Strait of Malacca to Sumatra, leaving behind a garrison force in Singapore. In the course of the next ten weeks,

Japanese forces rampaged through Sumatra, Java and Borneo. They seized the strategic base of Rabaul between New Guinea and the Solomon Islands; Japanese aircraft bombed Darwin in northern Australia; they overran the Philippines and laid siege to the fortress island of Corregidor, forcing American General Douglas MacArthur to flee to Australia; the Imperial Navy destroyed Allied naval forces in the Java Sea; the Combined Fleet, now based in Singapore, steamed into the Indian Ocean, forcing the British Eastern Fleet to withdraw, and attacked bases in Ceylon. The rays of the rising sun were now cast across one-sixth of the earth's surface. But conquering Southeast Asia would prove a lot easier than holding on to this territorial windfall. By as early as May 1942, the Japanese rampage was beginning to falter. The Battle of the Coral Sea stymied the push to Australia; in June the Battle of Midway ended Japanese ambitions to seize Hawaii; in August the Americans landed at Guadalcanal in the Solomon Islands and after protracted and ferocious fighting expelled the Japanese in February 1943, and from that moment on had the initiative in the Pacific War. But in an astonishingly short period, the Japanese transformed Southeast Asia. They brought fear and hope in unequal measure. For many Chinese Malayans, these were years of terror.

As the Japanese had approached Singapore in early 1942, the British had called on Chinese loyalists to resist the invaders. Special Force officer John Daley recruited over 2,000 Chinese students, clerks, dance hostesses and recently freed communists as 'Dalforce' and armed them with shotguns, hunting rifles and clubs, clad in hastily improvised uniforms and armbands. Many had fought bravely. Yamashita was shaken by the scale of Chinese resistance, and on 17 February ordered a 'mopping up operation' (*genju shobun*), meaning 'severe disposal', directed against 'anti-Japanese elements'. The precise nature of Yamashita's instructions and the massacre that became known as the Sook Ching, or 'purification by elimination', remains unclear. We know that master strategist Colonel Tsuji drew up a plan, the Dai Kenso, or the 'Great Inspection', and that the commander of the Singapore garrison, Major General Kawamura Saburo, passed the 'severe disposal' order to Lieutenant Colonel Oishi Masayuki of the Number 2 Field Kempeitai Group, to be carried out according to 'the letter and spirit of the military law'.

One Japanese officer, who left a short memoir of his experience in Malaya and Singapore as 'Mr Nakane', refers to 'cruising' the streets of Singapore to see how 'the personal examination is being carried on'. He casually alludes to 'those who were to be killed'. Tsuji visited the screening centres to demand his soldiers round up more suspects. He talked of cutting the entire population of Singapore in half. A Japanese officer bawled out a delegation of terrified Chinese leaders: 'You are our enemies. You know this. You have fought us for years. Now you know our strength!'

Yamashita gave Tsuji and Masayuki two days to complete the 'Great Inspection'. But the Sook Ching would turn into a months-long bloodbath that engulfed Chinese communities in Singapore and then the Malay Peninsula. The Kempeitai had clearly defined targets: British colonial personnel who had avoided detention; Chinese 'Dalforce' volunteers; civil servants and others who had worked for the colonial administration; members of the Kuomintang and Malayan Communist Party; secret society members, who could be easily identified by their signature tattoos; members of various anti-Japanese organisations.

On 16 February, Kempeitai sector heads spread out across Singapore to find suitable sites to use as so-called screening centres. Lieutenant Colonel Oishi, for example, selected the Supreme Court building; Major Onishi Satorou took over the Victoria School. Other commanders seized police stations and hotels. From the Japanese point of view, the 'Great Inspection' was a daunting task and the Kempitai officers called on the army to help. Soldiers with loudspeakers, notices and posters soon appeared all over central Singapore ordering Chinese men aged between eighteen and fifty to present themselves at the screening centres. Some were told to bring food, others not. Sometimes women and children turned up for screening as well as men.

Heng Chiang Ki remembered what took place at the screening centre in Victoria Street. 'Thousands were lining up to get clearance.... They had a long table there: high ranking Japanese officer ... and maybe one or two Chinese or Malays who were either informers or in the police force....' After a brief interrogation, Chiang Ki was 'chopped' (i.e. stamped) and allowed to go. He was lucky. When the selections had been completed, Japanese soldiers wearing Kempeitai armbands, drove parties of terrified men who had failed 'chopping' to execution sites in remote areas such as Changi, Punggol and Bedok. Japanese often carried out shootings on beaches where an ebbing tide would wash away the dead. Many were taken out to sea in launches, shot, then dumped in the water.

In early March, Colonel Tsuji ordered the Kempeitai squads to extend their campaign from Singapore to the Malay Peninsula. Here, too, they set up 'screening centres'. K. L. Chaye remembers that 'in every exit, there were masked men. And as we made to pass, if we are not wanted, we can go straight home. Don't turn back and look around. So many were stopped and asked to sit down on the field: they are the ones who were eventually all executed.'

The Japanese Sook Ching operations claimed tens of thousands of victims in Singapore and Malaya. It has proved impossible to quantify the exact number of victims and the Kempeitai did not compile meticulous records of specific operations. Estimates of the death toll have ranged from 6,000 to above 40,000. The numbers may even have been higher.

Establishing Syonan-to

After a few weeks, the Japanese killing spree began to burn out. The slaughter was over. In Syonan-to, the time had come for nation-building. The Japanese were now the civilisers, who presented themselves not just as the destroyers of European imperialism but, paradoxically, as its heirs. In Singapore in 1942, the Japanese must surely have been tempted to hurl the marble edifice of Sir Stamford Raffles into the river. And yet they did something more subtle. First of all, the Japanese authorities converted the old Raffles Museum and Library into the Syonan Museum. Then, in September 1942, they ordered a party of Indian labourers to remove the statue of Raffles from its pedestal in Empress Place and move it to the new museum. Here the *Syonan Times* reported it would have pride of place 'for all time', a tribute from the conquerors of Singapore to its founder. The symbolism was as exquisitely precise as any Japanese work of art. Raffles would be honoured, but tucked away in a museum, where he could no longer look out across the gleaming white administrative buildings, the bustling wharves and warehouses of the vanquished British emporium. The Japanese were now in the driving seat of history and building a new nation, the 'Light of the South'. As the 'Syonan Songbook' proclaimed:

> Let Asia greet the Rising Sun
> The herald of a greater day,
> When Asia's people shall like one
> Tread gloriously their destined way.

To this end, the Japanese declared war on the old 'habits and customs of the haughty and cunning English'. In Syonan-to, time became Tokyo time, one and half hours ahead of Singapore time. Days and years ran to Japanese time and the Japanese calendar. A blitz of Japanese signs replaced English ones. Streets and buildings were renamed. Japanisation would penetrate deeper into hearts and minds through the Japanese language. The *Syonan Times* became the *Syonan Shimbun* and began promoting lessons in Japanese, or 'Nippon Go'. The Japanese set up Radio Syonan to broadcast lessons, and office hours were shortened to allow the citizens of Syonan-to to perfect their skills.

The Japanese saturated Singapore with a relentless stream of propaganda. Newsreels and even music was harnessed to promote the spirit of Nippon. In classrooms, Japanese became a compulsory subject and Singaporeans who experienced the occupation as children can still remember interminable sessions of flag waving, singing Japanese songs, listening to uplifting speeches and performing callisthenic exercises to piped Japanese music. The Japanese believed that language and culture instilled Nipponese values of discipline, obedience and respect for the emperor. On the streets of Syonan-to, the Japanese reinforced these values at every moment. Everyone had to bow to any Japanese they encountered in their daily lives. Failure to show abject obeisance even to the lowliest sentry would be punished with a painful and humiliating slap.

The Japanese had vowed to build an Asia for Asians. Instead, they had raped, murdered and treated Syonan-to as a Japanese colony, crushing any hope of a brotherhood of diverse peoples liberated from the yoke of European colonialism. Nonetheless, the Japanese had exposed the French, British and Dutch as weak and vulnerable powers that could be swept away by a determined opponent. They had ignited the flame of nationalist aspiration, and that genie would never be forced back into the bottle. That flame burned brightest in the Indian communities and among Malays. Peoples who had been humiliated by Raffles and his successors and marginalised under European rule now stepped onto the stage of Asian history.

The Birth of Malay Nationalism

The founding father of Malay nationalism was Mustapha Hussain. You will not hear his name mentioned much in Malaysia today, but Mustapha was the true pioneer of a national movement among Malays. He had roots deep in Malay history. He was born the fourth in a family of ten children in Matang, Perak, on 21 August 1910. It was dusk, he tells us in his memoirs, and the Prophet's legendary 'Night Journey', the 'Lailat al Mi'raj', was being loudly celebrated at the village mosque. The family had roots in northern Sumatra; a distant ancestor was Sultan Alam Shah of Batu Barain who was a Nakhoda or 'trader captain'. 'Thankfully,' Mustapha remarks, his ancestors 'did away' with their titles when they crossed the Strait of Malacca to find a new life in the Malay Peninsula. He was a bright young man who, as he grew up, came to resent the fate of Malays in British Malay.

When he arrived in Kuala Lumpur in the early 1930s, Mustapha discovered an underground network of exiled Indonesians who had found refuge in the Malay settlement of Kampong Bharu in the heart of the city. Here he met Sutan Jenain, the revered seer of the anti-colonial movement, who preached that 'A nation is like a fish. If we are independent, we can enjoy the whole fish – head, body and tail. At the moment we are only getting its head and bones.' We, of course, meant Malays. Sutan explained: 'Every person in a colony, except those in the good books of the colonial masters, lives in misery. Who are the poorest people in Malaya? Are they not Malays? In Indonesia it is the Indonesians, except for those groomed by the Dutch: they are nothing more than horses the colonial masters ride on.' These were heady thoughts for young Malays like Mustapha Hussain.

It was from Sutan Jenain that Mustapha first heard of 'Melayu

Raya', or 'Indonesia Raya', a 'Greater Malaya' that put back together the old 'Malay Land' that had been filleted by the colonial powers. One evening in April 1938, Mustapha, Ibrahim Yaacob and a handful of young Malay radicals met secretly at a house in the kampong. That night, they formed the first Malayan anti-colonial nationalist organisation, the Kesatuan Melayu Muda (KKM), or 'Young Malay Union'. Membership was open, as Mustapha tells us in his memoir, 'to Malay youths, with Malay fathers, who practised Malay cultures and were Muslims'. The KMM would be the political saviour of 'nusa dan bangsa', nation and race. The KMM manifesto asserted the natural rights of Malays to possession of Tanah Melayu, the 'Homeland'.

When news came of the Japanese invasion at the end of 1941, Mustapha Hussain and other KMM disciples were thrilled. Mustapha looked on as the Imperial Army marched through Taiping. By then, the KMM leader Ibrahim Yaacob had already come to an agreement with the Japanese to support the invaders. He expected his fellow members to follow his lead. At the Raja Rest House in Taiping Lake Gardens, Mustapha met Major Iwaishi Fujiwara, who was chief of the Fujiwara Kikan, a Japanese intelligence unit that was recruiting Malays to attack the British. Fujiwara informed Mustapha that Ibrahim had boasted that the KMM had a huge membership who would join forces with the Imperial Army. A few hours later, Mustapha and a number of other Malay KMM supporters found themselves heading south towards the Perak capital of Kuala Kangsar on the Perak River, proudly wearing 'F Kikan' armbands.

Mustapha Hussain and his KMM followers would soon have their hopes dashed. The Malay F Kikan arrived in Kuala Lumpur on 11 January. Columns of Japanese troops and military vehicles rumbled along Batu Road, the city's main thoroughfare. There was no resistance. British forces had abandoned the city and retreated south. Kuala Lumpur was an open city. At the prestigious Selangor Club in the Lake Gardens, a symbol of British might, Mustapha and other KMM members tried to impress the Japanese with a 'national anthem':

> Japanese troops have arrived
> Let us assist them....
> They came to liberate us....'

Japanese officers listened stony-faced. One asked: 'Where is your national flag, national anthem and constitution?' He made the Japanese position very clear. 'Let the Japanese be the father. Malays, Chinese and Indians live like a family. However, if the Malay child is thin, and needs more milk, we will give him milk.'

For Mustapha Hussain, this was a bitter blow. In Singapore, after the British capitulation, he chose not to attend the humiliating surrender ceremony. A few months later, the Japanese banned the KMM, and in July 1943 they handed over the long-disputed northern Malay states of Kedah, Perlis, Trengganu and Kelantan to the Thai government. For ardent Malay nationalists, Japan was the god that failed.

A Malay Renaissance

New ideas, once they have gripped human imaginations, are much harder than organisations to crush. In Singapore, the Japanese obsession with moulding other Asians to become obedient servants of Nippon inadvertently inspired a vibrant new Malay literary culture. The Syonan-to authorities licensed a number of Malay language newspapers and periodicals, such as *Berita Malai* (Malay News), *Fajar Asia* (Asian Dawn) and *Semangat Asia* (Spirit of Asia), that daily pumped out a stream of stories about military feats and the inexorable rise of a new Asia. The Japanese were clever enough to permit the Malay editors to leaven the relentless fare of propaganda with what appeared to be innocuous short stories and poems. A new generation of writers made very creative use of this opportunity. Drawing on older Malay traditions of allusive imagery and metaphor, poets like Masuri S. N. scratched out a secretive language that expressed both a uniquely Malay consciousness and laid bare the harsh realities of occupation, where Malays were starving in the 'Light of the East'.

After the war ended, the British arrested Mustapha Hussain. He served time as a collaborator. When he was released, he set up a food stall in Kampong Bharu in Kuala Lumpur. He became famous for his food and his talk. Many years later, after a long silence, he gave a talk to students at a university in Kuala Lumpur. He said: '… bitter and gruelling experiences' flooded back, 'as a Malay Fifth Columnist leader, detained in several British lock ups and prisons, taunted and jeered by Malays who saw me hawking food on the roadside, humiliated by people who slammed their doors in my face ... even labelled as the Malay who brought the Japanese into Malaya....'

The Indian National Army

Under Japanese rule, Singapore became a laboratory of political experimentation and fervent hope. On 5 July 1943, a joyous crowd of young Indian men and women streamed down Orchard Road to the Padang. They had come to see the most charismatic of all Indian nationalist leaders, Subhas Chandra Bose. He was known all over Asia as Netaji, 'the leader'. As the huge crowd patiently waited in the blazing sun, the bespectacled and rather professorial Bose stepped onto a podium wearing a Japanese uniform. He led the huge crowd in chants of *Chalo Delhi! Chalo Delhi*, the cry of the Indian rebels in 1857.

For Bose, the road to that moment on the Padang had been a long and twisting one. He had emerged in the 1930s as the most radical of Indian nationalists who demanded an end to British rule. He had been frequently locked up by the British, ruining his health, and snapped at the heels of Gandhi's non-violent campaigns. Bose preached a war of liberation. In January 1941, Bose escaped from house arrest in Bengal and fled to Afghanistan. From there he journeyed to Moscow where he was cold-shouldered by the Soviets, and then to Berlin. In Nazi Germany, he found supporters in the Foreign Office and was put up in an opulent villa on the Tiergarten. He soon discovered that Adolf Hitler was a fervent admirer of the British Raj and had no interest in liberating India. When Bose read the German dictator's autobiography *Mein Kampf*, he was disgusted by Hitler's contempt for 'brown skinned peoples'. Netaji became ever more frustrated. Eventually, in 1943, he was put on board a German submarine and spirited away to Sumatra. Here, the Japanese occupiers tasked him with mustering an Indian army in Malaya to take on the British and liberate India.

Bose had enormous charisma. Standing in front of the huge crowds on the Padang, he eloquently set out his vision of leading a mighty Indian army to the borders of India to inspire the Indian

Army to turn against their British masters. He reached out to all Indians in Syonan-to – Muslim and Hindu, man and women. Since the Indian Mutiny in 1915, the British had clamped down on any talk in Singapore of the struggle for independence in India. Now, at these huge rallies, Bose opened the valves of decades of pent-up patriotism. Indian men, women and children were swept up by Bose's vision and rhetoric: *Chalo Delhi!* Tens of thousands volunteered the join his Indian National Army, the INA.

Bose's fantasies of leading an Indian army to conquer the Raj were extinguished in the jungle of Burma. In March, 1944, a young woman called Rasamma Bupalan, known as the Rani of Jhansi, who had joined the women's branch of the INA, boarded a train in Singapore that would take her and the other women of the regiment north through Malaya and Thailand to the Burmese border with India. By the time Rasamma and her comrades reached the front line, they discovered that the Japanese army was in full retreat as the British 14th Army led by Field Marshall William Slim pushed south. Rasamma remembered that 'we were given orders to retreat and we wept'. In August, 1945, Bose was killed when his aircraft crashed taking off from Taihoku in Japanese-occupied Taiwan.

The Return of the British

The Japanese occupation of Malaya and Singapore brought death and hardship to Asians. Thousands of women were forced into sex slavery. By the end of the war, as American forces threw the Japanese from their Pacific strongholds and the British forced them out of Burma, the people of Southeast Asia starved. The Japanese Co-Prosperity Sphere now turned into a land of living corpses. As many thousands starved, black marketeers, racketeers, pimps and gamblers prospered. Syonan-to, the 'Light of the South', was guttering out in chaos and despair. In August 1945, the American Air Force dropped two atomic bombs on Japanese cities. A few days later, Emperor Hirohito conceded that 'the enemy has begun to employ a new and most cruel bomb, the power of which to do damage is, indeed, incalculable, taking the toll of many innocent lives. Should we continue to fight, not only would it result in an ultimate collapse and obliteration of the Japanese nation....' The war with

Japan came to a terrible end in a brilliant flash of lethal energy. In the ruins of the Japanese Empire, the British, French and the Dutch former masters of Southeast Asia assumed that they could simply turn back the clock to colonial time before December 1941. They would soon understand that the world had utterly changed in ways that could never be reversed.

On 9 September 1945, extraordinary events unfolded at Morib Beach on the east coast of the Malay state of Selangor. Lord Louis Mountbatten, the supreme commander of Southeast Asia Command, or SEAC, had given the go ahead for 'Operation Zipper', the invasion of Malaya. Standing together at dawn looking out to sea were two men who had waged war on the Japanese in the jungles of the Malay Peninsula. One was John Davis, an old Malaya hand who had enjoyed family holidays on the very same beach. The other was a young Chinese man who had fought alongside Davis and called himself Chin Peng. He was one of the leaders of the Malayan Communist Party. Chin Peng and John Davis were fast friends. David recalled later that 'somewhere out at sea, in the darkness, we heard the sound of marine engines.... At first light, we saw the fleet. The horizon was filled with ships large and small, all shapes and sizes.' As the hot sun rose in the eastern sky, a flotilla of landing craft crunched onto the beach and began debouching Indian soldiers, trucks, and small amphibious boats known as 'ducks'. Nothing went as planned. The invasion had been badly mistimed. The tide was ebbing, and many vehicles were soon left stranded. The crust of sand that covered the beach concealed layers of silt. Scores of heavy military vehicles sank deep into viscous traps.

It was fortunate that the Japanese had already surrendered. The landings on Morib Beach would have turned into a bloodbath if the British had been resisted. As Chin Peng observed the chaotic spectacle with Davis, he overheard 'exuberant words of congratulation ... expressions of praise and jubilation....' He wrote later, 'I must have thought: we are letting them back unimpeded to reclaim a territory that they have plundered for so long.'

CHAPTER 17

Merdeka or Bust

I magine an aerial panorama of the world at the end of World War II. The scorching conflagration of the war that raged across Europe is guttering out, leaving in its wake a landscape of cities laid waste and churned-up battlefields criss-crossed by tides of weary refugees. Across Asia, the survivors of once-mighty Japanese armies are in sluggish movement across land and over sea in desperate flight to a homeland brought low by surrender. The fire-bombed city of Tokyo still smoulders, and in Hiroshima and Nagasaki traumatised survivors of nuclear Armageddon stumble through a radioactive wilderness.

Now let us turn south across the waters of the Southern Ocean. Even as the furnace of war cools in Indochina, Malaya and Indonesia, flames from new conflicts cast a lurid glow across plantations, cities and jungles. The British are resigned to abandoning India, the 'Jewel in the Imperial Crown', and then Burma, but in Saigon and Surabaya British soldiers, most of them Indian or Sinhalese, are ordered to turn their guns on other Asians who are demanding release from the rusted shackles of European rule. The old empires are bruised and battered, but the servants of empire will not be packing up and going home without a fight.

Singapore after the War

In the old Straits Settlements, conflicted and competing visions of the future vied for attention. Newspapers, radio stations and public spaces like Singapore's People's Park filled with the words and voices of communists, unionists and other leftists who found new readers and listeners among the young, the poor and the hungry. It was a time of tremendous excitement and experimentation. From this noisy turmoil, charismatic political leaders would step onto the stage of history to declare Merdeka – 'freedom'. For the returning British soldiers and administrators, this exuberant cacophony was troubling. They urged caution and restraint. Yes, talk about change by all means but let us make sure it works for us. The British government had been bankrupted by war and was under pressure from Washington to shut down its imperial shop. But in the offices of the Malayan Planning Unit at London's Hyde Park Gate, old colonial hands were in no doubt that beleaguered Britain must cling to Malaya and Singapore to stand any chance of surviving in the harsh new world of the Cold War. Profits from tin mines and rubber plantations would be needed to prop up the tottering British economy. In the political climate of the Cold War, Singapore remained a vital base for both fading Britain and ascendant United States.

A New British Plan

To set the scene, five million people inhabited Malaya and Singapore at the end of the war. Malays made up 50 per cent of the population; people of Chinese origin comprised 38 per cent; a diverse Indian community 11 percent, and the remaining 1 per cent was formed of several smaller ethnic groups. After a century of British rule, the different 'races' were locked in an intricate web of internecine conflicts. Malayan communists were committed to a broad-based 'race blind' struggle, at least in theory, but the majority of its 12,000 members were Chinese. Many Chinese Malayans and Indians joined the Pan-Malayan Federation of Trade Unions which called some 300 strikes in 1947 alone, but Malays remained aloof. The British wanted to impose order on a divided colonial society that was blighted by homelessness, rising unemployment, disease and semi-starvation. In the aftermath of the war, British policy in Malaya was driven by a desperate thirst for dollars. Britain had been bankrupted by the war and Malaya's lucrative rubber and tin industries were needed to replenish the depleted national coffers. Malaya had a trade surplus in dollars with the United States that exceeded all four of the empire's top dollar earning colonies combined. Malaya, it was said, was the empire's cash cow. To keep the rubber and tin flowing, it was vital to pour a great deal of oil on Malaya's troubled social waters. And in 1946, Malaya was rapidly plunging into crisis – and on many different fronts.

The Malayan Planning Unit (MPU) had been set up in July 1943 before the war ended. The chief planner was Major-General Herbert Ralph Hone, whose expertise was the Middle East, not Asia. He was also an officer of the Grand Office of the Rose Croix branch of the Freemasons. The idea he and his advisers came up with was to yoke together the former Straits Settlements, the Malay States, North Borneo, Sarawak and Brunei in a streamlined Malayan Union to be ruled directly from Britain. After James Brooke's acquisition of Sarawak, British involvement in North Borneo, present-day Sabah, had steadily deepened. In the latter part of the nineteenth century, the British North Borneo Company had won land concessions from the sultan of Brunei, and its territory was eventually declared a British protectorate in 1888. Both North Borneo and Sarawak became Crown Colonies after World War II.

It is not hard to detect in the plan hatched up by Major-General Hone and his colleagues in the MPU's scruffy offices that overlooked the tranquil green spaces of Hyde Park the stale odour of the old colonial civilising mission. The promise offered to the peoples of Singapore and Malaya was simple. If they proved themselves to be well behaved subjects of empire, they would be offered independence at some future date. Hone wanted to create not merely a new kind of colony but a new 'Malayan citizen' who would forget about his or her origins in India or China. The idea of a 'new Malayan' met with the full approval of Lord Mountbatten, the all-powerful supreme allied commander of the Southeast Asia Command (SEAC). 'I cannot help feeling that in the long run nothing could perhaps do more to perpetuate sectional antagonisms … than the giving of special recognition to one race…. If we can make a start in this way by getting people, whether Malays, Chinese or Indians, to combine together as citizens (and not as racial communities) … we may hope that one day they will come to look at the wider problems of Malaya in the same light.' The irony of the British proposal for a Malayan Union is stark. From the moment that Raffles had laid out his segregated masterplan for Singapore, the British had fostered, exploited and even *created* uneasy divisions between Malays, Chinese and Indians in the Straits Settlements. Now, in the aftermath of war, the MPU hoped to paper over the cracks. It was a daunting task, and Hone recognised from the start just how elusive this new 'Malayan citizen' might prove to be. The new plan did not include Singapore. Why? The reasoning went as follows. The MPU planners feared that incorporation in a Malayan Union might come to compromise the engine of Singapore's prosperity, its status as a free port. Second, the British wanted to retain direct control of the military and naval base. A third and equally powerful argument was that for the rulers and peoples of the Malay States, Singapore stood for the power of Chinese capital. The partnership between English merchants and Chinese towkays had been forged in the course of more than a hundred years and created an alliance of commercial and political power that was deeply resented by Malays. The MPU planners showed impressive clairvoyant powers. Singapore was a piece of the Malayan jigsaw that would never fit.

A Power Vacuum in Malaya

In the chaotic aftermath of the Japanese surrender, British forces took time to restore order, and for three bewildering weeks a whirlwind swept through the Malay States and Singapore. It was a time that would be remembered as the 'Interregnum'. The Malayan communists and their allies seized their chance. In the Malay States, nationalist Chinese unfurled Kuomintang flags, and from the jungles of the peninsula units of the communist guerrilla army, the Malayan Peoples' Anti-Japanese Army, the MPAJA, emerged to take control of cities and villages as Japanese soldiers vanished from the smaller towns and villages. The MPAJA had fought a long and bitter guerrilla war against the Japanese with British support. Now they wanted to reap the harvest of victory. They sought power, but first they wanted revenge. MPAJA officers became self-appointed judge and jury of anyone who had collaborated with the Japanese occupiers and then their executioners.

They all wore caps with three red stars, the Tiga Bintang. The traditional Malay administrations and police in the rural areas had, by and large, complied with Japanese rule. In the eyes of the MPAJA, they had collaborated. Now they lost protection overnight. There was no sign of the British and the only authority in some areas was the MPAJA. Many of the Chinese guerrillas who had lost families in the Sook Ching massacres thirsted for revenge and meted out brutal punishment to alleged informers and collaborators. Vengeful energies were directed at Malay policemen. 'It was a world gone mad,' recalled a survivor, 'a world turned upside down. Suddenly people seemed to remember every little wrong I did.'

Soon the MPAJA fighters crossed the Causeway into Singapore. Here, they hunted down Chinese businessmen who bought favour with the Japanese occupiers and women who had, for whatever reasons, become mistresses of Japanese officers. They had, as the French say, collaborated horizontally. Singapore was suddenly engulfed by wild justice, meted out by gangs who gave themselves names like the 'Exterminate Traitor Corps'. Many hundreds were abused, humiliated and murdered. Retribution was fatally mixed up with basic score-settling. Eye-witness Lee Kip Lin described the situation as 'totally out of control. There were murders everywhere and I knew some of the people who had been collaborators had been murdered. A lot of personal vendettas went on. You done me wrong. I don't like you. Now is the chance.'

In the smoking ruins of the Japanese Empire, new visions of the future began to form and new voices were heard above the din. One of those voice belonged to Lai Teck, the enigmatic secretary-general of the Malayan Communist Party. Enigmatic may not be quite the right word, for Lai Teck had led an astonishing life of intrigue and deceit. The man who became infamous as Lai Teck was born in 1903 in Saigon of a Vietnamese father and Chinese mother. In French colonial nomenclature, this made him a Sino-Vietnamese *métis* (or in Vietnamese *minh huong*). His real name was Nguyen Van Long. Lai Teck attended a Lycée, or high school in Saigon and joined the Indochinese Communist Party at an early age. He soon impressed his comrades with his fervour and knowledge of Marxist-Leninist doctrine. For reasons we will never know, when Lai Teck was arrested by the French 'Sûreté Générale Indochinoise', which did the same job as the British Special Branch in Singapore, he agreed to spy on his comrades. When later he fled to Singapore, he made contact with the head of the Special Branch, René Onraet, and made an offer to spy for the British. Showing remarkable cunning, Lai Teck rose fast through the ranks of the Malayan Communist Party, all the while feeding information back to the Special Branch as a special asset known as 'Mr Wright', his British code name. When the Japanese occupied Singapore in February 1942, Lai Teck was betrayed by a Chinese Special Branch detective and held at Kempeitai headquarters in Stamford Road. He seems to have 'broken' under interrogation and agreed to work for the Japanese as a special agent. And so it was that the secretary-general of the Malayan Communist Party became a triple agent who passed on high quality intelligence to the British Special Branch and the Japanese Kempeitai.

In late August 1945, as the MPAJA legions marched triumphantly through Singapore, Lai Teck circulated an 'Eight Point Programme' calling for the creation of a new Malayan nation 'drawn from all races of each state.' Lai Tek had made his play for a new Malaya weeks *before* the Malayan Planning Unit finally released its long-debated plan for a Malayan Union. This meant that when the British finally rolled up in Singapore, they faced a formidable political rival, formidable because the MPAJA guerrillas were, after all, war heroes. On 6 January 1946, Mountbatten put up Chin Peng and other MPAJA leaders at the prestigious Raffles Hotel. At a dazzling ceremony, Mountbatten, resplendent in gleaming white military dress, presented the guerrilla heroes with the Burma Star. In front of a large crowd and scores of photographers, Chin Peng and his comrades refused to acknowledge the British supremo's salute. Instead, they stood with clenched fists raised. Behind the ceremonial razzamatazz, wartime goodwill between the Malayan communists and the British was fast evaporating.

Now, to British dismay, it was the Malayan communists who hoped to win the hearts and minds of Malayans. Backed by the British, the MPAJA guerrillas had spilt blood for Malaya and believed that they were entitled to claim it as a homeland. On 2 October 1945, the MCP staged a rally to celebrate Gandhi's birthday at the Happy Valley Amusement Park. More than 7,000 celebrants turned up. When MCP and Kuomintang supporters marched through Singapore to commemorate China's National Day, the procession stretched for five miles through town.

The British Military Administration

History has no reverse gear. When the British came back to Singapore, even the most obtuse colonial administrators were left in no doubt that the peoples of the old Straits Settlements demanded a stake in their future. Instead, on 15 August 1945 they got the British Military Administration (BMA), the interim administrator of British Malaya, from August 1945 to the establishment of the Malayan Union in April 1946. After three years of occupation, the former 'Light of the South' was a battered ruin and many of its people were starving. Thousands squatted illegally on patches of land growing tapioca. So, the peoples of Singapore and the Malay States needed to be fed, watered and got back to work. This was the task allotted to the BMA, set up in Singapore. It was a Herculean undertaking, but the officials of the BMA made every mistake in the book. A young student who would soon dominate its political landscape, scorned the BMA as an 'education in the unfairness and absurdities of human existence.' None of the pompous brigadiers, majors and colonels who were in charge had any stake in the future of Singapore. They dreaded the moment they would be dismissed and returned to civvy street. The student wittily put it, 'their commissions would vanish like Cinderella's coach,' and at the back of their minds was the 'pumpkin of civilian life'. The student's name was Lee Kuan Yew.

The harsh reality was that British soldiers had not 'won back' Malaya and Singapore. The Japanese had not been conquered by feat of British arms but had surrendered. It was impossible to erase shaming memories of unconditional surrender and faint-hearted abandonment. The incompetent and often venal officials of the BMA further tarnished the reputation of the colonial power. For ordinary people, BMA came to stand for 'Black Market Administration'.

In a shockingly short period of time, the BMA made a desperate situation much worse. They abolished the Japanese wartime currency, the notorious 'banana notes', wiping out savings and driving up inflation. Rice hit 30–40 times its pre-war price. To try and make ends meet, the BMA resorted to the old colonial trick of importing opium. The BMA needed a vast army of labourers for reconstruction and was not scrupulous about how it was recruited. Japanese POWs were forced to work, and even some Malayans and Singaporeans were press-ganged by corrupt contractors for paltry wages. Although we talk of the British 'coming back' to Malaya and Singapore, many of the new invaders were not 'old Malay hands'. Few spoke Chinese or Malay, and many had no inhibition about expressing the nastiest kind of racist contempt. Rape, belligerent drunkenness, the trashing of shops and stores – the British return to Singapore was not a pretty sight.

The Battle for Union

In the Malay States, the British were dealt another blow. The Malayan Union Plan would have its moment in the sun and then be buried for ever. Why that happened and how has a lot to tell us about the new nation that would emerge after independence.

From the moment it was slapped on the table, the Union plan was that it was seen by many Malays as an affront to their identity and honour. And perhaps rightly, for after the end of the Japanese occupation, there was widespread distrust on the British side of supposedly 'traitorous' Malay nationalists like Ibrahim Yaacob and Mustapha Hussain, and a sense that only the Chinese had resisted the Japanese occupiers. There was, it was said 'an anti-Malay atmosphere', 'anti-Malay whispers' and 'anti-Malay sentiments'. SEAC supremo Mountbatten reinforced these sentiments when he awarded the MPAJA veterans those Burma Stars. The Chinese, it was implied, and not the Malays, had fought 'for Malaya' and were, by implication, true Malayans. For Malays, the British plans for the Malayan Union focused all their budding resentments.

A Multiracial Malaya

The most important elements of the Malayan Union Plan were, first, a centrally governed peninsular union comprising the nine Malay states, Penang and Malacca, but not Singapore; second, a common citizenship scheme for 'all who regard Malaya as their home,' and third, nine Malay states must abrogate their powers to the British Crown.

The MPU planners understood that each one of these proposals was potentially explosive. The Malay rulers had resisted centralised rule for more than half a century. The majority of Malays staunchly refused to accept Indian and Chinese 'birds of passage' as equal citizens. It was readily acknowledged that the Malay sultans and their Malay subjects would need a great deal of persuading. And persuasion would be laced with a strong dose of coercion. The diplomat chosen by the Colonial Office in London to make the long-gestated Malayan Union a reality was Sir Harold MacMichael, whose tenure as the high commissioner of Palestine and Transjordan had ended in the autumn of 1944. He seems to have understood his task with unflinching clarity. According to a cabinet minute, 'Sir Harold, ever since he was provisionally appointed for this task, has been very anxious to know how far he can go in making it clear to individual Sultans that H.M.G. intends to bring the policy into effect, notwithstanding possible resistance by any or all of them.'

MacMichael embarked on a tour of the Malay States to get to know his new fiefdom and persuade the wary sultans to sign up to the new plan. Many remained unpersuaded, but MacMichael used strong-arm tactics to get his way. Sultans who had become too close to the Japanese were either blackmailed or replaced by a relative. By the end of his tour, MacMichael seemed to have secured agreement to the Union plan and sent news of his success to the Colonial Office in London. It soon became all too apparent that the British had badly miscalculated. Rumours about MacMichael's bullying of the sultans had swept through the Malay community. If the British had studied the *Sejarah Melayu*, the 'Malay Annals' closely, they would have realised that if a sultan was insulted and humiliated, so too were his people, the *rakyat*. Ordinary Malays were galvanised as never before.

The force of Malay reaction caught the British on the back foot. The colonial myth of the docile Malay was ripped to shreds: 'Nature's gentlemen' were acting like tigers. Ire soon focused on the terms of the Union agreement. For what angered Malays most deeply was the proposal of equal rights for all races: 'a common citizenship scheme for all who regard Malaya as their home.' In a sentence, the British planners eviscerated the special status of Malays as 'sons of the soil', or Bumiputera. Any suggestion of ethnic equality was anathema, and remains so to this day.

In London, the Colonial Office stubbornly refused to compromise. It announced that the unloved BMA would be wound up on

1 April 1946, and plans were made to fly out Sir Edward Gent, who was head of the Eastern Department, to be installed as the first governor of the Malayan Union. Gent was seen as an expert on the Far East and a safe pair of hands. In 1928, he had taken part in a 'fact finding' tour of Ceylon, Java and Malaya, and during the early days of the MPU, he had insisted that the 'traditional apprehensions of the Malay sultans' had become a 'barren policy' which prevented Malays 'standing on their own feet' – and rode roughshod over the interests of the other races. Gent became one of the leading advocates of a new deal for British Malaya. The British had manufactured the fractured communal landscape of Malaya. Now it would seem they had a bad conscience about the repercussions.

A New Malay Political Party

In Malaya, the man who led the charge against the Malayan Union was the forcefully articulate journalist Onn bin Jafaar. Privately educated in England, Onn was close to the Johor royal family but snubbed his privileged family connections and launched a career as a campaigning journalist on the other side of the Causeway, in Singapore. Here, he was drawn into the early stirrings of Malay nationalism and began writing about Malay grievances. Like many politically aware Malays, he resented the way MacMichael had treated the sultans, and would do all he could to resist the British plan. But Onn was not, as the honorary title Dato' he received in 1940 from the sultan of Johor might suggest, an uncritical loyalist. If he was going to defend the sultans, he wanted payback for ordinary Malays, the *rakyat*. He expressed this in a famous slogan: 'The Rakyat have become the Raja, the Raja have become the Rakyat'. The sultans were the custodians of the Malay *bangsa*, or race: its servants, not its beneficiaries.

The solution, Onn concluded, was to found a new party to defend Malay rights and Malay privileges. On 1 March 1946, some nervous British officials and Special Branch officers unobtrusively entered the Sultan Suleiman Club in Kuala Lumpur to observe proceedings at the very first All Malay Congress that had been called by Dato' Onn. The British observers were astonished and then alarmed when Onn stood up to make an impassioned speech calling for a new party to lead the crusade *against the Union*. He proposed calling the new party the United Malays National Organisation, or UMNO.

UMNO was the first mass political movement in Malayan history. It was, as historian Cheah Boon Kheng emphasises, supported to begin with by all the key Malay groups. The emergence of the new party signalled serious trouble ahead. But in Singapore's Government House and King's House in Kuala Lumpur, British upper lips were stiffened. Gent was due to fly into Kuala Lumpur in a few weeks to take up his role as governor, and besides, it was assumed that Malays knew little about politics and had probably been swayed by religious propaganda. Gent and his cohort could not have been more wrong. They grossly underestimated the depth of emotions felt by the majority of Malays to the idea of giving non-Malays a stake in a future independent Malaya. On the British side, a few nervous voices questioned whether the Chinese and Indians were now being offered too much, but Gent and the union advocates pressed ahead regardless.

In the early hours of the morning of 31 March 1946, the aircraft carrying Sir Edward Gent, the 'father of the Malayan Union', touched down at the old Subang Airport in Kuala Lumpur. He was driven to 'King's House, the official residence and guest house of the British high commissioner in Malaysia, to prepare for the ceremony of inauguration. Soon, he was attired in all the ornamental finery of British colonial power. In the meantime, all nine sultans had gathered at the Station Hotel on the Padang. They listened as Dato' Onn bin Jafaar politely requested that they refuse to attend the ceremony. That afternoon, the rulers sent a telegram to King's House informing Gent that they would not participate. All the rulers had agreed that the British proposals were an unacceptable attack on their prestige. All nine sultans, led by the sultan of Perak, refused to meet Gent.

Behind his somewhat dithering manner, Gent was stubborn. But other British power brokers had run out of patience. As Gent flapped about King's House, Sir Malcolm MacDonald, the governor general designate in Singapore, could see that Gent's cherished Malayan Union was entering its death throes. In the meantime, the sultans threw the British a lifeline. There could be no union, but they might accept a federation. It was a straw – and MacDonald clutched it.

The Union Is Dead, Long Live the Federation

On 11 May, Gent threw in the towel. At the end of July, both he and MacDonald held secret talks with the Malay rulers, Onn and other UMNO representatives. The British agreed to reaffirm their commitment to the rulers' sovereignty and, crucially, the special position and rights of the Malays. Gent would no longer serve as governor but as high commissioner, a status that implied that his power was the gift of the sultans. The bitterly contested matter of citizenship for non-Malays was hurled far into the long grass. In the agreement drawn up with the British, no reference is made to Malayan citizenship. Instead, the word *Melayu* is used referring to individuals who spoke Malay, professed Islam and conformed to Malay custom. Singapore, with its huge Chinese population, remained a Crown Colony. Malaya and Singapore would take very different paths to independence.

On 1 February 1948, the sultans of the nine Malay states finally gathered together in their pomp at King's House. A long procession of luxury automobiles purred through the gates and crunched across the immaculate gravel drive. At the ceremony, the new high commissioner was in surprisingly good spirits: 'We had tremendous fun and games here yesterday with the signing of the State and Federation agreements ... with everyone dressed up to the nines and the Malays looking most magnificent and myself a picture of purity in my white uniform. The whole show was accompanied by a Hollywood atmosphere of brilliant lights and movie cameras.'

Dato' Onn bin Jafaar and UMNO had decisively won the first round. Or so it seemed. Privately, the British patted each other on the back, confident that the new Federation of Malaya still gave them '90 per cent of what they had wanted'. In the longer term, the consequences of the battle of the Malayan Union would be an uneasy entente between the British and the Malay elites. Onn would soon be squeezed out by a more conservative leader with roots in the Malay aristocracy – Tunku Abdul Rahman. The Tunku would become the leading architect of the struggle for independence. But Governor Gent's troubles were far from over.

The Malayan Communist Party Reacts

On the very same day that the Malay sultans paraded into King's House, Chin Peng and the Malayan Communist Party Central Committee were locked in debate at their Klyne Street headquarters in the heart of Kuala Lumpur's Chinatown. As British guns fired round after celebratory round on the Padang in Kuala Lumpur, sending flocks of startled pigeons clattering and wheeling into the warm and curdled tropical air, an MCP committee member rose to his feet. 'I feel we have tried our best.... We have used every peaceful means to further the cause of the masses.... Yet we have had no impact whatever.' The MCP was adjusting to some harsh realities. In the aftermath of the Japanese surrender, Secretary-General Lai Tek had urged restraint and in return the British promised the Malayan communists a role in post-war political planning as members of the government's Advisory Council in Singapore. Chin Peng and the other committee members dutifully followed Lai Tek's instructions to 'agitate peacefully'. Then in March 1947, Lai Tek disappeared. This was a blow for the British who relied on the party chairman to keep a lid on the party and its activities. After an astonishing run of good luck, a number of suspicious party members had rumbled Lai Tek and exposed his treachery. He fled to Thailand. Years later, Chin Peng would reveal in his autobiography that the man he had revered for so long had been murdered in Bangkok and dumped in a canal.

Chin Peng was swiftly appointed secretary-general. He had been radicalised by Lai Tek's treachery. The British had embraced the Malay rulers and closed the door to the other parties. The collapse of the Malayan Union was the death knell of multiracial liberalisation. For the MCP, it was a political nadir. Protest, strikes, demonstrations – these tactics were failing. The struggle had to be ramped up. But how? It would take months, perhaps years, to prepare for armed struggle – and who in any case would support an armed insurrection?

The Roots of the Emergency

During the Japanese occupation, Chin Peng and the MPAJA guerrillas had come to rely on the support of many thousands of Chinese who had fled towns and cities in Malaya and taken refuge in the countryside. Here they occupied land illegally, and so became known as 'squatters'. The word is pejorative since it implies indolence and squalor. But the majority of Chinese squatters were hard-working farmers who grew crops and raised livestock on parcels of abandoned land. A typical squatter could work miracles with just a handful of acres. By the end of World War II, the squatters were feeding many tens of thousands of starving Malayans. And their numbers continued to rise. In February 1949, an economist called Harry Fang wrote a report on the squatter economy for *The Malaya Tribune*. He estimated that an astonishing 95 per cent of Malaya's population had come to depend on the output of Chinese small-holdings for supplies of rice, vegetables, meat and eggs.

Trouble came when the British colonial government concluded that the Chinese squatters had outlived their usefulness. As the British revved up the economy, European companies lobbied for mass evictions to free up land for commercial cultivation. Malays also piled on the pressure. They wanted their reserved lands back. Soon the British began raiding squatter communities and launched mass clearance operations. These mass evictions began in the Kroh Forest reserve in the Kinta Valley in Perak, then expanded to the Sungei Siput area. Many squatters resisted, with backing from the communists – and a wave of strikes hit the mines and rubber plantations that were earning dollars for the beleaguered British government in London. The British had stirred up a hornet's nest. A young Malay communist called Hassan Saleh lamented: 'Our homeland has a lot of tin, gold and timber. This belongs to us. They take it all and take it back to England. Our wealth is taken to England. The prosperity is there, not in our homeland.'

The bitter reactions to the mass evictions laid down the kindling that would flare into an armed insurrection. The spark was struck in the little town of Sungei Siput in the Kinta Valley. In 1948, Sungei Siput was more roadside village than town. A cluster of huts and shophouses straddled the trunk road that led north to the Thai border and south to Ipoh. From Sungei Siput, a web of unpaved roads and forest paths radiated out to connect the tin mines and rubber plantations that fed the battered British treasury. At the northern end of town, the Lintang Road cut through the jungle for twenty or so lonely miles until it came to a dead end. On each side of the road lines of rubber trees marched monotonously into the distance, seemingly without end. The rubber trees belonged to the Sungei Siput and Elphil estates, two of the biggest plantations in Perak. It was here, on the morning of 16 June 1948 that a group of young men cycled into the Elphil Estate and dismounted outside the estate manager's office. They pushed open the door and shot dead plantation managers Arthur 'Wally' Walker and John Allison and trainee planter Ian Christian. The leader of the hit squad reassured Indian estate clerks: 'We are out only for Europeans. These men will surely die today: we will shoot all Europeans.'

As trouble flared in Malaya's lucrative plantations, the powerful associations of rubber planters and miners in Kuala Lumpur had complained incessantly to Gent, the high commissioner, to 'do something'. The *Straits Times* printed the infamous headline 'Govern or get out!' The killing of the three white 'Tuans' on a single day was a gift to noisy hardliners. Gent had few options. He had to act. Gent declared a State of Emergency in Perak, where the planters had been killed, which was extended to the whole of the Malay Peninsula two days later, on 16 June. The war without a name had begun.

Why did Gent and the high commissioners who followed him so staunchly resist calls to declare martial law? The most frequently cited reason is that the Emergency 'label' protected insurance claims made by the European owners of tin mines, plantations and other private colonial businesses for loss or damage to property. Under martial law, responsibility for financial compensation would have fallen not on insurance companies but on the British government, and the new British prime minister, Clement Attlee, was unwilling to shoulder such a burden. There was a second reason that favoured emergency ordinance over declaring martial law. Colonial governments often used martial law to put down rebellions, but it carried risks for officials and military commanders who could be indicted for murder if they overstepped the mark. So, martial law carried risks for the men who had to enforce it. In the view of a future high commissioner, Sir Henry Gurney, who was chief secretary to the mandate government, declaring martial law was a sign of weakness and the first victory for terrorists.

CHAPTER 18

Singapore's Struggle for Independence: Opening Moves

O n a day in 1955, Marjorie Doggett, a young English woman who had eloped to Singapore with her future husband to work as a nurse, climbed to the top of the Victoria Concert Hall clutching her beloved German-made Rolleicord camera. From her vantage point, she painstakingly adjusted her position until she could capture in a single image Empress Place, the Dalhousie Obelisk, the Fullerton Building and the Bank of China. Doggett, who was self-taught, was fascinated by Singapore's noble old buildings caught in velvety black and white under lowering clouds. In another striking image, Doggett set up her camera on Clifford Pier to capture the Fullerton again, symmetrically framed by a man reading a newspaper and a father and his young daughter looking out across the quay. Looking at the photographs today, the father and daughter seem to be caught between the past and the future. What is the man on the left reading about in his newspaper? What hopes and fears flicker in the minds of father and daughter on the right? Marjorie Doggett's beautiful photographs show a city in aspic. Mrs Doggett rarely ventured beyond the European town with her camera. There is a hidden Singapore behind Empress Place and the Fullerton, a realm of poverty and struggle. And under the same threatening skies, the world's superpowers compete for influence in the lands below the winds.

Demands for Change

In 1948, the population of Singapore was just over 900,000 people. Ten years later, it had risen above a million. In one fundamental way, the city had changed very little. Imagine waving down a taxi outside City Hall at the dawn of the new decade and crossing the city to reach the furthest reaches of Serangoon Road. The old rickshaw trade has been in steep decline since the 1930s and our garrulous taxi driver impatiently negotiates streets crowded with motor cars, trucks belching black smoke and shiny new trolley-buses. Over three-quarters of its population is still clustered within five miles of Raffles' landing place on Boat Quay. Outside the inner city, the poorer Chinese and Malays inhabited jerry-built villages or kampongs that seemed to spring up overnight to accommodate the still ceaseless flow of migrants from China. Even the inner city was pockmarked with overcrowded slums.

In the mid-1950s, sociologist Barrington Kaye began studying a single street in Chinatown. Dr Kay's book, simply called *Upper Nankin Street, Singapore*, plunges us into a crowded, dark and noisy world. Upper Nankin Street, a short walk from Speakers' Corner in Hong Lim Park, was first laid out in the mid-nineteenth century when Singapore was hitting its stride to become one of the richest port cities of Asia. Kaye meticulously recorded dialect, immigration status, education, occupation and living conditions. The hard facts he compiled still shock: '17% of the floors surveyed were without a toilet; the average pressure on those on the remaining floors was 20 adults per toilet; there were 15 households obliged to use toilets in which the pressure was 40 and more adults per toilet. All the toilets were of the open-bucket type; only 30% of them were emptied daily. For the most part, the toilet consisted of a small room (usually a cubicle) built in the corner of the same veranda that served as a kitchen.' There was only rudimentary ventilation and few windows. Few human actions could happen in private. The shophouses of Nankin Street were gloomy, noisy and often deadly. In the 1950s, there were many, many Nankin Streets in Chinatown.

The Singapore Improvement Trust

In the 1920s, the colonial government had established the Singapore Improvement Trust, the SIT, to do something about the dire living conditions for ordinary people. The problem was that from its founding, the SIT was chronically underfunded and lacked the power to do much more than clear some of the worst slums and build a few modest new developments. The SIT showpiece was constructed between 1927 and 1936 on 70 acres of swamp land known as Tiong Bahru, which in Hokkien means 'New Tomb'. The SIT planners evicted some 2,000 squatters to build Singapore's first public housing. Today, Tiong Bahru is a property hot spot for wealthy millennials, lured by the estate's Art Deco 'streamline moderne' design, but even in the 1930s when the project was completed, the SIT set such high rents that many of the flats stayed empty. Wealthy businessmen rented flats for their mistresses and the new estate became known as Mei Ren Wo, the 'den of beauties'. Tiong Bahru was a stylish dead end that did little for Singapore's poor. By the mid-1950s, the SIT was hobbled and impecunious. Few of its schemes were completed and rents were simply too high for many needy residents. The colonial government could not cope with such a fast-burgeoning population, which grew by 54 per cent between 1947 and 1957.

With so many residents living in crowded and unsanitary homes, the spectres of hunger and disease stalked the poorest streets of Singapore. Young people most of all suffered deadly outbreaks of measles, tuberculosis and smallpox. Many lives were spent in the debilitating shadow of malaria and dengue fever. The government supported a fragile network of clinics and military hospitals, but mortality rates remained stubbornly high. A smallpox epidemic rampaged through Singapore as late as 1959.

Far-sighted Asian men and women were ravenous for change. And change was demanded, and rights asserted by every community in Singapore, and not always with one voice. Communal strife would shape the struggle for independence. Learning how to manage and, it has to be said, to exploit simmering tensions between and within Chinese, Malay and Indian communities would preoccupy the new generation of political leaders who led the long struggle for independence. Whoever mastered the whirlwind would shape the future of Singapore and Malaya.

The Maria Hertogh Case

On the early morning of 11 December 1950, large numbers of Malays carrying banners and flags began gathering outside the imposing new Supreme Court on the west side of the Padang. The mood was volatile. Inside the court, a British judge was considering an appeal against a custody ruling. At stake was the fate of a young Dutch woman and the Malay woman who had raised her. Just after midday, it was announced that the judge had thrown out the appeal. He had considered the matter for just five minutes. As news of the judgement ripped through the crowds, reaction was immediate and angry. Groups of young men rushed away from the court and began attacking Europeans and Eurasians. Cars were overturned and set on fire. A British serviceman called John Davis was dragged out of a trolley bus and beaten to death in a roadside drain. Mobs rampaged through Singapore. That evening, the district officer commanding Singapore District, Major General Dermot Dunlop, deployed two Internal Security Battalions to reinforce the police and called in reinforcements from Malaya. It took three days to restore order. By then, 18 people had been killed and some 200 injured.

At the epicentre of the storm was a thirteen-year-old Dutch adolescent called Huberdina Maria Hertogh. It was her extraordinary story that led to a ferocious custody battle and triggered the riots that would take her name. Maria had been born to a Dutch family in Cimahi, not far from Bandung in the Dutch East Indies in 1937. Her parents, Adrianus Petrus Hertogh, a sergeant in the Royal Netherlands East Indies Army, and Adeline Hunter, a Eurasian of mixed Scottish and Javanese descent, were Catholics. They had five children and Maria was their third daughter. When the Japanese invaded Java in 1942, Adrianus had been captured and sent to a POW camp in Japan. For disputed reasons, Adeline sent Maria to stay with Che Aminah Mohammed, a Malay friend of the family from the Malay state of Trengganu. When Adrianus returned to Java at the end of the war, he and Adeline had tried to find Maria but there was no sign of their daughter. As it turned out, Che Aminah had taken Maria to Kampung

Banggol in the district of Kemaman, her home village in Malaya. She now had a new name, Nadra binte Ma'arof, and was being raised by her foster mother as a devout Muslim. She now spoke only Malay.

The Hertoghs appealed to the Red Cross and the Indonesian Repatriation Service to find Maria, and eventually she had been tracked down to the kampong. The Hertoghs turned to the Dutch Consul and the British authorities to seek custody of their daughter. But Che Aminah fought back. Her case was backed by Malay activists and a 'Nadra Action Committee'. In the mosques, there was talk of Jihad. There is no doubt at all that Maria was deeply attached to her foster mother and her kampong. She was devoutly Muslim. She barely knew her birth parents, Adrianus and Adeline. The case continues to fascinate and provoke to this day. Was Muslim Nadra still Catholic Maria? The British lawyers believed she was. The Hertoghs won their case and Che Aminah's appeals were thrown out. Malays had followed every twist and turn of the case and believed fervently that Nadra belonged with her mother and community. In the meantime, Maria had, willingly, married a young Malay teacher in a *nikah gantung* or truncated marriage ceremony, meaning the marriage would not be consummated until she reached the age of majority. Throughout the long and tortured proceedings, the British and Dutch authorities had trampled on Malay sensibilities. They had arranged for Maria to be photographed in a convent and overruled her marriage. There had been warning signs of a gathering storm but the British authorities had turned a blind eye. The dismissal of Che Aminah's appeal by a British judge threw gasoline on a smouldering fire. In Kuala Lumpur, Tunku Abdul Rahman had followed the case closely. He talked later of his rage when he heard that a Muslim girl had been forcibly taken from her foster mother and 'converted to Christianity'. But, the Tunku went on, 'I had gained much popular support for myself and the party I led as a result of this case.' The 'Maria Hertogh Riots' galvanised the energies of Malay nationalism and may well have accelerated progress to independence.

Culture against Race

We cannot view Singapore in the 1950s solely through the lens of conflict. On both sides of the Causeway, artists, film-makers and musicians took part in an explosion of creativity that swept aside ethnic or communal barriers. In Singapore, a vibrant film industry unselfconsciously projected a race-blind Malayan identity. To be sure, Malay writers, musicians and directors played the leading role shaping a richly diverse world of stories and characters drawn from Malay folk tales and Bangsawan traditions. But Chinese producers like the Shaw Brothers controlled Malay films and Cathay-Keris, the island's two main studios, and Filipino and Indian directors worked alongside Malay colleagues. Bestriding the Malayan renaissance was P. (Puteh) Ramlee, director, actor, writer and musician. Born in Penang, Ramlee was an astonishing talent who worked in Singapore throughout the 1950s. Today, Ramlee is claimed by Malaysia: he was posthumously awarded the honorific Tan Sri. As one fan site puts it: 'If Malaysia had a "Walk of Fame", his star would be the shiniest – you know, polished by the tears of fans and lit by the flashes of their cameras. When it comes to local show business, there really is no one who lives up to the legacy left by Teuku Zakaria bin Teuku Nyak Puteh'. The irony is that when Ramlee was lured away from Singapore to join the Merdeka Film Studios in Kuala Lumpur, his career fell into decline. He died far too young at forty-four, convinced that he was a 'has been'. At his creative peak, P. Ramlee was a truly *Malayan* star, who flourished in Singapore, and was loved unreservedly by Malay, Indian, Chinese and Eurasian audiences.

The Rise of David Marshall

Politics, too, is all about performance. In the mid-1950s, a handful of talented and competitive individuals strode onto the Singaporean political stage to lead the struggle for independence. As it turned out, only one of these ambitious and brilliant individuals had the stamina, sheer good luck and ruthless manipulative talent to navigate the treacherous and fast-moving currents of history to become the first prime minister of independent Singapore and the 'father of the nation'. The rise to power of the Hakka Chinese lawyer Lee Kuan Yew would have astonished most of the people who gathered in Empress Place or tuned into Radio Malaya on 21 March 1956 to listen to the stirring words of Singapore's new chief minister: 'Merdeka,

People of Singapore….' he began. The minister's voice was rich, deep and confident. At that moment, David Saul Marshall, politician and lawyer and the first chief minister of Singapore (1955–56), seemed to hold the fate of Singapore in his hands: 'I put before you a blueprint for a miracle.' As a 'Grand Old Man' many years later, Marshall liked to tell a story. As a Jewish teenager growing up in the British colony, he was dumbfounded when the family's soothsayer predicted that he would one day be 'the most important man in Singapore'. There was a sting in the tail: 'But you won't be the most important man in Singapore for long.'

That day, standing under an apple tree on Empress Place, Marshall skilfully played the crowd. Brandishing a pipe and using the agitated rise and fall of his bushy eyebrows to add grace notes to his words, Marshall promised his listeners 'a blueprint for a miracle'. He complained that when he was elected chief minister, he was astonished to be informed that he had 'no office, no clerk, no *thambi*' (male servant), and the crowd laughed heartily when Marshall explained that the 'heaven born' British chief secretary saw his new chief minister as 'the senior *thambi* among the *thambis*'. Marshall warmed to his theme, feeding on his listeners' belly laughs. Read the English press, he exhorted, 'we are a group of baboons … we want Papa and Mama colonialism….' Here Marshall imitated brattish infant: 'Mama colonialism! Mama! A lost boy….' Then his tome darkened: 'The communists are the ultimate danger to this country….' Referring to a dance sometimes performed by communist students, Marshall insisted, 'You don't want, I don't want a *yanko* Merdeka. We want a Malayan *merdeka!*' Marshall is one of the architects of modern Singapore. But his blueprint would be torn up by two charismatic younger men who would prove to be even more formidable opponents than the 'heaven born' British officials in Government House.

He had been born David Saul Mashal in 1908. His parents Saul and Flora were Sephardi Jews who had emigrated from Baghdad. They anglicised the family name in 1920. Jews from Iraq had been coming to Singapore since the time of Raffles, and Baghdadi Jewish traders were familiar figures in many Indian Ocean ports. At home, David had a traditional Orthodox upbringing but was schooled at Catholic Schools and the Raffles Institution. Marshall was often unwell and his twenties were overshadowed by bouts of malaria and tuberculosis which thwarted his early ambition to study medicine. He collapsed on the eve of his final exams. After that disappointment, Marshall was unclear what to do next. So, following the family trade, he studied textile manufacturing in Belgium, and back home in Singapore found work as a salesman. He was restless. He had learnt excellent French during his time in Belgium and tried his hand at teaching. Finally, in the mid-1930s, Marshall threw himself into studying law. Like many Asian law students before and since, he took a steamship to England and enrolled at the University of London. He was called to the Bar at Middle Temple and returned to Singapore in 1937 to launch a career in criminal law.

Marshall's experience as a lawyer in colonial Singapore made him a cynical observer of its British rulers. As a Jew, he despised racial segregation but he was sharply aware of the threat of Nazism. When Germany invaded Czechoslovakia in 1938, he immediately joined the Straits Settlement Volunteer Force in Singapore. He was not in the least cowed by his British officers and protested that Asian recruits were not paid as well as European volunteers. Marshall's experience of war was traumatic. When the Japanese army attacked Singapore in early 1942, he was captured and interned at Changi Prison. He was later transferred to a forced labour camp in Japan. His was a tough war. He explained: 'Three and a half years as a prisoner taught me humility.... I realised that mankind is capable of cold-hearted cruelty. I can be angry, and I have no doubt I can be cruel for five, ten minutes. But the Japanese cruelty was cold-blooded, permanent, and eternal. Man's inhumanity to man in fact, in real life, made its presence really known to me when I became a prisoner and saw it in action. Of course, I have known cruelty before. But wide-spread, long-term, cold-blooded, permanent cruelty, I've never experienced before, not even from the British imperialists no matter how arrogant they were. That was a major shock, the feeling that there were human beings who were not on the same wavelength as me at all, who were not even human from my point of view.'

Marshall's bitter experience in Japan seems to have deepened his contempt for the way the British governed colonial Singapore. From his school days, Marshall was made aware that as an Asian, and a Jew, he was an outsider in colonial Singapore. Interviewed late in life, Marshall spoke for the first time of the 'anger in his belly' goaded by the 'leprous concept' of racial superiority. He wanted, he said 'to break through the sonic barrier against Asians and especially Jews'. His politics were, in the best sense, *emotional*. There was nothing doctrinaire about Marshall: he was a socialist of sorts, who hated communism. When he returned to Singapore, Marshall focused on growing his very busy legal practice. 'I've got to build up my career!' he protested when the leftist Eurasian journalist Gerald de Cruz tried to persuade him to join his new party, the Malayan Democratic Union. Marshall was hesitant rather than reluctant to step onto the political stage. His charisma and sense of theatre had been honed in the courtroom. He knew instinctively that his voice would be heard.

A New Career

His opportunity came in the mid-1950s, and it was all to do with what was happening on the other side of the Causeway in Malaya. Let us recap briefly. After the war, the British had welded together the Malay States, Penang, Province Wellesley and Malacca as a federation. They had ring-fenced Singapore as a distinct Crown Colony. In 1948, the British had established a Singapore Legislative Council but only 6 of its 22 members were popularly elected. For the next few years, constitutional progress froze. The reason was that the British focused on combating the communist insurgency that had exploded in Malaya. By 1955, the British and their Malay allies had begun to drive the communist insurgents from their jungle hideouts. This brightening of the mood in Malaya had a knock-on effect in Singapore. In 1953, as violence waned, the British governor, Sir John Nichol, established the Rendel Commission to look into accelerating Singapore's progress to self-government. Self-government is not independence, of course, and the British wanted to make sure they kept a firm hand on the political tiller. The upshot of the commission was a plan to revive the moribund legislative council. In 1954, the governor announced that popular elections would be held the following year for a reformed assembly of 32 members, of whom 25 would be elected by the people of Singapore.

Marshall recognised immediately that a chink had been opened in the colonial armour. 'Hey, we are human beings! We've got a right to a voice in how we are to live.... Hey, we are standing on two legs.' He threw in his lot with the Labour Front, a coalition of socialist parties stitched together to contest the elections by trade union leader Lim Yew Hock and threw himself into campaigning. Now he discovered a talent as a magnetic and passionate speaker who rebuked the British in a cascade of barnstorming appearances and speeches. He recalled that he wanted to 'awaken the people', and you can't do that with 'somnolent sentences'. What was needed was a new *story*, and Marshall relished the idea that he was David taking on the colonial Goliath.

Marshall's fervour and hold on the huge crowds that gathered to hear him speak unnerved the British. His message was belligerently anti-colonial. Governor Nicholl gambled heavily on the British friendly Progressive Party (PP) to romp home with a majority. Marshall branded PP candidates as 'colonial stooges'. He accused European expatriates of draining the economy dry and turning Singapore into an 'exploiters' slag heap'. When the results came in, Marshall had turned the tables on Singapore's colonial masters. The Labour Front romped home to win a game-changing victory. The governor was in shock. Marshall had indeed 'awakened the people'. Recognising his unique political talents, the Labour Front candidates unanimously elected Marshall as chief minister. David had not felled Goliath, but he had given him a nasty shock.

The exultant, newly elected Labour Front members soon began shaking up the stilted, talking-shop formalities of the newly created Legislative Assembly which replaced the old council. Marshall led the way. When he was invested as chief minister, he provocatively wore an open-necked bush jacket: 'an insult to the Queen!' shrilled the horrified editor of the *Straits Times*. This was grist to Marshall's mill and he adopted the bush jacket as a kind of uniform. Francis Thomas, another Labour Front minister, took sartorial protest to another level. He donned a safari jacket and sandals for the official opening of the Legislative Assembly. The sight of his brazenly displayed and sockless feet heralded a provocative new style of politics. Marshall and his Labour Front colleagues had been proved right. The peoples of colonial Singapore wanted change, and offered the chance to vote for radical new ideas had rushed unhesitatingly to the polls.

Singapore politics had become exciting. Marshall played expertly to the packed public gallery. At a council of ministers meeting, he quarrelled with the governor about the traditional use of red ink to veto unwelcome decisions. Marshall insisted that his own green ink had equal power, and he would use green ink for the rest of his life. Bush jackets, ministers in sandals ... a little war of inkpots. Politics was lively and even fun. But Marshall's purpose was serious. He demanded free legal services and protection for trade unions. He drew on every rhetorical trick to force the government to take notice of poisonous inequalities in education, medical care and housing.

Marshall could not know that his political star had reached its zenith. The old family soothsayer was right. He would hold power, but not for long. For in the Legislative Assembly David faced another Goliath, a new foe who would overturn the Biblical myth and win the day.

The First Clash with Mr Lee

Marshall dominated the Legislative Assembly. He had the fine-tuned skills of a stage actor and the passion of conviction. He spoke for the many underprivileged people who had voted for the Labour Front. But he did not possess the stage alone. Marshall was soon made aware that he faced a formidable political rival in the Legislative Assembly for the 1955 election had transformed the fortunes of another new party and its alarmingly clever founder. Day after day, Marshall clashed with the leader of the opposition People's Action Party, the PAP, who day after day niggled at the chief minister's grandstanding histrionics with the sharpest inquisitorial sorties. Soon, reporters in the press gallery were thrilling readers with the war of words between the two big players in the assembly, the chief minister and Mr Lee Kuan Yew. And backing the sharp-tongued Mr Lee was a young man with 'a soft baby face' and a ringing voice. Lim Chin Siong and his friend Fong Swee Suan were young men, Lee remembered, who were 'well mannered, earnest and sincere', the 'kind of lieutenants I'd been looking for.' Lee, Lim and Fong would soon seize the political baton passed on, reluctantly, by the first chief minister.

CHAPTER 19

The Emergency War: The Malayan Front Line

T he Emergency war in the Malay Peninsula had started badly for the British. It was worse for Chinese plantation workers. On 11 December 1948, a patrol of fourteen British soldiers of the 7th Platoon, G Company of the 2 Scots Guards Battalion struggled through the semi-cultivated fringe of the Malayan rainforest 45 miles northwest of the colonial capital of Kuala Lumpur. They had set off some hours earlier from their barracks in Kuala Kubu Bahru. The target that day was a small Chinese settlement that had been built in a clearing on the Sungei Remok rubber estate. There had been reports of 'bandit activity' not far from the estate. The young British men, who were all doing national service, had received only the most rudimentary training in jungle warfare. It was fiercely hot and humid and they would have been tormented by mosquitoes and other biting insects.

When they reached the plantation, the Scots Guards began interrogating the Chinese workers. They could find no evidence of any contact with communist 'bandits'. The soldiers continued to harass the plantation workers and the following morning separated the men from the women and children. Then the shooting started. Years later, some of the soldiers gave interviews to a British newspaper: 'Then we heard shooting so instinctively almost, we opened fire. Once we started firing, we seemed to go mad. An old man died immediately from one bullet. The one that was furthest away at the time took about seven bullets before he finally stopped crawling.... I remember the water turned red with their blood. The incredible thing was that none of them spoke. They didn't shout or scream or anything…. The man who kept crawling – we shot in the head at point blank range. The man's brains spilled onto my foot.'

By midday, twenty-four young Chinese men lay dead on the Sungei Remok Estate. The British platoon set fire to the huts and returned to their base. One of the men, a private Fern, was reported to be 'distressed'. Major George Ramsay, the base commander, addressed the platoon. They must all stick to an agreed story. The men they had shot were MNLA bandits who had been captured and shot when they tried to escape. Journalist Harry Miller dutifully reported in the *Straits Times*: '… the biggest success occurred in Batang Kali…. Scots Guards numbering 14 shot dead 25 Chinese who they surprised yesterday morning.'

The British Way of Counter Insurgency

An insurgency has been succinctly defined as 'a contest between the insurgents and the colonial state to win political legitimacy in the eyes of the civil population'. After 1945 and 1967, the British fought anti-colonial insurgents in Palestine, Malaya, the Canal Zone, Kenya, British Guiana, Cyprus, Oman, Nyasaland, Borneo and Aden and, for a short period in 1948, the Gold Coast. These 'little wars' invariably blur the distinction between insurgent and civilian. In Malaya, the British faced the classic problem of counter-insurgency campaigns: uncertainty about the identity of the enemy. Malaya was a racially divided society, and a significant number of the Malayan National Liberation Army (MNLA) fighters were Chinese. There was just a single battalion of Malay insurgents. The problem was deepened in Malaya because the MNLA guerrillas were supported by a mysterious 'Masses Organisation' known as the Min Yuen. Before and since, it has proved impossible to gauge the numbers of people who were actively involved. From the British point of view, the secretive Min Yuen seemed to be everywhere. Just about any Chinese person you met might secretly be a Min Yuen. So, it was all too easy for government forces to suspect that any Chinese Malayan was a 'bandit' or 'bandit supporter'. Unusual behaviour by Chinese individuals could be construed as threatening, with deadly consequences.

Assassination

For the British, the nadir came in October 1951. The new high commissioner to Malaya, Sir Henry Gurney, who had replaced Gent, fell into despair. He reported that the Chinese were allowing the MNLA to 'get away with it'. Chinese leaders 'refused to help their own people resist Communism'. They were only interested in making money, Gurney complained. He left the report unfinished. Two days later, the High Commissioner and Lady Gurney set off for Fraser's Hill, the old British resort near Raub in Pahang, to escape the broiling heat in Kuala Lumpur. A few hours after setting off from King's House, Gurney's Rolls Royce, with its fluttering and eye-catching Union Jack pendant, sped ahead of military escorts to begin the long, winding climb into the hills. He had no idea that MNLA leader Siew Ma was camped out above the road with a platoon of thirty-six men. They had set up a 'killing box' on the road hoping to ambush a colony. That day, they got lucky. In fact, Siew Ma and his men were hungry and about to give up. But at about 1 p.m. they spotted the black Rolls Royce turning into the killing box and opened fire. The Rolls skewed to a halt and Gurney, wearing a light tropical suit, stepped out of the car to draw fire away from Lady Gurney and the rest of the party. The volley of fire reached a crescendo and the high commissioner fell dead by the side of the road.

The assassination of the high commissioner shattered British morale. In London, the new prime minister, Winston Churchill, who had ousted Clement Attlee's Labour government, demanded action. He sent a suave aristocrat to Malaya to find out what was going wrong. He did not mince his words: What is delaying progress? he asked. This was his reply: '... the answer is Communism. The answer is the terrorists. The answer is the Min Yuen and those who, partly from fear and partly from sympathy, create a passive but no less serious obstacle to victory.' On them, he promised, would fall the 'full severity which their betrayal merits'. The situation, he concluded, was 'appalling': 'I have never seen such a tangle as that presented by the government of Malaya.' Field Marshall, now Viscount Bernard Montgomery, brusquely advised: 'We must have a plan. Secondly, we must have a man. When we have a plan and a man, we shall succeed: not otherwise. Yours sincerely (signed) Montgomery (F.M.)'

The Briggs Plan

The man was World War II veteran General Gerald Templer and the plan was a new kind of war fought for hearts and minds. Templer was lucky. The MNLA was already reeling from the impact of a strategy developed by the former director of operations, General Sir Harold Rawdon Briggs, who had been sent to Malaya. Known as the 'General in a Trilby hat', Briggs grasped how the war could be won. He saw that the communists were sustained by 'uncontrolled squatter areas, unsupervised Chinese estates and small holdings'. The plan he proposed was daunting. It meant evicting huge numbers of Chinese peasants from their smallholdings and transferring them to 'resettlement camps'. The 'Briggs Plan' was utterly ruthless. It was war by means of starvation. And it worked. Eventually. When he left Malaya, Briggs believed his plan was failing, but resettlement would, in fact, transform the human landscape of Malaya.

The Catholic Belgian-Chinese novelist and doctor Han Suyin was an eye-witness. In her autobiography, *My House has Two Doors* (1982), and a semi-factual novel, *And the Rain my Drink* (1956), Han Suyin wrote searing accounts of the lives of the 'resettled'. Her reports caused such an almighty stink that her husband, Leon Comber, who was a member of the Special Branch, was sacked. The couple later divorced. Han Suyin saw that resettlement was deepening the divisions between the Malayan races: 'Whole villages, in some cases villages established for a century or more, in which Malays and Chinese had lived peacefully together, were now sundered, the Chinese taken away and put in "new villages" behind barbed wire'. As resettlement gathered pace, a barbed-wire barrier descended between the rural Chinese and other races, as well as the rest of the Chinese communities. Conditions for the uprooted squatters were often dire. Han Suyin describes visiting a resettlement camp with a Mr Winslow, who was 'in charge of resettlement' in the area. Whoever he was, Mr Winslow was proud of what had been achieved. It took four hours by jeep to reach the new settlement, the little party bumping along a new road slashed through the jungle. The first sign that they had reached their destination was a great barrier of barbed wire and a police post at the edge of a fetid mangrove swamp. Outside the wire was the 'sombre menace of the

jungle'. The new houses spread into the swamp: 'Four hundred beings, including children, huddled there: foot deep in brackish water.
There were some atap huts with rusty zinc roofs…. I shall never forget the pale, puffy faces: beri beri or the ulcers on their legs. Their
skin had the hue of the swamp. They stank. There was no clean
water anywhere. Mr Winslow, standing on a box … admonished
them sternly in Malay: a Chinese interpreter translated in Teochew
dialect. The villagers had been guilty of passing food to the bandits
and so they had been transported here. Now they must work hard
to redeem themselves.'

A War for Hearts and Minds

Templer was lucky in another way. In 1950, war had broken out in
the Korean Peninsula. When the army of North Korea backed by
China swept across the 38th Parallel, President Truman pledged to
support the South Korean government of Syngman Rhee and the
United Nations backed 'police action' to defend the South. Britain
was rapidly drawn into the conflict, and 90,000 Britons, many of
them national servicemen, would fight and die in Korea. By 1952,
the savage war in Korea had ground to a stalemate but the conflict
generated massive demand for tin and rubber and the Malayan
economy boomed. Estate managers now had ample funds to invest
in fortifying their estates against MNLA attacks. Templer lavished
money on accelerating resettlement and also splashed out on a propaganda war. Another 'man with a plan' was sent to Malaya to fight a
war of the mind. This was Hugh Carleton Greene, the older brother
of the famous novelist Graham Greene, a very tall, thin, shambling
and bespectacled gentleman with a razor-sharp mind. Ensconced
as head of the Emergency Information Services (EIS) in the appro-
priately named Bluff Road, Greene quickly realised that weaning
Chinese hearts and minds from communism had to be a priority.

Greene insisted that propaganda must be credible and stand up
to cross-checking. Don't, he insisted, underestimate the enemy.
Second, propaganda should have a positive message and not merely
threaten the enemy. Greene, for example, vetoed a proposed leaf-
let called 'Death to Min Yuen Workers'. Shrewdly, he argued that
information should be spiced with entertainment. Here spoke a fu-

ture director general of the BBC! Greene commissioned radio shows such as 'Spotlight on the Emergency' and 'This is Communism' that leavened hard news with spots for a radio doctor and well-known storytellers. Finally, Greene insisted, propaganda had to draw on the most refined, up-to-date and precise market research, culled from meticulous examination of MNLA documents. The EIS invested heavily in film and radio propaganda, and mobile projection units toured Malay kampongs and resettlement villages projecting films such as 'The New Life: Resettlement in Johor', 'Rewards for Information' and 'Communist Extortion Methods'. Greene made sure his producers spread the jam of entertainment on the bread of information.

This was the war the British won. Resettlement eviscerated the MNLA and the campaign to win hearts and minds slowly built a sense of national identity for Malayans – and shamed the communists. At the same time, British troops pushed the MNLA ever deeper into Malaya's rainforests and made sure ordinary people read about the rising 'kill rates' and saw the corpses of MNLA men and women that were displayed on roadsides and in villages. British soldiers habitually decapitated the MNLA men they killed to make sure they kept an accurate head count. By the time Templer left Malaya in July 1954, some 5,000 guerrillas were still under arms in the Malayan jungles, but MNLA numbers were in steep decline.

The road to independence now lay not through the barrel of a gun but along the long, bumpy road of communal reconciliation. The time had come to mend fences. The British view was that the peoples of Malaya had to deserve independence by resolving deeply felt and long-held communal antagonisms. The road to independence would be paved with good intentions that covered festering hatreds. It bears repeating that it was the British who had created and deepened ethnic divisions between races. Now they insisted that the price of independence was communal harmony.

CHAPTER 20

The Clever Mr Lee: The Rise and Rise of Lee Kuan Yew

L ike Singapore's first chief minister, David Marshall, Lee Kuan Yew was an outsider. Then, perhaps, all Asians were outsiders in colonial Singapore. Who, it might reasonably be asked, were the insiders? Marshall's family were Levantine Jews from Iraq. On his father's side, Lee belonged to the Chinese Hakka community. In her *Hakka Cookbook*, Linda Lau Anusasananan tells us that the Hakka have been seen as guests, gypsies, nomads, barbarians, outsiders, even Mongolians. The word 'Hakka' in Chinese is 客家, pronounced *kejia* in Mandarin, literally meaning 'guest people'. The word *zhu* 主, 'owner', is used to identify local or native residents. The Chinese nationalist Sun Yat Sen, Chinese leader Deng Xiaoping, Taiwan's Lee Teng Hui and Lee Kuan Yew were all Hakka. Lee's great-grandfather Lee Bok Boon or Li Muwen had emigrated from the tiny village of Tangxi in southern Guangdong, and the house he built there with money earned in Singapore has become a shrine for Chinese admirers of Lee Kuan Yew: 'We are still immensely proud that a world leader has come from our village,' the local Communist Party official told the *Straits Times* in 2016. According to historians, the Hakka Chinese never completely assimilated with southern Chinese. It was Hakka Chinese who incited the Taiping Rebellion that shattered China in the mid-nineteenth century. Lee's mother, Chua Jim Neo, was of Hakka and Peranakan descent, and is fondly remembered by many Singaporeans as the author of *Mrs Lee's Cookbook*, a collection of Peranakan recipes. At home, Lee grew up speaking English as a first language, in addition to Cantonese and Malay. It seems he learnt neither the Hakka dialect nor Mandarin until his political career took off in the mid-1950s and he began taking Chinese lessons.

Political Awakening

To begin with, he was Harry – Harry Lee, his English name – and a precocious schoolboy. Harry and his future wife Kwa Geok Choo were top-scoring performers at the Raffles Institution and Raffles College. Both aspired to continue their education at a top English university. In 1942, the Japanese Imperial Army hurled their ambitions off the tracks. Like many Asians who witnessed the humiliation of the British garrison by Japanese soldiers, Lee was astonished by the fragility of British rule. He knew that his own life was now in danger. This was the time of the Sook Ching, Japan's deadly onslaught on the Chinese communities in Singapore. When the Japanese military police, the Kempeitai, began rounding up Chinese men, Lee had a narrow escape. He gave the Japanese the slip and fled home. He was safe and the waves of mass killings slowly began to fade. For the next three years, Lee, like many other educated Asians in occupied Singapore, adapted well to life in Syonan-to. He learnt Japanese and was given a job at Sentosa Island listening in to Allied radio stations. By the end of 1943, he was in no doubt that the Japanese were losing the war.

Debating the Future

In 1945, the Japanese surrendered and the British were back. The British had been shamed by surrender, now they presided over a shabby peace. Lee described the years after the war as an 'education in unfairness and absurdity'. But the battered British Empire had not completely lost its allure for Lee and Geok Choo. They left for England at the end of 1946, and by the Lent Term of 1947 both were studying law in Cambridge, she at Girton College, he at Fitzwilliam. Both graduated with starred firsts. They discovered a nation that was experiencing a polite sort of revolution. In the general election of 1945, Clement Attlee had ousted the Conservative war leader Win-

ston Churchill and launched social reforms that promised a land fit
for heroes, including a National Health Service 'free at the point of
need'. Lee was impressed by the Attlee government, and while still
in Cambridge joined the campaign to elect his friend and fellow law
student David Widdicombe as Labour MP. He lost but Lee had got
his first taste of the hardships and frustration of campaigning. He
and Geok Choo had not forgotten Singapore. Britain and her allies
had won the war but the fate of the empire was uncertain. The Labour government was divided. India became independent in 1947,
but Britain was bankrupted by war and Attlee was reluctant to give
up lucrative colonial possessions like Malaya. Yes, the sun was going down on the British Empire but no one could be certain when
it would finally set.

For the subjects of empire like young Harry Lee, hope was laced
with frustration. When he was called to the bar at Middle Temple in London, Lee and Geok Choo joined the Malayan Forum in
London. This was no mere talking shop. It was founded by Abdul
Razak Hussein, who would later become prime minister of Malaysia, Goh Keng Swee and Maurice Baker. At meetings of the forum,
Malay and Chinese students could freely discuss and debate the future of Malaya. How could independence be won and what kind of
nation did Malayans want? In January 1950, Lee Kuan Yew stood
before his friends and delivered a speech of remarkable sophistication and prescience. Here is his conclusion: 'No sane man whether
he be English, Malay, Indian, Eurasian, or Chinese, can honestly
study the situation in that part of the world, and not come to the
conclusion that either with or without the opposition of the Western educated intelligentsia in Malaya, British imperialism will end.
At the moment it is clear that the only party organised to force the
British to leave, and to run the country, is the Communist Party.
They are not merely so many bandits, shooting and being shot at
in the jungle, and creating terror for the sake of terror. Theirs is a
tightly knit organisation making their bid for power.' The roots of
the PAP as a 'tightly knit' political organisation can be traced to the
Malayan Communist Party.

Becoming an Activist

By 1951, Lee was back in Singapore. He was no longer Harry. Now as Lee Kuan Yew, he and Geok Choo launched legal careers. For David Marshall, Lee and many others, English law was the pathway to political activism. Lee and Geok Choo joined the legal firm of Laycock and Ong and dabbled half-heartedly in politics. John Laycock was an unusual fellow, an ebullient, hard-drinking, former rock-climbing enthusiast who founded Singapore's first 'race blind' sports club, the Island Club. In 1948, Laycock had joined a group of other English-educated lawyers as well as Indian and Chinese business-men to found the Progressive Party and contest the first elections to the Legislative Assembly in 1948. In 1951, Lee was roped into Laycock's election team but he was unimpressed by the party's narrow vision and dirty campaigning tactics. At his Oxley Rise home, Lee and old friends from the Malayan Forum met to thrash out a loftier vision of the future. Lee and the other members of the 'Oxley Rise Set', as he called these gatherings, argued long into the night about how to win a mass base and build political muscle.

Then, early in 1952, Mr P. Govindaswamy and three Malay men stepped into the offices of Laycock and Ong and asked to see Lee Kuan Yew. By then, the Lees were well known for taking on litigation cases, often pro bono, for hawkers, unionists and other disadvantaged Asians. His visitors that day worked for the Singapore Post Office. They told Lee that they were planning strike action and needed a legal representative to make their case. The dispute was about pay, but the postmen were also defying embedded inequalities in colonial Singapore. They were protesting the fact that British expatriate employees had been awarded a much higher pay rise than Asian postmen. Lee agreed to take on the postmen's case even though, as he confessed to Laycock, 'there would not be much money in it.'

The Turning Point

The postal strike would be a turning point in the history of Singapore and a pivotal moment in the political career of Lee Kuan Yew: 'Little did I know,' Lee recalled, 'that I would be guiding union leaders in a strike that in two weeks changed the political climate.'

Lee did much more than put the postmen's cause on a firm legal footing. He shrewdly took charge of the press campaign; in other words, he took control of the narrative to put pressure on the employers and the government. His old friend Goh Keng Swee introduced Lee to S. Rajaratnam, a reporter for the *Singapore Standard*, who was well known for his fair reporting of strikes and disputes. At Oxley Rise, night after night for two weeks, Lee and Rajaratnam hammered out a press campaign to make the postmen's case and win sympathy for their cause. And it worked. The government agreed to arbitration and the two sides patched up their differences. Lee and the postmen had won, and thanks to Rajaratnam's stream of reports, Lee was a celebrity of sorts. Newspaper reports of the time often featured photographs that showed a confidently smiling Lee shoulder to shoulder with the striking postmen or striding into meetings with government officials. His offices at Laycock and Ong and the basement kitchen at Oxley Rise thronged with workers and union reps clamouring for Lee's 'counsel of last resort'.

A New Party

The political lessons were clear. Lee and the men and women who gathered in the basement of Oxley Rise to chew over the future of Singapore had no doubt that the mass membership and organisational muscle of the labour movement were the keys to power and change. Here was the road to independence – Merdeka. When Sir John Nicholl announced in 1954 that popular elections for the new Legislative Assembly would be held the following year, Lee and his closest associates, Goh Keng Swee, S. Rajaratnam and Toh Chin Chye, made a momentous decision. They would set up a new party to go head to head with the supine Progressive Party and the Labour Front to contest the elections. On 21 November 1954, the People's Action Party (PAP) was registered with the electoral commission. Lee's appointment as secretary-general was uncontested.

Later, Lee admitted that the infant PAP was a club of 'English educated colonial bourgeoisie'. It was all very well jaw wagging about independence. The funders of the PAP had to find a way to tap into the simmering cauldron of political energies that was welling up among Singapore's students and workers. We can see this happening in the early work of the poet Edwin Thumboo, who is admired by many Singaporeans today as a sort of unofficial poet laureate. His father was a Tamil schoolteacher, his mother a Teochew Chinese-Peranakan housewife. At school, Edwin was bullied. Precociously talented, Thumboo fought back with words. Inspired by his English teacher, Thumboo began writing poetry and entered the University of Malaya in 1953. He joined the Socialist Club where he met like-minded men and women who defined themselves as cosmopolitan Malayans. Thumboo joined the editorial board of the socialist journal *Fajar*, which means 'dawn' in Malay, and hatched up a local Esperanto he called 'EngMalChin'.

The Riots of 13 May 1954

On the evening of 13 May 1954, Thumboo and a group of university friends left the Cathay Cinema and began strolling home along the Penang Road. It was a dry, warm evening. As they approached the dark mass of Fort Canning, then known as King George V Park, large numbers of Chinese students rushed past and chained themselves to the park railings. Riot police, clad in wicker shields and waving wooden batons, followed in hot pursuit. For the first time, Thumboo and his friends caught the bitter taste of tear gas on their tongues.

The riots of 13 May 1954 had been provoked by the British introduction of national service for young Chinese men. The next day, the British ordered the closure of all Chinese schools, but students were having none of it. They locked themselves in their classrooms, organised their own lessons and went on a hunger strike. The students could not be prised from their barricaded classrooms for many weeks. It was only in the second week of June that the police restored order.

Thumboo and the other members of the *Fajar* editorial board were thrilled by the Chinese students' defiance. In his poem 'May 1954', Thumboo found the words for the moment:

Do not ignore, dismiss, pretending we are foolish;
Harbour contempt in eloquence. We know your
Language.

My father felt his master's voice, obeyed,
But hid his grievous, wounded self...
Depart Tom, Dick and Harry.
Gently, with ceremony;
We may still be friends,
Even love you ... from a distance.

Just a few days *before* the riots erupted, the editors of *Fajar* had published an article under the title 'Aggression in Asia'. The author branded Singapore a police state. When the Special Branch spotted the article, they put two and two together and made five. Police raided the Socialist Club, arrested Thumboo and the editors of *Fajar* and charged them with sedition.

Lee Kuan Yew sprang to the students' defence. He and his colleague, the left-wing barrister D. N. Pritt, made mincemeat of the government's case, and in a blaze of newspaper headlines succeeded in getting Thumboo and the other students released. Soon afterwards, Lee agreed to act for Chinese students arrested during the riots. He was already well known in Singapore. The camera liked his confident smile. Sympathetic reporters lapped up his sardonic put-downs. When Lee took on the cause of the Chinese students, he caught the attention of two Chinese firebrands. Lim Chin Siong and Fong Swee Suan had won the hearts and minds of many Chinese students and workers. A few weeks later, the two young men knocked on the door of Oxley Rise. They were, Lee remembered 'well mannered, earnest and sincere, simple in their clothes'. They came to Lee's home, of course, accompanied by an interpreter for neither Lee nor his visitors shared a common language. Lim's 'ringing voice,' Lee remembered, 'flowed in his native Hokkien.' Lee himself, of course, spoke in English.

This encounter between the highly educated English-speaking lawyer and the two young Chinese unionists still fascinates historians of Singapore's battle for independence. At the time, Lee's friend Goh Keng Swee feared that such a bond was 'reckless folly', but Lee instantly saw in Lim and Fong the 'kind of lieutenants he'd been looking for'. At that first meeting, he explained his plans for a new political party to speak for the 'workers and the dispossessed'. Lim and Fong left Oxley Rise unconvinced. That is not surprising. Lee

represented, as he admitted, the establishment, the 'colonial bourgeoisie'. Yet, this smooth-talking English-speaking lawyer with a
ready smile for the press photographers had taken on the British
establishment and won. Two weeks later, Lim and Fong were back,
with their interpreter. Yes, they would join Lee in the new party,
not to 'seek power', they insisted, but to expose the colonial regime
and the inadequacies of the Rendell Commission. They wanted to
'demolish the parties that would take office'.

The Charismatic Lims

This was a radical agenda, to be sure, and Lee must have realised
that talk of 'demolition' would not do in the long run. By 1954, the
communist insurgency was fizzling out on the other side of the
Causeway. The British would need to be persuaded and cajoled, not
bullied, into granting independence. This was not Lim and Fong's
vision of the future. They made no secret of their admiration for
Mao Zedong and had been thrilled by the 1949 revolution in China.
They were excited by the promise of the liberation movements that
were taking on the old colonial powers all over Africa and Asia. So,
Goh was right: getting into bed with Lim and Fong was high risk, a
gamble on Singapore's future. But Lee could see a lot more clearly
than some of his more cautious associates that if the new party had
any chance of breaking out of the 'English-educated bourgeois box',
he needed to get Lim and Fong on his side. He would describe this
later as joining up 'the disconnected bits of the anti-colonial movement' to become the movement's 'telephone exchange'.

To understand why Lee needed Lim and Fong, we need to understand the people they spoke for and represented or, to put it
another way, the energies they could connect to the fledgling new
party. Lim and Fong emerged from a Singaporean world that Lee
and his English-educated associates knew little about. This was the
Chinese-speaking Chinese-educated majority who in divided and
unequal colonial Singapore still lived precarious lives in the shadows. This was not, however, a silent or submissive majority. Fifty
per cent of Singapore's population was under twenty-one, and despite chronic underfunding many ordinary Chinese schools were
hives of hot-blooded dissent. Lim and Fong had met at the Chinese

High School. They had both, Lim recalled, 'loved reading'. Chinese schools and their bookworm students who ardently sucked up new ideas in Chinese translations were the foundries of the anti-colonial movement. Lim and Fong were both active members of the short-lived Anti British League, but for school principals their openly expressed sentiments were an embarrassment. Both had been expelled from the Chinese High School. They had taken jobs as bus workers and rapidly made their mark as highly articulate and astute union leaders.

Lee was the Cambridge-educated, English-speaking, media-friendly campaigning legal counsel who spoke up for the 'workers and the dispossessed'. Lim and Fong were the real thing: the current powering the 'telephone exchange'. The truly astonishing significance of the moment Lee and his Oxley Rise associates joined Lim, Fong and other unionists on the stage of the Victoria Memorial Hall for the inaugural meeting of the People's Action Party in November 1954, was missed by the *Straits Times* reporter who dutifully attended the event. He merely noted that the founders of the new party had to make way for the early afternoon screening of an 'absurd film' about a Persian princess. Lee himself admitted there was 'little electricity in the air'. Speeches declaring that the PAP would fight to secure Merdeka and banish inequality were duly and drily read out. The PAP did not spring onto Singapore's political stage bawling and bellowing. But very soon after that first tentative gathering in the Memorial Hall, Singapore's first minister, David Marshall, would feel the heat and sting of a vibrant new political force.

The Front Line

The front line was the Hock Lee Bus Company on Alexandra Road. When the bus workers voted to join Lim and Fong's Singapore Bus Workers' Union, the SBWU, the management had them fired. With the union's backing, the bus workers began picketing the depot by forming a human chain across the entrance and stopping buses. Some of the bus workers went on a hunger strike. When the police broke up the picket line, students and other sympathisers rushed to the Hock Lee depot to back the strikers. Across Singapore, workers in other companies struck. With May Day approaching, the government feared a nationwide stoppage. This was very bad news for First Minister Marshall. He backed workers' rights but was obliged as a member of the government to find a way to halt the slide into chaos. He rushed to Alexandra Road where he met with Lim and Fong and their legal representative, the PAP leader Lee Kuan Yew.

As Marshall struggled to persuade the strikers to show moderation and responsibility, Lee, Lin and Fong took their fight to the people. On May Day, Lee addressed a huge crowd that had crammed into the Oriental Theatre on New Bridge Road. He turned all his rhetorical gifts against the chief minister. He poured scorn on what he called 'half-past six democracy'. Lim went even further – there is bound to be bloodshed in the course of the revolution.

And bloodshed there was. On 12 May, huge crowds of students and workers mustered outside the gates of the bus company. The police ordered the crowd to go home. No one moved. At about 7 p.m., the police turned high-powered water cannons on the crowds, blasting people into drains and turning pebbles and glass into missiles that lacerated the faces of workers and students. Blood flowed. By the end of the following day, fourteen people and been injured and two killed, including the American correspondent Gene Symonds who found himself in the wrong place at the wrong time. The government began shutting down Chinese schools. Singapore's bus workers retaliated by calling a nationwide strike. Then on 14 May, Marshall announced that he had reached a settlement. As the strikes and stoppages erupted across Singapore, Marshall and Lee Kuan Yew had jointly thrashed out a deal with the Hock Lee management. It was an impressive achievement. Bus workers would be allowed to join unions and sacked workers would be reinstated. With Lee's backing, Marshall had won. He seemed to have quelled the bubbling cauldron of worker unrest and got the bus workers a good deal. He had, as it transpired, lost a much bigger war.

Marshall Fights Back

But not yet. After the Hock Lee riots, Marshall was in bad odour in government circles and denounced by the Singapore's conservatives and European expats in the pages of the *Straits Times* for 'surrendering' to the rioters. Like the British planters in Malaya who had rounded on Sir Edward Gent, they demanded that Marshall act or get out. He refused to resort to what he called the 'bullet and Emergency regulations'. As pro-government factions sharpened knives, Fong Swee Suan and the Bus Workers Union exulted in the victory they had won against the Hock Lee management and urged other unions to seize the moment. From April 1955 to the end of the year, Singapore witnessed a battery of strikes, walk-offs and stoppages that in one way or another united workers, leaders, communists and socialists. As Lee put it, Lim and Fong had 'a swing door to push', and push they did, day after day. Marshall dithered. He was reluctant to turn on the workers he had won office to protect. But then he lashed out. Using the Emergency regulations, he ordered the arrest of the most intransigent unionists. One of them was Fong Swee Suan. In the Legislative Assembly, Lim turned on Marshall: 'I share the same beliefs,' he proclaimed 'and the same aims as Fong Swee Suan.' He challenged the government to arrest him too.

Marshall was in grave danger of appearing to be a colonial stooge – the accusation he had flung at the Progressive Party. He made an audacious move to recapture the left. In early July, he proposed that the new governor, Sir Robert Black, agree to appoint new ministers to the cabinet who would take on powers that the colonial government still stubbornly kept for itself. Marshall threatened, as he put it, to tear the 'scraggy hand of death', the colonial government, from the 'breaks of progress'. When the governor dug in his heels, Marshall threatened to resign, thus recapturing his old role as David confronting Goliath. The rumour that Marshall was about to resign hit the newspapers all too soon and big crowds gathered outside the Legislative Assembly demanding 'Marshall must stay!' Hansard, the records of the British parliament, shows that Marshall had influential allies in Westminster. Fenner Brockway, a veteran critic of the British Empire spoke up: 'While hoping that Mr David Marshall will continue to serve as Chief Minister, may I ask the right hon. Gentleman whether he will convey to the Secretary of State, before the conversations take place, the feeling of many hon. Members of this House that the peoples of Singapore and Malaya are now as determined to end colonialism as the peoples of India were in 1946, and that steps should be taken for the realisation of full self-government in these territories?'

Fearing that if Marshall carried out his threat, Singapore might plunge ever deeper into chaos, the colonial secretary sent Marshall a mealy-mouthed invitation for talks in London about the constitutional future of Singapore. This was not quite Merdeka but it was nonetheless a victory for Marshall. He had won back respect from even his harshest critics. In the Legislative Assembly, he turned on Lim, demanding that he come clean about whether or not he was a communist. Marshall caught Lim's political ally Lee Kuan Yew on the back foot. Lee was forced into making a public statement that the PAP was committed to a democratic, non-communist Malaya. This was the first clear sign that Lee, sooner or later, would have to confront his two firebrand lieutenants. For now, in mid-1955, the ball was back in Marshall's court. After the humiliation of the Hock Lee riots, Marshall had found a second political wind, but before long his hopes of winning Merdeka would be sunk by an intransigent British government and a moment of slapstick farce.

CHAPTER 21

High Noon:
The London Talks

I n December 1955, Marshall headed for London to prepare for
negotiations scheduled for April the following year. On the
way, he stopped off in Delhi, describing himself as a 'pilgrim in the
land of Gandhi and Nehru'. He received, he reported, 'warm encour-
agement' from Prime Minister Nehru but recklessly 'swore to bring
down the selfish gods of the Colonial Office'. His words outraged
the secretary of state for the colonies, Lennox Boyd. Nor did his
rhetoric go down well in Singapore. Lee fulminated about the 'er-
ratic' first minister. When he finally met Boyd, Marshall pushed for
a maximalist version of independence that embraced the Federation
of Malaya and the states of Sarawak, Brunei and North Borneo as
well as Singapore. Boyd delivered, Marshall wrote later, a 'cold, angry reply'. Marshall was gambling on bolstering his reputation in
Singapore by acting tough in London. He was, it seems, tilting at
windmills. Early the following year, British Prime Minister Anthony
Eden agreed to send a parliamentary mission to Singapore to 'see
for themselves if Singapore was ready for independence'. Marshall,
the *Canberra Times* reported, hoped that the people of Britain would
see that the people of Singapore were human beings 'not monkeys
in trees'. Back in Singapore, Marshall called for a 'Merdeka Week'
to demonstrate to the visiting British MPs that Singaporeans were
indeed ready for self-government. The celebrations would reach a
climax with a mass rally at Kallang Airport. The visiting British MPs
would attend. The disaster that unfolded at Kallang Airport on 18
March 1956 doomed Marshall's crusade for independence.

Disaster at Kallang Airport

During the morning, huge crowds gathered at the airport. Many were supporters of the People's Action Party (PAP) who had come to hear their hero Lim Chin Siong address the rally. Many carried placards showing the communist dove of peace. Many were singing and performing the communist *yanko* dance. Marshall was driven through the crowds in an open-topped convertible, his arm raised in the Merdeka salute. Was this hubris, a politician flying too close to the sun? He stepped out of the car and walked, smiling broadly, towards a wooden dais that had been hastily constructed on the edge of the airport runway. Huge crowds pressed against police lines. Marshall was joined by Lee Kuan Yew, Lim Chin Siong and Ong Eng Guan. Inside the terminal building, the British delegation waited nervously. Marshall, Lee and the other PAP leaders climbed the rickety wooden stairs onto the stage and turned to face the crowd. Marshall raised his arm again and stepped forward to grasp a microphone stand. He summoned up all his rhetorical energies. Suddenly, as if the Merdeka salute had been a signal, the crowd surged through the police lines and stormed the stage. The fragile wooden structure crumpled and gave way – and all the microphones went dead. Under a surging sea of banners, angry young people turned on the police. Others began throwing bricks at the windows of the Kallang terminal building. The British MPs cowered inside as the glass shattered.

The catastrophe at Kallang was rich in unwished-for symbolism. Marshall's flimsy platform had collapsed. No one could hear him speak. The communist *yanko* dancers had won the day. In the demeaning language of the colonial rulers of Singapore, the unruly peoples of the Singapore were not 'ready for self-government'.

Showdown in London

It was a chastened Marshall who flew back to London in April accompanied by other representatives of the Labour Front, Lee Kuan Yew and Lim Chin Siong. In the aftermath of the Kallang disaster, Marshall was in a weakened position. He sternly denounced communism, but the British government was not convinced he could hold the ground against the leftists. Nor were the Americans. In London and Washington, fear that Singapore might become a communist bridgehead in the Far East was hard to counter. The 'Merdeka riots' stoked British and American anxieties that 'Fortress Singapore' was too volatile to trust. A profile in *Time* magazine portrayed Marshall as an untrustworthy tub-thumper, a pipe-smoking, bush-shirted and 'violently anti-colonialist'. Yet, to the discomfiture of the other delegates, Marshall could not resist playing up his anti-colonial credentials. He told Prime Minister Eden, 'I am no diplomat … I am a missionary of democracy.'

Negotiations were slow and frustrating. Discussion soon bogged down on the matter of internal security. Marshall insisted again and again that 'British control of internal security deprived us of the reality of internal self-government.' He was right, of course, but he had, recklessly, run up his flag as 'Merdeka or bust' and he had no room for manoeuvre. Since the British suspected that Marshall could not rein in the leftists, they refused to give way. Marshall had boxed himself even deeper into a corner by threatening to resign (again) if the London talks failed. His response to any setback was to bluster.

The British were not Marshall's only problem. His fellow delegates were running out of patience and Lee decided to act. Without consulting Marshall, Lee called a press conference and openly scolded the chief minister's 'ineptitude'. Lee's calm, rational and, above all, *pragmatic* performance was positively reported in newspapers and on the BBC. Here was a man the British government could do business with. Soon afterwards, Lee and Lim left London and returned to Singapore. The die was cast. The PAP leaders had crossed the Rubicon. Marshall bitterly complained that he had had no idea that the colonial secretary had 'already lined up a new government'.

In June, Marshall resigned. He would become a bit-part player in Singaporean politics before ascending to grand old man status. History has, perhaps inevitably, judged Marshall less fairly than his rivals. Lee Kuan Yew was not yet in the driving seat in that turbulent year and, if he had been, may not have succeeded in reconciling the clashing pressures of an intransigent colonial government and the cauldron of unrest on the streets of Singapore. Marshall had, as he promised, 'awakened' the people of Singapore and taken the first steps to reform Singapore's chronic social and ethnic inequalities.

There was a 'Marshall Plan' for Singapore and it laid the foundations of independence.

Independence in Malaya

In Malaya, the struggle for independence had taken a different course. As daylight faded on 30 August 1957, thousands of people began gathering on the Padang in the centre of Kuala Lumpur. They had come to witness 'the greatest moment in the life of the Malayan people', the words used by the prime minister designate, Tunku Abdul Rahman, to describe the handover of power by the British. In April 1949, the British government had made a commitment to Malaya's independence but insisted on a transition period of between fifteen and twenty-five years. Just under ten years later, Malaya became an independent nation in a few minutes of magnificent political theatre. Two minutes before midnight, the Tunku was driven onto the Padang to join members of the Alliance Party youth division. The lights on the Padang were doused. The crowd waited in silence. Then, as the hands of the clock on the façade of the government buildings chimed midnight, the lights were switched back on and the Union flag was lowered as a military band played 'God Save the Queen'. The new flag of Malaya was raised and the band played 'Negaraku' (literally 'My Nation'), the national anthem. The huge crowd chanted 'Merdeka!' ('Independence') seven times. A new nation had been born.

The grand theatre of Merdeka at the end of August 1957 papered over some harsh realities. The British had granted independence only to the Malay Peninsula. The government in London had not yet given up Singapore, and the status of North Borneo, Brunei and Sarawak was unresolved. Merdeka, it might be concluded, was only half won, a partial victory. The British still had the power to impose a kind of points system. Independence had to be *earned*. At the beginning of the 1950s, Dato' Onn bin Jaffar had tried to persuade the other UMNO leaders to open the party to non-Malays. He had failed. So, too, had the Chinese Malaysian Chinese Association (MCA) leader Tan Cheng Lock, who had similarly struggled to open his party to non-Chinese office holders. Under pressure from the British who insisted on ending communal politics, the Malay, Chinese and Indian leaders finally agreed to form a united front as the Alliance Party. None of the parties, which eventually included the Malayan Indian Congress, gave up their ethnic identity but agreed to form a coalition as the only viable candidate for government. A lot of communal cracks were papered over.

Another important milestone was passed in December 1955. Earlier in the year, the Malayan Communist Party had reached out to the Alliance to discuss 'peaceful co-existence'. Chin Peng saw which way the wind was blowing, and he wanted a stake in independence. Defying British advice, the Tunku agreed to talks. Accompanied by the chief minister of Singapore, David Marshall, and Tan Cheng Lock, he travelled to Baling in Kedah to confront Chin Peng in the classroom of a government school. The Tunku, strongly backed by Marshall, harangued Chin Peng about the evils of communism and made it very clear that the MCP and its military wing might only have a role in an independent Malaya on condition that they completely renounce communism. Since the British by 1955 had blunted the fighting capacity of the Malayan National Liberation Army, Chin Peng had no choice but to walk away from the talks and return to his beleaguered jungle stronghold. By agreeing to meet Chin Peng and insist on what amounted to surrender, the Tunku and his Alliance partners had convinced the British that they would never share power with communists. By then, the Emergency was merely a clean-up operation. The MNLA was a spent force. The Tunku and the Alliance had inoculated Malaya against the communist virus. For the British, Singapore still showed symptoms of infection.

The Promise and Price of Independence

For Lee Kuan Yew and the moderate wing of the PAP, the lessons of the London negotiations were all too clear and troubling. The Colonial Office would not give up more power unless political leaders in Singapore showed that they were prepared to take on the left and exorcise the demon of communism. The task was a daunting one. By the end of 1956, Singapore appeared to have begun a steep descent into anarchy. In October, Chinese students had once again taken to the streets: rioting claimed twelve lives and over a hundred injured.

The new chief minister, the tough-talking Lim Yew Hock, imposed a curfew; the British transferred troops from Malaya; and military helicopters throbbed over the streets of Chinatown. Lim was leader of the Singapore People's Alliance, which had been formed in 1958 as a merger of the Labour Front and the Liberal Socialists. The important point is that Lim and the Alliance were rivals, not allies, of Lee and the PAP. In September, Lim ordered arrests of leading leftists and outlawed the most vociferous student and labour unions. Lim had taken an enormous risk for he had struck at the PAP itself. He arrested Lee's allies Lim Chin Siong and Fong Swee Suan. For Lee, Lim's purge was both a dilemma and an opportunity.

The political storm soon burst. After the debacle in London, Lee Kuan Yew had come round decisively to realising that the British would never agree to relinquish control of Singapore's internal security until the nettle of communism was grasped. The price of independence would be purging the left and the cost to reputation could be very high. Lee's new-found pragmatism enraged the left wing of the PAP. Lee was accused of cowardice. The dilemma for the PAP was that, even with Lim and Fong behind bars, the left could still run rings round the moderates. Faced with a rebellion in the party he had founded, Lee and his allies resigned from the executive. The result, a stalemate.

Lee and the 'Oxley Rise Set' had forged an alliance with Lim, Fong and other firebrand leftists to tap into the human reservoir of the Chinese schools and unions. Many Chinese in Singapore were impressed by the feats of Mao Zedong's communist party in China. Communism was not yet a dirty word. Declaring war on the leftists could backfire by weakening the PAP's grip on its most important and numerous constituency of supporters. But Lee realised that there was a way out. In his memoirs, he reveals that he 'calculated' that the chief minister, who represented a different party, would take the necessary action. In other words, Lim Yew Hock would do the dirty work. He did just that, launching another round of arrests to strike even harder at 'communist fellow travellers'. With the left crippled, Lee and the moderates took back control of the PAP executive and began rebuilding the party from the ground up. They began weeding out anyone loyal to Lim and Fong. In the meantime, Chinese voters, appalled by the purge, deserted Lim's party in droves and began paying attention to the PAP.

Reassured by the purges, the British agreed to further constitutional reforms and a fresh election was called to be held in May
1959. Under new citizenship laws, the number of people eligible to
vote had swollen the register by some 300,000 voters, all required
by law to cast their ballots. These first-time voters were ordinary
Singaporeans from every ethnic community who had until this pivotal moment played bit parts in the battle for independence. Few
of these first timers had much interest in ideologies, unions or the
intricacies of constitutional reform. Many Chinese parents hoped
that their rebellious children would forsake the revolution, go back
to their desks and get good jobs. They would, in short, vote for better lives. Lee's great insight was that this once-silent majority would
speak with the voice of the PAP.

The PAP Storms to Victory

In a remarkably short period of time, Lee Kuan Yew and the moderates in the PAP had shed the burden of the leftists. In Changi Prison,
as Lim Chin Siong, Fong Swee Suan, Devan Nair, Sandra Woodhull
and the other PAP detainees pondered the future of Singapore, Lee
and his supporters got on with the job. They had cleverly left the
dirty business of roundups and arrests to the chief minister, and so
it was Lim Yew Hock who took the flak as a 'British stooge' or 'fas-
cist'. This was damaging enough. Then in 1958, Francis Thomas,
a minister in Lim's governing party, the Singapore People's Alliance, turned whistle-blower and exposed the shady doings of other
ministers who had pocketed illegal donations from the American
government to buy shares and new houses. Thomas resigned from
the government and in a moment of high drama strode across the
floor of the Legislative Assembly to join the PAP. Since 1954, Lee
and the PAP members had all worn white to proclaim the party's
unimpeachable purity. That short walk was a moment of exquisite
political theatre.

It is often said that elections are lost by incumbents rather than
won by the opposition. This does not apply to Singapore's general
election in 1959. To be sure, Lee and the PAP had been reinvented
as moderates and Lim's government was hobbled by scandal. But

Lee and the other PAP leaders fought a dazzling campaign. Few missed the eloquence of Lim and Fong when they heard rising stars like Ong Eng Guan, who won control of the Singapore City Council for the PAP, who showed he had the same crowd-pulling talents and gift for theatre as David Marshall. As soon as he had been appointed mayor, Ong insisted on the removal of the fusty old mayoral mace and refused to wear any of the pompous regalia that had traditionally come with the job. He was a fiery Chinese speaker who won the hearts and minds of the Chinese 'silent majority' who were voting for the first time. Lee Kuan Yew had realised also that English, however eloquent, would never win over the new Chinese voters. He could always draw large crowds, and for the first time nervously began using his rather basic Mandarin. He would not completely master the language for some time but his efforts went down well. Getting Chinese voters on board was a key strategy for the PAP, but fortunately Lee also spoke excellent Malay. The PAP's campaign seemed to bring under one tent roof all the ethnic communities of Singapore and speak with a single voice regardless of language or dialect. This was nation-building as much as electioneering. The future citizens of Singapore would not be defined only as Chinese, Indian or Malay but as Malayans.

On polling day, 30 May 1959, the PAP won a decisive, landslide victory. The party took 43 of 51 seats in the Legislative Assembly. Lee Kuan Yew became Singapore's first elected prime minister. Soon after the results were announced, some 60,000 party supporters gathered in the early evening to celebrate on the Padang in front of City Hall. The *London Times* rather patronisingly reported that the event was more carnival than political rally. It was, simply, very Singaporean. The Padang, where the British had strolled, gossiped and played countless games of cricket, was turned into a huge street market. Hundreds of food stalls were lit by a glowing constellation of paraffin lamps. Lee and the party leaders gathered beneath a huge PAP banner. Spotlights illuminated the bold red lightning stroke set in a blue circle.

Lee was daunted by victory. It was a victory, he remembered later, 'but I was not jubilant'. The people of Singapore had voted for a revolution. Could the PAP step up to the mark? Five days later, the last British governor of Singapore, Bill Goode, arrived at City Hall to

be received by the new leaders of self-governing Singapore. In the
not too distant past, the British governor would have donned the
ceremonial plumed hat of colonial power. On 5 June 1959, Goode
wore a sombre dark suit. The winds of change were beginning to
blow away the fusty cobwebs of empire. When Lee Kuan Yew and
the other ministers of the new government had been sworn in, the
new prime minister led his ministers, all clad in gleaming white, in
a solemn procession from City Hall to the Legislative Assembly. In
a victory speech, Lee had told his supporters that they had won 'a
victory over wrong, clean over dirty, righteousness over evil'. Fine
words, but how would the men in white haul colonial Singapore
into a new era of freedom?

CHAPTER 22

The Formation of Malaysia: Independence at Last

B y the end of a tumultuous decade, the communist threat was fading in Malaya. Singaporeans went to the polls in 1959, the Emergency was officially declared to be over. After more than twelve years, the undeclared war with the Malayan National Liberation Army had been won. Chin Peng and the other communist leaders fled across the Thai border; Chin Peng himself eventually ended up in Beijing. In Kuala Lumpur, however, anti-communist rhetoric did not diminish with victory and was refocused on the little island on the other side of the Causeway.

Among his United Malays National Organisation associates, Tunku Abdul Rahman often vented his fear that Singapore might 'go communist' and become 'the Cuba of Southeast Asia'. He acknowledged that Britain had given Singapore self-government while keeping a firm grip on defence and internal security. The problem was that this was a transitional settlement that would expire in 1963. At that point, Lee Kuan Yew's government would almost certainly demand full independence, with complete control over its own affairs. The nightmare scenario was an independent, communist Singapore joining forces with leftists in Malaya. There was, the Tunku believed, only one solution. Reluctantly he had begun to embrace the idea of a union of independent Malaya with 'Chinese' Singapore.

On 27 May 1961, he left Kuala Lumpur to make a speech to foreign journalists at the Adelphi Hotel in Singapore. He astonished his listeners by proposing to 'seek an understanding' with the people of Britain, Singapore, North Borneo, Brunei and Sarawak, in other words, to yoke together all the former British colonial territories in a single nation. It was not a new idea. But for the Tunku, in the anxious aftermath of independence, union made a lot of sense. It would put the lid on the Singapore leftists, and the huge risk of Malays being overwhelmed by the Singapore Chinese would be countered by the inclusion of the Borneo states, Sabah and Sarawak, as Malays in the peninsula viewed the peoples of Borneo as ethnic kin.

Social Revolution in Singapore

In the aftermath of the spectacular People's Action Party victory in 1959, Prime Minister Lee Kuan Yew set out an ambitious plan for the future in 'The Tasks Ahead: PAP's Five Year Plan' which, Lee insisted, promised 'a social revolution through peaceful means' but in some ears sounded like something Josef Stalin might have hatched up. Lee and his ministers, the men in white, were determined to rid Singapore of the evils of the past, the inequalities and divisions that blighted its history. Lee promised a revolution but knew all too well that if he wanted to keep Singapore afloat in the perilous waters of Cold War Asia he could not afford to get on the wrong side of the former colonial power and her much more powerful ally, the United States. The harsh fact is that the PAP government was on probation. The British still maintained a garrison on the island and could with little difficulty snatch away everything the PAP had won in 1959. Just as Lee's new government settled into power and prepared to shape the future, the old demons of leftist rebellion bubbled up inside the PAP.

As soon as all the Merdeka razzamatazz was over, Lee and his ministers rolled up their sleeves and got to work. The 'men in white' possessed formidable technocratic expertise, but to begin with the efforts of the PAP seemed to many Singaporeans to be largely cosmetic. As all Singaporeans and expats know, appearances count for a lot in Singapore life and culture. Get a taxi at Changi Airport and on the only route into town you will see scores of hooded workers busily clipping hedges. Singapore is a manicured 'garden city'.

The roots of all this clipping, shearing and pavement washing can be traced to the fragile early years of self-government. On 8 June 1959, the PAP launched a campaign against 'yellow culture', a literal translation of the Chinese phrase *huangse wenhua*, which refers to decadent behaviour such as gambling, opium-smoking, prostitution, pornography, corruption and nepotism that supposedly plagued China in the nineteenth century. The 'yellow culture' campaign was energetically pursued for many decades.

Spearheaded by then Minister for Home Affairs Ong Pang Boon and supported by the Ministry of Culture, the government launched a nationwide clamp-down on hedonistic 'foreign influences' that were supposedly promoting anti-social behaviour and lifestyles and corrupting Malayan youths.

Singapore's cultural revolution reached into every nook and cranny of society – and even as far as the hair follicles of its citizens. The Undesirable Publications Ordinance and the Cinematograph Film Ordinance banned obscene publications and films depicting crime, violence, sex, nudity, racial prejudice as well as those glorifying colonialism. The PAP outlawed pin-table saloons on the grounds that they allowed gangsters to corrupt young people. Chinese mutual aid associations and social clubs were also shut in a futile attempt to stamp out gambling. Very few cultural activities were left untouched by the government campaign: Radio Singapura banned rock and roll music, and in the late 1960s the government turned on hippie culture – in fact, any man with long hair. Long hair seemed to provoke especially intense anxiety since it was associated with drugs and promiscuity. On 1 November 1974, the PAP launched Operation Snip Snip to target subversive coiffure: men with long hair were served last at government offices and companies were discouraged from hiring long-haired men. Employees who transgressed were fired; long-haired tourists were forbidden entry.

Lee's cultural revolution was profoundly puritanical. As a reporter from *Time* magazine put it, the PAP was a party of 'zealous, tieless and coatless puritans'. In such a small city-state, Lee had the means to impose pervasive norms on Singaporean citizens. Singapore became a kind of experimental laboratory designed to manufacture well-behaved, productive citizens, who would become as manicured as the city's parks and freeways. Lee often roped in his ministers and government employees to join ordinary people in mass campaigns to clean up the streets, beaches and parks. To be a good Singaporean you had to get your hands dirty cleaning up the city. It was a kind of top-down state puritanism and for decades set the tone of a new Singapore rising from the dirt and squalor of its colonial past.

The Cost of Reform

Such a zealous top-down remaking of Singapore would be expensive. Lee took risks slashing the salaries of government employees who had to 'give up their maids', as he put it. Details mattered. He ordered air-conditioning installed in offices to promote alertness. As a student in Cambridge after the war, Lee, who was not especially fond of Singapore's colonial masters, was impressed by the achievements of Clement Attlee's Labour government which had nationalised failing industries and begun building a public welfare and health service. The PAP revolution would also be a government-led enterprise and the engines of change would be big new public organisations which would become familiar acronyms for Singaporeans: the Housing & Development Board (HDB), which replaced the ineffectual old Singapore Improvement Trust, and the Public Utilities Board (PUB). In its early years, the HDB was a well-oiled home-building machine. Slums were cleared and a new landscape of monolithic HDB blocks sprang up across central Singapore. The HDB blocks were not works of art, but as 'machines for living in' they worked. By 1963, the government was building forty housing units every minute.

Change on such a scale is rarely accomplished without breaking a few eggs. There were many Singaporeans who regretted having to leave behind the communal world of the kampong for new homes some ridiculed as 'rabbit hutches'. But there were just as many others who were thrilled by the HDB's 'streets in the sky'. This urban revolution took place in the lifetimes of Singaporeans who are still alive today. There was no point throwing up so many new homes and then neglecting the hearts and minds of the people who would rent or own the family homes of the next generation of Singaporeans.

Building a Malayan Culture

The task for the first minister of culture, Sinnathamby Rajaratnam, was to mould a new kind of citizen, weaned from his or her ethnic or clan identity as a true 'Malayan'. Rajaratnam identified communal tensions or, as he put it, the 'tragedy of racial conflict', as the biggest threat to a happy and harmonious Singapore: 'We must consciously set about inoculating society against such dangers...,' he insisted. This new Malayan culture would need to embrace difference from the get go. Inoculation meant multiculturalism. The PAP officially recognised four Singaporean languages – English, Chinese, Malay and Tamil – but Rajaratnam assumed that Malay would become a shared common language among the 'races'. The ministry actively promoted manufacturing this Multikulti Singapore, with events such as the People's Cultural Concerts at the Botanic Gardens which dutifully showcased songs and dances drawn from every ethnic culture. The prime minister and his government colleagues were often photographed at these worthy singalongs, sitting cross-legged with smiling ordinary folks.

Industrial Revolution

This was the soft edge of the PAP's cultural revolution. There was a harder battle to fight in the swamplands of Jurong and the little island of Pulau Samulan. It was here in Singapore's wild west that the PAP minister of finance, Goh Keng Swee, jump started an industrial revolution. Backed by a team of UN advisers led by the Dutch economist Albert Winsemius, Goh despatched armies of workers into the muddy world of the Jurong wastelands to construct from scratch a new world of factories, refineries and shipyards. Goh had a vision of a reinvented port city that would not only shift the world's cargoes but make stuff as well. On the front line, work was hard and not always safe. Goh feared that his 'Jurong Industrial Estate' would go down in history as 'Goh's Folly'. But as one of the pioneers put it, 'You are staying in Singapore. You are earning from Singapore. You sure support Singapore.'

Lee and his ministers could never forget that they had not yet crossed the finish line – and the big test would come in 1963 when the transitional constitution was due to expire. The umbilical cord that connected Singapore to London had not yet been cut. Lee understood that even now independence had to be deserved. The world was in the grip of the Cold War and Lee had to demonstrate that Singapore was a safe bet for the Cold War warriors in Washington and London – and for investors from anywhere. The new government needed to prove its loyalty to the global cause of anticommunism and offer a safe haven for capital. Lee concluded that it was time to summon up the spirit of Sir Thomas Stamford Raffles.

In the aftermath of the 1959 election, there were many Singaporeans who urged the government to forget Raffles once and for all. The old bronze statue should be pulled down. Raffles had once gazed sightlessly across the Padang providing sports fans with a convenient platform to watch beefy men in cricket whites play the old game of empire. The Japanese had dumped the statue in a museum. Now he stood awaiting his fate on Boat Quay on the spot where he and Major William Farquhar had stepped ashore to meet the Temenggong of Johor in 1819. Now Raffles' saviour turned out to be the Dutch economist and development guru Albert Winsemius. The mature decision, he argued, would be to hang onto Sir Stamford and leave him to stand gazing into the future. His argument, so persuasively put to Lee and Minister of Culture Rajaratnam, was simple. The preservation of Raffles would reassure foreign investors. Under its founder's marble gaze, Singapore was open for business.

The Enemy Within

What, then, was the prime minister of Malaya, Tunku Abdul Rahman, so worried about? How could this vibrant, new-fangled Singapore possibly turn into an Asian Cuba? To answer that question, we need to rewind to the beginning of June 1959, the moment Lee Kuan Yew proclaimed independence, Merdeka, standing alongside the other PAP leaders on the steps of City Hall. A few days later, a very different moment of political theatre unfolded outside the gates of Changi Prison. The PAP radicals detained two years earlier on the orders of Lim Yew Hock walked free out of the gates of Changi Prison. According to the *Straits Times*, a noisy crowd of thousands of supporters joyously greeted and garlanded their heroes – Lim Chin Siong, Fong Swee Suan, Devan Nair, James Puthucheary and Sandra Woodhull. The *Time* headline read 'OUT! ... WHAT A WELCOME!' Newsreel cameramen captured the moment Lim released a pair of doves, symbols of freedom, that ascended into the sky with a noisy clatter of wings. Dig deeper and we discover that these joyous moments had been orchestrated by none other than Singapore's new prime minister.

Lee was still Lim and Fong's legal counsel and he had often visited his clients in prison. During the election campaign in 1959, Lee had made it clear that he would take office only on condition that the PAP prisoners were released. It was a political balancing act that David Marshall failed to master. Lee had relied on Lim to purge the troublesome party radicals and then spoke up on their behalf when they were all safely locked away. They would be offered freedom on Lee's terms. He imposed two binding conditions. First, the prisoners would not be freed until the new government was sworn in and victory was celebrated in their absence. Second, as a condition of their release, the detainees each had to sign a manifesto entitled 'The Ends and Means of Malayan Socialism', literally 'signing on' to Lee's vision of the future. Only the best-known, most popular prisoners were released. As Lim, Fong and the other celebrity detainees walked free, twenty-eight leftists remained locked up inside Changi.

It did not take long for trouble to brew. After their release, the most prominent former detainees were given jobs in the new ministries. James Puthucheary was, after all, a respected economist who had spent his time in prison writing a book about the future direction of the Malayan economy, and so Lee put him in charge of the new Industrial Promotion Board. Lim and Fong were given backroom jobs as 'political secretaries' and quickly became disillusioned. Neither was allocated an office. All the former detainees were stripped of rights in the PAP. In 1960, the government set up a centralised trade union congress to inhibit unions calling strikes. For Fong, who was working for the Ministry of Labour, this was a step too far and he publicly attacked Lee, who promptly removed him from the ministry. The embers of rebellion were starting to glow ominously.

Lee under Fire

The first serious attacks on Lee Kuan Yew's position came from an unexpected direction. And pitted him against was an old foe. In July 1961, David Marshall spat out all his suppressed anger at 'Emperor

Lee Kuan Yew' whom he accused, in a bitter tirade, of 'humbug, hypocrisy, hate, vanity, arrogance and ruthlessness'. Marshall concluded, 'We are not the blind chicken you think we are. Resign!' Marshall had campaigned for immediate and full independence for Singapore. Lee had made another powerful enemy.

We last encountered Ong Eng Guan as the charismatic new mayor of the Singapore City Council who Lee praised as a 'crowd puller'. After the election, Lee rewarded Ong with the post of Minister for National Development, hoping to firm up government support in the Chinese communities loyal to Ong. But the new minister soon demonstrated that he was not prepared to kowtow to the PAP central committee. He moved his ministry lock, stock and barrel to his Chinatown constituency in Hong Lim, and rather than getting down to the hard graft of development, he reignited the campaign for full independence and attacked the influence of foreigners. Infuriated, Lee humiliated Ong by downsizing his ministerial brief but Ong fought back. He attacked Lee's leadership style and called for the release of the leftists who were still in prison. He began preparing a draft resolution for the PAP annual conference proposing reforms to democratise party policy-making by appointing a new watchdog committee with powers of veto. For Lee, Ong's resolution was an attack on the foundations of the PAP and tantamount to treachery. Moments after the conference opened, Ong was expelled from the party and lost his seat in the Legislative Assembly. But Lee was not yet rid of the troublesome Ong. In April 1961, Ong campaigned as an independent to win back his old stronghold in Chinatown and defeated the PAP candidate with a resounding 73 per cent of the vote.

The Tunku's Grand Design

In the wake of these political body blows, Lee took the customary step of offering to resign, and although his offer was rejected, Singapore politics again looked volatile and unpredictable. It certainly appeared that way to Tunku Abdul Rahman, and it was his and his government's fears of political turbulence in Singapore and a possible communist takeover there that persuaded him to make his 'Grand Design' speech to the Singapore Press Club at the end of May 1961. As British records show, it was the younger members of the

Malayan government, Deputy Prime Minister Abdul Razak Hussein and Minister of Finance Tan Siew Sin, who had pushed a hesitant Tunku to embrace the idea of merger with Singapore. The proposal of a Federation of Malaysia merging Malaya with Singapore and the Borneo territories killed two birds with one constitutional stone. The federal government in Kuala Lumpur would have the means to press the lid firmly down on the communists in Singapore. At the same time, by incorporating the non-Chinese peoples of North Borneo, Brunei and Sarawak as Malaysian citizens, the Tunku allayed Malay anxieties about the Chinese majority in Singapore. The British, for their part, accepted that the Borneo territories would be the price they would have to pay to persuade the Malayan government to accept Singapore as a base.

In the early 1960s, British Prime Minister Harold Macmillan and Colonial Secretary Iain Macleod were preoccupied with Africa and tardy in establishing any firm policy for the future of Singapore. Macmillan delegated this task to the new commissioner-general of Southeast Asia, 'Geordie' Selkirk, who had just been sacked as first lord of the Admiralty. When Selkirk arrived in Singapore, he was impressed by the PAP leadership but reported that Lee was 'depressingly pessimistic' about communist influence on Chinese schools and unions. He was 'obsessed' and 'rightly so'. Exasperated by his government's failure to come up with a coherent policy for Southeast Asia, Selkirk also embraced merger as the only viable outcome. He warned, tellingly, that 'Our ability to influence the course of events declines with the passage of time.' The truth of this became all too clear when in the aftermath of the Tunku's 'Grand Design' speech, Lim and five other trade union leaders loudly demanded complete autonomy for Singapore, a new constitution that abolished the Internal Security Council (ISC) and the end of all British privileges on the island.

Lee Campaigns for Unification

It is hardly surprising that Lee Kuan Yew, reeling from the bitter aftermath of those stinging by-election defeats, embraced the Tunku's proposal. Since the British clung to Singapore as a secure Cold War base in Asia, merger was the only way to achieve full independence.

Lee was fully backed by his cabinet. For Finance Minister Goh Keng Swee, merger offered a way to shore up his ambitious and as yet unproven plans to industrialise Singapore. Lee and the majority of his ministers were convinced that Singapore could not 'go it alone'. And so, discussions soon opened between the Malayan government and the PAP to thrash out the details of a Malaysian federation.

Merger with Malaya horrified Lim and the other PAP rebels. The Tunku made it clear that the new federal government in Kuala Lumpur would oversee Singapore's defence, international relations and internal security. Singapore would have its own assembly controlling education, labour legislation and, after a lot of squabbling, much of its revenue. In 1955, Marshall had been strong-armed into allowing the British to retain control of internal security. Now Lee agreed to hand it over to the Malayan government to secure merger. The PAP rebels would not have been in any doubt that the Tunku and his allies would use merger to crush the threat from the left.

What Lee feared most of all was a collapse in public order that would force the British to retake control. This would demolish his standing and scupper his political career for good. On 17 July, Lee approached Selkirk with a proposal that can only be described as worthy of Machiavelli. He explained to Selkirk that he planned to demand the release of all detainees to outflank the leftists by seeming to be anti-British. Secretly, he went on, the British and Malayans should agree to veto the releases. His political enemies would stay locked up while he could at the same time blame the ISC and bolster his anti-colonial kudos. And there was more. Lee proposed that Selkirk, as the Queen's representative, would prorogue the Legislative Assembly to disguise the PAP's loss of a governing majority. In the meantime, Lee and the Tunku would rush through the merger agreement. On the same day, former detainee James Puthucheary telephoned Selkirk and requested a meeting with 'a few friends'. The following morning, Lim Chin Siong and Puthucheary led a small party into Selkirk's offices at Eden Hall, his residence on Nassim Road. They wanted an assurance that if the Lee government fell, the British would refrain from declaring martial law. In other words, they were arguing that the PAP was not the sole guarantor of a stable Singapore. Selkirk replied that he would respect any new party that came to power through non-violent, democratic means. He seemed to be implying that he would support Lee's rivals.

When Lee heard about the 'Eden Hall Tea Party' he angrily accused Selkirk of 'flirting with the communists' and plotting to split the PAP. In the same speech, Lee claimed that he had a plan to release the detainees and now blamed his opponents for vetoing it.

The Birth of the Barisan Socialis

In the meantime, Singapore plunged into political turmoil. Lee narrowly survived a vote of confidence after the PAP's defeat in the Anson by-election but lashed out at the rebels. He openly denounced Lim and others as communists, a charge Lim famously denied: 'I am not a communist, or a communist front-man or for that matter anybody's front man.' Lee was a brilliant political strategist. By launching a frontal attack on Lim, he gambled on winning the approval of the Tunku. The consequence was that he tore the PAP apart. On 13 August 1961, Lim addressed, speaking in Mandarin and Malay, a crowd of 10,000 passionately noisy supporters at the Happy Valley Stadium to announce the formation of a new party, the Barisan Sosialis, or Socialist Front, of Singapore. Battle lines were drawn and the gloves were well and truly off. Lim promised his followers a 'democratic, non-communist, socialist Malaya'. The new party was not a malcontents' talking shop. The Barisan shattered the PAP, taking control of 35 local branches out of 51 and scored direct hits on the PAP leadership by seizing Tanjong Pagar, Lee's own seat, Rochor and Kampong Glam. There were open mutinies in the People's Association and Work Brigades, and Lim and Fong could count on the support of most of the Chinese unions. In the Legislative Assembly, the PAP's majority now hung by a thread.

The Battle for Merger

Lee Kuan Yew was now under intense pressure from both the British and the Malayan members of the Internal Security Council (ISC) to hit back hard. But Lee was much smarter. He appealed to the people of Singapore to back him or sack him. On 13 September 1961, tens of thousands of Singaporeans tuned into Radio Singapura as Lee delivered the first of a series of twelve radio talks called

'The Battle for Merger'. Lee's genius was to speak above and beyond squabbling party factions. He struck a reconciliatory tone to begin with and praised Lim and the others for courageously demanding independence, then rapped them on the knuckles for turning their backs on 'peaceful and democratic socialism'. Lee wrote later that his strategy was to be completely candid about the political infighting and betrayals, the riots, strikes and boycotts and even his own bonds with the communists. For many of his listeners, Lee's was a calm, reasoned and, for many of his listeners, fatherly voice that made sense of the confusing sound and fury of politics. In modern political terminology, Lee took control of the narrative. He told a story that might yet, if Singaporeans followed his advice and leadership, have a happy ending. At the end of each talk, Lee concluded with a cliff-hanger, convincing his listeners to tune in again and again as he painstakingly made the case for merger and, of course, his own leadership.

Meanwhile, British Prime Minister Harold Macmillan, who had not been impressed by Selkirk's machinations, wrote directly to the Tunku expressing support for the concept of a Greater Malaysia and inviting him and Lee to London for talks. Macmillan made it clear that he shared the Tunku's fears that independent Singapore might become a satellite of China. For both UMNO and the British government, merger was a means to guarantee that the pivotal city state would not fall into the clutches of Mao Zedong. He had concluded, he wrote, that it was essential to take a decisive step to secure the island's future. And that step meant federation. The ball of merger was rolling faster, and on 24 August 1961 the Tunku met Lee and reached agreement to create a Greater Malaysia. At the London talks that followed soon afterwards, Lee seized the initiative just as he had in 1955 when he had outmanoeuvred David Marshall. He won over reporters and got on famously with the abrasive Commonwealth Relations Secretary Duncan Sandys, who treated the Tunku and Abdul Razak Hussein with ill-disguised contempt. When he returned to Singapore, Lee easily won the vote for merger in the Legislative Assembly with votes from the PAP rump and Lim Yew Hock's supporters. All other parties joined a Barisan walkout. Lee was, for now at least, back in control. But the fight was not over yet.

Thorny Issues

The road to merger would be to be a bumpy one of many twists and turns. Tunku Abdul Rahman provoked the first quarrel by demanding immediate mass arrests of Singaporean opposition leaders. Selkirk resisted the Tunku's demands on the grounds that there was no convincing evidence at all that Lim and the Barisan Socialis (Singapura) leaders were planning violence and that arrests on any scale would 'arouse a storm of protest'. Lee, as we will soon discover, was not opposed to detaining his opponents but vetoed, with Selkirk's backing, any such action until 'Malaysia was completely tied up'. In March, Lee travelled to Kuala Lumpur to confront the Tunku but ended up agreeing to a new security agreement that seemed to satisfy the Malayan side. Taken by surprise, Selkirk refused to agree to the new plan and the Malayans withdrew from the ISC in protest. Once again, political temperatures in Singapore and Kuala Lumpur began to rise. In the aftermath of Lee's visit, UMNO (the United Malays National Organisation) launched a campaign of verbal threats directed at both Singaporeans and the British. When the Tunku returned to Singapore to lay the foundation stone for a new headquarters for his party, he made a number of provocative speeches threatening to 'cut the Causeway' if the government of Singapore now refused to go through with merger.

The Referendum Solution

The old issue of security was only one cause of friction. The other was citizenship. What status would Singaporeans have in the new federation? Under the terms of the agreement negotiated by Lee and the Tunku, Singaporeans would not be citizens but 'nationals' with no voting rights in Malaya. The very reasonable fear that Singaporeans might end up as 'second-rate' citizens in the federation soon became highly charged. In September, Lim Yew Hock proposed a way to take the heat out of the problem. He tabled a motion for a referendum on merger to be held on 1 September. Since no party in Singapore objected to merger in principle, it was a referendum not on the what but the how. Voters were then offered three options A, B and C, which were pinned to the different parties and their leaders. Option A was the PAP proposal for an autonomous Singapore within a Malaysian federation. This was Lee's policy and, Selkirk warned, he was taking a huge risk putting it to the popular vote. But Lee cunningly persuaded the Legislative Assembly to accept that all abstentions and blank ballots would be counted as votes in favour of Option A. Lee's grip on power had wobbled frequently since 1959 and the referendum would be the most decisive test of all. Selkirk and other pessimistic British officials feared that Lee had blundered, but the referendum result turned out to be his biggest triumph as 71 per cent of the electorate voted for merger on Lee's terms. As Goh confessed later, the party had taken back control of Singapore's destiny from a 'position of total collapse'.

Operation Coldstore

The triumph of the referendum results cleared the way for draconian action. Lee, with British and Malayan backing, now struck back against the Barisan Sosialis leaders. In the early morning of 2 February 1963, the government sent more than sixty police units to addresses across Singapore to round up the usual suspects. 'Operation Coldstore' had begun. 'There was a knock on the door. I opened the door, and it was an old neighbour of mine carrying a rifle,' recalled Fong Swee Suan, who had been born in Malaya and was now handed over to the Federal Government in Kuala Lumpur. The police had a list of 169 names. Quite a few managed to escape but 113 ended up in custody. As well as Fong, Lim Chin Siong, Sandra Woodhull, James Puthucheary and over twenty other leading members of the Barisan were all behind bars in Changi Prison. Lee had offered Lim the chance to flee to Indonesia, but he refused. They now faced years in prison without any prospect of a trial. Soon after the arrests, the ISC announced that the Singapore Special Branch had uncovered evidence that the Barisan leaders were plotting to overturn the government and establish a 'Communist Cuba' in Singapore. No hard evidence proving the existence of such a plot has ever been discovered.

Months of wrangling between Lee, the Malayan government, Selkirk and Duncan Sandys in London had preceded the decision to launch Operation Coldstore. Lee hesitated because he was anxious that once the Barisan leftists had been taken care of, the Tunku would lose interest in the creation of a federated Malaysia or walk away with the Borneo territories and leave Singapore to its own fate. After all, the Tunku was focused almost entirely on the supposed 'communist threat' in Singapore and if Lee neutralised the left, he might lose important leverage.

The British also stayed Lee's hand. What mattered was the appearance of fair play: there should be no mass arrests without evidence of a clear and present danger. And it was Lim Chin Siong who inadvertently provided cover. On the night of 7 December 1962, the People's Party of Brunei, backed by Indonesia and the Philippines, staged a revolt against inclusion in the Malaysian Federation. In Singapore, the Special Branch reported that two days earlier Lim had met Sheik A. M. Azahari, leader of the People's Party who was on his way to Manila. There is no evidence that Lim was involved in the Brunei revolt but Lim's meeting with Azahari was good enough for Selkirk to give the nod to Lee. On the morning of 2 February 1963, 113 leading figures in the Barisan, who were detained without trial, were interrogated and tortured at Changi Prison. Lim was put in solitary confinement and given psychotropic drugs. Long before, Lee had said of Lim that 'he will be the future prime minister'. Lim was not released from prison until 1969, when he was exiled to England, where for many years he worked as a grocer in Bayswater in London.

However, the government baulked at banning outright the Barisan Socialis (Singapura). Even with so many of its members locked up, the party was still a force to be reckoned with. On 22 April, Dr Lee Siew Choh, one of the party leaders who had not been arrested, led a crowd of supporters to City Hall to protest against the detentions. The protestors clashed with the police and Dr Lee and a number of others were arrested. The hearings were scheduled to start in August. Lee chose this moment, when the Barisan leadership was thoroughly distracted, to call a snap election. Even though the Barisan was hobbled by mass arrests, the PAP could not afford to take the outcome of the election for granted. Lee had launched a one-man election campaign at the end of 1962, and in the eleven months that followed, he reached out to every one of the island's fifty-one constituencies. He brought a simple message: 'The government's got to do the job. Homes must be built, clinics must be built, roads must be made, money must be saved – the people must be taken care of.'

Lee's insight was that the man himself could be the message. He had first discovered this power when he had spoken up in the court-room for the downtrodden and oppressed. He had rediscovered it on Radio Singapura and now he would go deep into Singapore's grassroots to demonstrate that he was the man to get the job done and 'look after the people'. Now, in 1963, Lee was not confined to radio. He could appear on television screens. Judy Bloodworth, a television 'sound person', whose husband Dennis was the corre-spondent in Singapore for the *London Observer* newspaper, provided a vivid account of the rallies: 'We would arrive in pitch darkness sometimes, then suddenly the lights would go up, the people would cheer and boo … [Lee] would be elated, push his way down among them, laugh at the lion dancers around him, careless of the roaring fireworks, never showing fear.' Lee spoke in market Malay, Chinese, English and even some faltering Hokkien. 'They were all cheering for me.' These scenes of a smiling, elated Lee in the midst of happy Singaporeans were splashed all over public television screens in coffee shops, community centres and a few more affluent homes. Lee, we discover in his memoirs, had been tutored by the best. In London for merger talks the year before, he had been introduced to BBC producer Hugh Burnett, who had won fame as the producer of a series of probing television interviews called 'Face to Face'. Lee admits that when he first viewed himself in television interviews, he had looked 'fierce'. Burnett's advice was simple: 'Be natural, be direct, be yourself.' Easier said than done, but somehow it worked. Television would make Lee, in his own words, a Singaporean 'every-man', 'a kind of political pop star'. He rather cattily noted that his Barisan opponents 'looked ugly and menacing'. In the early days of political television, many confident public speakers were undone by the merciless scrutiny of the camera lens.

Even though its leaders were locked up in Changi Prison, many Barisan candidates fought a determined campaign against over-whelming odds. Both sides played political hardball, and in the lead-up to election day, Selkirk suspected that the results might be too close to call. British officials debated how they would deal with a Barisan government. They had no need to be concerned. On 21 September 1963, the PAP won a landslide victory for a second time, winning 37 seats to Barisan's 13.

There can be little doubt that Operation Coldstore and the destruction of the Barisan leadership made the party's defeat almost inevitable. Nor can it be denied that the PAP and its leaders had campaigned on its record in government, in other words, the achievements of the social revolution it had promised in 1959. That revolution was unfinished, but many tens of thousands of Singaporeans now enjoyed new jobs, new houses, new utilities and new hospitals, schools and clinics thanks to Lee Kuan Yew and the 'men in white'. The people of Singapore had also, on 16 September, become citizens of a fully independent new nation, the Federation of Malaysia. Lee had gambled on merger and his bet seemed to be paying out. The PAP had delivered jobs, houses, hospitals and, at last, an undiluted Merdeka. Raffles still stood on Boat Quay, but the British yoke had at last been lifted.

CHAPTER 23

Together Apart: Singapore Goes It Alone

T roubled courtships do not always end in failure but the marriage of Malaya and Singapore was very soon on the rocks. Merger had enemies within and without. Its fiercest opponent was the first president of Indonesia, the vast archipelago nation to the south of Singapore. Sukarno had won the first great independence struggle in Southeast Asia, ousting the Dutch to create a sprawling new nation in 1949. By the end of the 1950s, Sukarno presided over an uneasy coalition of the huge Indonesian Communist Party (Parti Komunis Indonesia, or PKI), a few Islamic parties and the Army. Sukarno preached an ideology that he called Nasakom, an acronym that yoked together the Indonesian words NASionalisme (nationalism), Agama (religion), and KOMunisme (communism). To the dismay of the United States and Britain, the PKI flourished to become the largest non-ruling communist party in the world. In the early 1960s, Sukarno formally aligned Indonesia with Communist China.

As the governments of Singapore and Malaya edged closer to merger, Sukarno denounced the idea of a Malaysian Federation as a British-sponsored neo-colonial project. The flashpoint came in Brunei. In the early 1960s, the island of Borneo was divided between the Indonesian province of Kalimantan in the south and the hodgepodge of British Crown Colonies, North Borneo and Sarawak, and Brunei in the north. The idea of merger was already controversial here, and in February and March 1962 the Colonial Office sent a Commission of Inquiry, led by Lord Cobbold, to Sarawak and North Borneo to gauge public opinion about merger with Malaya. The Cobbold Commission discovered that about a third of the population was opposed, for different reasons, to the Malaysia project. There were many who wanted independence or a continuation of British rule. The Commission presciently reported that 'There will remain a hard core, vocal and politically active, which will oppose Malaysia on any terms unless it is preceded by independence and self-government: this hard core might amount to near 20 per cent of the population of Sarawak and somewhat less in North Borneo.' Nevertheless, Cobbold concluded that there was sufficient general support to go ahead with incorporating the Borneo territories. He confided to British Prime Minister Harold Macmillan, 'I have supported Malaysia in the report on the assumption that Singapore also joins in ... if Singapore were to drop out, a federation between Malaya and the Borneo territories without Singapore would have few attractions.'

The strongest resistance had come from within Brunei. Tunku Abdul Rahman had offered Brunei's ruler, Sultan Omar Ali Saifuddin III (r. 1950–67), the revolving post of the Yang Di-Pertuan Agong, or supreme ruler, that would be shared with the Malay sultans, but the sultan was reluctant to accept what he viewed as a 'demotion'. Even more importantly, he wanted to hang on to Brunei's huge offshore oil reserves that had already made him one of the richest individuals in the world. He was unwilling, in other words, to share his role or his wealth in a new state. Resistance to merger was also strong among the sultan's opponents. The Brunei People's Party and its leader, A. M. Azahari, despised the sultan and had long campaigned for a democratic revolution to rid Brunei of its despotic ruler. Azahari proposed creating a 'Unitary State of Kalimantan' in North Borneo which would hand the entire island to Indonesia. In December 1962, Azahari launched a rebellion in Brunei and adjacent regions of Sarawak and North Borneo. The British flew in Gurkha troops and the Brunei revolt was swiftly crushed. In the meantime, Sukarno and the PKI had backed the rebellion and begun broadcasting 'The Voice of the Freedom Fighters of North Kalimantan' from a transmitter near Pontianak in the south. When the rebellion collapsed, Azahari was offered asylum in Jakarta. It is easy to see why Lim Chin Siong's meeting with the Brunei rebel leader in Singapore was so imprudent.

Konfrontasi

The Brunei revolt was only the beginning of Sukarno's campaign against merger. A year later, the Indonesian foreign minister, Dr Subandrio, visited Beijing where he met with Zhou Enlai, the first premier of the People's Republic of China. Although relations between Indonesia and China had been upset by discrimination against Chinese citizens of Indonesia, Zhou Enlai indicated that China would support a 'national liberation war' in Brunei. On his return to Indonesia, Dr Subandrio announced Indonesia's policy of 'confrontation' with Malaysia, which was confirmed by Sukarno. The undeclared war of 'Konfrontasi', from 1963 to 1966, opposed to the formation of the Federation of Malaysia, had begun and it would be backed by Beijing.

At the southern end of the Malay Peninsula, Singapore was right on the front line. By mid-1965, Indonesian saboteurs had carried out at least forty terrorist bombings on Singapore, starting with an explosion near Katong Park on the east coast. It was the twenty-ninth attack that had the most chilling impact and lodged deep in Singaporeans' collective memories. Early in January 1965, two young men who served in Indonesia's Korps Komando Operasi (KKO), paddled a sampan across the narrow strait that separated Singapore from Batam, one of the Riau islands. They carried backpacks full of explosives and had instructions, they revealed later under interrogation, to 'bomb any place they liked'. From Changi, the two young commandos took a bus into town and ended up in Orchard Road. Here, they spotted an imposing 'red building' which they chose as a suitable target. They placed explosives next to a staircase, primed the fuses and calmly took the bus back to Changi. The sampan had vanished. At about 3 p.m., crime reporter Charles Tan Kok Siew, who was visiting the police station in Orchard Road, heard a loud explosion. Policemen rushed out of the station, 'all of them fully equipped' Tan remembered, and he followed. The imposing 'red building' the two commandos had chosen was MacDonald House, the headquarters of the Hongkong and Shanghai Bank. The explosion killed three bank staff, including two young women who were fatally injured by falling rubble. The news of the attack and the deaths of the bank clerks was shattering. The Konfrontasi war had reached with deadly effect into the commercial heart of Singapore. A few days later, a coastguard intercepted the two Indonesians who had tried to return to Bantam on a log. They were interrogated, tried and sentenced to death.

The MacDonald House bombing was traumatic. But even with support from China, Konfrontasi degenerated into a war of low-level conflict and infrequent skirmishes. The most violent phase began in April 1963 when Indonesian troops launched a surprise attack on the border village of Tebedu in Sarawak. This was followed by scores of raids over the next three years, which tapered off when British troops arrived to reinforce the border. On the other side of the South China Sea, Indonesian troops landed on the Johor coast followed by a team of parachutists. The 'invasion' was a humiliating washout. Most of the Indonesians were captured or killed. Many believed they had come as liberators but were astonished to discover that local people in Johor had no interest at all in being liberated.

Konfrontasi quietly fizzled out. In 1965, Indonesian army general Suharto turned on Sukarno and, with American and British backing, purged the communists from every corner of the Indonesian Archipelago, from Sumatra to the island of Bali. Army units killed at least half a million people suspected of being members of the KPI or supporters of the party. Many thousands more were locked away on island prison camps. This terrible period of Indonesian history was ignored by the international community and forgotten by most Indonesians. Government propaganda insisted that Suharto had saved Indonesia from communism. Half a century after the massacres, a documentary film by Joshua Oppenheimer called 'The Act of Killing' exposed Indonesia's long-overlooked period of mass murder to the world for the first time.

Sukarno had failed to 'crush Malaysia' and was ousted from power by General Suharto. A much deeper threat to the unity of Malaysia came not from external foes but from within the new federation and was fuelled by starkly opposed ideas of Malaysian identity. It was rather as if on the day after a rather strained wedding ceremony, the happy couple each woke up to realise that their new partner sitting opposite them at the breakfast table was a stranger with very different ideas about the future of their life together.

Crisis: The 1964 Federal Elections

The first signs of trouble came in April 1964 when Lee decided to contest a number of seats in Malaysia's Federal Elections. UMNO had fielded a few candidates in Singapore's elections in 1963 but the PAP's decision to take on Alliance candidates on the other side of the Causeway a year later provoked a storm of protest from UMNO: Tunku Abdul Rahman accused Lee of breaking a 'gentleman's agreement'. In the course of the campaign, the PAP candidates refrained from attacking UMNO directly but focused on its Alliance partner, the Malayan Chinese Association (MCA) and its president, Tan Siew Tin, who had succeeded his father Tan Cheng Lock, the founder of the party, and served as finance minister in the government. The PAP plan was to target the mass of Chinese voters by portraying the MCA as a party of 'silver spoon' elitists. Tan was indeed a millionaire. From the Tunku's side, it appeared that Lee and the PAP were proposing the same kind of leftist reforms they had pursued in Singapore. Was Singapore becoming the communist Trojan Horse he had always feared? Alarmingly, Lee attracted huge crowds at campaign meetings on the mainland but public interest failed to translate into actual votes. The Alliance won a sweeping victory with a crushing majority. The PAP gained a single seat.

For Lee and the PAP, the 1964 Federal Elections were a disaster. They failed to attract discontented Chinese voters and antagonised UMNO. As the dust settled, it was evident that the PAP and the Alliance were divided by a chasm that was both political and cultural. The PAP stood for peaceful social revolution, and the PAP government had already shown what that meant in real world terms with new flats, factories and community centres built for everyone regardless of ethnic identity. UMNO, the dominant party in the Alliance, was rooted in tradition, and staunchly committed to upholding Malay rights under the protection of a Malay king.

Communal Conflict Erupts in Singapore

The PAP had ventured across the Causeway and been rebuffed. In July, communal conflict erupted in Singapore. During the Federal Election campaign, the UMNO secretary-general in Singapore, Syed

Jafaar Albar, had attacked the record of the government which he accused of discriminating against Malays. He made very effective use of the Malay newspaper *Utusan Melayu* to draw attention to alleged unfairness in housing policy. The government was accused of 'resettling' Malays against their will. There is some irony in the fact that the founder of the *Utusan Melayu*, Yusof Ishak, had served as the Yang Di-Pertuan Negara or President of Singapore since 1959. The message pumped out on the pages of the newspaper was 'Do not treat the sons of the soil as step-children.' After the PAP humiliation in April, Syed Jafaar Albar and the other prominent UMNO representative in Singapore, Esa Almenoar, fired up Malay resentment against Lee, the PAP government and its Malay minister for social affairs, Othman Wok. On 12 July, Malays crammed into the New Star cinema in Pasir Panjang to listen to Albar calling for Malay unity against the PAP government to shouts of 'Kill him.... Kill him.... Othman Wok and Lee Kuan Yew.'

Just over a week later, on 21 July, Othman Wok made a courageous decision to lead a delegation of young PAP-supporting Muslims to join a mass celebration of Mawlid, the Prophet's birthday on the Padang. There were some seventy PAP delegates all dressed in white shirts and trousers among a crowd of 20,000 people. When Esa Almenoar rose to speak, he attacked 'cruel wrongdoers' whom he accused of driving Malays out of their homes – 'our castle, our place to live and our religion'. He called on the crowd to 'sacrifice their lives and properties for the sake of the country'. This was provocative talk, and Othman Wok became increasingly anxious when he heard angry young Muslims in the crowd proclaiming 'Allah-hu Akbar....'

After the speeches, the crowd began moving out of the Padang in the direction of Geylang Serai. It was, Othman Wok remembered, 'a very, very hot day'. He and the PAP delegation followed, their PAP banners fluttering to the beat of Malay drums. As the huge crowd turned into Arab Street, gangs of Malays began harassing the PAP youngsters, provocatively crying *Hidup Cina* ('Long live the Chinese') and *Mati Melayu* ('Death to the Malays'). At the Kallang Bridge, some of the marchers tried to find shelter from the brutal afternoon heat in the five-foot way along the route of the march. When the police intervened, the young Malays chased them away. The violence rippled through the crowds. Fearing the worst, Othman Wok led his party into the empty Kallang Airport to seek shelter. This was where David Marshall's Merdeka celebrations had gone so disastrously wrong a decade before. At about 6 p.m., Wok told the young PAP supporters to try and return to their homes; he also urged them to throw all PAP flags and banners into the river. In the meantime, the police declared a curfew. But the following day, the violence erupted again and this time did not end for four days. Twenty-two people were killed.

Negotiating Separation

The Malaysian marriage was now on the rocks. Quietly, behind firmly closed doors, divorce proceedings had already begun between Malaysian Deputy Prime Minister Abdul Razak Hussein and Goh Keng Swee, who had been the most enthusiastic advocate of merger on the PAP side. If there had been a battle for merger, the war of separation was now in full swing. As in any war, truth was the first casualty. In Kuala Lumpur, the Tunku and his deputy Abdul Razak Hussein suspected that Lee was hatching up a scheme to dump Malaya and join the old Straits Settlements and the Borneo territories in an alternative federation. And then came the shock that, according to the Tunku, 'broke the camel's back'. At the end of May, Lee travelled to Kuala Lumpur and made what would turn out to be his last speech to the Federal Parliament. He spoke first in English and then in Malay. He called on the government to respect the rights of all common people as Malaysian citizens and abandon what he provocatively called an obscurantist doctrine that offered rights to 'a few special Malays'. Lee proclaimed that 'We will wait and see – in 10 years we will breed a generation of Malays with educated minds, not filled with obscurantist stuff, but understanding the techniques of science and modern industrial management, capable, competent and assured the family background, the diet – health problems, the economic and social problems that prevent a Malay child from taking advantage of the educational opportunities which we offer free from the primary school to university. We will solve them, we will meet them, because in no other way can you hold this multi-racial society together.'

Lee always claimed that he fought tooth and nail for Singapore to remain part of Malaysia. His remarkable speech to the Federal Parliament tells a different story. He was challenging the fundamental principle of Malay political ideology, the privileging of Bumiputera (the 'sons of the soil'). Since the collapse of the Malayan Union in the 1940s, Malay political leaders doggedly insisted on Malay rights, and just as consistently Lee and the PAP rejected communal political ideologies. In this light, it is much more convincing to understand his speech as a forceful acknowledgement of irreconcilable differences. He knew that a leopard cannot change its spots. Tunku and his party were intractable. Lee was saying 'it's over'. In the early morning of 7 August, he summoned his closest colleagues, Toh Chin Chye and Sinnathamby Rajaratnam, to come immediately to Kuala Lumpur. When they arrived at Singapore House after a long, tense drive, Lee and Goh called them to a meeting. In the course of the days before Lee's dramatic call, he and Goh had thrashed out the terms of a divorce settlement with Abdul Razak Hussein and Eddie Barker, the minister for law, and Kadir Yusof, the attorney general. The party then proceeded to the Tunku's residence where the agreement was laboriously typed up and a great deal of whiskey was drunk. When the final Separation Document was presented to Toh and Rajaratnam the following day, both men were shaken and distressed. When the Tunku assured them that there was no going back, they agreed to sign. The Separation Document was then flown back to Singapore so that the rest of the cabinet could add their signatures.

Singapore Expelled from the Malaysian Federation

On 9 August, 1965 at 10 a.m., Singaporeans tuned in to hear the shattering announcement that Singapore had been expelled from the Malaysian Federation. At noon, Lee arrived at the studios of Singapore Radio & Television to explain to Singaporeans why the dream of merger was over. 'You see this is a moment of anguish,' Lee said. 'Would you mind if we stop for a while?' As he spoke, the most famous tears in Singapore history were shed. Lee's distress was genuine: he had been under severe stress for some time. But as ever, emotion served a political purpose. The truth was that negotiations for divorce had been going on for some time. Both sides had recognised that union was unworkable. The following day the front page of the *Straits Times* bluntly stated: SINGAPORE IS OUT. The Federation had lasted just twenty-three months.

Lee may have wept on television, but as he revealed in his memoir *The Singapore Story*, 'the merchants in Singapore's Chinatown were jubilant.' Crowds gathered to celebrate separation with the noise and spectacle of firecrackers. The day after the announcement, the streets of Chinatown were strewn with red-coloured debris. Separation set off a tremendous burst of activity in Asian stock markets. Investors had decided that separation was good for business. The second intriguing revelation in Lee's memoir is that throughout the fraught period of negotiation with the Tunku and Abdul Razak, no one had troubled to inform the British about what was going on. Lee says this omission filled him with remorse, but it was a clear signal that the peoples of Southeast Asia were making their own destiny. A few days later, Antony Henry Head, the high commissioner to Malaysia, called on Prime Minister Lee Kuan Yew at his official residence 'Sri Temasek' to discuss the implications of the new order of things. It was, Lee said, just a 'chit chat'. Lord Head was 'good at the stiff upper lip'. Lee explained the Malay fear that if they agreed to share power with non-Malays, they would be overwhelmed. Lee then writes: 'Despite the presence of 63,000 British servicemen, two aircraft carriers, 80 warships and 20 squadrons of aircraft ...' the British no longer had power or means to persuade the Malaysian government to abandon communalism, which was, in any case, the creation of the colonial power. On a global scale, the separation of Singapore and Malaysia as independent nations reflected the long withdrawal of British power 'east of Suez'. The ragged imperial flag was at last ready to be folded and taken home. The question was, what now?

CHAPTER 24

The Challenges of Independence: Singapore in the Cold War

L ee Kuan Yew and his government had no off-the-shelf model of development to go by and they faced a barrage of expert commentary that pronounced Singapore dead on arrival. For the PAP ministers, the hard question of survival was real and urgent. Goh Keng Swee admitted that the challenges that beset Singapore in 1965 were 'awesome and intimidating'. Singapore had prospered in the mid-nineteenth century by exploiting the riches of its hinterland in the mines and plantations of the Malay Peninsula. The island had few natural resources, and now the hinterland that had powered its rise to commercial power had been stripped away. Even water had to be imported from the reservoirs of Johor on the other side of the Causeway. In the early 1960s, Lee Kuan Yew had positioned Singapore as a member of the Non-Aligned Movement of developing countries that wanted independence from the power blocs of the Cold War. He sought out other non-aligned leaders like Nehru, Kenyatta, Nkrumah and Tito, and like them called out American aggression in Vietnam. His relations with the United States were often bumpy. In 1960, soon after the PAP's landslide election victory, a CIA agent was caught trying to buy information from a Singapore intelligence officer. When the bungled operation was exposed, the CIA offered to pay more than three million dollars to Lee to cover up the story. He, unsurprisingly, refused and the US secretary of state, Dean Rusk, apologised. In 1965, Lee talked about the incident in an interview, infuriating the American ambassador in Singapore. Lee did not mince his words. The CIA bribe, he said, 'may sound like James Bond and Goldfinger, only not as good but putrid and grotesque enough'. He drew a red line between his government and the pro-American Asian leaders: 'They are not dealing with Ngo Dinh Diem or Syngman Rhee. You do not buy and sell this government.' As Singapore steered into the waters of independence, Lee's commitment to a Non-Aligned policy would soon be put to the test.

The British Prepare to Pull Out

It was not only the Americans that Lee had to contend with after separation. The British still cast a shadow 'east of Suez' in Southeast Asia. In 1964, the Labour Party won power for the first time in over a decade and Harold Wilson became the new prime minister. Both Wilson and his defence secretary, Denis Healey, were foreign policy traditionalists who still acted as if Britain retained the status and privileges of a world power. The threadbare relics of Britain's Asian empire still mattered. Healey insisted that 'another 1,000 troops deployed east of Suez was a bigger contribution to world peace than another 1,000 in Germany'. The Konfrontasi war with Indonesia had not yet ended and British soldiers were fighting in the jungles of Borneo. In Malaysia and Singapore, some 90,000 British soldiers and ancillary staff accounted for about one-quarter of British overseas spending. But a year after taking office, Wilson's government was hit by an economic typhoon. There was a severe balance of payments crisis and sterling collapsed. In January, 1968, the British government acknowledged that it could no longer afford its commitments east of Suez. The sun was finally setting on the British Empire and Wilson set a deadline for withdrawal: Britain would pull out of Singapore in 1971.

For Lee and the PAP government, this was dismaying news. Since separation in 1965, the Singapore economy, far from tanking as Goh had feared, continued to be underwritten by British investment in its air and naval bases at Sembawang, which contributed 20 per cent of Singapore's national income and provided employment for 36,000 Singaporeans. Lee was hardened to accusations from other Non-Aligned leaders that 'the British had never really left' and that Singapore was a 'neo-colonial puppet'. He liked to claim that the bases stayed in Singapore only at the pleasure of Singaporeans and that the government could tell the British to leave at any time. But according to CIA reports, the British were pumping close to $200 million into the Singapore economy every year. Now the British decision to pull out threatened to damage the livelihoods of some 150,000 citizens.

Singapore Looks for a New Patron

Now, in 1968, Lee had no doubt that British withdrawal would damage Singapore's precarious economy. He had to find a new patron. In 1965, Lee had taken a sabbatical in Harvard to recover from the trauma of separation and was impressed by the supercharged American economy and the new thinking of economists like Milton Friedman. As the British prepared to pull out, Lee would devote all his efforts to luring the wealthy United States to replace bankrupt Britain. Ever since the Dutch economist Albert Winsemius had persuaded the Singapore government not to pull down the statue of Raffles, Lee and his ministers had worked hard to make Singapore investor-friendly. Now, the strategy was ramped up to appeal to American moneymen. The PAP passed new laws favourable to international corporate capital and unfriendly to the labour unions that had brought Lee to power. Lee's new guru, Milton Friedman, was horrified when he learnt that the government provided free hospital care in Singapore, so Lee dutifully ended the provision. The government also consolidated all trade unions into a single government-controlled union and set up the Central Provident Fund as a mechanism to control wages. These measures came with a further package of public order laws which punished spitting, graffiti and public urination with lashes and prison terms. Drug traffickers would be hanged. Lashing and judicial execution were old colonial punishments meted out to recalcitrant subjects of the British Empire. As Lee turned away from Singapore's old colonial masters, these draconian punishments would ensure that Singapore was an ordered, safe and obedient society that was open for international business.

The Singapore Government

It was the Cold War that made the plan work. As Britain began to withdraw from its old colonial bases, the global superpowers, America, the Soviet Union and China fought proxy hot wars in Indochina. At the beginning of the 1970s, the United States had been at war in Vietnam for nearly a decade. But in America, the war was increasingly unpopular and both North Vietnam and America stepped up negotiations in an effort to reach peace. But when peace talks failed once again, on 18 December 1972, President Richard Nixon, who had just been re-elected in a landslide victory, launched the biggest bombing campaign of the war. American bombers dropped over 20,000 tons of bombs to force North Vietnamese negotiators to resume talks. The two-week assault was known as 'The Christmas Bombing'. In the early 1970s, as the US Air Force rained explosives and napalm on the people of Vietnam, Singapore thrived as a war-based economy. By the end of the 1960s, 15 per cent of Singapore's national economy came from American military procurements for its war in Vietnam. Singapore began refining petroleum to feed the American war machine, and Lockheed, the huge American arms corporation, set up shop in Singapore to repair and maintain its huge fleets of aircraft deployed in Southeast Asia. By 1971, American investment in Singapore was growing at a spectacular US$100 million every year. Yet more American dollars gushed into Singapore from the pockets of free-spending American soldiers enjoying R&R breaks. Singapore had been hauled off the reef of disaster by the war in Vietnam.

On the political front, Lee abandoned any last shred of 'non-alignment'. He wrote to President Lyndon Johnson, Nixon's predecessor, that Singapore unequivocally supported the war. He cajoled American politicians in Washington to be resolute and stay firm on the side of the government in Saigon. He warned that Southeast Asia might fall to communism if America wavered and 'sold out'. In Kuala Lumpur, Tunku Abdul Rahman and his successors followed the same path as British power waned. So too did the Thai government and the new president of Indonesia, Suharto. Lee and the PAP government played their hand in the Cold War with consummate skill. The reward was a massive economic boom, with full employment achieved within a decade. Lee enjoyed escorting American CEOs around the island and often remarked that the roar of aircraft landing at Changi Airport was the sound of money.

The Americans abandoned Vietnam in 1973, but the dollars kept pouring in. Singapore led the region in electronics assembly, ship repair and food processing. This was a difficult trick to pull off because global capital chases low wages. In the 1980s, Singapore was faced with a shortage of workers and a strong Singapore dollar. As a consequence of this double economic whammy, hordes of global investors fled to new low-wage hotspots around Asia. Lee and Goh were forced to implement policies that suppressed wages, an economic policy Singapore has followed ever since. Singapore boasts of a 'Swiss standard of living'. The 'little red dot' is crammed with the spectacular villas of the superrich. But the *median* wage of Singaporeans today is roughly the same as the income of a street cleaner in Bern.

Pivot to China

In other post-colonial Asian economies, such as Taiwan and South Korea, the new states collaborated with wealthy local business leaders to establish protected firms that prospered under American protection. The Korean 'Chaebol' are huge conglomerates that are dominated by a family group. Since 1819, Chinese towkays had played a significant role in colonial society as businessmen and philanthropists, but it is a surprising fact that when it became independent, Singapore lacked a strong local capitalist class. The PAP plan for Singapore, ranging from housing to industrial development, was always top-down. The PAP elite ran the show and what has been called the 'cliquefication' of the PAP elite may prove to be the island's economic Achilles heel. On every National Day, the power of Singapore's superbly equipped armed forces, trained in the early days of independence by Israeli experts, is put proudly on display. Singapore's military has slowly become the seedbed for its civil administration, and many generals seem to end up running public institutions, including Singtel, the state telecommunications company, and the MRT public transport system.

The PAP continues to win elections, but even the Lee dynasty had its own apostate in the shape of the prime minister's younger brother, Lee Kim Yew, before his death in 2003, who joined the opposition party, Singapore Progress. More pressing than political squabbles among the elite is Singapore's pivotal relationship with China, the world's new superpower. It must surely be acknowledged that Lee Kuan Yew, Singapore's first prime minister from 1959 to 1965, and his successors proved to be skilled managers of competing global powers. Lee himself pivoted from Britain to the United States. His son Lee Hsien Loong, who has served as Singapore's third prime minister since 12 August 2004, is adroitly shifting the centre of strategic gravity away from Washington to Beijing, without breaking the US connection. Those bulging sovereign wealth funds now invest more in the Chinese mainland than any other country in the world. And with the old rival Hong Kong engulfed by pro-democracy protests and a Cantonese identarian revolt, Singapore basks for now in the golden glow of Chinese favour. To be sure, Singapore still conducts joint exercises with the United States Navy in the South China Sea, but if tension between the world's superpowers intensifies, Singapore may be forced to make a choice between a strategic rock and a hard place.

Forging a Singaporean Identity

As we have seen, Lee and the PAP seemed to regard Singapore as a kind of human laboratory designed to forge a new kind of Malayan identity. Nation-building was not just about investment and production, but hearts and minds. The purpose was to forge a Singaporean identity and shed older communal ones. When Singapore left the Federation, Malays went from being the Bumiputera to a minority. The architect of this new thinking was Sinnathamby Rajaratnam, a supple and articulate thinker, who had served as the first minister of culture and drafted the 'Singapore National Pledge' in 1966. He wanted the new Singaporean to become 'immune to the tugs and pulls of ancestral lands' and to identify with 'a modern, technological twenty-first century Singapore'. He coined the much-cited phrase that Singapore should be home to 'One united Singapore, regardless of race, language or religion'. In this utopian programme, citizens of the new Singapore would be required to remember differently and to recognise that the past mattered more than the future. Rajaratnam himself cited his own experience. He had no difficulty, he said, forgetting that he had been in succession a Ceylon Tamil, a Sri Lankan, a British subject, a Malayan, a Malaysian.

The idea of a pure Singaporean has proved a chimera. Singaporeans have turned out to be resolutely 'hyphenated'. Rajaratnam's purist thinking was to all intents and purposes abandoned in the 1970s. The peoples of Singapore were encouraged to take pride in their different cultures as loyal Singaporeans, and the 2019 celebration of the Bicentennial emphasised the many different streams of influence that had fed into Singapore's history before 1919. If Singaporeans are to recognise 700 years of history, they must also recognize its diversity. After all, Rajaratnam's famous use of the word *regardless* is double-edged. He meant the word to imply that a Singaporean identity could transcend race, language and religion. But 'regardless' can also mean indifferent, heedless or unmindful. Even in modern Singapore, ethnicity and its discontents lurk just below the manicured facades of the city state.

CHAPTER 25

Malaysia Takes a Different Road

T he story of Malaysia after 1965 continued to be shaped by the old rules and constraints of communal identities. After the merger in 1963, the 'sons of the soil' refused to share political power with non-Malays. Malaysia, to this day, remains a federation of sultanates whose citizens owe allegiance to a Malay king. It is often said that the British and other European colonial powers 'divided and ruled' by exploiting and deepening ethnic differences and favouring privileged 'races'. In Southeast Asia, as we have seen, colonial administrators formed close bonds with Chinese and Peranakan towkays and South Asian chettiars that marginalised Malays. Colonialism imposed the rule of the minority over the majority characterised by segregation, discrimination and racial superiority. It is therefore understandable that the new rulers of independent Malaysia sought to repair the inheritance of colonial rule. They chose, however, to remedy the problem by imposing constitutional inequality. This is embodied in Article 153 of the Federal Constitution that obligates the Yang di-Pertuan Agong to 'safeguard the special position of the Malays and natives of any of the States of Sabah and Sarawak and the legitimate interests of other communities in accordance with the provisions of this Article'. Tunku Abdul Rahman compared the constitutional insistence on Malay rights to a golfing handicap or a 'leg up'. In modern Malaysia, the privileges set out in Article 153 still remain in force. Although it was a temporary provision at the time of independence, Article 10 section 4 of the Malaysian Constitution makes it illegal for any party to question Article 153. There was no question of creating a 'Malayan' identity as Lee

Kuan Yew consistently advocated. In Malaysia, a single ethnicity would be privileged. And yet the Malaysian governments that have held power since 1957 have barely dented the persistent poverty of Malays in rural areas. Since 1969, political, economic and communal turbulence have dominated the lives of many citizens of Malaysia.

The First Decade of Independence

After independence, Malaysia inherited a robust export economy that was the envy of Southeast Asia and dominated the global market in the production of rubber, tin and palm oil. But the leaders of the new independent nation confronted chronic problems of unemployment and poverty, especially in rural areas. Here, Malays may have been privileged Bumiputera but were crushingly poor. Rural poverty was stubbornly resistant to government schemes, such as the Federal Land Development Authority (FELDA). Many Malays resented the way they were underrepresented in commerce and industry. At the same time, pouring development funds into Malay communities disadvantaged the Chinese who had been resettled in New Villages during the Emergency. Estate managers in the new nation added to the storm of deprivation by rationalising plantation holdings and sacking Indian estate workers. Neither the Alliance nor the Chinese political parties had solutions, and new political movements like the Gerakan or Malaysian People's Movement, the Democratic Action Party (DAP), the People's Progressive Party (PPP) and an Islamic party, Parti Islam Se-Malaysia (PAS) sprang up to offer a voice to the wretched of Malaysia. In June 1968, the Malayan Communist Party, now called the Communist Party of Malaya, formally announced that it would resume the armed struggle.

By May 1969, when federal elections were scheduled, Malay and non-Malay communities seethed with anger and disappointment. Each ethnic community saw its problems differently and somehow connected with the actions of the others, and so volatile ethnic tension smouldered in the cities, kampongs and New Villages. These tensions ignited during the elections in May.

The Events of May 1969

By 1969, Kuala Lumpur had become a cauldron of discontent. Many hundreds of Malay, Indian and Chinese men came to the city in search of work. If they failed, they blamed discrimination and ethnic prejudices. As the campaigns by different parties got under way, tensions became ever more volatile, and detonated when a young Chinese man caught painting anti-election slogans was shot by police. Ten thousand angry Chinese attended his funeral. When the new parties like Geranakan and the DAP humiliated the Alliance and deprived the government of a majority, euphoric supporters rushed into the streets of Kuala Lumpur to celebrate and, allegedly, taunted Malays with threats of winning future elections. UMNO supporters called a rally to counter the new parties. On 12 May, the different party factions clashed, provoking four days of rioting, looting and fighting. According to official reports, 196 people were killed and 409 injured. Most of the victims were Chinese. Some 6,000 residents of the city lost homes and property. Again, the Chinese community was hardest hit.

On 13 May, the government declared a State of Emergency and postponed elections in the Borneo states. A curfew was imposed and all newspapers shut down. Abdul Razak Hussein seized control of all administrative powers and set up a centralised National Operations Council, the NOC. At least 9,000 people were rounded up and detained. At the eye of the storm, Prime Minister Tunku Abdul Rahman blamed communist agitators, but there were many in his own party who blamed the Tunku himself for being too accommodating to the Chinese. The shrillest critical voice belonged to a then little-known party member from Kedah.

Dr Mahathir Mohamad had lost his political seat in the election and now demanded that the prime minister stand down. He had, Mahathir alleged, shown favouritism to his 'Chinese friends'. Many other UMNO party members sympathised with Mahathir's outburst, but the party closed ranks and he and his allies were expelled. Dr Mahathir used his time in exile to write *The Malay Dilemma*, which was immediately banned. Illegal copies were printed and circulated in Singapore. The argument made in the book is somewhat double-edged. Mahathir argues that Malays, the 'definitive people' of Malaya, are too good-mannered and tolerant to resist subjugation by other races. What upset the Tunku and other UMNO traditionalists was Mahathir's trenchant attack on the Malay rulers and the stubborn persistence of feudal servility.

A Change of Guard

The 1969 riots exposed a nation that was ill at ease with its identity. For some time, Malaysia would be governed by the NOC as a dictatorship by committee. Razak and his fellow members struggled to mend the broken fences of national identity. On 31 August 1970, the Yang di-Pertuan Agong, at that time the sultan of Kedah, announced the *Rukunegara* or 'Articles of Faith', that begins with belief in God and loyalty to the king. The following year, the Alliance won elections in Sabah and Sarawak with landslide numbers, and in Kuala Lumpur the NOC was confident enough to restore parliamentary rule. By then the ailing Tunku had been persuaded to retire, to be replaced by his deputy, Abdul Razak Hussein.

Razak has been called the 'father of development', but when Dr Mahathir won power at the beginning of the 1980s, very few of the problems that had beset Malaya since independence had been solved. Investment in rural areas benefitted a small minority of wealthier Malay villagers and left the northern Malay states untouched. In 1974, angry protests erupted in the Kedah districts of Baling and Sik as thousands of Malay farmers marched to demand government action. Islamic youth organisations backed the farmers under the leadership of a charismatic young politician called Anwar Ibrahim. The government swiftly quelled the disturbances in Kedah and Anwar was detained for two years. He would not stay quiet for long.

This was the situation Dr Mahathir confronted when he became prime minister in 1981. He had not changed his mind about Malaysia's ethnic inequalities. He was troubled by the student involvement in the Kedah protests and impatient with the lack of progress tackling rural poverty. Now, as prime minister, Mahathir could do something to resolve the 'Malay dilemma'. As it turned out, the new government broadened its development campaign to Malay and Chinese poor as well as the Tamil plantation workers who were plagued by alcoholism, drug abuse and other problems. Many were undocu-

mented. Rubber was now mainly produced by smallholders who preferred to recruit non-unionized Indonesians and Orang Asli. Many
indigenous peoples in Malaysia had been badly affected by development projects that targeted forest areas for dams, logging and road
building. Now they were required to become part of the Malaysian
mainstream. Not surprisingly, Orang Asli were forced to hire themselves out as labourers. Since independence, the indigenous people
of Malaysia have been pushed out of their forest domains to become
tourist attractions peddling wares to tourists at roadside stalls.

The Mahathir Plan

Slowly the government chipped away at rural poverty. But Mahathir
had much grander ambitions. His solution to the 'Malay dilemma'
was economic nationalism. By the time he took office, Malaysia's
economy had been given a massive shot in the arm by the discovery
of vast oil and gas fields off the coasts of Terengganu and Sarawak.
The revenues from these new natural resources funded investment
in deepening Malay ownership of companies that began developing joint ventures with foreign corporations to develop heavy industries. The most celebrated of these joint ventures was Perusahan
Otomobil Nasional (PROTON), which produced the famous Proton
Saga as a 'national car' in a joint venture with Mitsubishi. In 1984,
Mahathir appointed Daim Zainuddin, a successful businessman, to
oversee a radical plan to privatise transportation, utilities and communications. Mahathir was following the same economic playbook
promoted by American economist Milton Friedman and followed
by other Asian nations, most notably Indonesia. By the mid-1990s,
Malaysia was booming. In 1993, the World Bank issued a report on
the 'East Asian Miracle' and singled out Malaysia for 'getting the fun-
damentals right'. Some of the old demons had not been vanquished.
Government insistence that companies employ a quota of Malays
led to a capital flight of some two billion dollars from Chinese-
owned companies, but this hardly dented the Malaysian economic
miracle. By 1998, manufacturing accounted for 34.4 per cent of the
Malaysian economy with a striking emphasis on high technology.
Mahathir presided over the creation of the Multimedia Super Cor-
ridor and the incubator city of Cyberjaya.

The Asian Financial Crisis

Underneath the skin of the tiger economy, there were signs of rot. Privatisation on the scale Mahathir set in motion opened the gates to cronyism and nepotism, in a word, corruption. Government ministers favoured certain conglomerates and were rewarded in turn. In May 1997, pressure from speculators destabilised the Thai baht and set off a cascade of currency devaluations and capital flights. The infection spread rapidly. The Indonesian rupiah fell by 80 per cent and the Malaysian ringgit by 45 per cent. As currencies plunged and capital fled from the weakest economies, the Asian Financial Crisis sent tremors around the world. In Indonesia, the economic crisis led to a political conflagration and the downfall, after three decades in power, of President Suharto. As the crisis deepened, the Indonesian government had been forced to turn to the International Monetary Fund (IMF), which had imposed severe austerity measures sapping support for Suharto. The crisis pushed Malaysia into a depression, but Mahathir snubbed IMF assistance. He lashed out at Western banking systems and financiers and insinuated the existence of a cabal of 'Jewish financiers' manipulating global economies. Sadly, Mahathir's anti-semitic prejudices were convincing to many Malaysians.

As the storm of crisis raged, Mahathir clung to power. He turned his ire on his deputy and minister of finance, Anwar Ibrahim, who had called for international investment to drag Malaysia out of the doldrums of depression. Many Malaysians were shocked when Mahathir sacked Anwar and ordered his arrest on charges of corruption and committing sodomy, which is a criminal offence under Malaysian law.

Anwar had clashed with UNMO early on in his political career. So, too, it will be recalled, had Dr Mahathir, who persuaded the talented Anwar to join UNMO in 1982 to back his own campaign to reform the party. After Mahathir won power, Anwar advanced swiftly in the government, serving as minister of culture, youth and sports, minister of agriculture and, finally, minister of finance and deputy prime minister. He was very widely respected by international colleagues and Mahathir's draconian attack provoked outrage. His arrest, beating and conviction for 'acts of sodomy' was intolerant.

Reformasi!

Mahathir stepped down in 2003. Always a controversial figure, he angered many in the international community by making a major speech attacking 'Jewish financiers' a few days before his retirement. For unexplained reasons, Jews have been an obsession of Mahathir's for much of his life. Under his successor as prime minister, Abdullah Ahmad Badawi, the Malaysian High Court overturned Anwar's sodomy conviction, citing lack of evidence, and this intriguing political maverick was soon teaching at Oxford University and Johns Hopkins in the United States. In 2008, he returned to Malaysia to rally the fragmented Malaysian opposition in a coalition, the People's Alliance. Anwar himself was banned from seeking political office but used his charismatic reputation to campaign against corruption and economic stagnation. Thoroughly rattled by the strength of the opposition, Badawi accused Anwar of being a security threat and – the usual strategy – he was once again accused of sodomy. During the long period Anwar was on trial, Badawi was ousted by Abdul Najib Abdul Razak, the scion of a political dynasty. His father, Abdul Razak Hussein, was Malaysia's second prime minister from 1970 to 1976. His uncle, Hussein Onn, had led the country in the late 1970s. In the meantime, Anwar was acquitted, then rearrested, convicted and sentenced on appeal.

The clash between Anwar and a succession of Malaysian prime ministers, as well as the farcical accusations of sodomy, had long-lasting consequences for Malaysian political culture in the twenty-first century. The call for Reformasi has many times brought tens of thousands of young Malaysians onto the streets of Kuala Lumpur to demand an end to corruption. The youthful energy of the Reformasi movement proved resilient and created a vibrant political culture in Malaysia.

Reformasi and its successor movement Bersih, the Coalition for Clean and Fair Elections, were supercharged by the grotesque fall of Prime Minister Najib Razak in 2018. Rumours of corruption had begun to darken his reputation very soon after he won power. He was linked to dubious commissions – or kickbacks in less polite language – which accompanied Malaysia's purchase for 1.2 billion dollars of French Scorpène submarines in 2002 and the murder of a young Mongolian translator, Altantuya Shaaribuu, in 2006. Najib, of course, has persistently denied all accusations linking him to the Scorpène scandal and the killing of Altantuya. But in May 2018, Malaysian voters delivered a crushing blow to Najib and the Barisan Nasional, ending the party's six-decade hold on power. Within weeks of losing power, Najib was barred from leaving the county and charged with crimes linked to the 1Malaysia Development Berhad, the infamous IMDB, a Malaysian-owned investment fund. The scale of wrongdoing was astonishing. Swiss and American investigations separately concluded that some 3.5 billion dollars had been embezzled from 1MDB and laundered through various channels. Investigations referred extensively to 'Malaysian Official 1' as a key player. This 'individual' was, in fact, Najib Abdul Razak. The former prime minister has pleaded not guilty to forty-two counts of corruption and money laundering. In July 2020, he was found guilty of seven charges and sentenced to twelve years in prison – although appeals are still ongoing. The trial and conviction of Najib Abdul Razak was an inglorious end to a political dynasty that had witnessed the winning of independence and the rise of Malaysia as an 'Asian Tiger'.

The End of an Era

On 23 March 2015, Lee Kuan Yew passed away in Singapore's General Hospital. He was ninety-one and had ruled Singapore with an iron grip until 1990. The *Guardian* newspaper quoted Jennie Yeo, a teacher: 'He did everything for us Singaporeans regardless of race, language or religion … everything you can think of, he's taken care of for us.' His son, Prime Minister Lee Hsien Loong, declared a seven-day period of national mourning. His body was brought to 'Sri Temasek', the prime minister's official residence in the grounds of the Istana for a private wake. Two days later, the body was taken on a gun carriage to Parliament House to lie in state so that Singaporeans could pay their respects to the 'Old Man'. Nearly half a million people filed past the coffin after waiting for hours in the broiling heat. Undeterred by heavy rain, over 100,000 people lined a nine-mile route through the city-state to catch a glimpse of the funeral cortege. The coffin, draped in Singapore's red-and-white flag and shielded from the drenching rain by a glass case, lay on top of a

ceremonial gun carriage that was led slowly past the landmarks of
the city. Air Force jets roared overhead and a battery of howitzers
sounded a martial lament. The state funeral was attended by world
leaders, among them the former American president Bill Clinton
and that long-lived Cold War warrior, Henry Kissinger.

Not every Singaporean shed tears for the 'Old Man'. While many
feared for the future, others remembered the harsher sides of Lee's
inheritance. One leftist commentator summed up his achievements
in an article for *Open Democracy* (2 April 2015): 'He cleaned the
streets and waterways, selected the shade trees, imposed a somewhat robotic examination-driven meritocracy in education, and secured the comforts of investors, and tourists, and tiny Singapore's
70,000 resident millionaires (in U.S. dollars) and 15 billionaires
by importing more than 1.5 million virtually rights-less migrant
workers to keep wages down and instill fear and cultural sterility in
generations of Singaporeans.' Lee's son could not resist some Classical rhetoric: 'To those who seek Mr Lee Kuan Yew's monument,
Singaporeans can reply proudly: "Look around you."' And yet as
this brief history has, I hope, shown Singapore had many creators.

When the East India Company agent John Crawfurd clambered
the flanks of the Forbidden Hill 200 years ago, he knew that the
island had a long history that reached back many centuries. Crawfurd and Raffles were fascinated by the history of Temasek/Singa-
pura because the past added a patina of distinction to the island
they claimed for Company and Crown. Since medieval Singapura
lay in ruins, these English newcomers seized rights to the future.
Today, Fort Canning Park is a tranquil oasis ringed by the steel and
glass towers of Singapore's Central Business District. Beyond, on the
oily waters of the Strait of Singapore, stands an armada of container
ships and tankers. The city-state remains a pivot in a globalised
economy, standing, as it has for 700 years, between East and West.
The statue of Raffles still proudly gazes across the Singapore River.
During the Bicentennial celebrations in 2019, Raffles was joined
by figures from the longer history of the island – princes and merchants, sailors and soldiers, who all played their parts in the flow of
trade, ideas and culture along the Silk Road of the Sea.

Further Reading

I hope this brief history of Singapore and Malaysia will inspire its readers to delve deeper. I would like to thank many friends in Singapore and Malaysia who first introduced me to the intricacies of the history they are still living. It would be a cliché but nevertheless a truth to say that to write this brief history I have stood on the shoulders of giants. This is not an academic history, but I have sifted through numerous books and academic articles to ensure that the story told here is accurate and up to date. I first arrived in Malaysia in 2007 to make a documentary for National Geographic about the coronation of the Malaysian king, the Yang di-Pertuan Agong. I was shockingly ignorant of Malay culture and history, but as I became slowly accustomed to searing hot temperatures, drenching rainstorms and shattering detonations of thunder and lightning, I set off on a journey of understanding, with expert guidance from new friends and colleagues.

The two books by the late Christopher Bayly and Tim Harper, *Forgotten Wars: Freedom and Revolution in Southeast Asia* (Cambridge, MA: Harvard University Press, 2007) and *Forgotten Armies: The Fall of British Asia, 1941–1945* (Cambridge, MA: MIT Press, 2007), which were published the same year I came to live in Kuala Lumpur and remember finding in Kinokuniya in the Twin Towers in downtown Kuala Lumpur, were richly detailed explorations of the violent and fascinating history of the Malay Peninsula. I began to see how we, the British, had 'divided and ruled' with consequences casting long shadows into the present.

I subsequently worked on two History Channel documentaries about the Malayan Emergency and the Japanese occupation of Malaya with Malaysian producers Lara Ariffin and Harun Rahman, which significantly deepened my slowly evolving insights into history and culture and led to writing *Massacre in Malaya* (2010) about the Malayan Emergency. It was while writing this book that I became absorbed by the work of Benedict Anderson, above all *Imagined Communities: Reflection on the Origin and Spread of Nationalism* (London: Verso, 1983) and his wonderful study of Indonesia, *The Spectre of Comparisons: Nationalism, Southeast Asia and the World* (London: Verso, 1998), which deeply shaped the way we understand the history of the region and its peoples and how modern nations emerged from the old European empires.

Later, I worked in Singapore as an executive producer with Channel News Asia (International) and had the privilege of learning about Southeast Asian history from the brilliant Dr Farish A. Noor. So, my next recommendation is Dr Farish's *The Long Shadow of the 19th Century: Critical Essays on Colonial Orientalism in Southeast Asia* (Matahari Books, 2021).

Here, then, are a few of the books which I have come to value most deeply and would highly recommend to any reader who wishes to follow the same journey. Valerie Hansen's *The Year 1000: When Explorers Connected the World and Globalization Began* (New York, NY: Scribner, 2020), and David Abulafia's *The Boundless Sea: A Human History of the Oceans* (London: Allen Lane, 2019) provide richly detailed overviews of the flow of people and trade across and through Southeast Asia in the centuries before the arrival of Europeans. Professor John Miksic has made astonishing archaeological discoveries on and around Fort Canning, once known as the Forbidden Hill, and other sites in Singapore that lay bare the tantalising and complex world of medieval 'Singapura' and are thrillingly described in *Singapore and the Silk Road of the Sea 1300–1800* (Singapore: NUS Press and National Museum of Singapore, 2013). When I was researching and writing, I had on hand at all times *Singapore: A Modern History* by Michael D. Barr (London: Bloomsbury, 2018) and *Singapore: A Biography* by Mark Ravinder Frost and Yu-Mei Balasingamchow (Singapore: Editions Didier Millet, 2013). Close by on my desk were *A History of Malaysia* (3rd edn) by Barbara Watson Andaya and Leonard Y. Andaya (Manhattan, NY: Springer, 2016), *Singapore, Singapura: From Miracle to Complacency* by Nicholas Walton (London: Hurst, 2018) and *Crossroads: A Popular History of Malaysia and Singapore* (2nd edn) by Jim Baker (Singapore: NUS Press, 2010). For the all-important history of the East India

Company, the Honourable Company or simply 'John Company', I was most impressed by *The East India Company: The World's Most Powerful Corporation* (3rd edn) by Tirthankar Roy, Penguin Books (India, 2016) and *The Corporation That Changed the World: How the East India Company Shaped the Modern Multinational* (2nd edn) by Nick Robins (London: Pluto Press, 2012).

Let us not forget the fiction writers who take us back in time on the wings of imagination. Anthony Burgess's *Malayan Trilogy: Time for a Tiger* (1956), *The Enemy in the Blanket* (1958) and *Beds in the East* (1959) (all published by William Heinemann Ltd) may be rather outdated in its attitudes but is nevertheless a richly layered account of the author's time in Malaya before and after independence. Going back another decade, J. G. Farrell's *The Singapore Grip* (London: Weidenfeld & Nicholson, 1978) exposes the hedonistic complacency of the British community in Singapore on the eve of catastrophe in 1942.

In the decades since independence, Malaysian writers have created a notable modern literature represented at its best by Tash Aw's *The Harmony Silk Factory* (London: Harper Perennial, 2005) and *We, the Survivors* (New York: Picador, 2019) and Tan Twan Eng's *The Gift of Rain* (Quayside: Myrmidon, 2007). And to understand modern Singapore, no one can afford to ignore Kevin Kwan's hugely successful *Crazy Rich Asians* (Doubleday Canada, reprint, 2020).

Select Bibliography

Abulafia, David, *The Boundless Sea: A Human History of the Oceans*, London: Allen Lane, 2019.

Afonso D'Albuquerque, *Commentaries of the Great Afonso D'Albuquerque*, trans. Walter de Gray Birch, London: Hakluyt Society, 1875.

Anderson, Benedict, *Imagined Communities: Reflections on the Origins and Spread of Nationalism*, London: Verso, 1983.

Ban Kah Choon, *Absent History: The Untold Story of Special Branch Operations in Singapore, 1915–1942*, Singapore: SNP Media, 2001.

Barnard, Timothy P., *Contesting Malayness: Malay Identity across Boundaries*, Singapore University Press, 2004.

Bastin, John (ed.), *Travellers' Singapore*, Kuala Lumpur: Oxford University Press, 1994.

Bayly, Christopher, and Harper, Tim, *Forgotten Armies: The Fall of British Asia, 1941–1945*, Cambridge, MA: MIT Press, 2007.

————, *Forgotten Wars: Freedom and Revolution in Southeast Asia*, Cambridge, MA: Harvard University Press, 2007.

Bellwood, Peter, *Prehistory of the Indo-Malaysian Archipelago*, Honolulu: University of Hawaii Press, 1997.

Borschberg, P., *The Singapore and Melaka Straits: Violence, Security and Diplomacy in the 17th Century*, Singapore and Leiden: NUS Press and KITVL Press, 2010.

Bose, Ramen, *The End of the War: Singapore's Liberation and the Aftermath of the Second World War*, Singapore: Marshall Cavendish, 2007.

Brown, C. C. (trans.), *Sejarah Melayu, or Malay Annals: An Annotated Translation*, Kuala Lumpur: Oxford University Press, 1970; first published 1953.

Buckley, C. B., *An Anecdotal History of Old Times in Singapore, 1819–1867*, Singapore: Oxford University Press, 1984; first published 1902.

Burns, P. L. (ed.), *The Journals of J. W. W. Birch*, Kuala Lumpur: Oxford University Press, 1976.

Chan Heng Chee, *A Sensation of Independence: A Political Biography of David Marshall*, Singapore: Oxford University Press, 1984; reprinted 1992.

Cheah, Boon Kheng, *Red Star over Malaya: Resistance and Social Conflict During and After the Japanese Occupation of Malaya, 1941–1946*, 3rd edn, Singapore University Press, 2003; first published 1983.

Cortesão, A. (ed.), *The Suma Oriental of Tomé Pires: An Account of the East, from the Red Sea to Japan, written in Malacca and India in 1512–1515, and the Book of Francisco Rodrigues, Rutter of a Voyage in the Red Sea, Nautical Rules, Almanack and Maps, Writ-*

ten and Drawn in the East before 1515, vol. 2, Hakluyt Society, 1944; reprinted Ashgate, 2010.

Crawfurd, John, *Journal of an Embassy from the Governor-General of India to the Courts of Siam and Cochin China*, Kuala Lumpur: Oxford University Press, 1967; first published 1828.

Crisswell, Colin N., *Rajah Charles Brooke: Monarch of All He Surveyed*, Kuala Lumpur: Oxford University Press, 1978.

Dalrymple, W., *The Anarchy: The Relentless Rise of the East India Company*, London: Bloomsbury, 2019.

Elkins, Caroline, *A Legacy of Violence: A History of the British Empire*, New York: Alfred A. Knopf, 2022.

Emerson, R., *Malaysia: A Study in Direct and Indirect Rule*, Kuala Lumpur: University of Malaya Press, 1964; first published 1937.

Farish A. Noor, *The Other Malaysia: Writings on Malaysia's Subaltern History*, Kuala Lumpur: Silverfish Books, 2002.

Farrell, B. (ed.), *The Defence and Fall of Singapore, 1940–1942*, Stroud, UK: Tempus, 2005.

Frei, H., *Guns of February: Ordinary Japanese Soldiers' Views of the Fall of Singapore*, Singapore University Press, 2004.

Frost, Mark Ravinder and Balasingamchow, Yu-Mei, *Singapore: A Biography*, Singapore: Editions Didier Millet, 2013; first published National University of Singapore and Hong Kong University Press, 2009.

Hack, K. and Blackburn, K., *Did Singapore Have to Fall? Churchill and the Impregnable Fortress*, London: Routledge, 2004.

Hale, C., *Massacre in Malaya: Exposing Britain's My Lai*, Stroud, UK: History Press, 2013.

Harper, T. N., *The End of Empire and the Making of Malaya*, Cambridge, UK: Cambridge University Press, 1999.

Haughton, H. T., 'Landing of Raffles in Singapore by an Eye-witness,' *Journal of the Straits Branch of the Royal Asiatic Society*, 10 (June 1882), p. 286.

Heng, D., *Sino-Malay Trade and Diplomacy from the Tenth through the Fourteenth Century*, Athens, OH: Ohio University Press, 2009.

Jackson, R. N., *Pickering: Protector of Chinese*, Kuala Lumpur: Oxford University Press, 1965.

Kenley, D. L., *New Culture in a New World: The May Fourth Movement and the Chinese Diaspora in Singapore, 1919–1932*, New York: Routledge, 2003.

Keppel, Henry and Brooke, James, *The Expedition to Borneo of H.M.S. Dido*, Singapore: Oxford University Press, 1991; first published 1846.

Kratoska, Paul H., *The Japanese Occupation of Malaya: A Social and Economic History*, Honolulu: University of Hawaii Press, 1997.

Kwa, C. G.; Heng, D. and Tan, T. Y., *Singapore, A 700-year History: From Early Emporium to World City*, National Archives of Singapore, 2009.

La Motte, E., *The Opium Monopoly*, New York: MacMillan, 1920.

Lau, Albert, *A Moment of Anguish: Singapore in Malaysia and the Politics of Disengage-*

ment, Singapore: Times Academic Press, 1998.

Lee, Edwin, *Singapore: The Unexpected Nation*, Singapore: Institute of Southeast Asian Studies, 2008.

Lee Geok Boi, *The Syonan Years: Singapore under Japanese Rule, 1942–1945*, National Archives of Singapore and Epigram, 2005.

Lee Kuan Yew, *From Third World to First: The Singapore Story, 1965–2000: Memoirs of Lee Kuan Yew*, Singapore: Marshall Cavendish, 2009. HarperCollins, 2000. Singapore: Times Media, 2000.

Lee Poh Ping, *Chinese Society in 19th Century Singapore*, Kuala Lumpur: Oxford University Press, 1978.

Lim Yew Hock, *Reflections*, Kuala Lumpur: Pustaka Antara, 1986.

Loh, F. K. W., *Beyond the Tin Mines: Coolies, Squatters and New Villagers in the Kinta Valley, Malaysia c. 1880–1980*, Singapore: Oxford University Press, 1988.

Low Ngiong Ing, *When Singapore Was Syonan-to*, Singapore: Eastern Universities Press, 1973.

McNair, J. F. A., *Prisoners Their Own Warders*, London: Archibald Constable and Co., 1899.

Miksic, John N., *Archaeological Research on the 'Forbidden Hill' of Singapore: Excavations at Fort Canning, 1984*, Singapore: National Museum, 1985.

———, *Singapore and the Silk Road of the Sea, 1300–1800*, Singapore: NUS Press and National Museum of Singapore, 2013.

Milner, Anthony, *The Invention of Politics in Colonial Malaya*, Cambridge, UK: Cambridge University Press, 2002.

Murfett, Malcolm H.; Miksic, John N.; Farrell, Brian P., and Chiang Ming Shun, *Between Two Oceans: A Military History of Singapore from First Settlement to Final British Withdrawal*, Singapore: Oxford University Press, 1999.

Mustapha Hussain, *Malay Nationalism Before UMNO: The Memoirs of Mustapha Hussain*, trans. Insun Sony Mustapha; ed. K. S. Jomo, Kuala Lumpur: Utusan, 2005.

Onraet, René, *Singapore: A Police Background*, London, Dorothy Crisp and Co., 1947.

Percival, Arthur E., *The War in Malaya*, London: Eyre & Spottiswoode, 1949.

Pham, P. L., *Ending 'East of Suez': The British Decision to Withdraw from Malaysia and Singapore, 1964–1968*, Oxford, UK: Oxford University Press, 2010.

Proudfoot, I., *Early Malay Printed Books*, Kuala Lumpur: Academy of Malay Studies and Library University of Malaya, 1993; first published 1925.

Raffles, Lady Sophia, *Memoir of the Life and Public Services of Sir Thomas Stamford Raffles*, intro. John Bastin, Singapore: Oxford University Press, 1991.

Rajaratnam, S., *The Prophetic and the Political*, eds Chan Heng Chee and Obaid ul Haq, Singapore: Graham Brash, 1987.

Reid, Anthony, *Imperial Alchemy: Nationalism and Identity in Southeast Asia*, New York: Cambridge University Press, 2010.

Ricklefs, M. C.; Lockhart, Bruce; Lau, Albert; Reyes, Portia, and Maitrii Aung-Thwin, *A New History of Southeast Asia*, Palgrave Macmillan, 2010.

Roff, William R., *The Origins of Malay Nationalism*, Kuala Lumpur: Oxford University Press, 1994; first published 1967.

Sareen, T. R., *Secret Documents on Singapore Mutiny, 1915*, New Delhi: Mounto Publishing House, 1995.

Shinozaki, Mamoru, *Syonan, My Story: The Japanese Occupation of Singapore*, Singapore: Times Books International, 1992.

Stockwell, A. J. (ed.), *Malaysia: British Documents on the End of Empire*, 3 vols, London: Stationery Office, 2004.

Swettenham, Frank, *British Malaya: An Account of the Origin and Progress of British Influence in Malaya*, London: George Allen & Unwin, 1948; first published 1906.

Tan Jing Quee and Jomo, K. S., *Comet in Our Sky: Lim Chin Siong in History*, Selangor Darul Ehsan: Insan, 2001.

Tarling, Nicholas, *The Burthen, the Risk and the Glory': A Biography of Sir James Brooke*, Kuala Lumpur: Oxford University Press, 1982.

———, *Piracy and Politics in the Malay World: A Study of British Imperialism in Nineteenth- Century South-East Asia*, Singapore: D. Moore, 1963.

Trocki, Carl A., *Opium and Empire: Chinese Society in Colonial Singapore, 1800–1910*, Ithaca, NY: Cornell University Press, 1990.

———, *Prince of Pirates: The Temenggongs and the Development of Johor and Singapore, 1784–1885*, Singapore University Press, 1979.

Tsuji, Masanobu, *Singapore, 1941–1942: The Japanese Version of the Malayan Campaign of World War II*, Singapore: Oxford University Press, 1988.

Turnbull, C. M., *A History of Singapore, 1819–1988*, 2nd edn, Singapore: Oxford University Press, 1989.

Wallace, Alfred Russel, *The Malay Archipelago: The Land of the Orang-Utan, and the Bird of Paradise. A Narrative of Travel, with Studies of Man and Nature*, Cambridge, UK: Cambridge University Press, 2010; first published 1869.

Walton, Calder, *Empire of Secrets: British Intelligence, the Cold War and the Twilight of Empire*, London: Harper Press, 2013.

Warren, James F., *Ah Ku and Karayuki-san: Prostitution in Singapore, 1870–1940*, Singapore: Oxford University Press, 1993.

———, *Rickshaw Coolie: A People's History of Singapore, 1880–1940*, Singapore: Oxford University Press, 1986.

Yeoh, Brenda S. A., *Contesting Space in Colonial Singapore: Power Relations and the Urban Built Environment*, Singapore University Press, 2003

Yong, C. F., and McKenna, R. B., *The Kuomintang Movement in British Malaya 1912–1949*, Singapore University Press, 1990.

INDEX